Management for Professionals

The Springer series *Management for Professionals* comprises high-level business and management books for executives. The authors are experienced business professionals and renowned professors who combine scientific background, best practice, and entrepreneurial vision to provide powerful insights into how to achieve business excellence.

More information about this series at http://www.springer.com/series/10101

Volker Nestle • Patrick Glauner •
Philipp Plugmann
Editors

Creating Innovation Spaces

Impulses for Start-ups and Established
Companies in Global Competition

Editors
Volker Nestle
LifeTech/Medical Technologies
Festo SE & Co. KG
Esslingen, Germany

Patrick Glauner
Applied Computer Science
Deggendorf Institute of Technology
Deggendorf, Germany

Philipp Plugmann
Interdisciplinary Periodontology
and Prevention
SRH University of Applied Health Sciences
Leverkusen, Germany

ISSN 2192-8096   ISSN 2192-810X   (electronic)
Management for Professionals
ISBN 978-3-030-57641-7   ISBN 978-3-030-57642-4   (eBook)
https://doi.org/10.1007/978-3-030-57642-4

This Springer imprint is published by the registered company Springer Nature Switzerland AG.
The registered company address is: Gewerbestrasse 11, 6330 Cham, Switzerland

Foreword

After the successful IPO of our Australian startup Amaysim in 2015, I embarked upon a journey to identify a winning formula for the best environment of a successful tech startup. I was convinced that the right setting would have a tremendous impact on producing better ideas, talent, and outcomes. For over two years my journey led me to the East and West Coast of the USA, Europe, and Australia. I visited co-working spaces, accelerators, incubators, and high growth startups and engaged in inspiring exchanges with seasoned founders and young entrepreneurs.

The varied attributes of different locations which excelled quickly became clear to me: cities with top universities satisfied the unquenchable thirst of high growth tech companies for young talent and forward-thinking academics. Metropolitan areas blessed with multiple generations of successful entrepreneurs stood out through the continuous passing on of knowledge and capital to their young hopefuls. Places where international exchange is commonplace and talent from all corners of the world were welcomed and integrated secured an exceptional advantage. All this laid the groundwork for institutional investors to ensure a broad, deep, and lucrative field in which risk capital achieved outstanding returns and companies could secure funding for their capital needs.

But what determined a successful innovation environment on a micro level? Launching Venture Lane Boston, my startup hub for early-stage tech companies, provided firsthand experience: a dedicated, open, and innovation-driven culture, which the participants of the ecosystem cherished. It has its foundation in the concept of "Give First," where all members participate in a collaborative manner without asking for or expecting immediate return. In addition, there is one fundamental tenet that binds the community members: that behind the beginning of every idea, there is a relevant and identifiable problem, worth spending resources on and bearing economic return. Finally, it is the firm belief that innovation and progress are only possible if you accept failure as an integral part of the creative process.

We are at the beginning of the golden age of automation and biotech. The powerful combination of human values and the right environment provides the perfect opportunity to grow jointly as an individual and a society.

Venture Lane, Boston, MA, USA   Christian Magel

Preface

Our world is currently undergoing a major multidimensional transformation. In many industries, traditionally stable and controllable value chains are beginning to break up and get increasingly dematerialized by ongoing digitalization. At the same time, market shares are shifting due to increasing globalization. In these volatile, uncertain, complex, and ambiguous (VUCA) times, companies have to simultaneously get along with different areas and speed of change. On the one hand, the established core business has to be kept competitive for new challenges; on the other hand, completely new business ideas have to be tested and developed in order to remain viable for the future. It is nothing new that in times of exponential change, companies find it very difficult to address these challenges sufficiently and to address all relevant dimensions of the necessary transformation properly.

But how do you innovate and reinvent yourself in a VUCA world and which successful concepts are already there in science and business?

If this question has sparked your interest, then you should read this book. This innovative book reflects the recent developments stated above while providing comprehensive outlooks on what companies need to do in order to remain competitive in the future. It provides an unparalleled mix of expertise of respected international authors from academia and the industrial world. The authors present their work on and expertise in how to be innovative, spanning from the fields of human aspects of change through leadership, digitalization, and artificial intelligence to corporate entrepreneurship and corporate accelerators. This book aims at innovators, investors, decision makers, entrepreneurs, researchers, and students. It offers readers novel impulses and productive takeaways for their future design of innovation.

Each chapter is self-contained and provides the necessary respective prerequisites. Some chapters are more business-oriented while others are more technical in order to address a diverse audience. In their chapters, the authors also make concrete recommendations on how to innovate and demonstrate the potential of their approaches to create economic value in real-world applications.

This book would not have been possible without Ms. Rocio Torregrosa and Dr. Prashanth Mahagaonkar, our commissioning editors. We would like to thank them and all the other Springer staff, in particular Ms. Sayani Dey, involved for their professionalism, tireless ability to read multiple drafts, and help improving the book. Our deepest thanks also go to our families, friends, and partners for their patience and support in writing this book.

Esslingen, Germany   Volker Nestle
Regensburg, Germany   Patrick Glauner
Leverkusen, Germany   Philipp Plugmann
July 2020

About the Book

The international competitiveness of companies depends on their strength to innovate and develop new products and services in an increasingly volatile, uncertain, complex, and ambiguous world with exponential changes. Take, for example, the increasing dematerialization of value chains using new digital business models and platforms based on artificial intelligence. There are more and more signs that only companies that are able to adapt to the changes by (re-)innovating themselves will survive in the long run. Especially for startups, the innovation strength is a benchmark to attract investors and grow successfully. Both startups and established companies have their own individual path to create innovation environments for their workforce. These environments allow them to interact and exchange ideas, create prototypes, and brainstorm new solutions for customers. This book provides respective novel impulses from different industries. A number of established authors share their experiences in how they deal with innovation processes. Whatever the storyline of an innovative organization, the creation of innovation environments in the organization has the highest priority and requires different competencies to manage it. This book aims to offer readers novel impulses and productive takeaways for their future innovation processes.

Contents

1 Innovation Management for Artificial Intelligence 1
Patrick Glauner

2 Extracorporate Innovation Environments: An Example Lead
User Approach Applied to the Medical Engineering Industry 15
Philipp Plugmann

3 Innovation Management and Digitization: Will Everything
Remain Different? 33
Volker Nestle

4 Raising Innovation Potential Through a Well Indoor Climate 49
Alexander Buff

5 "It's not about the Room, it's about the Mind-Set!": How
to Create an Integrated Newsroom with Digital Workflows
and Cross Border Collaboration 59
Marie Elisabeth Mueller and Devadas Rajaram

6 The Role of a Leader: Transformational Efforts in Innovation
and Change 71
Christian Kastner

7 On Corporate Innovation 85
Victor Paraschiv

8 Designing Innovative Ecosystems and Introducing Digital
Smart Services Using Examples of the Value Chain
from Building Investor to Facility Management 99
Christoph Jacob

9 How to Radically Innovate While Utilizing a Firms'
Capabilities: Practical Aspects of Corporate Entrepreneurship 119
Christof Siebert

10 Experience as an Architect in an Agile Environment.................. 133
Annegret Junker

**11 Why Emotional Intelligence Is the Key to Survival
in an Ever-Changing Digital World** 145
Franziska Stubbemann

**12 Professional Social Media and Innovation:
How You Start Leveraging on Your
Innovation through Strategic Content
Creation on LinkedIn** 153
Ilkay Özkisaoglu

13 High Quality with Statistical Process Control 4.0 in Automation 169
Johannes Bernstein

14 Digital Platforms as Drivers of Innovation 183
Philip Meier

**15 Expatriate and Expat-Preneur Ecosystems: Innovation Spaces
Away from Home** 193
Alexander Ruthemeier

**16 The Role of Law in Creating Space for Innovation:
An Example from the Healthcare Sector in Germany** 209
Roman Grinblat

17 Start-Ups Meet SMEs 221
Michael Krause

**18 The Five Elements of AI to Leverage Data and Dominate Your
Industry** 235
Alexander Thamm

19 Leveraging the Human Factor through Holarchy: A Case Study 259
Habib Lesevic

**20 Designing a Corporate Accelerator: Enabling
the Collaboration of Incumbent Companies and Start-ups
to Foster Innovation** 281
Marcel Engelmann

21 Leadership in Transformation: How to Lead in the Digital Era? 293
Dana Goldhammer

22 How to Exploit Me as Much as Possible 305
Tamim Al-Marie

23 An Entrepreneurial Approach to Designing Innovation Space 317
Jamshid Alamuti

**24 Augmenting Machine-Human Intelligence
with Human-in-the-Loop** 327
Karina Grosheva

25 Innovation Spaces in the Global Environment 335
Karl H. Ohlberg

About the Editors

Volker Nestle has an engineering background in precision and micro technologies and worked many years for Festo AG & Co. KG as a research engineer before he joined an Executive Master of Business Innovation program and consecutive doctoral studies at the EBS University in Oestrich-Winkel. In 2010, he received his doctoral degree for his research about open innovation processes in technology clusters. Until the end of 2016, he was Head of Research Future Technology at Festo and subsequently joined TRUMPF GmbH + Co. KG as Head of Corporate Research and Development. In 2018, Volker Nestle received his honorary professorship for Innovation and Technology Management at the EBS University. In July 2020, Volker Nestle switched back to Festo SE & Co. KG to build up the new business unit for LifeTech/Medical Technologies as Head of Product Development. Since 2014, Volker Nestle is also Chairman of the Board of Hahn-Schickard Gesellschaft for applied research, running three research institutes for application-oriented research on innovative solutions in micro technologies. Beyond his activities in technology and trend scouting for production technologies, his current fields of interest are about the implications of digitization on medical technologies and the subsequent transformation in business innovation and the working environment.

Patrick Glauner is the Founder & CEO of skyrocket.ai GmbH, an artificial intelligence consulting firm based in Bavaria, Germany. In parallel, he is a Full Professor of Artificial Intelligence at Deggendorf Institute of Technology, a position he is honored to hold since the age of 30. His research on AI was featured in *New Scientist* and cited by McKinsey and others. He is also Area Editor of the *International Journal of Computational Intelligence Systems* (IJCIS). Previously, he held managerial positions at the European Organization for Nuclear Research (CERN), at Krones Group, and at Alexander Thamm GmbH. He studied at Imperial College London and also holds an MBA. He is an alumnus of the German National Academic Foundation (Studienstiftung des deutschen Volkes).

Philipp Plugmann has been doing multidisciplinary work for the last 20 years in parallel to practicing as a dentist in his own clinic in Leverkusen, Germany. He is also Full Professor for Interdisciplinary Periodontology and Prevention at SRH University of Applied Health Sciences. His first book on innovation in medical technology published in 2011 was reviewed by Cisco. His second book on innovation published with Springer in 2018 got more than 50,000 chapter downloads in its first fifteen months. Previously, he held multiple adjunct faculty appointments for more than twelve years and has won multiple teaching awards. He also holds an MBA, an MSc in Business Innovation, and an MSc in Periodontology and Implant Therapy (DGParo) and is currently pursuing his third doctorate. Plugmann has given research talks in the field of innovation at conferences at Harvard Business School, Berkeley Haas School of Business, Max Planck Institute for Innovation and Competition, and Nanyang Tech University, Singapore. Plugmann is a serial entrepreneur and advisor to several companies, including a global technology consultancy—DataArt.

Innovation Management for Artificial Intelligence

Patrick Glauner

1.1 Introduction

What exactly is artificial intelligence (AI)? Humans make decisions dozens of times an hour such as when we have a coffee break, picking a marketing strategy or whether to buy from vendor A or B. In essence, humans are great in making a lot of very different decisions. While we have seen automation of repetitive tasks in industry for about the last 200 years, we had not experienced automation of multifaceted decision making. That is exactly what AI aims at. In our view, a simple definition of AI would therefore be:

> AI enables us to automate human decision making.

The aim of this chapter is to share our experience in AI innovation management with you. As a consequence, you can replicate our best practices in order to make sure that you build concrete AI-based products rather than getting bogged down with mere proofs of concept. The beginning of this chapter provides a description of how we define innovation and innovation ecosystems. We then provide a brief introduction to the field of artificial intelligence, its history and its key concepts. Next, we present how we do innovation management in a joint industry-university research project on the detection of electricity theft in emerging markets. The deliverables of that project are concrete outcomes that are used by the industrial partner. We then discuss some recent advances in AI as well as some of the related contemporary challenges. Those challenges need to be solved by researchers and practitioners in order to make sure that AI will succeed in the long term in industry.

P. Glauner (✉)
Deggendorf Institute of Technology, Deggendorf, Germany
e-mail: patrick@glauner.info

V. Nestle et al. (eds.), *Creating Innovation Spaces*, Management for Professionals, https://doi.org/10.1007/978-3-030-57642-4_1

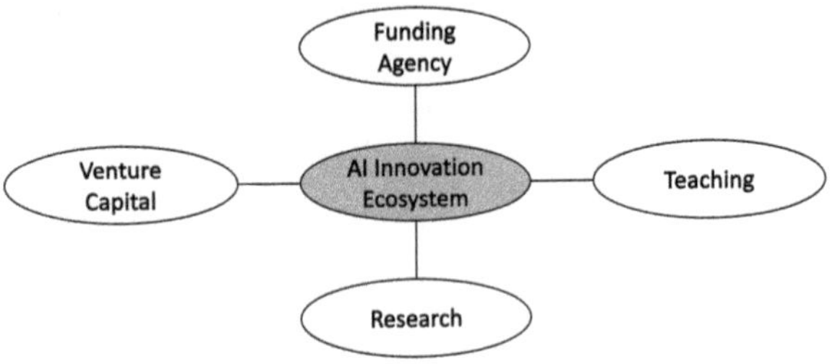

Fig. 1.1 Composition of an
AI innovation ecosystem.
Source: author

Last, we discuss why China is leading in AI innovation management and what we can learn from China.

1.2   Innovation Ecosystems

What is an innovation ecosystem? A fruitful, cutting-edge and sustainable innovation ecosystem consists of a functioning and dynamic combination of research, teaching, industry, research funding and venture capital, as depicted in Fig. 1.1, which we explain below.

A large part of all innovations in the field of artificial intelligence originally started in academia. Most of that research is funded by third parties, which therefore requires active collaboration with research funding agencies and industrial partners. In order for new research findings to become a reality, and not just to be published in journals or conferences, these results must be exposed early to interaction with industry. In industry, however, there are predominantly practitioners and less scientists. Modern university teaching must thus ensure that today's computer science graduates are prepared for the challenges of tomorrow. Interaction between academia and industry is possible both with existing companies and through spin-offs. A close integration with funding sources such as research funding agencies or venture capital is indispensable for the rapid and competitive transformation of research results into value-adding products.

1.3   Artificial Intelligence

This section provides a brief introduction to the field of artificial intelligence, its history and key concepts.

1.3.1   History

The first theoretical foundations of AI were laid in the mid-twentieth century, especially in the works of British mathematician Alan Turing (Turing 1950). The actual year of birth of AI is the year 1956, in which the 6-week conference Summer

Research Project on Artificial Intelligence at Dartmouth College took place. For that purpose, an application for funding was made in the previous year. The research questions contained therein proved to be indicative of many of the long-term research goals of AI (McCarthy et al. 1955). The conference was organized by John McCarthy and was attended by other well-known scientists such as Marvin Minsky, Nathan Rochester and Claude Shannon.

Over the following decades, much of AI research has been divided into two diametrically different areas: expert systems and machine learning. **Expert systems** comprise rule-based descriptions of knowledge and make predictions or decisions based on input/data. In contrast, **machine learning** is based on recognizing patterns in training data.

Over the past decades, a large number of innovative and value-adding applications have emerged, often resulting from AI research results. Autonomously driving cars, speech recognition and autonomous trading systems for example. Nonetheless, there have been many setbacks. These were usually caused by too high and then unfulfilled expectations. In that context, the term of an "AI winter" has been coined, with which periods of major setbacks in recent decades, the loss of optimism and consequent cuts in funding are referred to. Of course, this section can only provide an overview of the history of AI. The interested reader is referred to a detailed discussion in Russell and Norvig (2009).

1.3.2   Machine Learning

A machine learning algorithm finds ("learns") patterns from examples. These patterns are then used to make decisions based on inputs. Both, expert systems and machine learning, have their respective advantages and disadvantages: Expert systems on the one hand have the advantage that they are understandable and interpretable and that their decisions are therefore comprehensible. On the other hand, it often takes a great deal of effort, or sometimes it even turns out to be impossible to understand and describe complex problems in detail.

Example 1.1 (Machine Translation) To illustrate this difficulty, an example of machine translation, the automatic translation from one language to another, is very helpful: First, languages consist of a complex set of words and grammar that are difficult to describe in a mathematical form. Second, one does not necessarily use languages correctly, which can cause inaccuracies and ambiguities. Third, languages are dynamic as they change over decades and centuries. Creating an expert system for machine translation is thus a challenge. The three factors of complexity, inaccuracy and dynamics occur in a variety of fields and prove to be a common limiting factor when building expert systems.

Machine learning has the advantage that often less knowledge about a problem is needed as the algorithms learn patterns from data. This process is often referred to as "training" an AI. In contrast to expert systems, however, machine learning often leads to a black box whose decisions are often neither explainable nor interpretable.

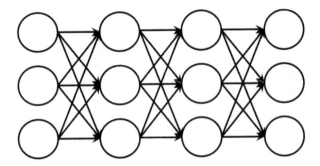

Fig. 1.2 Neural network. Source: author

Nonetheless, over the decades, machine learning has gained popularity and largely replaced expert systems.

Of particular historical significance are so-called (artificial) neural networks. These are loosely inspired by the human brain and consist of several layers of units—also called "neurons". An example of a neural network is shown in Fig. 1.2. The first layer (on the left) is used to enter data and the last layer (on the right) to output labels. Between these two layers are zero to several hidden layers, which contribute to the decision making. Neural networks have experienced several popularity phases over the past 60 years, which are explained in detail in Deng and Yu (2014).

In addition to neural networks, there are a variety of other methods of machine learning, such as decision trees, support vector machines or regression models, which are discussed in detail in Bishop (2006).

1.4 Example AI Innovation Ecosystem: Detection of Electricity Theft in Emerging Markets

In this section, we present an AI innovation ecosystem in which we have built AI-based products that create value for utilities.

1.4.1 Non-technical Losses

Power grids are critical infrastructure assets that face non-technical losses (NTL), which include, but are not limited to, electricity theft, broken or malfunctioning meters and arranged false meter readings. In emerging markets, NTL are a prime concern and often range up to 40% of the total electricity distributed. The annual world-wide costs for utilities due to NTL are estimated to be around USD 100 billion

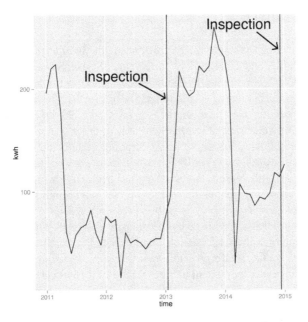

Fig. 1.3 Typical example of electricity theft (Glauner 2019). Source: author

(Smith 2004). Reducing NTL in order to increase revenue, profit and reliability of the grid is therefore of vital interest to utilities and authorities. An example of what the consumption profile of a customer committing electricity theft may look like is depicted in Fig. 1.3.

The consumption time series of the customer undergoes a sudden drop in the beginning of 2011 because the customer's meter was manipulated to record less consumption. This drop then persists over time. Based on this pattern, an inspection was carried out in the beginning of 2013, which detected an instance of electricity theft. This manipulation of the infrastructure was reverted and the electricity consumption resumed to the previous level. One year later, the electricity consumption dropped again to about a third, which led to another inspection a few months later Even though the pattern of a sudden drop is common among fraudsters, this drop can also have other causes. For example, tenants can move out of a house or a factory can scale down its production.

Note that in developed and economically wealthy countries, such as the United States or Western Europe, NTL are less of a topic in th news. Reasons for this include that the population can afford to pay for electricity as well as the high quality of grid infrastructure as argued in Antmann (2009). However, there is still some fraction of NTL in those countries. Given the overall large consumption of electricity in those countries, the absolute costs of NTL may still be considerable.

1.4.2 Stakeholders

Now we present our research project between the Interdisciplinary Center for Security, Reliability and Trust (SnT),[1] University of Luxembourg and the industrial partner CHOICE Technologies.[2] That project has led to the author's PhD thesis on the detection of NTL using AI (Glauner 2019). CHOICE Technologies has been operating in the Latin American market for more than 20 years with the goal of reducing NTL and electricity theft by using AI. In order to remain competitive in the market, the company has chosen to incorporate state-of-the-art AI technology into its products. Today, however, much of the innovation in the field of AI starts at universities. For this reason, the company has decided to work with SnT, which specializes in conducting hands-on research projects with industrial partners. The aim of these projects is not only to publish research results, but also to develop concrete outcomes that can be used by the industrial partners. The third stakeholder is the Luxembourg National Research Fund (FNR),[3] a research funding agency that contributes to the funding of this research project through a public-private partnership grant under agreement number AFR-PPP 11508593.

1.4.3 Collaboration

The activities of this innovation ecosystem are shown in Fig. 1.4, which we explain below.

At the beginning of a project iteration, the university staff and the company's employees agree on the requirements to be met. Next, the staff of the university prepare an extensive literature review, which describes in detail the state of the art of research. Based on the literature review and the company's requirements, project goals are agreed on to deliver both new research results and concrete results that the company can exploit. Afterwards, the staff of the university carry out the research tasks and receive data from the company, which consists among other things of electricity consumption measurements and the results of physical on-site inspections. Throughout a project iteration, both sides regularly consult with each other and adjust the requirements as needed. After completing the research, the university staff present the research results to the company, including a software prototype. The use of the results is now divided into two different directions: First, the results are published by the university staff in suitable journals or presented at conferences. The publications also refer to the support of the research funding organization, which can also use these publications for marketing its research funding. In addition, the university staff are able to integrate their new research findings into their courses, preparing the next generation of researchers and developers for future

---

[1] http://snt.uni.lu.

[2] http://www.choiceholding.com.

[3] http://www.fnr.lu.

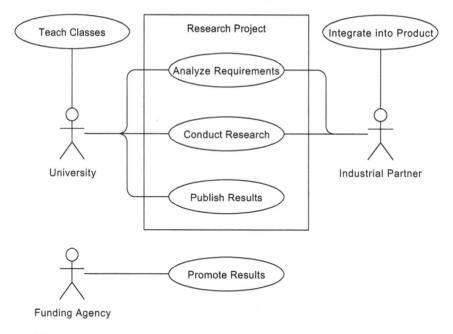

Fig. 1.4 Activities and interactions in this innovation ecosystem. Source: author

challenges with state-of-the-art lecture content. Second, the company integrates the relevant and usable research results into its products. As a result, it can use the latest research results to not only to maintain its competitiveness, but also to expand their business. After that, the next project iteration begins, in which new requirements are identified. Ideally, these also contain feedback from customers that use the new product functions resulting from the research results.

1.5 Recent Advances in AI

Although AI research has been conducted for over 60 years, many people first heard of AI just a few years ago. This, in addition to the "Terminator" movie series, is largely due to the huge advances made by AI applications over the past few years. Since 2006, there have been a number of significant advances, especially in the field of neural networks, which are now referred to as deep learning (Hinton et al. 2006). This term aims to ensure that (deep) neural networks have many hidden layers. This type of architecture has proven to be particularly helpful in detecting hidden relationships in input data. Although this was already the case in the 1980s, there was a lack of practical and applicable algorithms for training these networks from data first and, secondly, the lack of adequate computing resources. However, today there is much more powerful computing infrastructure available. In addition, significantly better algorithms for training this type of neural network have been derived since 2006 (Hinton et al. 2006).

As a result, many advances in AI research have been made, some of which are based on deep learning. Examples are autonomously driving cars or the computer program AlphaGo. Go is a board game that is especially popular in Southeast Asia, where players have a much greater number of possible moves than in chess. Traditional methods, with which, for example, the IBM program Deep Blue had beaten the then world chess champion Garry Kasparov in 1997, do not scale to the game of Go, since the mere increase of computing capacity is not sufficient due to the high complexity of this problem. It was only until a few years ago the prevailing opinion within the AI community that an AI, which plays Go on world level, was still decades away. The UK company Google DeepMind unexpectedly revealed their AI AlphaGo to the public in 2015. AlphaGo beat South Korean professional Go play Lee Sedol under tournament conditions (Silver et al. 2016). This success was partly based on deep learning and led to an increased awareness of AI world-wide. Of course, in addition to the current breakthroughs of AI mentioned in this section, there have been a lot of further success stories and we are sure that more will follow soon.

While many recent accomplishments are based in part on deep learning, this new kind of neural network is only one of many modern techniques. It is becoming increasingly apparent that there is a hype about deep learning and more and more unrealistic promises are being made about it (Dacrema et al. 2019; LeCun et al. 2015). It is therefore essential to relate the successes of deep learning and its fundamental limitations. The "no free lunch theorem", which is largely unknown both in industry and academia, states that all methods of machine learning averaged over all possible problems are equally successful (Wolpert 1996). Of course, some methods are better suited to some problems than others, but perform worse on different problems. Deep learning is especially useful for image, audio, video or text processing problems and when having a lot of training data. By contrast, deep learning, for example, is poorly suited to problems with a small amount of training data.

1.6   Contemporary Challenges in AI

We would now like to discuss what we feel are the most pressing challenges in AI. We have previously introduced the notion of an AI winter—a period of great setbacks, the loss of optimism and consequent reductions in funding. It is to be feared that the current and hype-based promise could trigger a new AI winter if those challenges are not solved in the foreseeable future.

1.6.1   Interpretability of Models

It is essential to better understand deep learning and its potential and not neglect other research methods. A major limitation of deep learning—and neural networks in general—is that these are black box models. As a consequence, the decisions made by them are often incomprehensible. Some advances have been made in this area recently, such as local interpretable model-agnostic explanations (LIME) (Ribeiro et al. 2016) for supervised models. However, there is still great research potential in this direction, as future advances may also likely increase the social acceptance of AI. For example, in the case of autonomously driving cars, the decisions taken by an AI should also be comprehensible for legal as well as software quality reasons.

1.6.2   Biased Data Sets

For about the last decade, the big data paradigm that has dominated research in machine learning can be summarized as follows: "It's not who has the best algorithm that wins. It's who has the most data." (Banko and Brill 2001) In practice, however, most data sets are (systematically) biased. Generally, biases occur in machine learning whenever the training data (e.g. the set of inspection results) and production/test data (e.g. the set of customers to generate inspections for) have different distributions, for which an example is depicted in Fig. 1.5.

The appearance of biases in data sets imply a number of severe consequences including, but not limited to, the following: First, conclusions derived from biased—and therefore unrepresentative—data sets could simply be wrong due to lack of reproducibility and lack of generalizability. This is a common issue in research as a whole, as it has been argued that most research published may actually be wrong

Fig. 1.5 Bias: Training and test data sets are drawn from different distributions. Source: author

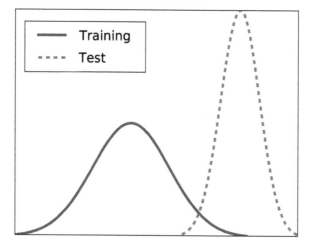

(Ioannidis 2005). Second, these machine learning models may discriminate against subjects of under-represented categories (Curtis 2015; Wang and Kosinski 2017).

Historically, biased data sets have been a long-standing issue in statistics. The failed prediction of the outcome of the 1936 US presidential election is described in the following example. It is often cited in the statistics literature in order to illustrate the impact of biases in data. This example is discussed in detail in Bryson (1976).

Example 1.2 (Prediction of the Outcome of the 1936 US Presidential Election) The Democratic candidate Franklin D. Roosevelt was elected President in 1932 and ran for a second term in 1936. Roosevelt's Republican opponent was Kansas Governor Alfred Landon. *The Literary Digest*, a general interest weekly magazine, had correctly predicted the outcomes of the elections in 1916, 1920, 1924, 1928 and 1932 based on straw polls. In 1936, The Literary Digest sent out 10 million questionnaires in order to predict the outcome of the presidential election. The Literary Digest received 2.3 million returns and predicted Landon to win by a landslide. However, the predicted result proved to be wrong, as quite the opposite happened: Roosevelt won by a landslide. The Literary Digest compiled their data set of 10 million recipients mainly from car registrations and phone directories. In that time, the households that had a car or a phone represented a disproportionally rich, and thus biased, sample of the overall population that particularly favored the Republican candidate Landon. In contrast, George Gallup only interviewed 3000 handpicked people, which were an unbiased sample of the population. As a consequence, Gallup could predict the outcome of the election very accurately (Harford 2014).

Even though this historic example is well understood in statistics nowadays, similar or related issues happened for the elections in 1948 and 2016. Furthermore, biases appear every day in modern big data-oriented machine learning. As an outcome, biases may cause severe impact every day dozens of times, such as in the following example:

Example 1.3 (Auto-tagging Images) It has been argued that most data on humans may be on white people and thus may not represent the overall population (Podesta 2014). As a consequence, the predictions of models trained on such biased data may cause infamous news. For example, in 2015, Google added an auto-tagging feature to its Photos app. This new feature automatically assigns tags to photos, such as bicycle, dog, etc. However, some black users reported that they were tagged as "gorillas", which led to major criticism of Google (Curtis 2015). Most likely, that mishap was caused by a biased training set, in which black people were largely underrepresented.

The examples provided in this section show that having simply more data is not always helpful in training reliable models, as the data sets used may be biased. As a consequence, having data that is more representative is favorable, even if the amount of data used is less than just using the examples from a strongly biased data set. We published an extended survey and discussion of biases in big data sets in Glauner et al. (2018).

1.7 AI Innovation in China

You may wonder whether you should actually invest in AI so soon. Probably your business is going very well at present time. On top of that, there may be a limited number of competitors that so far have not been able to outrank you. All of that may be true-today. In the coming years, however, completely new competitors will emerge. Most likely, they will be based in China. I often feel that most people in the Western world, including decision makers, see China mainly as an export market or a place for cheap labor. In the last couple of years, however, and unnoticed by most Westerners, China has become the world's leading country in AI innovation. You can learn more about China's AI innovation ecosystem and its strong support from both the government and industry in Kai-Fu Lee's book "*AI Superpowers: China, Silicon Valley, and the New World Order*" (Lee 2018). Lee's book is both, encouraging and shocking in our opinion.

How Quickly is China Innovating in AI?

Let me tell you more about my own experience. I travel to Shanghai at least once a year. I kept noticing an old factory in the Yangpu district. It seemed to have been closed down a long time ago and the land appeared unused. Every single year I passed by, nothing had changed. In 2017, however, the factory was suddenly gone. Furthermore, the factory was not only teared down, the entire land has been turned into an AI innovation hub named "Changyang Campus". The office space also already seemed to be entirely taken, predominantly by startups. All of that had happened in less than 12 months! Imagine how many years it even takes in the Western world in order to tear a factory down and get a new construction permit.

In my opinion, we need to radically rethink innovation and agility in the Western world in order to remain competitive. AI's ability to automate human decision will play a crucial role in the future of nearly every company's value chain, be it in research and development, procurement, pricing, marketing or sales, just to name a few parts. Therefore, the companies that invest in AI early on will be the leaders of their sector in the coming decades. Those that do not invest now are likely to be put out of business by a new AI-driven competitor. After I share the insights of Lee's book and my own experience, I typically manage decision makers to rethink their business and how AI can help them to remain competitive in the long term. Take some time to read Lee's book, it will be a truly rewarding experience.

1.8   Conclusions

The first part of this chapter provides a description of how we see innovation
ecosystems that lead to fruitful, cutting-edge and sustainable results. We then
provided a gentle introduction to the field of artificial intelligence, its history and
fundamental concepts. In the second part, we presented an innovation ecosystem
of a joint industry-university project on the detection of electricity theft, a USD
100 billion business annually. We showed how concrete AI innovation management
works and how it leads to cutting-edge outcomes that are used in software products.
In the third part, we discussed recent advances in AI, its contemporary challenges
and its most relevant questions for its future. We also looked at Chinese AI
innovation ecosystems. As an outcome, Western decision makers in any industry
should understand that they have to invest in AI as soon as possible in order to
remain competitive.

References

Antmann P (2009) Reducing technical and non-technical losses in the power sector. World Bank,
    Washington
Banko M, Brill E (2001) Scaling to very very large corpora for natural language disambiguation.
    In: *Proceedings of the 39th annual meeting on association for computational linguistics*, pp 26–
    33. Association for Computational Linguistics, Stroudsburg
Bishop CM (2006) *Pattern recognition and machine learning.* Springer, Berlin, Heidelberg
Bryson MC (1976) The literary digest poll: making of a statistical myth. Am Stat 30(4):184–185
Curtis S (2015) Google photos labels black people as gorillas. Telegraph. http://www.telegraph.
    co.uk/technology/google/11710136/Google-Photos-assigns-gorilla-tag-to-photos-of-black-
    people.html. [Online]. Accessed 28 December 2017
Dacrema MF, Cremonesi P, Jannach D (2019) Are we really making much progress? A worrying
    analysis of recent neural recommendation approaches. In: *Proceedings of the 13th ACM
    conference on recommender systems (RecSys 2019)*
Deng L, Yu D (2014) Deep learning: methods and applications. Found Trends Signal Process
    7(3–4):197–387
Glauner P (2019) Artificial intelligence for the detection of electricity theft and irregular power
    usage in emerging markets. PhD thesis, University of Luxembourg, Luxembourg
Glauner P, Valtchev P, State R (2018) Impact of biases in big data. In: *Proceedings of the 26th
    European symposium on artificial neural networks, computational intelligence and machine
    learning (ESANN 2018)*
Harford T (2014) Big data: are we making a big mistake? FT magazine. http://www.ft.com/intl/
    cms/s/2/21a6e7d8-b479-11e3-a09a-00144feabdc0.html. [Online]. Accessed 15 January 2016
Hinton GE, Osindero S, Teh Y-W (2006) A fast learning algorithm for deep belief nets. Neural
    Computation 18(7):1527–1554
Ioannidis JP (2005) Why most published research findings are false. PLoS Med 2(8):e124
LeCun Y, Bengio Y, Hinton G (2015) Deep learning. Nature 521(7553):436
Lee K-F (2018) AI superpowers: China, Silicon Valley, and the new world order. Houghton Mifflin
    Harcourt, Boston
McCarthy J, Minsky ML, Rochester N, Shannon CE (1955) A proposal for the dartmouth summer
    research project on artificial intelligence. AI Mag 27(4):12
Podesta J (2014) Big data: Seizing opportunities, preserving values. White House, Executive Office
    of the President, Washington

Ribeiro MT, Singh S, Guestrin C (2016) Why should I trust you?: Explaining the predictions of any classifier. In: *Proceedings of the 22nd ACM SIGKDD international conference on knowledge discovery and data mining*, pp 1135–1144. ACM, New York

Russell SJ, Norvig P (2009) Artificial intelligence: a modern approach, 3rd edn. Prentice Hall, Upper Saddle River

Silver D, Huang A, Maddison CJ, Guez A, Sifre L, Van Den Driessche G, Schrittwieser J, Antonoglou I, Panneershelvam V, Lanctot M et al (2016) Mastering the game of go with deep neural networks and tree search. Nature 529(7587):484

Smith TB (2004) Electricity theft: a comparative analysis. Energy Policy 32(18):2067–2076

Turing A (1950) Computing machinery and intelligence. Mind 59(236):433–460

Wang Y, Kosinski M (2017) Deep neural networks are more accurate than humans at detecting sexual orientation from facial images. J Personal Soc Psychol 114(2):246–257

Wolpert DH (1996) The lack of a priori distinctions between learning algorithms. Neural Comput 8(7):1341–1390

Extracorporate Innovation Environments: An Example Lead User Approach Applied to the Medical Engineering Industry

Philipp Plugmann

2.1 Introduction

Technology companies are in the midst of unflagging competition, on both the national and international levels. Innovation must give rise to new products and services at short intervals of time. This unvarying pressure to perform needs structured processes. A company applies innovation processes within its boundaries for the purpose of establishing and optimising a structured process. The intended outcome is the development of products and services that fulfil the needs of users and therefore the market demand.

In the process, companies are ready and willing to follow up their customers' tips and ideas, and especially those provided by specifically qualified, progressive customers (the so called lead users), that facilitate the company's developments of new products and services and improvements to its present portfolio (Herstatt et al. 2007).

The lead user approach is an organisational process that helps technology companies to optimise the generation of its ideas and the improvement of its products and services. Yet this process must also help to overcome barriers. In this respect, the lead user functions as an external research and development department. This chapter is not intended to detail how the remuneration agreements are organised between lead users and companies. Rather, a strategic view is taken that explores how the lead user approach can be established permanently as an integral constituent of the company strategy and the innovation processes. Finally, also the issues involved with the innovation environment and the satisfaction of the

P. Plugmann (✉)
SRH University of Applied Health Sciences, Leverkusen, Germany
e-mail: philipp.plugmann@srh.de

© The Editor(s) (if applicable) and The Author(s), under exclusive license to Springer Nature Switzerland AG 2021
V. Nestle et al. (eds.), *Creating Innovation Spaces*, Management for Professionals, https://doi.org/10.1007/978-3-030-57642-4_2

lead users themselves are scrutinised, and the findings translated into the permanent and successful maintenance of the interaction flow.

The empirical study presented later was intended to examine scientifically whether the SMEs on Germany's medical engineering sectors had established a sound basis for interaction with lead users or whether this basis was only temporary, i.e. more or less informal and therefore unstructured. Furthermore, the exploratory preliminary examination raised questions at the last minute, which also require consideration.

2.2 Domestic Situation in the Innovation Field: A Ten-Year Analysis

The present economic situation and the future of Germany hinges on the performance capabilities of its industries (DIW 2008). Specifically, the innovation capabilities of companies in the international competitive arena can afford a key contribution in the form of new product and service developments towards preserving and building on this status quo in 2018 and for the future. In their book "Innovationsindikator 2017: Schwerpunkt digitale Transformation"—published as part of the series "ZEW-Gutachten und Forschungsberichte", a collaboration between the German Academy of Science and Engineering (acatech), the Federation of German Industries e. V. (BDI), the Fraunhofer Institute for Systems and Innovation Research (Fraunhofer ISI), and the ZEW—Leibniz Centre for European Economic Research (ZEW)—Weissenberger-Eibl et al. (2017) note that education, research, and knowledge transfer should be geared more thoroughly to future challenges. This book reveals that Germany is in fact lagging behind other countries in all subfields. For instance, the innovation performance of the German economy is shown to fall behind that of South Korea and the USA. According to the authors, the educational system is still a very long way behind the top countries, such as South Korea and Finland, and this in spite of improvements introduced in recent years. Of interest here is the particular emphasis placed on Singapore. According to the Innovation Indicator 2017: "The high score achieved by Singapore in second place according to the Innovation Indicator 2017 can be put down specifically to wide reaching state subsidisation. This includes generous, direct state research incentives, tax incentives for corporate research and development, and a high state demand for new technologies providing incentives for innovations. In terms of percentage of university graduates among employees and quality indicators for its educational system and educational results, Singapore achieves the highest values in international comparisons. The science system is rated the second best, after Switzerland."

Today—as eleven years ago—there are initial indications warning of the inadequate general conditions, environment, educational programme, and funds for innovation in Germany and of Germany's remoteness from a top position, as evidenced by some analyses in international comparisons. As early as 2008, a strength–weakness profile was presented in the study "Rückstand bei der Bildung gefährdet Deutschlands Innovationsfähigkeit" ("educational deficits jeopardise Germany's innovation capabilities") published by the renowned German Institute for Economic Research (DIW 2008).

Whereas this study named among the strengths the marketing of new products (DIW 2008, p. 717) and the intermeshing of university and non-university research, the greatest weakness proved the educational field (fifteenth place in a comparison of seventeen industrial nations). The authors saw here the danger of erosion to future innovation capabilities if the innovation system could not be supplied with adequately qualified personnel. Further weaknesses were identified in the funding of innovation, specifically in the provision of risk capital for corporate startups.

The DIW study of 2008 judged the cultural innovation climate to be particularly serious, a finding which the authors put down to the people's attitude to change and to the new and their (un)willingness to accept risks and collaborate on novel solutions. The international comparisons even placed last the willingness of startups in Germany to accept risks. In conclusion, the study (DIW 2008, p 724) criticised the supply of highly trained personnel from Germany's educational system, which produces too few tertiary graduates.

In his book "Design Thinking" (Plattner et al. 2010), Hasso Plattner, SAP cofounder, cited precisely this DIW study, listing the findings over several pages. Also the portfolio of the Federal Ministry of Education and Research (BMBF) for innovation strategy (BMBF 2010), high tech offensives as well as research strategies reveals that Germany's innovation strengths can be improved, and a wide range of measures has now been initiated on the international level.

Improving the weaknesses in the educational system will take years. And it will be years before these qualified academics will become available to German companies. This is an assessment of the future. Hence, at the same time, it becomes all the more important to assign and steer the existing innovation forces to even better effect at companies and to quantify these force's success.

The empirical study presented later in this chapter is intended to elaborate a theoretical concept and a practical recommendation for action based on the SMEs in Germany's medical engineering fields as the research objects. The findings are then to be provided as current scientific figures that the management boards of technology companies can utilise as a basis for their decisions affecting innovation teams with lead users.

In October 2013, SPECTARIS, the Berlin association of high tech industries in Germany SPECTARIS criticised the EU regulation relating to medicinal products. SPECTARIS stated that the medical engineering industry in Germany was "shocked" and "deeply disturbed" by the draft of the "new medicinal products regulation of the European Parliament". SPECTARIS criticised that the apparently large number of responsible MEPs were unaware of the effects this will have on medical engineering SMEs and that this administrative hurdle in the form of numerous approval boards will prove detrimental to the competitive strength of Germany's medical engineering industry. Also the opinion "Kommissionsvorschlag für eine neue EU-Dual-Use-Verordnung März 2017" ("Commission's proposal for a new EU dual use regulation of March 2017") that SPECTARIS published in March

2017 (SPECTARIS 2017) served to underscore the current criticism issued by the association for this sector with respect to the compounded complexity of the general conditions and the greater administrative needs that corporate innovation teams will now have to face.

At the time, this assessment by the professional association SPECTARIS was substantiated by the findings of the BMBF (2008) and BMBF and VDE (2009) studies serving to "identify obstacles to innovation in medical engineering". These studies had been conducted as updates to their predecessors of 2002 and 2005 concerning the medical engineering situation. The study design chosen included a survey among 45 experts in the various medical engineering fields. These expert interviews made use of a questionnaire with 6 question levels of 5–6 subquestions each. There were therefore about 30–35 questions. Also case examples were presented, e.g. "Dental Navigation, Case Example No. 9" (BMBF and VDE 2009, p 119), as a means to illustrate better the obstacles to innovation in the various medical engineering fields.

The summary (BMBF and VDE 2009, pp 4–8) points out the complexity and very high costs involved in the development of new technical products and services for the medical engineering fields. The companies see that the entire process, from the idea to the refinancing of a medicinal product, demands more and more time on the German market. It is stated that in particular smaller companies are able to meet this trend only with limited financial means and that these obstacles to the innovation process in medical engineering will steadily increase. The findings returned by this study's expert survey also revealed that the great challenges of the future will be posed by the whole financing aspect in conjunction with reimbursement issues raised by statutory health insurance (SHI) on the one hand, and the availability of highly qualified personnel, above all from interdisciplinary fields, for virtually all phases of the innovation process on the other.

The DIW (2008) and BMBF and VDE (2009) studies confirm that the demand placed on German companies to assemble, direct, and quantify the success of innovation teams will become greater in future if they are to deliver the required performance. One success factor here will be the continued integration of lead users. In this context, the refinancing strategy pursued by these companies will continue to be a great challenge at the same time as the personnel problem. In conclusion, the performance capabilities of corporate innovation teams will become a key factor for their companies' survival on the international market—and lead users can contribute to this. The empirical study presented later is intended by means of surveys among SMEs in Germany's medical engineering fields to derive for these research objects theoretical findings and practical options for action. It is also to explore the issues presented by the discussion of "radical innovation" (Gemünden et al. 2007) and "breakthrough innovation" (Herstatt et al. 2007) discussed in more recent literature, which focuses on the interaction with lead users and their satisfaction.

2.3   Innovation Process Models

Standardised innovation processes facilitate intracorporate flows and regulate operations. Hence there are various models of differing historical backgrounds for the design of corporate innovation processes. Their names seem to be never ending, but the following presents a selected excerpt of model nomenclature based on corporate innovation processes and their integration:

Phase Review Process (Hughes and Chafin 1996), Ulrich and Eppinger Process Model (Ulrich and Eppinger 1995), 3rd Generation Stage Gate Process (Cooper 1996), Innovation Process based on Simultaneous Activities (Crawford 1994), Value Proposition Cycle (Hughes and Chafin 1996), Phase Model for Operative Innovation Processes (Thom 1992), Brockhoff Phase Model (Brockhoff 1999), Witt Innovation Process (Witt 1996), Vahs Innovation Process (Vahs and Burmester 1999), Overall Process of Performance Requirements (Ebert et al. 1992), and Herstatt Innovation Process (Herstatt 1999). At the same time, there are also application based empirical figures from a great many companies and entrepreneurs that reveal highly individual trends during the birth of innovative technologies (Glauner and Plugmann 2020).

In textbooks and specialist publications, the above innovation process models are depicted as flowcharts that illustrate the building block processes from the generation and assessment of ideas to development, production, and marketing. These historical process depictions make virtually no allowance for the integration of lead users. This is one starting point for specific research to supplement the conventional depictions. How do technology companies interact with lead users today? How would lead users themselves rate their satisfaction with this interaction? Do they see their proposed ideas realised? Are they satisfied with the way the companies supervise this realisation? Is the interaction temporary, structured, or formal to some extent?

However, the implementation of one or more of these models (Cooper 1983, 1994; Cohen et al. 1998; Herstatt 1999) does not warrant the market success of products or services. These models describe solely the possible flows. It is here that the lead user approach can be applied and implemented. Often, lead users are customers of the company and experience daily the use of products the company sells. No one is closer to the customer than the customer himself.

2.4   Definition and Concept of "lead user"

Lead users were first described in the pertinent literature in the seventies. At that time, Von Hippel (1976, 1977a,b) and Allen (1986) described the relevance of "leading users" whose suggestions for the improvement of existing products and services served to influence the innovation process to a positive extent. Von Hippel also stated that lead users could be both companies and individual persons. Individuals can develop and implement innovative solutions for the most diverse reasons. This can be born of the need to help a loved one suffering from an illness, physical disability, or other issues.

At the beginning of the innovation process, the lead user persists in trying out a solution until he has developed a prototype or method that works to such an extent that it can be shared with other affected persons or users. This so-called peer to peer principle causes other individuals in the affected community to apply the new products or methods and to use and improve them for themselves. Once the number of users reaches a certain "critical mass" allowing a producer (manufacturer) to enter series production, the innovation can be produced and marketed in large numbers.

2.4.1   Market Vicinity and Future Orientation of Lead Users

Often, lead users are described as specifically qualified users (von Hippel 1978, 1982, 1986). Yet there are also users, although they do not possess the requisite technical expertise or skills, who are nevertheless driven by a mixture of intrinsic dedication and persistence to realise innovative ideas. Also self-education forms part of this makeup. Yet another characterising feature of lead users is that they are a step ahead of other users on the market. They gear themselves to future needs and trends, and want to see their ideas realised. They focus on the solution of a problem affecting the lead user directly or indirectly. The element of market research, otherwise favoured by industry, cannot compete with the activities of lead users: a survey among customers often contributes to the definition of problems, but does not necessarily promote the generation of ideas comparable with an innovation process.

2.4.2   Detecting Lead Users: Research in Literature

Lead users can be individuals or companies. Individuals can be users or the company's employees. A study by Lüthje (2000) examining outdoor products revealed that users adopted a leading role in the development of ideas and improvements. Shah (2001) arrived at the same conclusion after examining skateboard and snowboard products. Shaw (1985) verified this for medical engineering companies which integrated medical personnel as lead users in their innovation process. Herstatt (1994) could demonstrate the relevance of lead users in the construction industry, e.g. HILTI. Riggs and von Hippel (1994), von Hippel and Riggs (1996) and von Hippel et al. (1999) could demonstrate that breakthroughs in the innovation process were also achieved in collaboration with lead users, and these from differing industries.

A further possibility takes the form of lead users embedded in the company itself. Here, Schweisfurth and Raasch (2014) define embedded lead users (ELUs) as employees at a company who are lead users of the products and services this company produces. Oliveira and von Hippel (2011) could describe users as service innovators, taking as their basis a case example from the banking services sector. Hienerth et al. (2012) compared in the personal sector the innovation efficiency of consumers and producers. Von Hippel et al. (2011) published in the MIT Sloan

Management Review the article "The Age of the Consumer-Innovator". Morrison et al. (2000) investigated the determinants of user innovations and the sharing of innovations on local markets. Hence, research into the economy has been analysing for decades and to a very great extent the innovation processes of various industries, their champions, and user influence. This provides a very broad scientific foundation for further analyses. The changes induced by global digital transformation in the general conditions will provide a very wide and deep research field for the coming decades.

2.4.3 Interaction between Lead User and Company: Research in Literature

User innovation passes through various phases in which one or more users engage in collaborative evaluation, replication, and improvement. Finally, in the so-called peer to peer diffusion phase, it is spread by word of mouth among similar users, where it establishes itself to an increasing extent. Once a critical mass has been reached, it may prove interesting to a producer to enter series production of the innovation now established among the users. This cycle between the user (innovation designs) and producer (innovation support) can lead to mutual satisfaction (Raasch and von Hippel 2012a,b).

Raasch and von Hippel (2012a,b) describe interactions between innovations by (lead) users and producers. For their example, they take four different forms of the innovation process: the design changes and proposals submitted by users, and the innovation supported by producers, complementarity, or competition. Furthermore, they present two ways of developing and disseminating innovations, either free of charge over the peer to peer channel, or over market channels associated with high costs. This study sheds light on a fascinating aspect: that, from the producer's viewpoint, the analysis of competition treats the user as the abrupt emergence of an optional competitor, should he start producing himself. In this context, artificial intelligence is gaining in strategic significance for companies (Iansiti and Lakhani 2020).

It demonstrates how a user contested market can reduce prices and hence exercise a positive effect on the public good. If user ideas can no longer be diffused continuously into the producers' development process, but remain within the user environment which develops and markets products from these own ideas, the producers may have to face a competitor that is stronger than other producers. This underscores the relevance of lead users' satisfaction with producers in innovation collaboration, and so we have integrated this aspect as well, among others, in the study now presented in the following.

2.5   SCIENTIFIC STUDY: Integrating the Innovation Process of Lead Users in Germany's Medical Engineering SMEs

Whereas large companies, owing to their size and payroll, are compelled to make use of structured, formalised innovation processes, small and medium sized enterprises (SMEs) in Germany's medical engineering industry (GMEI) may also choose from unstructured, spontaneously emerging, or individualised innovation processes.

IfM (2018) defines SMEs in Germany either as small enterprises employing up to 9 persons and achieving an annual turnover of less than EUR 1 million or as medium sized enterprises employing up to 499 persons and achieving an annual turnover of less than EUR 50 million.

This study is to present the extent to which GMEI SMEs are open to innovation processes with lead users and the level of their integration. The hypothesis underlying this scientific empirical study assumed that lead users afford a key contribution to the production of new, innovative products and services and represent a fixed constituent of innovation processes at SMEs in Germany's medical engineering industry.

2.5.1   Exploratory Preliminary Examination

Before we could draw up the questionnaire, we first had to conduct an exploratory preliminary examination. This involved sending an email to about 150 managing directors of SMEs in the medical engineering industry from our network in Germany, Austria, and Switzerland, requesting them for a fifteen minute interview by telephone. In the end, 18 managing directors declared their willingness, and the following focal points emerged, listed in the following as (an unprioritised) "Top Ten":

1. 7 of 16 companies interact in a standardised form with lead users
2. 9 of 16 companies interact in an unstructured, sporadic form with lead users, relying primarily on their own research and development department
3. Fixed and unstructured formats are combined during interaction with lead users
4. Project management IT has often integrated "lead user integration" in its software, but this is activated only for specific projects
5. Exhibitions, congresses, and sector events were often the places of first contact with lead users
6. Many lead users assume a proactive role in contacting companies
7. Some lead users are no longer available for the exchange of ideas after a number of years
8. Both national and international lead users are integrated
9. Products and services are developed jointly with lead users

10. In isolated cases, subsidiaries were set up with lead users of many years' standing

The above "Top Ten" represented the first leads to occupy SME managing directors in the medical engineering industry with respect to lead users.

2.5.2 Material and Method

The exploratory preliminary examination revealed that there are standardised and unstructured innovation processes and that interactions with lead users sometimes had a fixed format, and sometimes did not. The innovation ideas of lead users support innovation projects and are incorporated partially in project management IT. Following the exploratory preliminary examination, it became clear that a large number of company cases was needed to obtain meaningful data. After collection, these can be analysed with IBM SPSS Statistics software.

Between March 2015 and October 2017 we surveyed 114 companies from the medical engineering sectors in Germany, Austria, and Switzerland. The predefined inclusion criteria were small and medium sized enterprises (SMEs), German speaking economic areas, medical engineering companies at least five years on the market, interaction with lead users, and no more than 499 employees. The 114 surveyed companies participating in the study received an email and a reminder email fourteen days later. Contacted were 357 companies, of which 186 replied and ultimately 114 took part.

2.5.3 Questionnaire

The final questionnaire listed the following ten questions:

1. Is the integration of lead users in your company's innovation processes relevant to your creation of value?
2. Does more than 25% of your created value depend on the successful integration of lead users in your innovation processes?
3. Are lead users integrated according to formal criteria, or is this process more or less unstructured?
4. Would you say that lead users are satisfied with how their ideas are realised?
5. How often do you confer with lead users?
6. Could you translate the ideas of lead users into new, innovative products and services?
7. Did it come to conflicts between the management board and the research and development department during lead user integration in the innovation process?
8. Have digital technologies like Skype, WhatsApp, or the social networks altered your interaction with lead users?

9. From literature, you are acquainted with structured, building block innovation models. Would you say that these are still of topical relevance in the digital age?
10. Are there classical standard users, i.e. "non-lead users", among your external input providers?

The questionnaire was sent to the participating companies in January 2017, together with a request to reply within three months. In early April 2017, we sent out reminders granting a four week extension, so that we could begin with the statistical analysis in May 2017.

2.5.4 Findings

The results in Table 2.1 were returned for the frequency distributions based on each of the ten questions.

Also of interest to us was whether digital technologies were used in the evenings or at the weekends as well to communicate with lead users (question 8) on the subject of their integration in the innovation process. These statistics we now present in Table 2.2.

Table 2.1 Frequency distributions based on each of the ten questions ($n = 114$)

	Questions	Findings (Total $n = 114$)
1	Is the integration of lead users in your company's innovation processes relevant to your creation of value?	Yes 40.35% ($n = 46$)
2	Does more than 25% of your created value depend on the successful integration of lead users in your innovation processes?	Yes 47.37% ($n = 54$)
3	Are lead users integrated according to structured, formal criteria?	Yes 66.67% ($n = 76$)
4	Would you say that lead users are satisfied with how their ideas are realised?	Yes 89.47% ($n = 102$)
5	Do you confer regularly with lead users?	Yes 79.82% ($n = 91$)
6	Could you translate the ideas of lead users into new, innovative products and services?	Yes 82.46% ($n = 94$)
7	Did it come to conflicts between the management board and the research and development department during lead user integration in the innovation process?	Yes 13.16% ($n = 15$)
8	Have digital technologies like Skype, WhatsApp, or the social networks altered your interaction with lead users?	Yes 92.11% ($n = 105$)
9	From literature, you are acquainted with structured, building block innovation models. Would you say that these are still of topical relevance in the digital age?	Yes 88.60% ($n = 101$)
10	Are there classical standard users, i.e. "non-lead users", among your external input providers?	Yes 15.79% ($n = 18$)

Table 2.2 Crosstab table distributions for questions 11 and 12

11	Do you use digital technologies to communicate with your lead users in the evenings or at the weekends as well?	Yes 82.86% ($n = 87$) based on $n = 105$ from question 8
12	Do you think this is a problem for the lead users?	No 96.55% ($n = 84$) based on $n = 87$ from question 11

2.5.5 Discussion and Summary of the Study

40.35% ($n = 46$) of the companies surveyed in this study stated that lead user integration in their innovation processes is relevant to their creation of value. From this it can be easily inferred that the competition between medical engineering companies depends not only on the performance of their own research and development departments, but also on their expertise in gaining and integrating permanently the lead users on the market for collaborative purposes. Only 47.37% ($n = 54$) confirmed that collaboration with lead users contributed more than 25% to the value created.

66.67% ($n = 76$) of the surveyed companies confirmed that their collaboration with lead users was based on structured, formal criteria. 89.47% ($n = 102$) were of the opinion that the lead users were satisfied with how their ideas were realised. The satisfaction of lead users with how companies realise their ideas in the development of new, innovative products and services is a crucial factor for their permanent integration in these companies. In most cases, the ideas submitted by lead users are the outcome of laborious thought and work. They want considerable improvements to existing products and services or to create something new. They make every effort to work out and submit a practicable proposal to the company they are collaborating with. If this is not appreciated or finds little response, this will lead over the long term to demotivation and the lead users' increasing unwillingness to collaborate further with this company. The lead user will continue to work on his ideas, but this time alone or with competitors. The problem here is that the lead user approach encompasses a certain amount of open innovation, in that the collaborating company must open itself to the lead user when integrating him in the innovation process. The crucial roles here are trust and integrity.

79.82% ($n = 91$) confer regularly with their lead users, and 82.46% ($n = 94$) were able to translate their lead users' ideas into innovative products and services. This conversion rate, too, is relevant because it is a measure of the efficiency underlying the company's collaboration and performance. The decision of SME managing directors in the medical engineering industry in favour of integrating lead users in the existing innovation process can give rise to conflicts between the management board and R&D personnel. In this study, however, this was confirmed by only 13.16% ($n = 15$) of the companies surveyed. Of course, a management decision of this kind in favour of implementing lead users must be supervised and organised in such a manner that the R&D department does not take offence. Greater acceptance is therefore obtained, and so smooth running collaboration made possible.

92.11% ($n = 105$) state that they use digital technologies (Skype, WhatsApp, and social media) to communicate with lead users, and that the interaction has changed as a result. Today, text, images, videos, and messages can be sent without further ado over these fast channels. This accelerates the process and improves the efficiency of sharing ideas. 88.60% ($n = 101$) confirm that the structured innovation models known from literature continue to be of relevance to the company in spite of the digital age. This testifies to the stability and durability of these models as an underlying structure for innovation processes and collaboration at companies. The question concerning the input from classical users was affirmed by only 15.79% ($n = 18$), a relatively small number, which in turn underscores the relevance of lead users. Then we also became interested in the number of companies that communicate with the lead users in the evenings and at the weekends as well. This proved to be quite large, at 82.86% ($n = 87$ of $n = 105$ from question 8). In addition, 96.55% ($n = 84$ of $n = 87$ from question 11) or most companies thought that this was no problem to the lead users. This could explain the above average stress levels and the many working hours accepted by lead users.

In summary, this study shows that the interaction between producers and lead users, based here on SMEs in Germany's medical engineering sector, signifies a key constituent for these companies' creation of value. Industries in the competitive arena support the diffusion of ideas for innovative products and services from the user to the producer domains. Industry also makes every effort to maintain lead user satisfaction. This in turn consolidates the lead users' ties to companies and prevents them from turning into competitors, as described by Raasch and von Hippel (2012a,b).

2.6 User Driven Case Examples

Presented in the following are two interesting user driven projects in the healthcare sector which benefited from the power of user innovation. Particularly the platform PATIENT INNOVATION I find fascinating, and wish to share this with the reader. The concluding example on the birth of cardiac catheterisation is somewhat exotic and risky, but should be included if only for historical reasons.

2.6.1 Patient Innovation: Sharing Solutions, Improving Life

Two words, and a huge social innovation. On its website, PATIENT INNOVATION describes itself thus: "An open platform for patients and their carers, for all kinds of illnesses, worldwide. This platform lets them share the solutions they have developed themselves for health issues. It therefore helps patients to a better acceptance of challenges posed by their illness" (PATIENT INNOVATION 2018).

I first learned of PATIENT INNOVATION in August 2014 at Harvard Business School (Boston, USA). I had the honour of attending the 12th Open and User Innovation Conference (OUI) organised by Professor Eric von Hippel (Massachusetts

Institute of Technology) and Professor Karim Lakhani (Harvard Business School) to present briefly my own scientific research findings in the innovation field.

Professor Eric von Hippel (MIT, Sloan School of Management) is also one of the advisers for PATIENT INNOVATION. For decades he has been conducting research in the innovation field on user innovation, lead users, and the social impact of changing innovation processes. On account of my activities at the time as a lead user and adviser of many years' standing for various German medical engineering companies and of my work at my own surgery in Leverkusen, my many researches in literature repeatedly drew my attention to Professor Eric von Hippel. Now both my wife and I found the prospect thrilling of getting to know him personally at the OUI conference in the USA. At the OUI conference were about 200 international researchers, including many from Germany, Austria, and Switzerland, representing the fields of innovation, entrepreneurship, and management.

A further adviser for PATIENT INNOVATION, also from the Massachusetts Institute of Technology (MIT), is Professor Robert Langer who, in the field of biomedical engineering, runs the world's largest research laboratory (Langer's research lab at MIT) with over 100 researchers. Also on board as adviser is Sir Richard Roberts, 1993 Nobel Laureate in physiology or medicine, Chief Scientific Officer of New England Biolabs in Beverly, Massachusetts (USA).

The directors of PATIENT INNOVATION are Professor Pedro Oliveira (Católica Lisbon School of Business and Economics, Lisbon, Portugal) and medical practitioner Professor Helena Canhao (Nova Medical School, Nova University, Lisbon, Portugal).

The idea of the lead user is extrapolated here into the motivated "user", whose intrinsic motivation, free of financial interests but with colossal commitment, drives him to realize his innovative idea. The motivation may arise from the illness suffered by the user himself, his loved ones, or others he feels close to. Yet it may also stem from the inner, untrammelled drive to benefit society with this idea that can lead to better prevention and health. It is a platform for those who want to give and help. I was immediately captivated by this idea and the platform. For the best ideas realised, there is an annual award. The objective "is a platform and social network allowing patients, loved ones, and medical personnel to share with others their solutions to health issues" (PATIENT INNOVATION 2018), hitting the nail right on the head.

This website also hosts patient groups, provides alphabetically ordered lists of illnesses for searches, presents ideas and solutions submitted by other users, includes a forum for sharing ideas, and supports a community of members. How the platform works is self explanatory. For instance, the keyword "diabetes" returns 64 suggestions, from innovative equipment to online videos for nutrition and improved quality of life. Also the subgroups under each of the illness types are differentiated between, simplifying the user's search for ideas or solutions relating to his specific illness.

I would like to present here now extracts from a great idea that has received the PATIENT INNOVATION Award: One of the previous winners of the PATIENT INNOVATION AWARD invented the talking stick for the visually impaired. When interviewed, the inventor Pavel Kurbatsky describes how he designed it for the world, for the seeing and the visually impaired, in order to make life easier for them. "I could see that blind or deaf people, although exactly like everyone else, have great difficulty in moving in an environment not designed for them". On being asked about his motivation for developing this idea, he said: "I decided that I could help them in some way or other". The PATIENT INNOVATION (2018) website provides this interview in its entirety, which goes on to say:

> Some years before, this young genius had already started researching into possibilities of applying technologies to help people with disabilities. Aged nine, Pavel Kurbatsky invented a special thermometer for the visually impaired. Today, aged 18, he has developed a special stick and special glasses. The stick is fitted with sensors on three levels: head, hips, and feet. The sensors scan the environment and emit an acoustic warning when an obstacle is approached. The glasses feature an integrated headset and GPS that can store details of particular places for future reference. This is especially helpful in places like hospitals, government authorities, and public transportation.

Many other ideas and solutions can be viewed there as sources of inspiration. After this inspiration in 2015, I have developed at my own expense my "Dr. Dr. Plugmann APP", which is available free of charge to all on the internet. At any rate, I now know of a number of doctor's and dental surgeries that use this app as a playful option of assisting patients in their everyday routine. The app was designed with high user friendliness in mind, and in my view the combination of healthcare and gamification has huge potential when it is realised in user friendly and reliable form. For me, too, it was a kind of learning curve when realising this app idea to put myself in a better position to experience what app developers have to deal with, including communication with computer scientists, the legal bases, data protection, cybersecurity, and user friendly design.

2.6.2   Cardiac Self Catheterisation

I heard about the birth of cardiac catheterisation while I was studying dentistry at the University of Cologne, as part of the course "History of Medicine" in the first clinical semester. This is what happened, as was also reported in the "Ärzte Zeitung" (Ärzte Zeitung 2004). Born in 1904 in Berlin, Werner Forssmann wrote a new page in medical history when he was awarded the Nobel Prize for performing cardiac catheterisation on himself. The article describes this as follows: "In the summer of 1929, the 25 year old medical assistant Werner Forssmann decided to be the first person to perform on himself cardiac catheterisation, by inserting a catheter through a vein of his forearm into his right atrium. Forssmann's superior at Eberswalde forbade him from attempting this experiment for medical reasons. Thereupon, when alone during his lunchbreak, Forssmann, assisted by a nurse, inserted a catheter 30 centimetres into a vein of his arm, descended, with the catheter still inserted, the steps to the X ray department in the basement, advanced the probe another 30 centimetres, and recorded on X ray film the tip of the catheter in his right atrium."

This experiment on himself did not meet with any approval, and, like many other pioneers ahead of their time, he had to wait several decades for acknowledgement, when in 1956 he and two American colleagues were awarded the Nobel Prize for medicine. Of course, medical experiments on one's own person can also bring about negative results, and should not encourage anybody to follow suit. This extreme example, also familiar to medical students, was simply too good to be missing on a list of wide ranging illustrative examples in the nomenclature of lead users, users, and innovation.

2.7   Own Experiences as a Lead User

In the introduction to this work I related my initial experiences of fifteen years ago when I was an incipient lead user in various user pools and taking part in projects. The feeling of being on a team that doesn't want to hear any ideas from you is unpleasant, but for the company it is much worse. For today, the survival of companies hinges on internal and external ideas that help to produce products and services whose innovativeness exceeds that of the competitors in the global arena.

Whether as lead users or users with great ideas. The underlying procedure is similar: intrinsic motivation drives efforts to make something better which ultimately benefits patients. This can be a method, an app, a device, an instrument, a material, a combination of all these, or simply an idea that a community of others can evolve further.

Working as a lead user in addition to the chosen profession gobbles up time, and you have to be prepared to sacrifice what free time you have available. The ideas that I could submit personally and see realised were highly pleasing on an emotional level. And, of course, there were also many ideas that were not realised, but that shouldn't be taken personally. It is obvious that, when ten ideas are communicated to a company in the medical engineering industry, perhaps one or two of them are shortlisted for the project planning stage. Just take it easy when responding. After all, the commitment as lead user should be fun. Owing to my additional adviser activities in various sectors for companies like e.g. Ryskex, XignSys, and DataArt, I can integrate in my lead user role a whole range of approaches to solutions in my handling of problems and innovations.

This is also the right place now in this book in the year 2021 to offer my most heartfelt gratitude to my surgery manager of many years' standing, Ms Bettina Zirwes-Weinberg, who has covered me for over eighteen years at our dental surgery in Leverkusen by managing patients and surgery with unvarying excellence on the one hand and, on the other, by coordinating the communication between me, the dental laboratory we run at our own surgery, and medical engineering companies. Without a strong and motivated team, no lead user can take an active role in addition to his chosen profession. All success is a joint performance.

The design of innovation environments remains a highly individual process for every company and every founder. Samples from other companies can be transferred only within certain restrictions and do not constitute any warranty of future success in the cutthroat global arena for customer and user acceptance of innovative products and services. The strategic lead user approach is an instrument promising a great many possibilities for the sustained, long term survival of companies in this competitive environment.

References

Allen T (1986) Managing the flow of technology: technology transfer and dissemination of technology information within the R&D organization. MIT Press, Cambridge

ÄRZTE ZEITUNG (2004). https://www.aerztezeitung.de/panorama/article/315957/herzkatheter-selbstversuch-dichtung-wahrheit.html. Accessed 29 Apr 2020.

BMBF and VDE (2009) Identifizierung von Innovationshürden in der Medizintechnik, Bonn-Berlin.

BMBF—Bundesministerium für Bildung und Forschung (2008) Identifikation von Innovationshürden in der Medizintechnik. commissioned by BMBF, Berlin.

BMBF—Bundesministerium für Bildung und Forschung (2010) Ideen. Innovation. Wachstum. Hightech-Strategie 2020 für Deutschland, Referat Innovationspolitische Querschnittsfragen, Rahmenbedingungen, Bonn–Berlin.

Brockhoff, K. (1999) Forschung und Entwicklung: Planung und Kontrolle, 5. Aufl. Oldenbourg, München et al.

Cohen LY, Kamienski PW, Espino RL (1998) Gate system focuses industrial basic research. Res Technol Manag 41(7–8):34–37

Cooper RG (1983) A process model for industrial new product development. IEEE Trans Eng Manag 30(1):2–11

Cooper RG (1994) Third-generation new product processes. J Prod Innovat Manag 11:3–14

Cooper RG (1996) Overhauling the new product process. Ind Mark Manag 25(6):465–482

Crawford CM (1994) New products management, 4th edn. Irwin, Burr Ridge

DIW—Deutsches Institut für Wirtschaftsforschung (2008) Rückstand bei der Bildung gefährdet Deutschland, Berlin.

Ebert G, Pleschak F, Sabisch H (1992) Aktuelle Aufgaben des Forschungs- und Entwicklungscontrolling in Industrieunternehmen, In: Gemünden HG, Pleschak F (Hrsg.) Innovationsmanagement und Wettbewerbsfähigkeit. Gabler, Wiesbaden.

Gemünden HG, Hölzle K, Salomo S (2007) Role models for radical innovations in times of open innovation. J Creativity Innovat Manag 16(4):408–421

Glauner P, Plugmann P (2020) Innovative technologies for market leadership—investing in the future. Springer International Publishing

Herstatt C (1994) Realisierung der Kundennähe in der Innovationspraxis. In: Tomczak T, Belz C (eds) Kundennähe realisieren. Verlag Thexis, St. Gallen, pp 291–307

Herstatt C (1999) Theorie und Praxis der frühen Phasen des Innovationsprozesses. io Manag 68(10):72–81

Herstatt C, Lüthje C, Lettl C (2007) Management der frühen Innovationsphasen. In: Fortschrittliche Kunden zu Breakthrough-Innovationen. Springer, pp 61–75

Hienerth C, von Hippel EA, Jensen MB (2012) Efficiency of consumer (household sector) Vs. Producer innovation. SSRN eLibrary, September 1.

von Hippel E (1976) The dominant role of users in the scientific instrument innovation process. Res Policy 5(3):212–239. https://doi.org/10.1016/0048-7333(76)90028-7

von Hippel EA (1977a) The dominant role of the user in semiconductor and electronic subassembly process innovation. IEEE Trans Eng Manag EM-24(2):60–71

von Hippel EA (1977b) Transferring process equipment innovations from user-innovators to equipment manufacturing firms. R&D Manag 8(1):13–22

von Hippel EA (1978) Successful industrial products from customer ideas. J Mark 42(1):39–49

von Hippel E (1982) Appropriability of innovation benefit as a predictor of the source of innovation. Res Policy 11(2):95–115

von Hippel EA (1986) Lead users: a source of novel product concepts. Manag Sci 32(7):791–805 von Hippel E, Riggs W (1996) A lead user study of electronic home banking services: lessons from the learning curve Sloan working paper. Sloan School of Management, Massachusetts Institute of Technology.

von Hippel E, Thomke S, Sonnack M (1999) Creating breakthroughs at 3M. Harvard Bus Rev 77(5):47–57

von Hippel E, Ogawa S, de Jong PJ (2011) The age of the consumer-innovator. MIT Sloan Manag Rev 53(1):27–35

Hughes GD, Chafin DC (1996) Turning new product development into a continuous learning process. J Prod Innovat Manag 13:89–104

Iansiti M, Lakhani KR (2020) Putting AI at the firm's core. Harvard Bus Rev 98(1):59–67

IFM—Institut für Mittelstandsforschung Bonn (2018). http://www.ifm-bonn.org/ueber-uns/forschungsprogramm/. Accessed 29 Apr 2020.

Lüthje C (2000) Kundenorientierung im Innovationsprozess: Eine Untersuchung zur Kunden-Hersteller-Interaktion auf Konsumgütermärkten. Gabler-Verlag, Wiesbaden

Morrison PD, Roberts JH, von Hippel E (2000) Determinants of user innovation and innovation sharing in a local market. Manag Sci 46(12):1513

Oliveira P, von Hippel E (2011) Users as service innovators: the case of banking services. Res Policy 40(6):806–818

PATIENT INNOVATION (2018) Patient innovation sharing solutions, improving life. https://patient-innovation.com/?locale=de&language=de. Accessed 29 Apr 2020.

Plattner H, Meinel C, Weinberg U (2010) Design thinking—Innovation lernen, Ideenwelten öffnen. S.36. mi-Verlag.

Raasch C, von Hippel E (2012a) Innovation effort as 'Productive Consumption:' The power of participation benefits to amplify innovation. MIT Sloan School of Management Working Paper (October) (SMR forthcoming).

Raasch C, Von Hippel E (2012b) Modeling interactions between user and producer innovation: user-contested and user-complemented markets. SSRN eLibrary.

Riggs W, von Hippel E (1994) The impact of scientific and commercial values on the sources of scientific instrument innovation. Res Pol 23(4):459–469

Rost K, Hölzle K, Gemünden H-G (2007) Promotors or champions? Pros and cons of role specialisation for economic process. Schmalenbach Bus Rev 59:340–363

Schweisfurth TG, Raasch C (2014) Embedded lead users—the benefits of employing users for corporate innovation. Res Policy 44:168–180

Shah S (2001) Sources and patterns of innovation in a consumer products field: innovations in sporting equipment. Working Paper, WP 4105; Sloan School of Management, Massachusetts Institute of Technology, Cambridge, MA.

Shaw B (1985) The role of the interaction between the user and the manufacturer in medical equipment industry. R&D Manag 15(4):283–292

SPECTARIS (2017) Stellungnahme: Kommissionsvorschlag für eine neue EU-Dual Use-Verordnung.   http://www.spectaris.de/uploads/tx_ewscontent_pi1/SPECTARIS-Stellungnahme_DualUseVO_03.pdf. Accessed 29 Apr 2017.

Thom N (1992) Innovationsmanagement. Schweizerische Volksbank, Bern

Ulrich KT, Eppinger SD (1995) Product design and development. McGraw-Hill, New York et al

Vahs D, Burmester R (1999) Innovationsmanagement. Schäffer-Poeschel, Stuttgart

Weissenberger-Eibl MA et al (2017) Innovationsindikator 2017: Schwerpunkt digitale transformation. ZEW-Gutachten und Forschungsberichte

Witt J (1996) Grundlagen für die Entwicklung und die Vermarktung neuer Produkte. In: Witt J (ed) Produktinnovation. Vahlen, München

Innovation Management and Digitization: Will Everything Remain Different?

3

Volker Nestle

3.1 Introduction

> Innovation management is the conscious design of innovation processes and their framework conditions. A core insight of innovation research is that innovation management is something substantially different than the management of repeated routine decisions. Translated from (Fichter 2015)

Such—or similar—definitions of innovation management are often found in the innovation literature. And as simple and logical as they may appear at a first glance, the more complex are the actual facts behind them, which become particularly apparent in the increasingly accelerated digitized world. After all, if more than 20 billion objects become connected in the Internet of Things by 2020 (Gartner 2017), it is easy to see that today's producers of "things" will face demanding challenges in the future. Beyond the innovation of purely physical products, the decentralized acquisition and pre-processing of machine data, the networks between machines and systems and the intelligent evaluation of data will provide the basis for completely new business models, but as a first consequence—and therefore immediately present—for completely new "digitized" products.

In addition to the design of innovation processes, the adequate consideration of framework conditions for innovation is crucial for successful innovation activities. Although the framework conditions also can partly be influenced by companies, they are largely determined by exogenous factors. Today, it might be fair to say that the ongoing digitization represents an unprecedented change in the framework conditions for innovation in the manufacturing industry—but are we sure this is the case? This question will be examined on the following pages. First of all, we

V. Nestle (✉)
Festo SE, Esslingen, Germany
e-mail: volker.nestle@festo.com

V. Nestle et al. (eds.), *Creating Innovation Spaces*, Management for Professionals, https://doi.org/10.1007/978-3-030-57642-4_3

will recapitulate, on the basis of a retrospective view, the exogenous changes that manufacturing companies have been subject to since the middle of the twentieth century and the methods with which innovation management has reacted to them. Subsequently, the challenges for innovation management implied by progressive digitization will be discussed and methodological approaches will be proposed to meet these challenges.

3.2 Innovation Management in the Course of Time

A fundamental understanding of innovation as a process shapes the way innovation is initiated, implemented and controlled. This understanding has changed significantly over the course of time. In early process models, innovation was understood and implemented as a linear sequence of functional activities. Unfortunately, these Technology Push and Market Pull processes are still widespread today and show the mental imprint and the stored understanding of innovation in the company. However, the limitations of such approaches are obvious: in practice, innovation is always a coupling and adaptation of solutions to needs, in which interaction is the decisive element. Recent scientific studies and practical experience recognize these limitations of linear models and try to counter the high complexity as a product of a multitude of endogenous and exogenous influencing factors by flexible process models with a high degree of interaction.

3.2.1 Rothwell's 5G

The British sociologist Roy Rothwell is considered one of the pioneers of industrial innovation with his work on understanding innovation management. Using a historical overview of industrial innovation management beginning with the 1950s, Rothwell extracted five generations of innovation generation (Rothwell 1994). He found that each new generation was a reaction to significant changes in the framework conditions for innovation, e.g. growth, competition, inflation, stagflation or scarcity of resources. Rothwell's five generations are thus a vivid model of how manufacturing companies have structured their innovation processes over time. The focus of his research was on technological innovations in multinational corporations as well as high-tech start-ups (Provenmodels 2020).

3.2.2 First Generation (1950 to mid-1960s): Technology Push

Technology Push simply means linear and sequential innovation with a strong focus on R&D and the market as the pure recipient of the generated results. The rapid economic growth in the period from 1950 to the mid-1960s was based on a strong technology push and industrial expansion especially in the Western world. Scientific breakthroughs and an understanding of "more R&D in, more new products out" were seen as a proven means of solving social problems. R&D was part of the company's overhead costs and had little interaction with other business units: this image of R&D in an ivory tower was shaped in this generation and has unfortunately persisted in many companies until today. Due to the—if at all—late inclusion of market information, the results were often purely technically driven inventions that often could not be brought to market.

3.2.3   Second Generation (mid-1960s to mid-1970s): Market Pull

As a result of an intensified competition in the struggle for market share from the mid-1960s onwards, the constant expansion of technical change that had previously been pursued weakened increasingly and gave way to rationalization with a strong focus on the actual needs of the market (Mensch et al. 1980). As a result, market needs became a source of new ideas and displaced R&D into a reactive role. The resulting linear, sequential process was characterized by an intensive interaction of R&D with other divisions. Product managers had the responsibility to react to market needs quickly within the company, which led to a large number of projects with a high degree of coordination effort.

3.2.4   Third Generation (mid-1970s to mid-1980s): Coupling of R&D and Marketing

The aim of the close coupling of R&D and marketing was to reduce the operating costs of companies as a reaction of the companies to a constantly increasing pressure to rationalize in an environment of inflation and stagflation of the markets. In the integrative, process-based marketing approach, innovation is rarely the result of Technology Push or Market Pull, but usually the result of the exchange process between supplier and buyer and the requirements for integration and feedback loops (Mattmüller 2012). Models of this third generation are still in use today and—although in principle sequentially structured—can for the first time be described as rather open models due to the feedback loops provided (Berkhout et al. 2006). However, the focus is on product and process innovations and not (yet) organizational or business model innovations.

3.2.5   Fourth Generation (1980s to mid-1990s): Integrated Business Processes

With the recovery of the Western economy, a significant shortening of product life cycles was observed for consumer goods and consequently also for capital goods. Innovation management increasingly focused on integrated processes and the development of overall concepts. The fourth generation is also referred to as the model of parallel lines: the innovation process is no longer understood as a sequential shift from function to function, but rather as a parallel development process across different divisions of a company, which in particular also takes into account upstream and downstream stages of the value chain in the form of key suppliers and leading customers, allowing for rapid learning and targeted improvements in the generation of innovation (Graves 1987).

3.2.6 Fifth Generation (from 1990): System Integration and Networking

The fifth generation process adds three essential features to the fourth generation:—Firstly, the time-cost compromise is becoming increasingly important as product life cycles continue to shorten and technological change accelerates. Pure "fast innovators" turn out to be no longer adequate, since with increasing scarcity of resources the acceleration of innovation activity leads to higher costs just as much as a delay in projects.—Secondly, business processes have increasingly been automated by merchandise management and production information systems. These allow for efficient processing of the parallel lines of the fourth generation.—Thirdly, the strategic partnerships with upstream and downstream value-added partners already known from the fourth generation were expanded and made more permanent, and research collaborations were initiated as "open innovation" approaches to enable further learning effects in the pre-competitive environment (Chesbrough 2006).

Rothwell particularly emphasises the role of IT in the fifth generation:

> Many of the features of 5G are already in place in innovators that have mastered the 4G process; parallel and integrated operations, flatter structures, early and effective supplier linkages, involvement with leading customers and horizontal alliances. The most radical feature of 5G is the use of a powerful electronic toolkit to enhance the efficiency of these operations. While electronic measuring and computational devices and analytical equipment have for many years been important aspects of industrial innovation, 5G represents a more comprehensive process of the electronification of innovation across the whole innovation system. (Rothwell 1994)

With regard to the 4G and 5G process models, Rothwell noted that technological innovation is not a sequential process but is inherently cross-functional and recursive. These findings from Rothwell's research are important because they help to find an adequate understanding of innovation as such and consequently for effective and efficient innovation management. Limited mental models regarding the innovation process will also limit the possibilities of innovation. Typical examples are (Tidd et al. 2005):

- Innovation is understood as a linear Technology Push (focus on financing R&D, combined with neglecting customer interests) or Market Pull (one-sided focus on customer interests, neglecting the R&D perspective) process.
- Innovation is only understood as a breakthrough innovation, which means that the significant potential of incremental innovation is faded out.

- Innovation is only seen as a single isolated change, without complementary effects and effects on higher-level systems.
- Innovation is understood as a pure product or process innovation, without recognizing the interrelation between the two.

Rothwell's empirical studies ended with 5G in the late 1990s, but all the innovation patterns discussed are still in use today. With the rapidly advancing digitization at the beginning of the twenty-first century, not only was the use of IT-based innovation management tools intensified, but increasingly the growth potential for existing and new business areas based on digitization was recognized. Under the term "Industry 4.0", for example, similar leaps in potential are being held out for the fully networked digitized production as they have been realized through the introduction of mass production (Industry 2.0) or through the use of information and communication technology ICT (Industry 3.0) (see Geissbauer et al. 2014; Heinze et al. 2016). In addition to product innovations like cyber-physical components, process innovations and new digital or hybrid value creation are made possible along the horizontal integration across company boundaries or in vertical integration with networked production systems. As a result, increased networking does not only take place between "things", but also involves people along the value chain in various ways. The combination of innovative products and processes gives rise to completely new service approaches and business models that focus on customer needs and on interaction with the customer (Gleich et al. 2015). Innovation management in the environment of digitization must therefore increasingly focus on interorganizational interfaces and cooperation with external partners—but where does a company begin and where does it end at all? This question of the effective company boundary is of fundamental importance in modern innovation management.

3.3 A Little Bit of Theory Never Hurts . . .

In contingency theory, the emergence of an organization and its structure is regarded as a reactive measure for coping with uncertainties that may arise, for example, from environmental heterogeneity, the complexity of the production process or the size of the company (Schreyögg 1978). This assumption of a given corporate strategy is also found in transaction cost theory and is directly related to the determination of corporate boundaries. If the transaction cost approach is taken as a basis, the organizational structure that causes the lowest coordination costs is chosen to achieve the (given) profit potential (Williamson 1996). The coordination cost determinants frequency, specificity, uncertainty and risk therefore determine which activities of value creation are carried out within the enterprise (hierarchy) and which are purchased from outside the enterprise (coordination). The company boundaries are thus located where, with a given strategy, the lowest coordination costs arise.

However, the assumption of a purely reactive organization hardly corresponds to the reality, since it can be assumed that companies strive to proactively develop and implement an enterprise strategy in some form. In this respect, Chandler showed as early as the 1960s that organizational structure and strategy are closely linked and that any change or implementation of strategy requires new coordination and/or organizational structures to realize the profit potential (Chandler 1962). In addition to reducing coordination costs, the strategy of a company must also take into account the profit potential that can be achieved. On the one hand, company-specific resources that are the basis for Ricardian rents are decisive in this respect (Peteraf 1993). In addition, Schumpeterian innovation rents can emerge if the innovative capabilities of the firm are improved on the basis of greater resource dynamics (Teece et al. 1997).

Figure 3.1 shows the interdependence of strategy and organization, which at the same time provides a comprehensive approach to defining the boundaries of the enterprise: the strategy of the enterprise is efficient if the difference between strategic rents and coordination costs is maximized, or in other words: the efficient enterprise strives to maximize rents on the one hand and minimize coordination costs on the other, and therefore adopts a dual structure (March 1991).

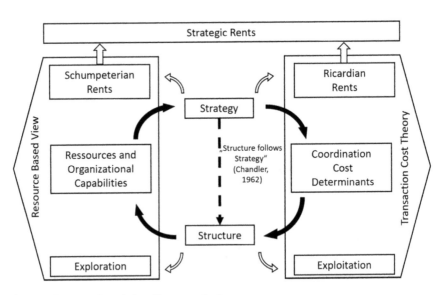

Fig. 3.1 Corporate boundaries. (Source: author)

3.4   Innovation Management and Ambidexterity

It is not only in high-tech industries that it can be observed that the speed of change and competition are constantly increasing due to the ongoing digitization (D'Aveni 1994). Companies are forced to build up new skills alongside the use of existing skills (Floyd and Lane 2000).

However, companies seem to have a preference for short-term success: the returns that can be achieved on the basis of existing business activities are less risky, can be developed in the short term and are therefore closer than exploratory activities (Levinthal and March 1993, p. 106). In addition, empirical knowledge in existing knowledge domains makes future exploitation in the same domain increasingly efficient (Rosenkopf and Nerkar 2001). For this reason, companies tend to progressively specialize their skills and develop them first into core competencies and later into core rigidities, also known as the lock-in effect (Leonard-Barton 1992): Companies thus develop themselves into a competence trap that no longer allows them to react adequately to environmental changes.

The focus on exploratory activities supports a company's ability to renew itself continuously. This characteristic seems to be of particular advantage in the rapidly changing environment of digitization. However, there is also the danger of reacting too quickly to environmental changes and making quick mistakes that do not result in any benefits (Volberda and Lewin 2003). Permanent organizational change can also lead to destabilization of the core business (Levinthal and March 1993, p. 106). The sustainable existence of organizations therefore depends on their ability to continuously exploit and develop their core business on the one hand and to carry out sufficient exploration on the other hand to ensure future success (Levinthal and March 1993, p. 105). It is empirically shown that companies that pursue exploration and exploitation simultaneously are more successful than others (Gibson and Birkinshaw 2004). Such ambidextrous organizations use dual structures to make the initiation and implementation phase of the innovation process more flexible and faster. Accordingly, ambidexterity can also be understood as the ability of firms to simultaneously drive both incremental and discontinuous innovation (Tushman and O'Reilly 1996, p. 24). Ambidextrous organizations reconcile seemingly contradictory demands from revolutionary and evolutionary change or exploration and exploitation.

Large companies such as ABB or Hewlett-Packard, for example, have been able to sustainably establish and maintain their position in established and mature markets with incremental innovations and at the same time successfully open up new market segments with discontinuous innovations (Tushman and O'Reilly 1996). At present, the example of Siemens shows how companies, driven by digitization, are subjecting themselves to major structural changes in their organization and future target markets in order to remain competitive in the long term, despite of great success in their current core business. Siemens should "become an agile fleet association" (Handelsblatt, December 27, 2017).

3.5 How to Master Ambidexterity?

The above argumentation shows that although much scientific research on ambidextria has been and is being done, few concrete solutions have been developed so far. In the meantime, however, companies have learned to deal with the phenomenon of ambidexterity. In this context, various strategies have been observed (Jansen 2005, p. 37):

– Accepting the paradox and learning to live with it without concretely planned activities
– Countering ambidexterity through spatial separation
– Countering ambidexterity through spatial separation
– Balancing and dissolving ambidexterity

What does that mean exactly?

3.5.1 Accept Ambidexterity and Learn to Live With It, Without Concretely Planned Activities

Companies can counter ambidexterity by accepting the paradox but avoiding open discussion of it. In this environment, innovation management means avoiding potentially divisive confrontations and promoting tolerance if all participants concentrate intensively on the tasks assigned to them. The acceptance of the paradox between exploration and exploitation results from the commitment of all participants combined with the realization that their own organizational structure is less effective and/or efficient than a structure that strives for one of the two solutions. Alternatively, the paradox between exploration and exploitation can be understood as either-or, so that either mechanistic or organic structures are set up with the aim of implementing the corresponding strategy. Such companies therefore accept ambidexterity but do not believe in resolving the paradox within the company. What cannot be covered within one's own company is outsourced and purchased from third parties (Baden-Fuller and Volberda 1997). Innovation managers are thus called upon to implement suitable open innovation activities that make the missing resources accessible externally.

3.5.2 Countering Ambidexterity Through Spatial Separation

Instead of accepting ambidexterity reactively, avoiding discussions about it and possibly resolving it by integrating external partners, companies can also take a proactive approach by clarifying structural relationships and connections between exploration and exploitation. The paradox is thus proactively countered by pursuing exploration and exploitation simultaneously in different parts of the organization.

Such a spatial separation can take place according to organizational level, function and/or location (Volberda 1998). If separation is made according to organizational levels, the processes of strategic renewal, e.g. in the area of competence adjustment, can be correlated with the responsible managers. The areas of definition, change, adjustment and deployment of competencies are assigned to different management levels: Managers of operative divisions experiment with new solutions for emerging problems and are thus explorative. In middle management, long-term consequences of this possible change in competencies are assessed on the basis of a deeper understanding of the strategic context. Top management finally adopts permanent competency adjustments on the basis of this understanding, balances the expanded knowledge base of the company and thus focuses on exploitation (Floyd and Lane 2000, p. 161).

However, there are also approaches in top management to pursue exploration and exploitation simultaneously. In a guided strategic renewal, the top management can set appropriate goals, observe the corporate environment and trends, look for alternatives and attempt to cope with ambidexterity by specifically supplementing competencies in individual areas while simultaneously exploiting existing competencies in others.

The separation of exploration and exploitation can also be carried out along functions or via spatial separation. In both cases, new organizational units are created that are inconsistent with previous units. Units pursuing exploration tend to be smaller and more decentralized, with a high degree of autonomy and loose culture and processes. Exploitation is more likely to be successful in larger, centralized units with tightly managed cultural and procedural constraints (Benner and Tushman 2003). Such separation along functions is particularly common in larger companies. Centralized and standardized production competences are geared to exploitation, while other corporate divisions such as R&D or marketing are tasked with developing new technologies and markets to ensure the company's success in the long term.

3.5.3 Countering Ambidexterity Through Temporal Separation

With temporal separation, identical divisions pursue exploratory activities during one period and then switch to exploitation in other periods. Such time-dependent dual organizational structures use mechanistic structures for routine decisions and switch to organic structures for non-routine decisions. This allows the company to adapt quickly to changing conditions. This strategy appears to correlate well with empirical findings, since studies show that technological progress is evolutionary in nature and is cyclically interrupted by discontinuous changes (Widmaier 2000). In evolutionary phases, on the other hand, organizations gradually change existing products and services in order to be able to cope with the framework conditions of the markets (Tushman and Anderson 1986).

Major discontinuous technological breakthroughs are rare, but there is now a consensus that Industry 4.0 will have to cope with even greater changes than in previous phases of industrialization, mass production or ICT. For example, the German Academy of Science and Engineering Acatech names the following far-reaching effects of progressive digitization not only on technological topics (see Acatech 2015, p. 8):

- Standardization and open standards for a reference architecture for cross-company networking and integration via value-added networks—Mastering complex systems and using models to automate activities and integrate the digital and real worlds.
- Comprehensive broadband infrastructure for industry to ensure that data exchange requirements in terms of volume, quality and time are met.
- Security to ensure operational safety, data protection and IT security.
- Work organization and workplace design: Clarification of the implications for people and employees as planners and decision-makers in the Industry 4.0 scenarios.
- Formulation of contents and innovative approaches for education and training.
- Legal framework for the legally secure design of new production processes and horizontal business networks.
- Responsible use of all resources (human and financial resources as well as raw materials and supplies) as a success factor for future industrial production.

This list shows that digitization represents a discontinuous change with such significant progress that older technologies will no longer be competitive in the long term. In such phases of change, companies are particularly challenged to temporarily increase their innovation activities in order to remain competitive.

3.5.4 Balancing and Resolving Ambidexterity

The fourth option for dealing with ambidexterity attempts to resolve the emerging paradox between exploitation and exploration by balancing seemingly contradictory tensions (Gibson and Birkinshaw 2004). This requires the creation of structures and control mechanisms that make exploration and exploitation manageable simultaneously within one and the same organizational unit. Such organizational units combine organic and mechanistic features and must develop a collective organizational context. Therefore, they may exist of contradictory organizational elements and avoid a fixed structure in favour of a combination of structural dimensions (McDonough and Leifer 1983).

3.6 Accompanying Cultural Change

Frequently, the innovation patterns built up over the past decades increasingly prove to be an obstacle in companies. "[Are you] prisoners of your past?"—this is how, for example, Pisano (2015) questions the dynamic abilities of companies to establish new products, services or business models on the basis of radically new innovation patterns and processes (Pisano, 2015). It is interesting to note that such implementation hurdles are deeply rooted in the corporate culture of successful companies in particular. Schein (2004) describes corporate culture as "a pattern of shared basic assumptions that was learned by a group as it solved its problems of external adaptation and internal integration, that has worked well enough to be considered valid and, therefore, to be taught to new members as the correct way to perceive, think, and feel in relation to those problems" (Schein 2004, p. 17). For successful innovation activity it is therefore important that innovation management in the sense of Schumpeter's definition of creative destruction (Schumpeter 1931) initiates and moderates the intensive questioning of established products and processes and accompanies the change in corporate culture. According to Schein's definition (Schein 2004), the competencies, characteristics and social skills of employees are basic cultural prerequisites for understanding innovation. A positive basic attitude towards change can only develop if the challenges that arise can be perceived and evaluated and appropriate measures can be taken to enable employees to cope with the necessary changes. On the basis of these basic values of innovation culture, long-term behavioral norms and patterns emerge which have a lasting influence on process effectiveness and efficiency and thus represent major implementation levers for successful innovation activity.

3.7   New Processes for New Products

In order to meet the challenges posed by digitisation, the German Academy of Science and Engineering Acatech emphasises the aspect of work organisation and process design explicitly:

> What is needed in this context is a socio-technical design perspective in which work organisation, further training activities as well as technology and software architectures are developed in close mutual coordination "from a single mould" with the focus on enabling intelligent, cooperative, self-organised interactions between employees and/or technical operation systems along the entire value chain. Translated from (Acatech 2013, p. 57)

Empirical insights of 278 companies in the manufacturing industry are provided by a survey conducted by VDMA, ZVEI and Bitcom on the perspective of Industry 4.0, in which the topic of process and work organization is seen as the second biggest challenge for the implementation of Industry 4.0 (Acatech 2013, p. 29).

In the management of innovation projects, agile methods are increasingly replacing the well-known stage-gate and waterfall models. Although agile methods originally come from software development, they have now been adapted by many industries for the development of specific products and services. The reason for this is obvious: in times of progressive digitization with ever shorter product life cycles and development times, efficient development is at the top of the priority list, a demand that can be ideally met by the collaboration-promoting and efficiency-enhancing effect of agile methods. Agile methods should standardize and improve the process of software development by identifying problems faster and thus being able to react faster to possible errors. In contrast to the well-known waterfall model, agile methods enable developers and teams to deliver better, because more suitable, products along iterative and interactive sprints. The traditional methods of project management mentioned above require phase-related meetings in which complete teams come together to discuss individual goals. Agile methods use requirements analysis and functional decomposition to pursue very specific goals under clear time constraints with smaller, focused teams that coordinate at regular intervals. As a result, statements can be made very quickly about the achievement of goals and goals can be adjusted along possibly changing customer needs in the ongoing project via iteration loops. The teams thus work more agile, flexible and efficient in terms of time, costs, quality and customer requirements.

Agile methods have become very popular and have rapidly spread beyond the software world into almost all industries. As an emergent approach, the methodology offers alternatives to the major disadvantages of the so-called "Big Design Up Front" (BDUF), the classical development of new products based on preceding requirement and functional specifications with waterfall models. The criticism of the BDUF is essentially based on the following points (Oestereich 2012):

– Not all important design decisions can be determined reliably in advance—> BDUF is more or less speculative
– The effort required to secure design decisions before implementation is often underestimated
– The effort to correct missing or deficient design decisions after an initial realization is often overestimated
– Test automation, test-driven development, constant direct communication with the customer (or product owner) and feedback institutionalized in short iterations (incremental reviews) and other agile techniques contribute significantly to correct design decisions much more cost-effectively and to validate design decisions at a very early stage after realization
– An objective statement on the usefulness of design decisions can only be made after the realisation has been checked
– Many decision-relevant findings only emerge in the practical examination of the problem object, i.e. during its realization, and cannot be theoretically anticipated or anticipated

The implementation of agile methods confronts innovation managers with great challenges, especially in large companies with a long tradition and established behavioral norms. Beyond learning new methods, it is also important to accompany necessary changes in the corporate culture and thus to shape the agile transformation. In this environment, internal corporate communication is becoming increasingly important.

3.8   Innovation and Communication

> Companies need a communication system that not only conveys information and knowledge, but also motivates all players to generate innovations and manage their effects cognitively and emotionally. (Mast 2009, p. 271)

Although innovation culture and understanding of communication are closely linked, research on innovation communication has only become increasingly important in recent years (see Duwe 2016). In this context, innovation communication is defined as "the systematically planned, implemented and evaluated communication of innovations with the aim of developing understanding of and trust in the innovation and positioning the organisation behind it as an innovator". (Zerfass et al. 2004, p. 4). As a cross-sectional function between R&D, corporate management and the communications department, innovation communication is increasingly becoming a success factor for companies, particularly in the case of large and far-reaching changes such as those associated with digitisation. In the future, innovation managers will be strongly challenged to build up and fill the communication interfaces to the company's internal innovation communication, innovation marketing and innovation PR. This is the only way to identify missing or incorrect information at an early stage and develop options for action to eliminate conflicts of interest (cf. Zerfass et al. 2004, p. 9).

3.9   Conclusion: Ambidextrous Innovation Management

So does everything remain different in innovation management? The answer to this question is as ambivalent as the question itself: Much remains (preliminary), much will (quickly) change. The ongoing digitzation of the economy increasingly requires new forms of cooperation. In its recommendations for action for Industry 4.0, Acatech therefore recommends a "socio-technical approach to the future project" (Acatech 2013, p. 28). This also applies to a large extent to the scope of and the demands on innovation managers. The successful integration of digital future technologies requires "intelligent embedding in an innovative social (company) organization" (Acatech 2013, p. 56).

6G in innovation management, however, means foremost and above all overcoming the seemingly insoluble conflicts of ambidexterity. For this purpose, however, the innovation manager needs to be able to set up and use the important implementation levers along the social company organization. This extends the classic understanding of the innovation manager's role significantly and essentially includes:

– Co-designing the creation of corporate and divisional strategies
– Organizational development through iterative adaptation of the organizational design
– Management of the company's resource base (internal vs. external)

- New method and process competence (agile vs. classic)
- Building and maintaining the culture of innovation
- Implementation and promotion of innovation communication

Coping with ambidexterity becomes the success factor of the sixth generation of innovation managers. More and more companies are already recognizing the need for change towards mastering the two worlds of exploitation and exploration, thus creating the basic prerequisite for ensuring competitiveness in an increasingly digitized environment. Innovation managers are called upon to expand their own competencies with regards to the socio-technical requirements mentioned above and thus to continue to develop their role as promoters and brokers of innovation in companies of the future.

References

Acatech (2013) Umsetzungsempfehlungen für das Zukunftsprojekt Industrie 4.0: Abschlussbericht des Arbeitskreises Industrie 4.0. Frankfurt am Main

Acatech (2015) Umsetzugsstrategie Industrie 4.0: Ergebnisbericht der Plattform Industrie 4.0, April 2015. Frankfurt am Main

Baden-Fuller C, Volberda HW (1997) Strategic renewal in large complex organizations: a competence based view. In: Heene A, Sanchez R (eds) Competence-based strategic management. Wiley & Sons, Chichester, pp 89–110

Benner MJ, Tushman ML (2003) Exploitation, exploration, and process management: the productivity dilemma revisited. Acad Manage Rev 28:238–256

Berkhout AJ, Hartmann D, van der Duin P, Ortt R (2006) Innovating the innovation process. Int J Technol Manage 34(3/4):390–404

Chandler AD Jr (1962) Strategy and structure, Cambridge

Chesbrough HW (2006) Open innovation. The new imperative for creating and profiting from technology. Harvard Business School Publishing, Boston

D'Aveni R (1994) Hypercompetition: managing the dynamics of strategic maneuvering. The Free Press, New York

Duwe J (2016) Kommunikation als Mikrofundierung dynamischer Fähigkeiten im Innovationsmanagement ambidextrer Technologieunternehmen. Gabler, Wiesbaden

Fichter K (2015) Grundlagen des Innovationsmanagements. Oldenburg

Floyd SW, Lane PJ (2000) Strategizing throughout the organization: managing role conflict in strategic renewal. Acad Manage Rev 25:154–177

Gartner, Inc (2017) Gartner says 8.4 billion connected "things" will be in use in 2017, up 31 percent from 2016. Pressemitteilung vom 7.2.2017. Online available at http://www.gartner.com/newsroom/id/3598917. Accessed 27 May 2020

Geissbauer R, Schrauf S, Koch V, Kuge S (2014) Industrie 4.0? Chancen und Herausforderungen der vierten industriellen Revolution. PriceWaterhouseCoopers Aktiengesellschaft Wirtschaftsprüfungsgesellschaft. München

Gibson CB, Birkinshaw J (2004) The antecedents, consequences, and mediating role of organizational ambidexterity. Acad Manag J 47:209–226

Gleich R, Schwarz M, Munck JC, Deyle N (2015) Industrie 4.0—zwischen Evolution und Revolution—Potenziale, neue Geschäftsmodelle und Auswirkungen auf das Controlling der Zukunft. In: Horváth P, Michel U (eds) Controlling im digitalen Zeitalter. Schäffer-Poeschel, Stuttgart, pp 101–121

Graves A (1987) Comparative trends in automotive research and development, DRC Discussion Paper No. 54, Science Policy Research Unit. Sussex University, Brighton.

Handelsblatt (2017) Siemens will kein Konglomerat mehr sein. Pressemitteilung vom 9.11.2017. Online available at http://www.handelsblatt.com/my/unternehmen/industrie/konzernumbau-siemens-will-kein-konglomerat-mehr-sein-/20561756.html?ticket=ST-2160913-b9iNcZvYb3AeiIjbKBNb-ap3. Accessed 27 May 2020

Heinze R, Manzei C, Schleuper L (2016) Industrie 4.0 im internationalen Kontext. Kernkonzepte, Ergebnisse, Trends. Beuth; VDE Verlag, Berlin

Jansen JJP (2005) Ambidextrous organizations: a multi-level study of absorptive capacity, explorative and exploitative innovation and performance. Erasmus Research Institute of Management (ERIM), Rotterdam

Leonard-Barton DA (1992) Core capabilities and core rigidities: a paradox in managing new product development. Strateg Manage J 13:111–125

Levinthal DA, March JG (1993) The myopia of learning. Strateg Manage J 14(S2):95–112

March JG (1991) Exploration and exploitation in organizational learning. Organ Sci 2:71–87

Mast C (2009) Mitarbeiterkommunikation, Change und Innovationskultur: Balance von Informationen und Innovationen. In: Zerfass A, Möslein KM (eds) Kommunikation als Erfolgsfaktor im Innovationsmanagement. Wiesbaden, Gabler, pp 271–288

Mattmüller R (2012) Integrativ-prozessuales marketing. Gabler, Wiesbaden

McDonough E, Leifer R (1983) Using simultaneous structures to cope with uncertainty. Acad Manag J 26:727–736

Mensch G, Kaash K, Kleinknecht A, Schnapps R (1980) Innovation trends and switching between full- and under-employment equilibrium, 1950–1978. Discussion Paper Series, International Institute of Management, Berlin

Oestereich, B. (2012): GPM-Blog. Online unter http://gpm-blog.de/bduf/. Accessed 1 Jan 2018

Peteraf MA (1993) The cornerstones of competitive advantage: a resource-based view. Strateg Mange J 14:179–188

Pisano G (2015) You need an innovation strategy. Harv Bus Rev 93(6):44–54

Provenmodels (2020) Online available at https://www.provenmodels.com/575/five-generations-of-innovation/roy-r.-rothwell/. Accessed 27 May 2020

Rosenkopf L, Nerkar A (2001) Beyond local search: boundary-spanning, exploration, and impact in the optical disc industry. Strateg Manage J 22:287–306

Rothwell R (1994) Towards the fifth-generation innovation process. Inter Market Rev 11(1):7–31

Schein EH (2004) Organizational Culture and Leadership. Third Edition. Josey-Bass, San Francisco

Schreyögg G (1978) Umwelt, Technologie und Organisationsstruktur. Bern, Stuttgart

Schumpeter JA (1931) Theorie der wirtschaftlichen Entwicklung: Eine Untersuchung über Unternehmergewinn, Kapital, Kredit, Zins und den Konjunkturzyklus. Duncker & Humblot, München

Teece DJ, Pisano G, Shuen A (1997) Dynamic capabilities and strategic management. Strateg Manag J 18:509–533

Tidd J, Bessant J, Pavitt K (2005) Managing innovation: integrating technological, market and organizational change, 3rd edn. Wiley

Tushman ML, Anderson P (1986) Technological discontinuities and organizational environments. Admin Sci Q 31:439–465

Tushman ML, O'Reilly CA (1996) Evolution and revolution: mastering the dynamics of innovation and change. Calif Manage Rev 38:8–30

Volberda HW (1998) Building the flexible firm: how to remain competitive. Oxford University Press, Oxford

Volberda HW, Lewin AY (2003) Co-evolutionary dynamics within evolution to co-evolution. J Manage Stud 40:2111–2136

Widmaier U (2000) Der deutsche Maschinenbau in den neunziger Jahren. Kontinuität und Wandel einer Branche. Campus, Frankfurt am Main, New York

Williamson OE (1996) The mechanisms of governance, New York

Zerfass A, Sandhu S, Huck S (2004) Innovationskommunikation: Strategisches Handlungsfeld für Corporate Communications. In: Piwinger M, Schönborn G, Bentele, G (Hrsg.) Kommunikationsmanagement (Lose Blattsammlung Bd. 1.24). Luchterhand, Neuwied, p 1–30

Raising Innovation Potential Through a Well Indoor Climate

4

Alexander Buff

4.1 The Office as Space for Innovation

Only upper management get air conditioning.

This was the answer I received to the question: "Why is it so hot in the R&D department?" as I sat with my co-founder in the development department of a German car manufacturer. Our meeting was not actually about the temperature in the R&D department, but our thoughts naturally turned to this topic after a short while. Despite the pleasant autumnal outdoor temperature, the indoor temperature in the stuffy office had risen to almost 30 °C.

Inwardly, we asked ourselves how hot it must get in the summer. Just how much innovative potential can employees really contribute under these conditions? What did the decision to not equip the office with suitable temperature control cost the company? Were perhaps considerations of power consumption and initial investment cost an obstacle? Does it make sense to save energy yet, as a consequence, to tolerate a potentially unproductive climate in the workplace? This and many other queries were raised in the follow-up to this meeting.

Just on gut feeling, it appears obvious that an uncomfortable indoor temperature can have a direct effect on an individual's performance. Personal factors such as level of fitness and age are significant, but environmental factors also matter. Numerous studies have been conducted on this topic since the middle of the nineteenth century, mostly on students or small groups. Normative planning frameworks for minimum indoor climate standards were created using these studies. While growing

A. Buff (✉)
interpanel GmbH, Gera, Germany
e-mail: alexander.buff@interpanel.com

industrialization, the active control of indoor climates and standards for indoor climate conditions in buildings drew more attention.

The situation previously described makes it clear that workspaces must guarantee an indoor climate that is agreeable to humans at the very least. An uncomfortable indoor temperature affects our concentration after only a very short time. Companies and parties involved in construction projects are often unaware that not only can unfavourable indoor climatic factors cause a considerable proportion of working hours per year to become unproductive, but that this can also have significant economic impact. The consequences can include hidden personnel costs, due to low productivity or discontent, that usually exceed the potential savings in energy costs many times over.

4.2   Aspects on the Impact of Climate Change on the Design of Buildings and Workspaces

Climate change and its multifarious implications is one of the most pressing problems of our time.

Urbanization and its effects in highly industrialized cities, such as smog, ozone, noise and life-threatening temperatures (Xu et al. 2020) during the day and night, will soon be a substantial challenge for billions of people. This particularly affects city planners, building planners, investors and, ultimately, the users of offices and commercial buildings (Buranyi 2019).

The construction and building sector produces approx. 40% of total global emissions (UNEP 2019) and so contributes significantly to climate change. To counteract these dramatic developments, the World Green Building Council has called for all buildings to reach net zero operating emissions by 2050.

The last few years were the warmest ever recorded in Europe. Outside temperatures over 40 °C on successive days and tropical nights in which the temperature does not drop below 20 °C between 6 PM and 6 AM undermine previous building concepts. Even with forced night-time ventilation, buildings cannot cool sufficiently if night-time temperatures remain high, and buildings without active cooling measures can be as hot as saunas from the early hours of the next morning. As a result, they cannot be used as productive workplaces.

Berlin, for instance, is expected to have a prevailing climate like that of Toulouse in southern France within the next few decades. In consequence, the number of heat waves and days with temperatures over 30 °C will increase from currently approx. 10 to 40.

Air conditioning in buildings is swallowing up an increasing proportion of power and thus producing more emissions. It amounts to 10% of global electricity consumption and 1/3 of the annual increase in energy consumption, it is a crucial means for improving the energetic quality of buildings as well as for enhancing comfort and hygiene factors.

It is estimated that 5.6 billion new air conditioning devices will be installed by 2050, in addition to the 1.6 billion air conditioners that already exist. According to recent data, approx. 20% of all energy required in buildings is expended for interior cooling (IEA 2018).

The emissions include not only the buildings' power consumption, but also the required materials and transport processes. Energy consumed by materials throughout their life cycle is referred to as "grey energy" (Trachte 2012).

Heating the buildings, which is mainly achieved using fossil energy sources, is also a significant cause of air pollution in winter. Air pollution resulting from combustion, e.g. particulate matter and the accompanying emissions, contribute to pollution of outdoor air, particularly in densely populated towns and cities. A significant percentage of thermal energy is still generated on site, for instance by burning oil, gas or biomass. From an energetic point of view, it is extremely costly to heat interiors to the low level of 20 °C with industrial combustion temperatures of >1000 °C. For this reason, heat pumps using climate-compatible coolants will increasingly replace fossil energy sources and contribute to reducing air pollution.

On a global scale, the rising levels of CO_2 in the atmosphere (416.2 ppm in April 2020) also affect the technical facilities in buildings. Before industrialization, the concentration was approx. 280 ppm. Every year, CO_2 content increases by approx. 2–3 ppm (Global Monitoring Laboratory—Carbon Cycle Greenhouse Gases 2020). Recommended maximum CO_2 levels in indoor air are in the range of approx. 600–1000 ppm (Caul and Dawkins 2016). As CO_2 concentrations in the outdoor air rise, higher air exchange rates must be planned to ensure that the air quality is acceptable.

4.2.1   Indoor Climate and the Enhancement of Productivity

The development and market penetration of effective filtration, ventilation, heating and cooling systems and new construction materials for airtight and insulated building envelopes has made it possible to build interiors that are both healthy and comfortable, in any climate zone. Milestones such as the development of the air conditioning system at the beginning of the nineteenth century made large building complexes possible for the first time. They have been considered a cornerstone of globalization for over 100 years. In many regions of the planet, air conditioning systems are not a convenience, but absolutely essential (Cox 2010).

The Economist William Nordhaus stated that individuals living and working in cooler climates generate up to 12 times the economic production, versus other individuals living in the hottest climate across the globe (Harford 2017; The Economist 2013).

A huge number of international and national recommendations, standards, guidelines and workplace ordinances are aimed at regulating the indoor climate in workspaces. As a rule, these define a minimum standard that must be maintained. In my own experience, planners then use the normatively stipulated minimum standards as their maximum target parameters.

This can cause a multitude of problems. For one, the defined minimum standard is generally a legally binding parameter. For another, it is not always possible to access technologies, experience and recommendations that would argue for higher standards of facilities.

A comment on the standardisation of fresh air supplies in line with ASHRAE (Allen and Macomber 2020):

> "The ASHRAE standard is called "Ventilation for Acceptable Indoor Air Quality." The key word here is "acceptable." This is not a standard for "healthy" indoor air quality, nor is it a standard for "optimal" air quality. It is a bare-minimum standard, by name and definition. (ASHRAE is quick to acknowledge that it's a minimum standard.) Think about this for a minute. We have learned that ventilation is critical for health and productivity, yet nearly every indoor space where you spend your day—from multifamily homes to offices to restaurants and schools—is guided by this minimum standard for ventilation, despite study after study showing the benefits of increasing ventilation above this minimum. This standard of "acceptable" is not acceptable!

The construction process is generally a major challenge in the construction industry. As a rule, design teams are rewarded for finding the cheapest construction products and constructing the building at the lowest possible cost. Companies are often additionally rewarded for finding supposedly cheaper solutions. After a short warranty period, nobody is responsible for the actual performance of the building in later stages due to the complex contractual relationships. New building projects then must be renovated earlier than expected.

Examples include the failure to install cooling systems. These must then be retrofitted after the first or second summer, which costs many times more and involves lengthy installation times. These facilities are axed during the construction stage for supposedly being too costly and then the buildings must be expensively refurbished down the line.

It is rather disconcerting that the exclusive focus is on construction costs and possible short-term savings. When viewed over a period of 30 years, the typical useful life of a building, the highest expense is the cost of personnel, amounting to approx. 92% of the total cost. This is followed by the operating and maintenance costs at approx. 6%, and by construction costs at approx. 2% (Caul and Dawkins 2016). The company Jones Lang LaSalle, one of the world's leading suppliers of property services and a Fortune 500 company, arrived at a similar comparison, the well-known 3–30-300 rule. The rule states the costs incurred per m^2 or square foot of constructed building. The costs are €3 for utilities, €30 for rent and €300 for the payroll (JLL 2016).

Good interior conditions seem even more important when we consider that people today spend up to 95% of their life indoors. And a large proportion of value-added activities are performed in workspaces and offices.

So, we can see from the examples and ratios mentioned above that cutting corners on the cost of a good indoor climate is a false economy for the users, operators and investors.

This particularly affects companies who employ a large proportion of knowledge workers, whose performance depends on suitable working conditions.

(Allen and Macomber 2020) summarized the factors that influence a healthy indoor climate based on current information. After over 40 years of research, the factors are divided into the following points, according to a report from the Harvard T. Chan School of Public Health:

- Ventilation
- Air QualityThermal Health
- Moisture
- Dust & Pests
- Safety and Security
- Water Quality
- Noise
- Lighting & Views

4.2.2   Temperature, Humidity and Ventilation as Influencing Factors on Productivity

Unlike the other factors for healthy buildings indicated above, the temperature of a room is usually directly perceptible. Depending on acclimatization, outside temperature and personal influencing factors, humans are only comfortable and productive in a working environment within a narrow range of temperatures. Even short periods of overheating result in a significant drop in mental capacity and an increase in error rates.

In some offices, temperatures of over 30 °C are common during the summer and many companies are unaware of the costs that this can incur.

A study conducted in a controlled environment showed that a temperature of 30 °C lowers performance by 6% compared to a temperature of 22 °C (World Green Building Council 2014).

The challenge begins during the planning phase, in which energy balance calculations are confused and jumbled together with considerations of comfort. For instance, high-performance air cooling in an office can dissipate the necessary heat, but the question of whether the user is then comfortable is usually not considered. For example, the air can become dry if air cooling is used exclusively. Cold drafts can make areas of the room unusable.

Humidity should be maintained between 40 and 60% to minimize both the transmission of influenza viruses (Noti et al. 2013) and health hazards, such as a dry throat, stinging eyes or dry skin.

In contrast to overheated offices, rooms can become too cold and engender the same loss of productivity. (Hedge and Gaygen 2010)

However, overall it is not only the temperature that is important, but the regulation of indoor temperatures and the ability to control the temperature. (Tse and So 2007)

In addition to the measurable radiation temperature and air temperature, psychological factors can also exert an influence. One strategy was discussed in which a trustworthy third person, e.g. the caretaker, is charged with controlling the indoor temperature. This person is then centrally responsible for the indoor temperature. When requested to adjust the temperature, they assure the caller that they will do just that. However, no real physical change is made. The mere act of making the call and relying on the trustworthy contact is intended to induce a higher acceptance of the indoor temperature without any true and involved adjustments being made. And this appears to work well, according to statements made by project participants. Therefore, in addition to measurable qualities, psychological effects must not be disregarded. Similar strategies are pursued using modified temperature displays and controls on room thermostats.

Thus, the perception of the indoor temperature comprises both subjective and individual psychological components.

There are two basic principles of transmitting heat and cooling for controlling the indoor temperature.

Convective systems either cool or heat the air. Heat is added or removed from the room via air movement and a cooling block.

An alternative principle is to heat or cool the room using thermally active surfaces. These surfaces are normally heated or cooled using water. Using this method, the main heat transmission mechanism is no longer convective air movement; instead it is the physical phenomenon of a constant exchange of thermal radiation between surfaces. Thermal radiation spreads constantly and evenly in all spatial directions at the speed of light without air circulation. This creates a pleasant indoor climate that is conducive to physiological comfort.

4.2.3   Circadian Rhythms and Biologically Effective Lighting and Control Concepts

Much has changed since artificial illumination first created a consistent source of indoor light almost 150 years ago. The typical spectrum ranges from 3500 K (warm white) to 6500 K (cold white). Most office lighting uses a medium range of approx. 4000 K, often called neutral white. Photographers make use of very warm white light during the "golden hour". At dusk and dawn, the sunlight has a very warm white colour of 2000 K.

Generally, cold white light is conducive to higher levels of alertness, better concentration and faster cognitive processing speeds. Mood and concentration improve, and this is also true for office workers. New technologies allow us to control the light colour and to measure the biologically effective light intensity, known as the melanopic lux. This parameter reflects the photopic response of the human eye (Allen and Macomber 2020).

The relevant directives for recommended light intensities can be used as a guideline. The normal lighting intensity requirements of 500 lx for a typical office workspace can be easily achieved thanks to the technological development of LEDs with high efficiency, high light quality and variable light colours. Some system concepts combine motion sensors, timers and daylight sensors with intelligent controllers to ensure that their operation is optimised to suit circadian rhythms and natural lighting conditions.

From a physiological point of view, it has been proven that humans from approx. 35 years of age require higher lighting intensities to experience the same levels of brightness, due to lens clouding in the eye. For this reason, it can be advantageous to equip workstations with lighting intensities above 500 lx. HCL lighting influences visual, emotional and biological sensations (Licht.de 2020). This makes it a holistic light management method.

Ever more stringent requirements for energy efficiency and compliance with the personal needs of users will make intelligent lighting solution controllers indispensable for workstations of the future. User-specific and digital control is of growing significance for workspace facilities now that economical, high-quality and durable LED chips have been developed and established. Numerous variants are available, e.g. for automated brightness control in areas with natural light and for changing the colour temperature between warm white and cold white lighting scenarios based on the natural gradients of the solar spectrum. They can be standard solutions for individual rooms or centrally controlled solutions connected to Smart Building interfaces controlled via apps using tablets or smartphones.

The trend towards equipping new buildings and workplaces with biologically effective lighting, also known as human-centric lighting (HCL), is growing steadily. In this approach, a holistic lighting solution is adapted to suit the requirements of the user profile. In these concepts, the most essential influencing factors are illumination level, light intensity, duration, size of the luminous surface and the light spectrum throughout the course of the day. While blue light can have a stimulating effect in the morning, it is undesirable in the evenings and the system adjusts to a warmer white light with lower biological effect. Further options allow the ceiling to be illuminated in a bluish colour while workstations are lit in warmer whites, which is intended to replicated a natural lighting scene. In this way, human-centric-lighting can make a significant contribution to improving the indoor climate.

Lamps can be controlled by digital protocols, smartphones, tablets or wired or battery-free wireless technologies such as EnOcean. It is also possible to combine multiple concepts.

4.2.4   Influence on Company Success

The relationship between indoor climate and employee performance has been researched in numerous studies. It is understandably difficult to condense or formulate universally valid and independently applicable values due to classification systems, boundary conditions and various specific factors.

However, the economic value of possible improvements can be estimated using relatively simple calculations based on representative studies.

Calculations performed by (Allen and Macomber 2020) are based on a company with 40 employees working 250 days for $75,000 annual pay, with 50% of the payroll as revenue, with rental costs of $300,000 and utility costs of $30,000. The net income of the company is calculated to be $1,169,000.

If we assume an increase in productivity of 1%, e.g. through improved ventilation and a more pleasant temperature level, the company would save 250 days x 1% = 2 days/year of potential absence per employee. This very conservative assumption of reduced sick days changes the net income by plus 1.8%.

An additional increase in performance of just 2% thanks to improved employee satisfaction raises the net income by 9% compared to the baseline scenario.

As also calculated in (Allen and Macomber 2020), a further general overview postulating a 3% increase in employee productivity, 10% higher rental costs and a $40/person hike in electricity costs results in an operational result of plus 10.7%, or $1,293,880 instead of the $1,169,000 calculated in the baseline case. The higher rental costs are due to the improved interior facilities that would be financed by the property investor. With only a 2% increase in productivity and with the same outgoing costs, the net income at the end of the fiscal year would be $1,251,880. This is still an improvement of 7.1% despite expenditure remaining the same.

So we can see that it is certainly useful to take scenario analyses into account when choosing to invest in spaces and rental properties that must be equipped. In this way, investment decisions can be considered from a holistic angle that considers more than the direct investment costs alone.

4.3   Conclusion

A pleasant and healthy working climate has a significant effect on innovative ability, company performance and company appeal. The global skills shortage and innovative pressure mean that highly qualified employees are demanding workplaces that provide a better indoor climate than workspaces in the home or than stuffy, unpleasant office environments.

Therefore, the quality of workplaces is an essential factor for improving the innovative capabilities of employers and companies alike. Home workspaces, co-working spaces and flexible work environments all have different climatic qualities. Centralised workplaces must create a positive climate to promote both innovative power and networking amongst employees. In the future, smart technologies will make a vital contribution to analysing, optimising and customising indoor climates in the workplace. Future building operators will no longer control a building's systems purely passively. And it will be possible to measure consumption on the fly, not only after the end-of-year statement. Instead sensors, 5G, networks, the IoT and machine learning will enable operators to measure building performance in real time. It will then also be possible to create personal comfort profiles and to incorporate efficiency benchmarks.

In addition to the installed technological hardware, the focus will be on user-centric control and influence, and on monitoring energetic quality and indoor climatic quality. In this way, productive working environments can be created on the basis of a systematic approach with reference to the physiological perceptions and climatic criteria. By generating attractive working environments, companies can break away from their market competitors and exploit a direct competitive edge. Due to the growing skills shortage and more ambitious and flexible concepts, these factors must be included in the agenda to ensure the sustainability of the company.

References

Allen JG, Macomber JD (2020) Healthy buildings: how indoor spaces drive performance and productivity. Harvard University Press, Cambridge, MA

Buranyi S (2019) The air conditioning trap: how cold air is heating the world. https://www.theguardian.com/environment/2019/aug/29/the-air-conditioning-trap-how-cold-air-is-heating-the-world. Accessed May 16, 2020

Caul F, Dawkins M (2016) Indoor Air Quality (IAQ). http://www.energycork.ie/wp-content/uploads/2016/12/ASHRAE-IAQ.pdf. Accessed May 5, 2020

Cox S (2010) Losing our cool. Uncomfortable truths about our air-conditioned world (and finding new ways to get through the summer). The New Press, New York

Global Alliance for Buildings and Construction, International Energy Agency and the United Nations Environment Programme (UNEP) (2019) 2019 global status report for buildings and construction: towards a zero-emission, efficient and resilient buildings and construction sector. https://www.unenvironment.org/resources/publication/2019-global-status-report-buildings-and-construction-sector. Accessed May 16, 2020

Global Monitoring Laboratory—Carbon Cycle Greenhouse Gases (2020) Annual mean growth rate for Mauna Loa, Hawaii. https://www.esrl.noaa.gov/gmd/ccgg/trends/gr.html. Accessed May 16, 2020

Harford T (2017) Fifty things that made the modern economy. Little, Brown Book Group, London

Hedge A, Gaygen D (2010) Indoor environment conditions and computer work in an office. HVAC&R Research 16(2):123–138. https://doi.org/10.1080/10789669.2010.10390897

IEA (2018) The future of cooling. https://www.iea.org/reports/the-future-of-cooling. Accessed May 20, 2020

Jones Lang LaSalle IP, Inc. (2016) A surprising way to cut real estate costs. https://www.us.jll.com/en/trends-and-insights/workplace/a-surprising-way-to-cut-real-estate-costs. Accessed May 16, 2020

Licht.de (2020) licht.wissen 21—Guide to Human Centric Lighting (HCL) for design and implementation. https://en.licht.de/fileadmin/Publications/licht-wissen/1809_lw21_E_Guide_HCL_web.pdf. Accessed May 20, 2020

Noti JD, Blachere FM, McMillen CM, Lindsley WG, Kashon ML, Slaughter DR, Beezhold DH (2013) High humidity leads to loss of infectious influenza virus from simulated coughs. PLoS One 8(2):e57485. https://doi.org/10.1371/journal.pone.0057485

The Economist (2013) No sweat: Artificial cooling makes hot places bearable—but at a worryingly high cost. https://www.economist.com/international/2013/01/05/no-sweat. Accessed May 16, 2020

Trachte S (2012) Grey energy of buildings materials. https://www.ashrae.gr/perch/resources/hellenicchapter-teeenergyinbuildings2012trachte.pdf. Accessed May 16, 2020

Tse WL, So ATP (2007) The importance of human productivity to air-conditioning control in office environments. HVAC&R Research 13(1):3–21. https://doi.org/10.1080/10789669.2007.10390941

World Green Building Council (2014) Health, wellbeing & productivity in offices. https://www.worldgbc.org/sites/default/files/compressed_WorldGBC_Health_Wellbeing__Productivity_Full_Report_Dbl_Med_Res_Feb_2015.pdf. Accessed May 16, 2020

Xu C, Kohler TA, Lenton TM, Svenning J-C, Scheffer M (2020) Future of the human climate niche. Proc Natl Acad Sci 117(21). https://doi.org/10.1073/pnas.1910114117

"It's not about the Room, it's about the Mind-Set!": How to Create an Integrated Newsroom with Digital Workflows and Cross Border Collaboration

5

Marie Elisabeth Mueller and Devadas Rajaram

5.1   The Third Pedagogue

Have you heard of the room being described as the "third pedagogue"? School architects introduced this concept in recent years, when responding to the need of providing more agile spaces for learners and teachers. They follow the observation that the pace of new knowledge, new professions and innovations coming into being is speeding up and transforming formerly permanent elements, roles and strategies into fluid entities. Adoption to permanent change and uncertainty is now a key competence which has to be implemented in teaching methods.

The third pedagogue joins the first who is defined as the peers and the social network online and offline and the second who is represented by teaching staff and the creation of assignments blending different types of learning activities as solitary readings, remote self-assessments, peer group brainstorming and peer group discussions or instructor-led classes with presentations, for example. As the perspectives, roles, tasks, monitoring, assessment and evaluation of learners and teachers are constantly changing, the concept of open, agile rooms becomes a necessity.

As often in the history of socio-political developments new fabrics of communication and networking engineered by emerging technologies can be at first spotted in the fine arts. Looking back to Weimar, shortly after World War I, now almost exactly hundred years ago, the third pedagogue played a central role in the "Bauhaus School" initiated and managed by architect and school director Walter Gropius and his circle of friends and colleagues in the area of fine arts.

M. E. Mueller (✉)
Bonn, Germany

D. Rajaram
Asian College of Journalism, Chennai, India
e-mail: devadas.rajaram@gmail.com

© The Editor(s) (if applicable) and The Author(s), under exclusive license   59
to Springer Nature Switzerland AG 2021
V. Nestle et al. (eds.), *Creating Innovation Spaces*, Management for Professionals,
https://doi.org/10.1007/978-3-030-57642-4_5

Fig. 5.1 Sketch of a room
without a central perspective.
(Source: authors)

Fig. 5.1 Sketch of a room without a central perspective. (Source: authors)

With their holistic approach to arts education as well as to a human-centered (later turned functional) architecture, the approach to integrate all crafts and arts into a deconstructive spatial structure of interwoven wings and rhombuses in a school building without a central view, came naturally to Gropius and his friends during their early years in Weimar and then in Dessau. Early drafts of rooms without a central view remind us of the form of a diamond, see Fig. 5.1.

But it would take decades for mainstream educational architecture to embrace an integrated method of translating agile functions into liquid forms and spaces.

5.2   Digital Eats the World

> What I've chosen to call, more to the point, 'liquid modernity', is the growing conviction that change is the only permanence, and uncertainty the only certainty. A hundred years ago 'to be modern' meant to chase 'the final state of perfection'—now it means an infinity of improvement, with no 'final state' in sight and none desired,

wrote British-Polish sociologist Zygmunt Bauman right at the beginning of the twenty-first century and coined the notion "liquid modernity" in his book of the same name (2000, p. 82). While our tiny computers and digital tools started to eat and digest the world, the third pedagogue was deconstructed and dispersed into a "liquid space", now on and off merging physical and virtual realities in real-time. Consequently the famous argument "form follows function" no longer holds true, as functions are first and foremost turned into 'invisible' code and forms are freely created and dissolved at our fingertips with the use of digital tools and emerging XR- and AI-based technologies.

In this article we elaborate this context not as an ontological question but as a practical one. As we're currently living, learning and telling stories in the framework of Bauman's "liquid modernity", we can't rely on a state of permanence or certainty of neither our knowledge and stories nor the ways we organize communication as well as teams and groups. The main point here is that we as educators in digital literacy, journalism and communications have to align our teaching strategies and expected learning outcomes accordingly. In concrete we have to map out an

Technological Pedagogical Content Knowledge

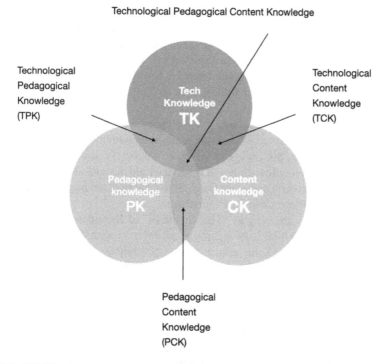

Fig. 5.2 TPACK model, inspired by (Serhat 2019). (Source: authors)

agile framework based on the model TPACK, see Fig. 5.2, merging Technological Knowledge with Pedagogical Knowledge and Content Knowledge.

When few first movers among educational institutions in the second decade of the twenty-first century started to offer blended learning and introduced a combination of instructor-led offline and self-learning online segments, some students would suspect that teachers went online to reduce their workload, while some teachers would suspect students would delegate workload to Google and Co. It is still a challenge to build mutual trust and align communication, feedback and assessment efficiently to adopt an agile learning environment outside of the traditional four wall classroom with its central perspective.

If this changing mode affects really all educational subjects with demanding a new and regularly updated framework of the three core TPACK dimensions, see Fig. 5.2, as such: 1. The use of emerging technologies for knowledge transfer, 2. Teaching content knowledge with the use of emerging technologies, 3. Aligning a pedagogical system which efficiently merges technologies and content—the subjects of journalism and communications are not only profoundly affected, too, but also offer in some ways an ideal model to implement TPACK and translate education into real-time simulation and experiments.

Although the many hurdles of hierarchical editorial managements, resistance to change and lack of resources hold many newsrooms back from change in reality, in education we can look at digital newsrooms in themselves as liquid learning environments. Because journalists are storytellers who translate invisible incidents, facts, voices and things into a comprehensive visible communication product for masses through the use of technology, their profession predestined them for the "liquid modernity".

However large parts of the industry, for many reasons we're not mentioning them in this article, preferred to stick to the traditional methods of news packaging and revenue streaming. So, change in the news industry is slow, exposing the news industry and the democratic societies they serve within the constitutionally protected right of freedom of speech and press freedom to an almost unchecked dominance of profitable global platforms and data capitalism.

Yet, some newsrooms such as "The Guardian" of Britain with then Editor-in-chief Alan Rusbridger—in 2019 making more revenue with digital products than with print products—and some educational institutions as the "Asian College of Journalism" in Chennai, India, with its Founder Sashi Kumar and, the author of this article, New Media Professor Devadas Rajaram, responded progressively, embraced the change and started working agile in so-called "integrated newsrooms", adapting step-by-step and term-by-term to an efficient TPACK framework to tackle the accelerating concepts of applied "liquid modernity" with "liquid newsroom spaces".

In the next paragraphs we'll briefly elaborate on the most important aspects of an "integrated newsroom" as a liquid educational environment within the TPACK framework.

5.3 Immersive Technology

Digital eats and digests the world by shooting, recording, scanning and editing everything with smart devices in live and real-time as well as transmitting anything from anywhere at any time to smart devices or shape it in physical smart forms, for example, 3-D augmented layers or 4-D printed things. In the recent months, with better graphic cards, applied ML to multimedia output und higher performance of tiny computers, we see the emergence of synthetic media production efficiently becoming the real thing, editing becoming the real shooting, in fact, more relevant and powerful than shooting and recording.

All of that is what we understand under the umbrella notion "immersive": the physical world reproduced as a virtual story environment, users becoming co-creators, immersed into virtual stories with more control about navigation and outline, stories turning into experiences, journalists starting to listen and having conversations with their audiences and users, happening anywhere, online and/or offline as well as linear and/or non-linear.

Newsrooms and news stories were for centuries built around a news pyramid with a linear central view on news packages in the form of containers. In the digital ecosystem, there is no longer a permanent news story and no central—or

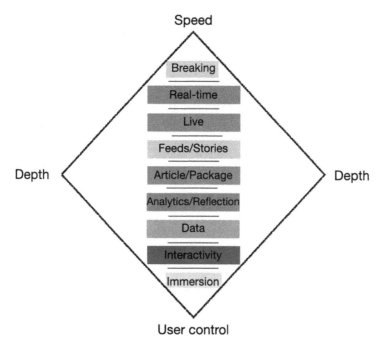

Fig. 5.3 News Diamond, inspired by (Bradshaw 2007). (Source: authors)

'impartial'—view on the story, instead we can envision a "news diamond", see Fig. 5.3, as digital journalism educator Paul Bradshaw suggested. Instead, each story unfolds on an ongoing timeline, defined by three basic metrics: 1. speed, 2. depth of research and time, 3. level of user control dependent on the chosen linear and non-linear (multimedia) storytelling methods related to the timeline and resources.

5.4   User Journey Into The Story

As applied skills are becoming more relevant than knowledge in containers, educators and educational institutions must address learners' needs in a diversified and fragmented approach with using emerging technologies to create efficient learning environments which offer simulated experiences, offline and online.

> Theirs (GenZ) is not a future of falling enrollment, financial challenges and closing campuses. It's a brighter world in which students subscribe to rather than enroll in college, learn languages in virtual reality foreign streetscapes with avatars for conversation partners, have their questions answered day or night by A.I. teaching assistants and control their own digital transcripts that record every life achievement,

describes Jon Marcus in a "New York Times" article on changing higher education with AI-based labs for GenZers, really turning learning into the experience of a life-long journey owned by the professional learner. (Jon Marcus 2020)

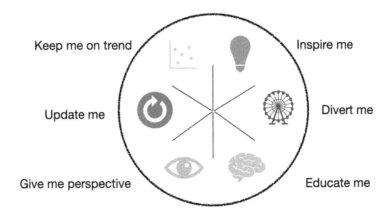

Fig. 5.4 Six user needs, inspired by (Shishkin 2018). (Source: authors)

While we find the newsroom pendant of the learners' journey in fragmented users' habits and needs across platforms, journalists must identify and address the different steps of users' journeys and habits in their story angles, headlines and captions to better connect with more and more diverse users and communities across demographics and platforms.

As users become co-creators and participants at each steps of a news story, it's imperative that journalists and storytellers share their process and navigation control with their audiences and start each story with first listening to their users— meaning to having online or offline conversations, conducting interviews, research and market metrics—to better understand how to serve their audiences best.

According to a survey in 2018 by BBC World service, which is for many users around the world the third or fourth stop when searching for news content, meaning that users are already updated on the most recent and most talked about news when they'd come to the BBC, we can identify six explicit users' needs, see Fig. 5.4, which journalists and content creators need to address in their choice of story angles based on the demographics and platforms they want to serve.

To come up with a useful editorial strategy based on data analytics, metrics and feedback iterations, we recommend for newsroom educators to apply a design thinking and listening first approach to news reporting and storytelling, transforming news stories into products which address and solve user needs.

Any newsroom and content creation unit in enterprises can work with these six users' needs and translate them into their audience building and content creation strategies.

5.5   Stories Travel Across Platforms

While learners and users are undertaking a much more self-owned journey into learning and communications, also journalists and content creators make their stories travel, underscoring the social/mobile-first approach in the digital ecosystem and the user behavior in it.

The first step is to listen and find a good story with an umbrella theme, for example, disruption of education by the Covid19 pandemic.

Then the second step is to break the story down into fragmented micro-stories with diverse angles for different platforms and work on it on a longer timeline. For example, an infographic on Twitter comparing the use of remote tools before and after March 17, 2020, a quick photo gallery with quotes of teachers and students on Instagram feed, a three minutes explainer video comparing Adobe Connect with Zoom on Facebook, a live-panel with experts and journalists asking hard questions about post-Covid19 education on Facebook, YouTube, Twitch and the Web, followed by a long immersive, multimedia and interactive data-story for the Web.

As stories travel across platforms on a longer timeline, interested users will also travel along and connect in a deeper relationship. The multiplatform content creation strategy is key for newsrooms and newsroom education moving into a virtual environment, see Fig. 5.5, blurring the lines between offline and online activities and environments.

In that sense, newsroom education gives us a great model for experiential learning environments in other subject areas, too.

Fig. 5.5 User journey across multiple platforms. (Source: authors)

Although space still matters for all participants in educational and newsroom environments to socialize, interact, group, discuss, collaborate, what now matters is a hyper-agile, liquid third pedagogue, embracing emerging technologies to merge physical environment (with a blending in 3-D and 4-D immersive environments), as for example educator Steven King (2020) explores in modules included in the curriculum.

Blending real and virtual spaces serves learners and educators best in fast adapting to new skills and applicable knowledge through experiences as well as include data-based forecast scenarios.

5.6   The Flipped Classroom

The "Bauhaus School" famously declared a community-driven vision transforming learning into a learning together approach, which was subsequently challenged by gender restrictions and hierarchical attitudes. But the idea surfaced in many variations over the last hundred years. At the beginning of the twenty-first century it was scientifically and practically shaped under the new notion "the flipped classroom" that explores how educators are reorganizing the classroom to share instruction and knowledge online, outside of class and using class time for homework and feedback.

In 2003 an OECD-led survey noted that the interactive digital ecosystem becomes ubiquitous in an adequate learning environment, focusing on three new key skills: 1. "act autonomously", 2. "interact in heterogeneous groups" and 3. "use tools interactively".

The accelerated speed of innovation and knowledge development, makes learning together, participation and collaboration, locally and internationally, a necessity, enabling the most productive outcomes for learners, educators and for journalists and content creators alike. As mentioned above, space now matters as a liquid enabler for education and newsrooms, blurring the lines between offline and online methods, aligning all activities around five dimensions: 1. social presence, 2. cognitive presence and leadership, 3. purpose and clear instruction, 4. skill development to working in a team, 5. seamless technology.

Seamless international collaboration is baked into liquid learning environments which embrace emerging digital tools and blended learning pedagogy shaping knowledge content anew. Since everything that happens somewhere on the globe affects other world regions, international collaboration is important for both educational institutions and newsrooms. Both authors have therefore worked over the last decade with a network of international collaborators on four continents who created the "Global Pop-Up Newsroom" (on Twitter, Facebook, Web)—a cross border collaborative multimedia reporting project for students. The project involves student reporters, citizens as sources and independent reporters across many world regions working together on a defined global theme to produce multimedia stories with local angles and having an interactive reporting and conversations in the live segment from multiple locations all over the world. (See Marie Elisabeth Mueller and Devadas Rajaram 2019).

Each event involves diversely skilled international teams who experiment and apply the most recent and updated digital tools available for all participating reporters and hosts, based in different world regions, with different access to technology and resources. This is part of the liquid newsroom preparation and realization and included in the conversation among participants, hosts and guests. An important part of the learning goals and the expected outcome is that participants lean into uncertainty, overcome technical hurdles and find solutions on the fly by collaborating and exchanging ideas and get to know each other better without physical travel.

It's worth noting that the concept of the Global Pop-Up Newsroom can be used as a blue-print model for international collaboration with agile methods and liquid spaces in many subject areas. Most prominently a similar concept was applied and realized by one of the most laudable and successful international collaborative newsroom projects in recent years, the "Panama Papers" in 2016, investigating international finance and tax crimes, blending online and offline activities and using emerging technologies. It was conducted by an international consortium of investigative journalists, with as much as 100 partners from as much as 70 countries, analyzing more than 11.5 million leaked documents.

5.7   The Integrated Newsroom

Using a simulated newsroom as an educational model also in other subject areas, we can look at the "integrated newsroom" model, see Fig. 5.6, as the adopted version of the "flipped classroom" for journalism and communications education.

> This new educational experience must be built around shorter, more intense bursts of co-learning that put a premium on collaborative, creative problem-solving. This may be hard for some people to accept, but education needs to learn from the success of social media and gaming companies and not simply dismiss them as childish or evil",

explains Erik P.M. Vermeulen, a Professor of Business and Financial Law at Tilburg University (Erik P.M. Vermeulen 2020).

Working successfully in an integrated newsroom simulation needs participants, students and teachers to be open and willing to develop a shared liquid mind-set which allows everyone to lean in uncertainty, embrace new technologies for better connecting with users as co-creators as well as with international collaborators, to blend self-organised work with group work in diversely skilled teams, to merge online and offline activities and, last, not least, to overall communicate efficiently. Surely project managers and editors who are willing and able to structure, guide and manage hyper-liquid processes while applying emerging technologies and are able to keep their cool, are the icing on the cake.

Fig. 5.6 Liquid newsroom. (Source: authors)

5.8   Conclusion/Learnings

It is one of a small but growing number of places where experts are testing new ideas that will shape the future of a college education, using everything from blockchain networks to computer simulations to artificial intelligence,

predicts Jon Marcus in the New York Times (Jon Marcus 2020).

After participating in an entire cycle of a newsroom simulation, we have quickly laid out above, individual student-reporters will equip themselves with two most important competences:

First, each student-reporter is able to master a treasure trove of practical skills, including how to find, experiment and apply digital tools and workflows for reporting and for seamless, location-independent collaboration.

Secondly, each student-reporter is able to master the entire user journey by building a complete story journey, including how to listen first to users, to research, find, define and verify a story, break it down into fragmented micro-stories for different platforms and demographics, and to produce multimedia stories for multiple platforms and distribute them across multiple platforms.

At the end of the day, it's not about tools or rooms, it's about the mind-set and the ability to make full use of hyper-liquid spaces for experiential environments in education, newsrooms and media.

References

Bauman Z (2000) Liquid modernity. Polity, Cambridge

Bradshaw P (2007) Online journalism. Wordpress.com. Accessed 6 June 2020

Jon M (2020) How technology is changing the future of higher education. Labs test artificial intelligence, virtual reality and other innovations that could improve learning and lower costs for Generation Z and beyond. In: Medium: https://www.nytimes.com/2020/02/20/education/learning/education-technology.html. Accessed 10 June 2020

King, S, Space Matters (2020) The value of 3D virtual reality classrooms. In: Medium. https://medium.com/@steven_king/space-matters-the-value-of-3d-virtual-reality-classrooms-c0a236be4762. Accessed 8 June 2020

Mueller, ME, Rajaram D (2019) Reimagining crossborder journalism with social TV. In: Medium: https://medium.com/@marieelisabethmueller/reimagining-crossborder-journalism-with-social-tv-a5eedb7b1157. Accessed 7 June 2020

OECD Effective Learning Environments Program (ELE) (2003). http://www.oecd.org/docment/38/0,3746,en_21571361_38481278_46322150_1_1_1_1,00.html. Accessed 9 June 2020

Serhat K (2019) TPACK Technological Pedagogical Content Knowledge Framework, 16.9.2019. https://educationaltechnology.net/technological-pedagogical-content-knowledge-tpack-framework/. Accessed 7 June 2020

Shishkin D (2018) Talk at the Google news initiative (from 33'04"), 11.12.2018. https://youtu.be/9NjLFG1LOhw. Accessed 5 June 2020

Vermeulen, EPM (2020) The classroom of the future? A total disruption of education. https://medium.com/@erikpmvermeulen/the-classroom-of-the-future-a-total-disruption-of-education-c8952564c980. Accessed 3 June 2020

Wall M (2017) *Liquid journalism for the next generation.* In Global Journalism Education: Challenges and innovation, pp. 327–342

The Role of a Leader: Transformational Efforts in Innovation and Change

Christian Kastner

6.1 Introduction

> If the rate of change on the outside exceeds the rate of change on the inside, the end is near.
> (Jack Welch [cited in Allison 2014])

Jeff Bezos, the founder of Amazon once said: '...Amazon is not too big to fail ... if you look at large companies, their lifespan tends to be 30-plus years, not hundred-plus years...' (Bezos 2018, cited in Brier 2018). Bezos went on to speak about the constant need for renewal and change. He insisted on disruptive behaviour of his employees to keep Amazon agile and relevant in a world of constant change and the threat of new competitors and imitators. Living in a VUCA world (volatility, uncertainty, complexity and ambiguity), change is happening constantly. As such a world is more unpredictable and uncertain, it also creates new challenges for companies. They have to question, change and transform established practices, leaving familiar paths, with the ultimate goal to remain relevant and profitable.

As such assessments and evaluations are not happening without the initiative of people, the key difference to being innovative (both as a company as well as individuals) is made by leaders and key employees, who are agile enough to adapt themselves and act (instead of reacting). They cannot just command change and innovation as a top-down order: rather it is more likely a process of renewal. Therefore, those in charge must find out the individual strengths of their employees and channel those strengths towards the achievement of the company goals.

C. Kastner (✉)
ORCID, Stuttgart, Germany

V. Nestle et al. (eds.), *Creating Innovation Spaces*, Management for Professionals, https://doi.org/10.1007/978-3-030-57642-4_6

6.2   Innovative Changes in Sales

For many years the innovation-focus of SMEs was on production-related issues ("how can we make our manufacturing more productive?"—issues like sourcing, production and logistics) as well as horizontal diversification ("what else can we make and sell?"). Here, the Value Chain Model (as shown in Fig. 6.1) of Michael Porter (1991) is probably one of the best-known concepts of the individual physical production process (= primary or upstream activities): how a company can link its internal capabilities and resources (= Resource-based view) to the supply chain of other suppliers to make the production of goods most efficient. Value creation is primarily evaluated by what the customer was willing to pay for and how a company could control the parameters necessary to create such value, (= value caption) (Priem and Swink 2012). However, the customer was not really the centre of the attention, the focus of leaders was more inward-looking towards capabilities and what its competitors were doing (Porter 1985).

Over recent years, it appears that the focus of the source of competitive advantage has been shifting from product and production capabilities towards the customer. This is happening both in Business-to-Business (B2B) sales and in Business-to-Customer (B2C) sales. Instead of "what product can we produce or sell?", it is now "what can we do for the customer to make their life better, easier and more enjoyable (= experience)?"

While costs (and so the price for the end customer) is still one important way of differentiation (Porter 1985), the focus of companies, especially in the Western world, is now more on differentiation (as other countries such as China are more competitive on costs).

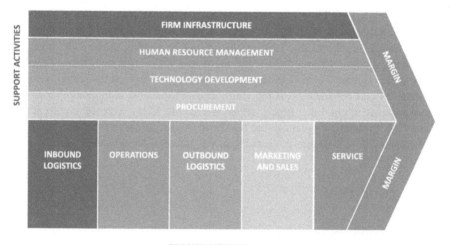

Fig. 6.1 Value chain-framework. Inspired by (Porter 1991). (Source: Author)

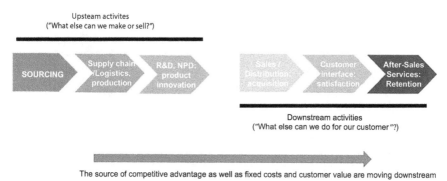

Fig. 6.2 The upstream/downstream orientation of company. Inspired by (Dawar 2013: 103). (Source: Author)

Dawar (2013) shows such a shift (or a different way of looking at the Value Chain) as shown in Fig. 6.2, separating the activities of a company into upstream (i.e. production, sourcing and logistics) and downstream activities (i.e. shaping customer perception). He makes the distinction that in the "old" world (upstream-focused) innovation was centred around physical products (i.e. cars, phones etc.), while in the downstream, the innovation-focus is all about the customers: reducing their risks and costs, and increasing their quality of life by making their lives easier and better.

Dawar expanded the ideas of Porter's Value Chain, shifting the attention of companies towards their possibilities in innovation-based differentiations. The differentiation in the upstream part of the value chain can come either through upgraded products or through an upgraded understanding of the activities within. Instead of selling their products just to customers, now customers or customer-groups (Stabell and Fjeldstad 1998) give proactive information to the suppliers on product volumes, the life cycle of products, and a forecast of delivery times. The focus here is not on selling but rather on working together and cooperation, creating a bond of trust between the partners (Wong 2001).

On the downstream side, one option for differentiation is shown in Fig. 6.3. Brenner (2011: 78) shows a possible way for incremental change: the organisation develops from a purely manufacturing company to a service/solution-focused company at a similar speed as the internal knowledge/competence creation (or collection of existing knowledge) is built up to become innovations and resources.

The observations of Brenner (2011) and Dawar (2013) show the need for leaders to move their organisations from reaction to action, from product life-cycles to a proactive involvement with customers as demands and challenges change much faster than in former (more product-oriented) times (Merchant 2012). Today it is important to act fast when you have a new idea of what the market might need. Sometimes just the way you package things, and especially how you market your products and services, are more important than (or at least equally important as) the product or service itself. Amazon, for example, sells the same books and goods as everyone else. Their speciality was firstly, the comfort of the customer in not

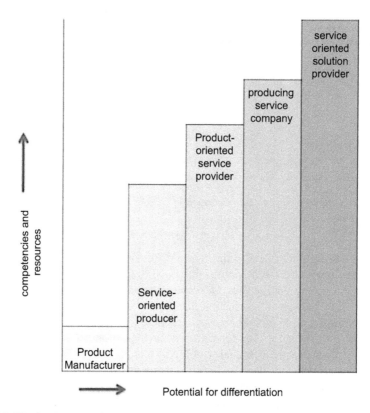

Fig. 6.3 The development of an organisation from pure manufacturing towards a service-oriented company. Inspired by (Brenner 2011: 78). (Source: Author)

having to leave the house to get the products, then the fast delivery, and now the ability to anticipate (with Artificial Intelligence and modern software) what you need, and when. It is not necessarily that the customer requires a physical product, but rather Amazon guides the need, organising all activities inside the value chain and delivering the goods to the customer's doorsteps. The trust of consumers in Amazon is so high that people are willing to pay higher prices, not even comparing them with competitors, purely for convenience. Therefore, the differentiation of Amazon is not in costs or physical goods but rather in the downstream side of shaping customers' perceptions (safe shipping and payment, trust, easy return of goods, fast delivery). Notably, these competitive advantages involve upstream parts as well (such as warehousing, products and logistics), but these factors are taken more or less as a kind of prerequisite by customers (there are many other companies online with similar upstream possibilities).

The difference is made in how Amazon puts it all together, creating trust in its brand and value proposition, forming a perception of the brand as customer-friendly and solution-focused.

If a company can raise awareness amongst its customers (or potential clients) in a similar way with its downstream components, sales discussions with its customers will soon move away from price towards the value the company can create for the client. It is much more difficult to compare the often intangible value propositions on the downstream side than it is to compare prices on the upstream offering. Merchant (2012) summarised it thus '...everything what is undifferentiated is going to be delivered in an ever more efficient, low-cost way. Porter's value chain is well suited for this mass-market, cost-driven approach...' For anything which can be adapted and customized (products and experiences), a down-stream-focused business (with hopefully higher prices) as a better chance of being unique and non-comparable.

To summarise the changes regarding sales, Gattorna and Waters (1996, cited in Dani, 2019) offer a great view of the four components of strategic fit a company needs in order to align its sales to the changing environment:

1. Leaders need to have a proper understanding of their market and the organisation's external environment. What are the changes in demand, customer behaviour, product features etc.? It is pivotal to reach as many of your customers yourself in order to obtain as much first-hand, unfiltered information as possible. Don't just rely on external sources or your marketing department to avoid bias and "filtered" information.
2. The external environment influences the possible strategy of a company. If you want to move from upstream to a more downstream focus, it will most likely involve a culture change, different people (or at least a different mindset) and also a different leadership style. All of those components need to support the sales effort.
3. The culture of the organisation, which is now more downstream-oriented, centred around intangible things and less around physical products. It involves more creativity, freedom, and a spirit of entrepreneurship on all levels. It also involves your willingness as a leader to "let go" and allow trial and error.
4. And finally, a new mindset, leadership and management style to support both strategic changes and the new culture. It will be less direct but probably more centred around objectives, leaving the details to be worked out at an operational level.

6.2.1 Practical Approaches to Establishing a more Downstream-Oriented Sales Approach

- The reasons your customer buys your product/service is either that you help him to save money (avoiding costs), to make more profit and more revenue, or to make his life better/easier/more comfortable (preventing risks). Focus your communication on how you're meeting these needs. Customers are willing to pay higher prices if you can show them not only WHAT you are selling but also HOW you will deliver it to them.

- Conduct a detailed (face-to-face) evaluation with your existing customers as to why they buy from you. Find out also why people are not buying from you. What are the "deal-breaker" components of your offer? Don't be afraid to challenge widely accepted industry practices as to how things are to be done. Uber disrupted the whole taxi industry by transferring power from the taxi companies to the consumers without owning a single car.
- Analyse the value chain of your customer together with them. As soon as you do that, you are moving away from being "just" a supplier towards more of a consultant and advisor.
- The shift from an upstream to a downstream-focus is a whole culture change from an inside-focus to an outside-focus (Dawar 2013). Instead of having control over supply issues like production and physical products, your field of competition is now whether you have the right market information, a great relationship with your customer, and how the customer perceives your company.

Other than the sales side and the components involved in the upstream process, which we have discussed in this first section, the task of downstream orientation involves the even more difficult task of changing the existing culture of a company. This will be explored in the next part of this article.

6.3   Innovative Changes in the Culture of a Company

In the previous section, we described the need for a different market orientation and customer focus. A change from the upstream to the downstream market-focus most likely needs changes to take place within an existing company culture. How can this be done and what is the role of a leader in creating a culture of innovation? Plugmann (2018) identifies the creation of a company culture of flexibility and innovation as an essential task, to create a common mindset among all leaders for facing the upcoming challenges of competition and general social changes within our societies.

It is, therefore, a top priority for leaders to conduct an ongoing, honest assessment of the current state of the organisation and the company culture: are there any demands upon or threats to the organisation, the current business model, the product or the services? Is the market share, profit and turnover declining or increasing? Are we seen as innovators by our customers and the market in general?

One of the first things to do in order to learn something new and to be innovative is to challenge and unlearn previous experiences (Huikkola and Kohtamäki 2017). Many SMEs appear to be imprisoned by their manufacturing, product-based history. What was good when the company focused on the production of physical goods might not be good when you try to sell complete solutions, software or services. Along with a change from physical resources to intangible success factors comes a necessary change related to the mindset of the stakeholders. The focus is no longer on just a physical product; it goes deeper. It questions and challenges the very identity of the company, progressing from a product/manufacturing culture to a more open/entrepreneurial culture. It is now trying to understand the real needs and value chain of the customer in selling more complex combinations of products, solutions and services. Here it is necessary to assess all current structures, procedures and policies to see if they are adding value to the company and the customer (Matzler et al. 2010; Barrett 2017).

Matzler et al. (2010) highlight seven leadership areas which are pivotal for innovation and change:

(a) Innovation orientation of top management: encouraging employees to think continuously about new approaches, then allocating sufficient funds; being prepared to take risks and try out unusual approaches.
(b) Culture of entrepreneurship (within the company): values and priorities focus on dynamic, growth and innovation
(c) Intensity of culture
(d) Core competencies: skills, technologies, resources and processes are unique, valuable to the market, and cannot be easily imitated or substituted
(e) Competence-based management: build core competencies and turn them into competitive advantages
(f) Market innovation: generate and constantly collect relevant information from the market; circulate it within the company as a basis for future decisions
(g) Innovation in products and services (or innovative ability) that gives an edge over competitors

While Matzler et al. (2010) maps the final stage of an innovative company, the 8-stage model of Kotter (1996) provides some practical steps for how to begin to move a project or an organisation towards this end goal. Kotter states the need for communication with all stakeholders as the starting point in a change process. The goal is to align team members, with a sense of urgency, around a common goal to create a guiding coalition (i.e. a new downstream-oriented company culture). So, once the leadership is convinced that changes are necessary, the key is to communicate this fast, often, and with the necessary combination of passion and facts to every stakeholder affected. The positive benefits for both the individual and for the whole organisation (Kouzes and Posner 2010) need to be highlighted. People do not want to follow an intangible vision of a leader or an organisation. They want to know that they are heard, cared for and understood; they also want to know what might be the benefit in the process for them.

Therefore, leaders have to demonstrate the potential for individual participation, the benefits of the change, and how the changes can be anchored in the culture (Hughes 2018:43–44). The key is to awaken hidden resources (i.e. knowledge, talents, ideas) among employees, to bring those resources out and to motivate the individual to participate in the innovation and change process. To make the change process more tangible, Avery and Bergsteiner (2011) suggest breaking down the desired end-result into key performance drivers and supporting practices. At this stage, it might be necessary to discuss the issue of individual values, the current

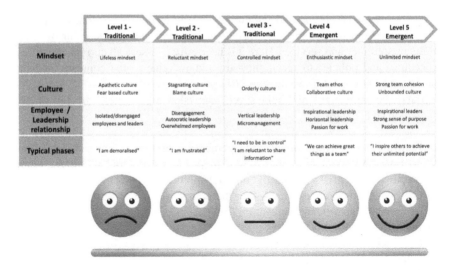

	Level 1 - Traditional	Level 2 - Traditional	Level 3 - Traditional	Level 4 Emergent	Level 5 Emergent
Mindset	Lifeless mindset	Reluctant mindset	Controlled mindset	Enthusiastic mindset	Unlimited mindset
Culture	Apathetic culture Fear based culture	Stagnating culture Blame culture	Orderly culture	Team ethos Collaborative culture	Strong team cohesion Unbounded culture
Employee / Leadership relationship	Isolated/disengaged employees and leaders	Disengagement Autocratic leadership Overwhelmed employees	Vertical leadership Micromanagement	Inspirational leadership Horizontal leadership Passion for work	Inspirational leaders Strong sense of purpose Passion for work
Typical phases	"I am demoralised"	"I am frustrated"	"I need to be in control" "I am reluctant to share information"	"We can achieve great things as a team"	"I inspire others to achieve their unlimited potential"

Fig. 6.4 The 5 stages of cultural change. Inspired by (Gallo and Hlupic 2019). Source: author

culture, and how the desired new culture might look with all involved stakeholders (Barrett 2017).

It is important to note that the leader (or management board) cannot achieve innovation and change just by ordering it top-down. The process will fail if it does not have the support of (at least) some opinion leaders within the company, who then have the power to convince others to follow. Therefore, innovation, first of all, is connected to people: if you have the right people with the right mindset in the right place, innovation will follow almost instantly. Figure 6.4 makes such a transformation—from a more traditional culture towards an emergent, innovative one—visible.

Notably, good examples and behaviour (role models at every level including leadership) will work towards the new approach. As (according to Gallo and Hlupic) the ' . . . organisational culture of a company is a reflection of the leaders' culture, ethics (or lack of them) and consciousness . . . ', the work and change have to start here, but not stop there. Individual awareness and change need to be implemented at an organisational level as well. This needs help, facilitated discussions and coaching at all levels about shared values, the "why" of the company (mission), the now-situation, and what a possible new culture, values and behavioural practices might look like.

6.3.1 Practical Approaches to Establish an Innovation-Friendly Company Culture

- Assess and evaluate the current state of the company culture (both formal, written down, and the unofficial culture). This includes values, beliefs, behaviour, mission and vision, as well as the purpose of the organisation. Most of these items are intangible and not obvious. It is recommended that you analyse the complete value chain of the organisation and ask your stakeholders questions about what is going well for them and where there might be areas for improvement. The first level of suggestions will most likely be operational issues—after addressing these, try to go one level deeper and find out the root of the problem. After that, try to think in a more complex way from upstream (physical, operational problems) to downstream issues. Make sure that you as a leader get first-hand feedback by talking to an unfiltered selection of your customers (that means that you select whom to talk to), and visit industry fairs to discover new trends. You should particularly focus on trends from the United States and China as they are the innovation hubs for new downstream trends and technology (think about disruptive companies like Uber, TikTok, Skype, WhatsApp, Tesla etc., changing industry standards within a very short space of time).

- Identify and address possible driving and restraining forces for innovation and change inside of your organisation (Lewin, 1951, cited in Fisher, 2007:131).
- Define improvement areas and shared values. People will not buy from you because of a nice-sounding value statement but rather because of how they are treated by your staff and whether or not you solve their problems. This implies that you as a leader serve as a role model. Your people will watch you very closely and imitate your good or bad behaviour.
- Praise and reward good employee behaviour. Put good practice in front of everyone. You can use town hall meetings, company newsletters and emails to share positive examples of how employees acted in line with the new values. Ask stakeholders (and especially customers) for regular feedback if they perceive changes as an advantage.
- Create innovation time for the individual employee. You can allocate a certain percentage of the monthly working time to "unaccounted innovation time"— during this time employees are encouraged to "dream" about innovation practices, helpful changes in the organisational value chain and possible product/service improvements. Have regular meetings where you collect all those ideas. Make sure that this is not killed but rather encouraged by department heads. If you have the chance, link part of the annual bonus for leaders to the number of innovation/change suggestions from their department. Be patient in this respect, you will not create such a culture overnight.
- Install regular feedback loops and continuously challenge the status quo. Often this is easier to do with an outside coach who is helping to facilitate this without being biased.

In this second section, we have discussed the evaluation of the current company culture, intending to see if it serves the purpose and future of the organisation. As mentioned already, this change will not come about without someone taking the first step. We will, therefore, look at a change-supporting leadership approach in the third part of this article.

6.4 Innovation in Leadership Style and the Understanding of Leadership

Historically, the role of a leader (both of a country and of a company) was seen as one person having total power to lead (called "heroic" or "transactional" leadership). Northouse (2009) described it as a form of authoritarian style with high interference from, and high influence of, the leader. It was a top-down approach with clearly expected outcomes from followers (Bass, 1981, cited in Vito et al. 2014).

This idea is still prevailing in certain parts of the world (countries influenced by the Anglo-Saxon working culture such as the UK and the U.S. as well as many countries in Asia). However, disruptive and changing markets, along with a different understanding of leadership especially among younger people, have also initiated a change in the general understanding of leadership. Maxwell (2019: 19) describes this change as '...it is from Soloist to Conductor...', it is from directing to connecting, from serving a company to serving a customer.

This new understanding of leadership (both in academia and in public opinion) is shown by different expectations of staff have about their leaders. While, decades ago, it was enough for a leader to produce results, it is now also expected that the leader care for his/her team members.

In a recent article in the Harvard Business Review, Giles (2016) surveyed what followers expect from their leaders, asking 195 leaders from 15 countries. The interesting outcome was that, while the top expectations from followers of their leaders were still traditional (clear goals and objectives, high ethical standards), more than half of the answers were more relationship-oriented ('...committed to my ongoing training, creates a feeling of succeeding and failing together, helps me to grow as a leader...' Giles 2016).

This is a new understanding not only of the leader as a person but also of what a leader has to do. It is further based on mutual trust: the leader is doing something for me and I do something for him/her (and the organisation).

This type of connection and relationship becomes more and more necessary as changes within the competitive environment (market) occur more frequently and people have to act. Interestingly enough, even in organisations like the Army, the understanding of leadership is changing from a former top-down-command leadership style to a more common, two-way style of communication. For example, the Army Leadership Code of the British Army (Anon 2015) reveals its understanding of leadership, executed by its officers, no longer to be an entirely top-down-command style but rather an evolving journey towards a two-way process. Officers enable followers, giving them space to develop and to act boldly. This is still within the command chain (and every organisation needs some clear leadership structure), but with much more responsibility and freedom delegated to the individual team member. Those team members respond (within a framework of loyalty and discipline) by acting boldly and independently to achieve their goals within a messy situation like a crisis or a battlefield.

How can a leader achieve such a level of trust, common understanding and support?

To begin with, an honest evaluation of the current leadership approach within a company is necessary. It might reveal that changes in both understanding and the leadership practice might be necessary—first, the understanding of what is expected from the leader, as well what he/she can do to enable followers within the company to be more innovative and positive towards change.

So, it is about introducing leadership ideas which integrate support, coaching and guidance rather than detailed (often micromanaging) instructions, while employees have to accept more self-responsibility, ownership, innovation and commitment (Ibarra and Scoular 2019). External coaches can help leaders to adapt to their new tasks of coaching and mentoring employees, but the real work of creating a learning and innovative culture has to come from inside the organisation.

6.4.1 How Leaders Can Foster a More Transformational Leadership Style

- Address and evaluate the current state of the leadership within the organisation. Most likely you will get very different opinions. Here the help of external coaches and, for example, 360° feedback (= feedback from all stakeholders/team members connected to the individual leader) can give a more complex and honest picture.
- Build the new leadership around a specific task to perform: to align the organisation to create an innovative culture, not for the sake of doing this but to make the organisation more customer-focused and competitive.
- Encourage leaders and followers to share their knowledge. This could create a new atmosphere and spirit of win-win, of learning together. Allow older staff members to share from their lives, the history of the company and success stories from the past. Give younger leaders and team members the possibility to share their experiences, and perhaps also how to use new technology with older team members. Every generation has something to give, and this sharing approach creates a more trusted platform of win-win for everybody.
- Be an example, and encourage other leaders to be an example as well. Reward a culture of knowledge sharing among employees and stakeholders both with praise and by making it part of individual bonus agreements. It is often "just" about the "freeing of minds", encouraging of new ideas and repackaging of current offers to disrupt existing practices. Through this transformational leadership style, it is possible to combine organisational knowledge with innovation to obtain a competitive advantage (Alowais, 2018).
- Make sure that peer development, coaching and mentoring are embedded in leadership expectations (this effort should be monetised and part of the flexible payment of senior leaders). Hire new people who have already practised these things in the past—this will speed up your change process.

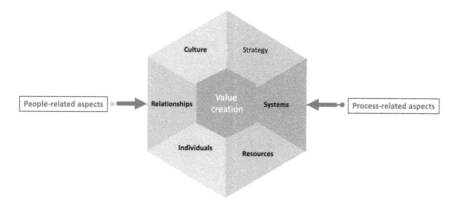

Fig. 6.5 The six dimensions of leadership. Inspired by (Gallo and Hlupic 2019). (Source: Author)

6.5 Conclusion

The model in Fig. 6.5 summarises the points we have highlighted throughout this article in one picture: to align people and processes around a common theme (i.e. value creation) and to create a culture, sales approach and leadership structure supporting this mission.

The organisational focus, as seen in Sect. 1, moves away from upstream-orientation towards value creation in the downstream. The existing systems, and especially the more static upstream culture and strategy, are challenged by a new approach to people. Section 2 reveals how empowered people take more responsibility, become more engaged and committed, and so change the existing culture. And finally, in Sect. 3 we have highlighted the new understanding of a leader in guiding and challenging this process, moving away from old behaviour towards a new, upgraded idea of leadership.

My personal experience with change is that people within an organisation are most often willing to go along with change as long as it is clear what their role and benefits will be. As employees today are looking for a job that provides not only money but also meaning, there is a huge potential for value in many SMEs to make a positive contribution in the coming years towards downstream solutions.

References

Allison S (2014, February 10) The responsive organization: coping with new technology and disruption. https://www.forbes.com/sites/scottallison/2014/02/10/the-responsive-organization-how-to-cope-with-technology-and-disruption/. Accessed June 13, 2020.

Alowais TM (2018, December 30) Influence of transformational leadership style on global competitive advantage through innovation and knowledge. Mod Appl Sci, 13(1), 183. https://doi.org/10.5539/mas.v13n1p183

Anon A (2015) The army leadership code. The Centre for Army Leadership, The Royal Military Academy Sandhurst, UK

Avery GC, Bergsteiner H (2011) Sustainable leadership practices for enhancing business resilience and performance. Strateg Leadersh 39(3):5–15. https://doi.org/10.1108/10878571111128766

Barrett R (2017, July) Building a conscious culture. http://edition.pagesuite.com/html5/reader/production/default.aspx?pubname=&edid=42a3e94d-8716-4c81-b242-c58f15c18c59. Accessed May 11, 2020.

Brenner M (2011) Vom Produzenten zum Lösungsanbieter—Reifegrade und Entwicklungsstufen basierend auf einer empirischen Studie. https://www.diplom.de/document/228599. Accessed June 13, 2020.

Brier E (2018, November 17) Do Big Businesses Die Young? Fact-checking Jeff Bezos. https://www.forbes.com/sites/elisabethbrier/2018/11/16/do-big-businesses-die-young-fact-checking-jeff-bezos/. Accessed June 13, 2020.

Dani S (2019) Strategic supply chain management: creating competitive advantage and value through effective leadership. Kogan Page

Dawar N (2013) When marketing is strategy—why you must shift your strategy downstream, from products to customers—HBR Reprint R1312G. https://hbr.org/2013/12/when-marketing-is-strategy. Accessed June 16, 2020.

Fisher C (2007) Researching and writing a dissertation: a guidebook for business studies, 2nd edn. Pearson Education

Gallo P, Hlupic V. (2019, May 15). Humane leadership must be the fourth industrial Revolution's real innovation. https://www.weforum.org/agenda/2019/05/humane-leadership-is-the-4irs-big-management-innovation/. Accessed June 13, 2020

Giles S (2016, March/April) The most important leadership competencies, according to leaders around the world. https://hbr.org/2016/03/the-most-important-leadership-competencies-according-to-leaders-around-the-world. Accessed June 13, 2020.

Hughes D (2018) The Barcelona way: unlocking the DNA of a winning culture. Macmillan

Huikkola T, Kohtamäki M (2017) Solution providers' strategic capabilities. J Bus Ind Mark 32(5):752–770. https://doi.org/10.1108/jbim-11-2015-0213

Ibarra H, Scoular A (2019, October 25) The leader as coach. https://hbr.org/2019/11/the-leader-as-coach?autocomplete=true. Accessed June 13, 2020.

Kotter JP (1996) Leading change. Harvard Business Review Press

Kouzes JM, Posner BZ (2010) The truth about leadership: the no-fads, heart-of-the-matter facts you need to know. A Wiley Imprint, Jossey-Bass

Matzler K, Bailom F, Anschober M, Richardson S (2010) Sustaining corporate success: what drives the top performers? J Bus Strateg 31(5):4–13. https://doi.org/10.1108/02756661011076273

Maxwell JC (2019) Leadershift: the 11 essential changes every leader must embrace. HarperCollins Leadership

Merchant N (2012, July 23) Why Porter's model no longer works. https://hbr.org/2012/02/why-porters-model-no-longer-wo. Accessed June 13, 2020.

Northouse PG (2009) Introduction to leadership concepts and practice. Sage Publications

Plugmann P (2018) Innovationsumgebungen gestalten: Impulse für Start-ups und etablierte Unternehmen im globalen Wettbewerb. Springer Gabler, Wiesbaden, DE

Porter ME (1985) Competitive advantage. https://www.ifm.eng.cam.ac.uk/research/dstools/porters-generic-competitive-strategies/. Accessed June 13, 2020.

Porter ME (1991) Towards a dynamic theory of strategy. Strateg Manag J 12(S2):95–117. https://doi.org/10.1002/smj.4250121008

Priem RL, Swink M (2012) A demand-side perspective on supply chain Management. J Supply Chain Manag 48(2):7–13. https://doi.org/10.1111/j.1745-493x.2012.03264.x

Stabell CB, Fjeldstad ØD (1998) Configuring value for competitive advantage: on chains, shops, and networks. Strateg Manag J 19(5):413–437. https://doi.org/10.1002/(sici)1097-0266(199805)19:53.0.co;2-c

Vito GF, Higgins GE, Denney AS (2014) Transactional and transformational leadership. Policing: An International Journal of Police Strategies & Management 37(4):809–822. https://doi.org/10.1108/pijpsm-01-2014-0008

Wong A (2001) Leadership for effective supply chain partnership. Total Quality Management 12(7):913–919. https://doi.org/10.1080/09544120120096043

On Corporate Innovation

7

Victor Paraschiv

7.1 A Better Definition

"It is inconceivable that we should allow so great a possibility for service, for news, for entertainment, for education, and for vital commercial purposes to be drowned in advertising chatter." declared Herbert Hoover, then United States Secretary of Commerce, at the first National Radio Conference in 1922. This statement is referring to the emerging radio technology, which was at the time on the brink of becoming mainstream and possibly open for commercial purpose. For everything that is created and man made, there is a decisive moment when the purpose and the objectives of this new creation is chosen. So was at the time the case for the radio. Within years from this statement the new Federal Radio Commission divided the radio spectrum in commercially available bands, and managed it in ways that favoured the commercial interests for this new technology over other dramatic improvements in the social spheres. Advertising became thus the core financial instrument of financing radio stations which set the radio amateurs and home enthusiasts on a path to disappearance. They were forced to decide if they either turn their hobby in a commercial enterprise or shut it down.

Artificial Intelligence is at the moment in the middle of a very debated topic where all possible advantages are being stacked against the remote possibility of bringing an end to the humanity and life on earth. It's yet up to us to jointly decide what we would like to turn AI into and control how much the commercial interests get represented when weighting in more of the social benefits.

Similarly "innovation" is currently at a turning point. I don't mean here innovation as in the sum of technologies and advancements. I merely refer to the term "innovation" and the meaning we associate with it. The meaning is vague and

V. Paraschiv (✉)
London, UK

© The Editor(s) (if applicable) and The Author(s), under exclusive license   85
to Springer Nature Switzerland AG 2021
V. Nestle et al. (eds.), *Creating Innovation Spaces*, Management for Professionals,
https://doi.org/10.1007/978-3-030-57642-4_7

thus two people can hardly have the same understanding of it. We also project individually, our expectations of what we would like to see on the term itself. However, we can all agree that intuitively everyone gets the idea of where the innovation points at: progress or advancement through new methods, ideas and technologies.

In companies that spread the full spectrum from nascent start-ups to big corporates, innovation is increasing its presence in the PR and marketing narratives in an attempt to convince the audience that novelty and advancement is happening indeed despite staying invisible, for now. We rarely get the chance to see the progress and conclude ourselves innovation is right here.

"Innovation" is now at a crossroads. It can become another proud member of the wooden language. Or it can be a claim that we take at face value and expect to see clear, reputable evidence of progress and advancements that leave little room for debate and doubt. The more we get accustomed to the use of this word in a misleading, self interested, self promoting, campaigning or a manipulative context the more it will decay it's meaning and worthiness. Do we use it when we speak about ourselves individually or collectively, as a team or as company for example, or perhaps it's mostly acceptable to use it when referring to a 3rd party entity in the same way we use compliments today. Complimenting oneself can hardly leave the realm of fun and amusement and establish itself into the business etiquette.

The use and meaning of this concept changes quickly. To guide ourselves in this journey we must first assign a meaningful, unambiguous interpretation ourselves. It's only then, when we are able to find and follow our path towards innovation.

What do you think innovation means to companies? What does it mean to you? In this chapter I can tell you what it means to me and then provide some reference points so that you can decide and build your own worldview and opinion.

7.1.1 The Ultimate Objective

It is of utmost importance to state and understand the results we seek to achieve through our actions, policies, processes or plans and why is that so important. Knowing at all times the ultimate objective and its importance is the key element that provides the context needed when assessing our actions, policies, processes or plans or when in doubt.

Too many times the objective and its importance is implied, not discussed, guessed or presumed. A blurry vision over the ultimate objective makes it difficult to assess, at a later point in time, if one achieved the objective already or judge how close to it the business arrived.

The emphasis in the dictionary's definition for "innovation" is on the novelty aspect (Cambridge 2020). The dictionary suggests that any new method is always an innovation. It doesn't tell us how to separate a new way of building a mobile microprocessor from a new method of cooking fried eggs using a mobile phone's battery or if there is any merit in separating the two at all.

What about the context? Does it have to be a completely new method in the human history similarly to what we call today an invention? Does the concept of "first to the patent office" apply to innovation too? We have been shooting rockets to the moon, other planets and even galaxies for decades now. Is SpaceX an innovative company? If the answer is "it depends." the immediate question I follow with is "It depends on what?".

What I would argue the current definition is missing is a measure of usefulness and the context it applies. Novelty alone doesn't mean much unless it is useful for something or to someone. Usefulness is just another proxy for what gets us closer to our objective. This is why having a clear understanding what we are set to achieve is so important. We can chose at any point in time elements that are useful for our mission. We can even compare and rank them based on their usefulness. If the objective is accurately defined and introduces measurable signals, we would then be able to measure each element's contribution in terms of its usefulness and given the context. The better job we do at defining our ultimate objective the more enabled we become in all our following actions.

The context and the measure of usefulness are too often intertwined, squashed together or even implied. When it gets difficult, not knowing what the company is after can become a terminal factor.

In the western world there are a few competing paradigms that describe a set of objectives. The free market participants that compete for revenue and ultimately profit. The government, who's objective is to devise and implement the policies it stood for during the general elections. The judiciary is trying to interpret the law and resolve disputes in a fair and unbiased way for all its parties. The social system is ensuring the basic needs of all its citizens are met.

Each objective, depending of how well defined it is, leads to a corresponding set of actions. Is GDP alone a good metric for government performance? Should the government even be looking at the GDP at all? Should there be a moral and social responsibility component included in any company's ultimate objective along side profitability? Since this element is not yet mandatory by law, why are some companies taking it into consideration? Does it translate to profit? How do we measure contribution in areas where the benefit is not directly quantifiable in profit such as education, health and the environment?

In the rest of this chapter, for simplicity, I am going to assume the position of a free market participant, a company, and see the world from their perspective. The reasoning and the judgments can be translated to equivalent terms for the other parties and paradigms operating in the society with some adjustments to their individual context.

The ultimate objective of a company is to bring in the next customer.

A customer here stands for an independent unit of revenue increment that needs to pass through your sales cycle from pitch to signing the dotted line. It may be the same customer purchasing an additional product from you or a completely new one.

7.1.2 Who is Your Customer

Who is your customer, it depends on your industry, business model and profession. Every company that aspires to be profitable and grow must have a good understanding of who is their target customer. Read the sales books, listen to your sales coach or talk to your sales manager. It's right there in sales and marketing 101: define your customer profile and understand its personas. Do that well and you know where to find your adopters, biggest spenders and top champions. If you want to give yourself the best chance of keeping them happy and for the long run, understand their habits and their motivation for choosing your products and services instead of your competitors'.

Whatever methodology gets your first customer it doesn't work for the 101st. It is also significantly different from your magic customer number 1 million. The approach changes and it's so fluid that it requires constant tinkering and adjustment of your entire sales pipeline, product, operation model, pricing and company.

Especially in its infancy, companies have to pull all their resources together to bring in another client. Some mature companies might have clients lined up at the door but they lack capacity. Can you remember an amazing restaurant with a long queue at the door? For them to bring one more client it may require a bigger kitchen or a larger seating area. Perhaps they lack the raw materials so they need to improve their supply chain. A solution that addresses the immediate bottleneck will permit an extra customer to be seated in. That's innovation right there. The new changes to your business that make room for one more client is innovation.

Most problems get solved over and over again, especially in the substitutable services and products because each individual context is slightly different and operated by managers with different understanding of the business and experience. From the outside we can also observe how the solutions eventually converge and start looking the same. Restaurants have to solve about the same problems to become financially sustainable. Newcomers to an industry may learn it the hard way. Seasoned business owners understand the scaling recipe, apply it and own multiple chains that have different branding and proposition. As they expand the business, the growth momentum breaks in new different ways. To grow an independent coffee shop to a Starbucks or McDonalds it requires bringing in a few extra million new clients. It's not just the capital that separates a small chain from a global franchise. It's the innovation gap and the expansion of the business context.

7.1.3 Innovation is One

Sometimes you need a bigger server but you are already using the largest existing server you can find in the cloud. Overcoming this challenge lets your next customer in. Your developers have to innovate to keep you in business.

You might have completely captured your initial market and the next customer lives across the border or in a new segment. You can only cross the market border when you create a new product adjusted to your new customers. That's innovation through new product creation!

There may be people dying of an incurable disease. They are willing to spend money to extend their lifespan or cure themselves for good. Create that new treatment and you have your next customer. Innovation through pharmaceutical R&D. Approve it in a new jurisdiction and you've got even more customers. That's business and regulatory innovation. Make it globally available and you've captured the entire planet. Do you have a monopoly? That requires changes in how your treatment gets successfully approved and passes scrutiny through diverse, independent methodologies, followed by branding, marketing and operations innovations. That's innovation step by step in more than one field.

The banking services in your geography are expensive, slow and convoluted. Come up with a better way of doing banking and you get your first client. Scale it out cheaply and you've got more clients that couldn't afford to use the traditional services or are ready to pay for a completely new user centric experience. That's business, tech and banking innovation.

Your local ISP hires 10 security network admins to monitor the traffic. Develop and deploy an AI monitoring tool, raise your sensitivity level higher and make sure don't miss anything. That's innovation indeed, through AI, technology and business as few employees could always actively monitor the entire network traffic 24/7.

Regardless of the nature of the breakthrough, as long it allows your next customer to join your business it is innovation. As your business grows you need to bring in solutions to problems few or none had. Scientific research, the development of new methodologies, new tactics, architecture, design, new business models and challenging existing solutions from first principles are all means to achieve your one ultimate objective: your next customer. That's innovation. That is also what got Amazon, Google, Apple, Microsoft, Tesla and SpaceX where they are today.

7.1.4 Monopolies

Monopolies, duopolies and cartels dominate an entire market segment. There are no more new customers to win. They are all captive. "Job done!". Market owners can now relax and increase their product prices. Stagnation kicks in for as long the status quo is maintained. If the government shoulders these companies as a result of their lobby and influence then it's nothing to be done regardless of the new, unexplored approaches available. The Holy Grail of capitalism is to become a monopoly, as monopolies are the ultimate innovation. Running a monopoly is capital efficient, market efficient and favours incredible profits. Radical innovation or government's intervention is needed to perturb the status quo so that the market players leave the Nash equilibrium. Small, incremental tweaks and adjustments are likely to be insufficient to change the pulling forcer within the entire marketplace.

7.2   Becoming Innovative

7.2.1   Call Me Change

It's time to stop calling it "innovation". Let's call it change instead.

When is the last time you woke up one morning and did some progress? We cannot do innovation in the same way we cannot do progress. We make changes through our actions and later on, we observe their consequences. We can only declare our actions a success a posteriori. While we are in the process of making those changes we can never tell precisely how much of progress or how much of a leap we are making, if any.

Looking backwards at historical activity, one might be able to conclude a product is innovative or tell which changes led to progress. It never happens when looking forward. Having high hopes that our actions mean something has nothing to do with the real, tangible results we get in the end. The outcomes of our actions and changes brought into this world is yet to be observed and assessed, by the history!

7.2.2   Culture of Change

Since innovation happens through change, we now need to design cultures where change is one of the core pillars. Why cultures? Because changes to the business cannot be the outcome of random chance nor people of an organisation left to their own devices and whims. To be meaningful it must be guided, directed and pointed in a direction that matters given the current context. Is everyone within the company aware of the ultimate objective?

Change is risky and it might lead to uncapped losses of all kinds. Change is unpredictable and it never guarantees any results. In spite of all these, the winning companies are those that embrace change and make it first class citizen in how they operate. How do they do that?

However risky, change as the outcome of our actions can be managed and turned into an effective tool for producing the desired effects while being in control. Continual improvement processes, lean management, Kaizen and agile methodologies propose a diverse set of frameworks and systems for managing the continuous process of introducing changes to a company so that clear objectives are met while the associated risks mitigated.

7.2.3   The Critical Path or Where to Innovate

The largest leverage actions have, within a company, lies on the critical path of its core products. Successes and failures on this path don't add up, they multiply. Have too many half-baked pieces stringed together and your largest advantage cannot prevent your business from becoming irrelevant. Great companies are winning big on their critical path by using technologies, processes and methodologies to make this path's flow as effective as possible, at capturing their next customer. Of course!

This is one place where change matters the most.

Have this in mind when you look at companies that claim that something doesn't work for their business. Have you ever heard anyone saying they brought in the company a new team specialized in a discipline such as digital transformation, artificial intelligence, data science, visionaries or agile experts that didn't manage to move the needle in terms of business ROI? Most recently the innovation gold rush started to reach the highest levels of leadership across all industries: the executives of big companies. The executives at the top, had clear strategies about how to innovate since 2013, surveys show. The objectives are an increase in profitability through business growth, higher cost reduction, new operational efficiencies, new products in new markets through more incremental and radical innovation (PWC, Unleashing the power of innovation, 2013). Every big company now has a well-defined strategy to innovation. The only difficulty they face is the execution (McKinsey 2020). Companies also struggle to find the right skills that can execute on these clear strategies (PWC, CEO Survey 2019 Report 2019). In the mean time, the bulk of the organizations are lining up for "silver bullet" innovation (Accenture 2015).

A culture of change that focuses on the critical path of the product might lead to innovation.

7.2.4   The Practice of Change

When a change framework is wired directly into your business' pulling forces, the lag time between the environmental change and company's response decreases rapidly. It is 100% certain, problems are going to appear on each company's road to success. What is always unknown is when and where this is this going to happen. For your company to react in a timely fashion with an appropriate response, it must first become aware of the new difficulties and then have the tools to naturally respond to the environmental change as soon as possible.

The word "naturally" stands here for the practiced discipline of applying your own thinking, calculations and judgements to the problem, starting from the first principles and yet considering the existing available options. Not responding to the pressure to stay within the boundaries of the "best practices" evangelised by your own industry, consultancies and experts, gives you the chance to take different paths when the standard solution becomes inadequate or a drag. Practising and applying what is known or actively implemented in the industry, without questioning its worth, can only take you to crowded places.

This is not reinventing the wheel. It's rediscovering the wheel!

This practice of independently solving problems keeps you aware of the trade-offs, the value of the existing approaches and the appreciation for why they are still in use today, as well as the right circumstance for their use. A good understanding for the state of the art methods provides a robust, reference framework to assess and analyse the current or new solutions. A good framework leads you to consistently picking the right options for your critical path. Good choices where it matters, multiply their value together to create disproportionate results: a great product many customers line up to buy and your ability to satisfy the demand.

A good example of this thinking is in Jeff Bezos' interview (CNBC 1999) when talking about the warehouses vs. high street shops. He's seeing something everyone else didn't even consider from its logical standpoint ("bad math"), which got immediately flagged as "arrogance" by the reporter.

More often than not, your team has already discovered the business and technical realities that surround your specific product, covering everything from challenges to strengths. This happened organically, as a by-product of them doing their daily jobs. Unless there is a pulling force to bias the team members to speak up, take action and fix the problems as soon as they appear, these insights will die unfulfilled. A winning culture facilitates the process that connects these random insights of your team and blends them in a viable solution. Since all your employees are caring, smart and well intended then you should ask yourself, *what is your culture and who are your leaders being that stand in the way of change?*

A culture that establishes a disciplined change methodology of the critical path of a product might lead to innovation.

7.2.5 Innovation is About Your Product

Maybe it comes as a surprise to know that companies perceived as the epitome of innovation have no innovation departments. None at all. Zero. This class of companies spends disproportionately more effort talking about their fast evolving products than selling the world the "we are innovating" spiel. Theirs conferences, events and marketing campaigns focus solely on the product, the roadmap, their vision and how that changes the world. The product, not "innovation" is their story.

For them, innovation doesn't exist independently at the fringes of the business or as an add-on to products that can be turned on and off as the board, stakeholders or investors decide.

Think about Tesla. Tesla created an electric car that gives people the freedom to travel anywhere. All the efforts in Tesla's public talks and press release focus on how they made their car, car's future developments or the challenges on their attempt to have a fully automated manufacturing process. Today we have books covering their journey as a company to overcome issues with the battery, the motor, the massive display screen placed in the main console and even the door handles. It's all about the car and the obsession with the ultimate goal.

Netflix on the other hand is all about "delivering excitement and entertainment". They survived the expansion of the Internet, which killed the DVD rental market by changing medium. Their engineering blog covers how many tools they invented to improve the entertainment delivery such as machine learning algorithms for user recommendations way back in 2007, a distinct user interface design and fast content delivery on multiple types of devices. This is why they are a leader and have been so for more than a decade. How do they respond to the demand for more variety in their video entertainment? Netflix starts their own TV series, enter the movie production and challenges Hollywood's status quo. Later on even Amazon started copying them. Attempting such bold moves, will likely make people think you are crazy rather than a sound business thinker. How much of a crazy person sounds Jeff Bezos in the previously mentioned interview (CNBC 1999). Real innovation lives by definition outside the box. To lead means to put everyone behind you and head into the darkness for new answers. Leaders show how to do it differently and own it, seeking no place to hide, excuses or someone else blame.

Here's Amazon's Jeff Bezos talking about his company's ambitions in 1999 and responding to questions about investors expectations, what clients want and the corporate arrogance to take on Walmart with a company only 3000 employees. Amazon had to expand their business to accommodate for the wildest crowd of customers. The necessity of staying in business made them become "customer centric" for real. For decades, they have delivered a world-class customer experience that other companies still look up to and some only now start to get it. How many times did he use the word innovation during this interview? Who is Jeff going to blame for failing to change the industry? What can you read in his body language?

Apple built a smart phone average people can use, far better than anyone else's. Just listen to Steve Jobs talking about the problems they had to solve to create a better phone than all of the competitors (Apple 2007). With the new iPhone's design he completely challenges the established market on their design decisions and tells them off publicly. They are all wrong. The market is wrong too. Here's a product that does it differently and this is why it's going to work now. He doesn't say it's innovative but it opens up the phone and let's you know how many things had to change so you get a great product experience.

7.2.6   The Amazon Approach

Let's turn to Amazon career's website. They do call their product "innovative" in the job spec. Today, April 19, 2020, there are 22,205 jobs listed that contain the word "innovation" either in the title or description. Software developers and the engineering positions amount to 13,945 while the rest are distributed across the entire business from administrative support, warehouse and fulfilment associates to legal, customer service and corporate operations. See Table 7.1 created from https://www.amazon.jobs/en-gb/search?base_query=innovation.

There is neither an innovation department nor innovation specialists. Or differently said, everyone is responsible for trying new ideas and delivering change within the business from warehouse staff to lawyers and the CEO.

When you start your interviewing process with Amazon you immediately run into their 14 principles of leadership (Amazon 2020). They are published on their main career website. That's their framework for bringing change to the world. During the interviewing process you get to absorb, discover and rediscover these principles over and over again. They grill you on them as well to make sure you can flexibly manipulate these concepts in logical thinking too. This is how they manage

Table 7.1 Open positions within Amazon that mention innovation

Category	Count
Software Development	6897
Solutions Architect	2336
Project/Program/Product Management—Non-Tech	1572
Project/Program/Product Management—Technical	1496
Operations, IT, and Support Engineering	1319
Sales, Advertising, and Account Management	1170
Fulfillment and Operations Management	1123
Human Resources	896
Systems, Quality, and Security Engineering	647
Marketing and PR	514
Finance and Accounting	505
Business Intelligence	426
Business and Merchant Development	406
Design	365
Machine Learning Science	310
Buying, Planning, and Instock Management	301
Customer Service	262
Supply Chain/Transportation Management	248
Hardware Development	217
Corporate Operations	165
Leadership Development and Training	141
Research Science	141
Data Science	137
Editorial, Writing, and Content Management	103
Investigation and Loss Prevention	92
Facilities, Maintenance, and Real Estate	86
Legal	83
Medical, Health, and Safety	63
Audio/Video/Photography Production	34
Administrative Support	32
Fulfillment Associate	28
Public Policy	28
Economics	24
Database Administration	19
Fulfillment/Warehouse Associate	19

change. These are for everyone that works at Amazon, regardless of where they sit in the corporate hierarchy. To me, these principles create a gravitational pull for the entire company towards a continuous focus on change. Amazon's change is fast, of good quality, simple and obsessed to satisfy their customers. This is the simplest explanation for how they get new customers and why the existing ones never leave.

If you're new to Amazon's principles there is an abundance of analysis on Internet for what they mean and their impact on the culture and the products. These principles have been around for nearly two decades. It is surprising to see how far their reverberations reach. It proves a well-designed culture can scale its success globally to even when the company has more than 100,000 employees worldwide.

Amazon decided to bring the next customer in through an intense culture that promotes everyone's thoughtful changes towards customer satisfaction. As of June 2020, Tesla doesn't even use the word "innovation" in the about or in the career section for any of their positions. Netflix doesn't have an innovation department either. Instead of a big picture role they mention innovation in the context of "core engineering" if that makes any sense at all. They expect new hires such as a Senior Data Scientist or Program Managers to change their product's content discovery system and the payment systems.

7.2.7   Imported Innovation

Some companies seek "innovation" externally. New problems are approached either via hiring new skills, contracting big consultancies or going to an external third party provider. The deep-pocketed corporations purchase patents in batches or even their competitors. Change may come from everywhere.

Their forward movement comes from adopting externally developed leverage. When done effectively it can deliver steps forward and keep the enterprises in the top echelon of the market. The adoptions of these novelties can actually work despite not being developed in-house. It's a different approach to making change and it requires a different set of skills and risks. The surveys show it's not easy to follow this path either.

7.2.8   The Perception of Innovation

The most intriguing, fascinating and yet disappointing approach is to do none of the above and spend your effort creating the perception innovation. One can go down the path of PR. It might work associating your brand with shiny, cool, new technologies or phenomena that are being perceived as futuristic or amazing. Despite being technologies in an exploratory stage or "innovations" at the brink of adoption they are not market ready. The focus is not on today's actions that move company's product forward but on the huge potential for altering humanity's lifestyle through possible new products that lie, for now, beyond the horizon or visionary, silver bullets for short.

When one cannot be part of the action then the second best thing is being part of the conversation about the action. When played as such, innovation is a spectators' sport. Many can give advice in abundance but few can actually play the game in the field, the only place where it matters.

When done right, this approach creates an aura of a forward thinking vision and progressive attitude. By sharing the spotlight with the actual game changers, the makers and the doers, the brand gets the benefit of the halo effect. The cognitive bias works as expected. Such industries of increased interest for supporters' cheering are the augmented and virtual reality, artificial intelligence, blockchain, IoT (Internet of Things), quantum computing, nano-technologies, electric cars, racing events, F1, genetics and space exploration to name just a few.

Alternative ways of being around the action is financing VC funds or start-up accelerators to display some logo or branding (just like in most sports), organising events, conferences and proposing industry wide boards of all kinds that review, curate, accelerate, oversight or facilitate access of these disrupting technologies.

Innovation in this approach is an outward looking exercise focused more on the story, narrative, branding and perception than the actual change they seek to bring in the daylight and to the status quo.

An interesting yet congruent picture is depicted by the job characteristics of roles within the "innovation" departments of such institutions. Most of them actually do have an innovation department in control of innovation adoption and rollout, so they say. The focus is on policies, strategy, governance, risk, communities, project management, industry threats, opportunities or investments. It is an interesting exercise to analyse the companies' standpoint of innovation. Press releases, PR campaigns, product presentation, job adverts all share the definition of innovation and how the company thinks it impacts their products and customers.

A good place to start understanding a company's understanding of "innovation" is their website. Careers section is equally invaluable. When the perspective of a company in regards to innovation matters to me, I would try to answer the following questions for myself.

Another example would be the number and types of jobs created in an organisation under the "innovation department" umbrella and their profile.

- What is innovation to this company?
- What is not innovation?
- How do they know what you did is innovation indeed?
- Is the company's approach to innovation inner or outer looking?
- Where does the company think innovation comes from?
- What is the context in which they talk about innovation?
- Can I clearly name one of their top innovations?
- Do they have an innovation department?
- Do they have a set of tasks, directions and responsibilities for the innovation department?
- If yes, who runs it and what do they do?
- How many new approaches did a manager try today, last week, last month? How many of them failed and why? What worked? Was anyone fired or promoted?
- What gets you fired in this company?
- Are they in a pursuit for any magic technology to get ahead the competition or they focus on improving their status quo through diligent and intelligent effort.

7.3   Conclusion

In all companies, assigning innovation to a special department that simulates activity and stands as PR props is unjust towards the employees working hard, on a daily basis to keep the business going and make it competitive. These employees and teams that focus on the daily operations are the real innovators and their effort is what companies should keep praising in its "innovation section". "Every organisation has somebody who has successfully launched a commercial product, but they are not always involved in the innovation hierarchy". Or even better, drop the "innovation section" altogether and let the customers use the adjective "innovative" spontaneously when talking about your product or service. Just like Tesla, Amazon, Apple, Netflix or Google does.

Most companies are already doing innovation. They just aren't aware of it. Innovation is how a company stayed in business for so many years. They don't know it because it happens at grassroots and the employees saw the effort as being part of their daily business. When successful, high-fives in the team were given around their desks not and at the C level suite followed by a big promotions and an internal newsletter with a word from CEO praising them.

Innovation is not a master insight delivered from a special bureau of thinkers that gets constantly enlightened by divine inspiration.

It starts with the daily sweat and it is made of the cumulative, daily adjustments of the business intricacies, the history of mistakes made and the viable solutions brought forward to pressing matters that threatened the business over the time. The surprising element when you get closer to the grassroots is that business survival and development has never been a direct consequence of the innovation department's proceedings, ever!

How did it happen?

Most likely these critical changes occurred through the good shepherding of common individuals that operate the business as usual without fanfare or being anointed into prestigious titles.

The employees improve things without asking for permission. Isn't this what everyone asks for in every new job they begin: the ability to make a difference, make the company they serve a bit better and be recognised for it.

As I am preparing to close this chapter Tesla issues a press release letting everyone know their flag ship car, Model S just got better and cheaper. Here's an excerpt from the press release itself synthesizing the innovator's mind-set or how they think about innovation. Bring small incremental changes to your critical path so you can bring in your next customer (Tesla 2020).

If you are wondering, they stay strong in their stubbornness of not calling themselves innovative, yet!

. . .

While each of these changes are relatively small in individual impact, our unique ability to introduce them into active manufacturing lines enables significant gains in efficiency, range, and overall value when combined.

Model S Long Range Plus has also recently received a price reduction of $5,000. Paired with these range improvements and gains in efficiency, customers now receive more value than ever when purchasing a new Tesla, and as with our other products, all of our vehicles will continuously improve over time with over-the-air software updates. Order today at Tesla.com.

References

Accenture (2015) Innovation: clear vision, cloudy execution. 2015 US Innovation Survey. https://www.accenture.com/t20180705t112257z__w__/us-en/_acnmedia/pdf-10/accenture-innovation-research-execsummary.pdf. Accessed 19 June 2020

Amazon (2020) Leadership principles. Amazon. https://www.amazon.jobs/en-gb/principles. Accessed 16 June 2020

Apple (2007) Steve Jobs introduces iPhone in 2007. YouTube. https://www.youtube.com/watch?v=MnrJzXM7a6o&t=305. Accessed 16 June 2020

Cambridge D (2020) Innovation definition. Cambridge Dictionary. https://dictionary.cambridge.org/dictionary/english/innovation. Accessed 12 June 2020

CNBC (1999) Jeff Bezos in 1999 on Amazon's plans before The Dotcom Crash. YouTube. https://www.youtube.com/watch?v=GltlJO56S1g. Accessed 16 June 2020

McKinsey (2020) Growth and innovation. Strategy and corporate finance. https://www.mckinsey.com/business-functions/strategy-and-corporate-finance/how-we-help-clients/growth-and-innovation#. Accessed 18 June 2020

PWC (2013) Unleashing the power of innovation. https://www.pwc.co.uk/assets/pdf/achieving-business-growth.pdf. Accessed 19 June 2020

PWC (2019) CEO Survey 2019 Report. https://www.pwc.com/gx/en/ceo-survey/2019/report/pwc-22nd-annual-global-ceo-survey.pdf

Tesla (2020) Model S long range plus: building the first 400-mile electric vehicle. (Tesla, Producer). https://www.tesla.com: https://www.tesla.com/blog/model-s-long-range-plus-building-first-400-mile-electric-vehicle. Accessed 16 June 2020

Designing Innovative Ecosystems and Introducing Digital Smart Services Using Examples of the Value Chain from Building Investor to Facility Management

8

Christoph Jacob

8.1 What is a Digital Ecosystem?

Digital technologies and transformation, Big Data, Virtual Reality and Smart Services are on everyone's lips and have started to change our world considerably: at companies, at home office, at customers, suppliers or even when we are travelling, due to available cloud connections and mobile devices we can work anywhere. Through network connections and access to virtual workspaces, we can access necessary documents and information everywhere. These technologies have also changed business models and significantly optimized our working processes. These digital processes and the ability to generate data and information about procedures, products and systems in real time provide us with decisive new information and advice at an early stage. In addition, new digital services also offer attractive benefits to customers and are therefore also used and paid for by them.

Based on these technologies, a digital ecosystem describes the networking of all active market participants with each other. Employees, customers, suppliers, subcontractors, partners, but also potential competitors, as well as machines and products: In the corporate ecosystem, all processes can be linked together and form a centre of shared know-how. Although many companies still believe that they need to protect their own knowledge and skills, the trend is that this type of business management is lagging far behind the speed requirements of markets, as expectations of product development cycles are increasing year by year and the time windows for market launches are becoming ever shorter.

Networking ecosystems create connections beyond a company and also link, for example, the product development departments of various competitors or industrial

C. Jacob (✉)
CASEA AG, Neu-Isenburg, Germany
e-mail: Christoph.Jacob@casea.com

© The Editor(s) (if applicable) and The Author(s), under exclusive license
to Springer Nature Switzerland AG 2021
V. Nestle et al. (eds.), *Creating Innovation Spaces*, Management for Professionals,
https://doi.org/10.1007/978-3-030-57642-4_8

partners. These temporary development project partnerships enable market-ready products to be developed in the shortest possible time. Digitization brings people into harmony even in several places, in different time zones and with different data, tasks and machines.

The cooperation takes place on an interdisciplinary level and overarching networks. The different skills of the participants result in a pool of expertise that delivers results faster, easier and more cost-effectively.

This means that a digital ecosystem is characterized above all by the dynamic and joint determination, compilation and evaluation of all available data and access to a common digital platform (von Engelhardt et al. 2017).

This results in a natural selection and evaluation of new services and attractive solutions that create benefits for participants in the value chain that were not available before. Ultimately, these new service offerings are adapted to local requirements and customer wishes, represent a significant competitive advantage for a few years and ensure a more intensive, networked supplier or customer relationship. The more digital the networking of value chains is, the more this has an impact on corporate competencies, prioritized activities, partnerships and the use of offices, apartments, warehouses, work and production facilities, sales and showrooms, shopping, sports and leisure facilities, churches and other buildings.

8.2   What are the Success Factors for the Creation of Future Innovations?

Digital networking increases the speed of innovation.

Innovations are not a matter of course. The top management of a company is responsible for the creation, development and implementation of innovations and innovation processes. Products, processes, systems and procedures that ensure and increase the competitiveness of a company are considered innovations.

An active innovation culture ensures that solutions for future challenges and trends are actively addressed. The basic prerequisite is that the costs for professional idea development are budgeted and are an integral part of a dynamic corporate strategy.

With a clearly formulated strategy, companies have the opportunity to communicate their goals and priorities in an understandable way, cascade this information at all levels and ensure that all managers and employees are working in the same direction.

The next important success factor is a consistent selection of corporate values that drive innovation and are recognized within the organization. The values creativity, courage and curiosity are the right companions. To be allowed to think all ideas and as well to accept a productive and solution-oriented error culture are further prerequisites. It is about using the entire potential of all employees in a company and taking calculated risks.

The active and consistent living of these values by managers promises a secure further development of the innovation culture to achieve sustainable results.

Team diversification with a wide range of complementary skills as well as the admission and promotion of disruptive thoughts significantly increase the quality of innovation. Lateral thinking is desired and rewarded. Targeted incentive systems support these qualities.

Departmental thinking is a thing of the past. Always focusing on the common goal, open communication supports the fast and uncomplicated exchange of information at all hierarchical levels of the organization.

In the past, companies have built high walls around their research departments. Their goals and projects were secret, and they wanted to develop new products and processes alone and exclusively. As a result, innovation cycles were very long and characterised by periods of several years. These time horizons were no longer sufficient to meet the demands of global and more educated customers. Today, the speed of innovation and disruptive quality are decisive success factors.

The structures are undergoing a paradigm shift. Digital technologies and the Internet are creating innovation platforms that make it possible to link different companies, experts, customers and suppliers together with the same identified goal and to form an alliance for innovation development.

Innovation platforms are also characterised by the fact that start-ups are part of the network alongside established companies. Start-ups can often develop smaller partial services of innovations in a more agile and flexible way at a significantly higher speed and at significantly lower costs than research and development departments in large established groups.

Start-up incubators and accelerator programs connect with universities, industry and expert networks together on innovation platforms. Start-up companies act as idea pools and implementation generators. In cooperation with established companies, they generate new technologies and advanced prototypes from ideas. The subsequent application and quality tests as well as the preparation for series production are usually continued by the companies themselves until market readiness is ensured.

Innovations decide on the continued existence of companies and are of fundamental importance, as the following examples from the construction sector also show.

8.3   Which Industries or Sectors are Part of the Construction Value Chain?

The world population will have grown to more than 10 billion people by 2050, and for years the trend has been observed that large cities in particular are becoming ever larger. The main growth is already noticeable today in conurbations. The demands on the cities and buildings of the future are determined by this development and differ massively from those of today. Not only is the population growing, but also the fact that people are getting older and older determines the use of buildings. Climatic conditions increase the time spent in rooms to more than 90% of their lifetime. Other drivers for change are the growing need for security, energy efficiency, indoor climate and comfort: the need for security has increased significantly in recent years due to aggressive terrorism and crime.

Sustainability also plays a major role. More than 40% of the energy used worldwide is used for buildings. This makes this segment even more important than mobility and industry.

Permanently rising costs in the construction, acquisition and operation of buildings are another influencing factor.

Networked cooperation between all those involved in the building construction process and—after completion—building operation management is a necessary prerequisite for the optimal use of resources.

Which areas in buildings are important elements to consider?

Of course, building protection plays a special role with aspects such as fire, smoke and gas detection, evacuation and extinguishing. The second area describes security through access control, video surveillance and intrusion detection. Comfort is described by heating, ventilation, air conditioning, lighting, shading and parts of the building automation, such as access solutions. An important cost and environmental factors are achieved through energy efficiency and requires a more detailed consideration.

The questions as to what conditions buildings must meet in order to be able to meet the requirements for fire protection, security, maximum energy efficiency, comfort and indoor climate are not changing with new digital technologies, but remain the existing ones.

The improvement of the demanded building physical properties, guided by intelligent and networked building monitoring, requires a networked and integrated basis of sensor technology. This is rarely possible at present, since most suppliers of building equipment use their own sensor technology with their own digital platforms. A further aspect is the additional assistance systems that record and evaluate user data and develop proposals for optimized use.

Facility Management (FM) represents integrated processes for the effective and cost-optimized operation and maintenance of buildings with multiple functions such as real estate, environmental, planning and project management, building services engineering, energy and quality management (Jones Lang LaSalle IP, Inc. 2016).

Facility management is a life cycle approach and considers the holistic processes in buildings with the aim of reducing operating and maintenance costs and networking with optimizing technical systems.

Facility Management workplaces include building automation, monitoring, control, regulation and optimization equipment, video technology, electro-acoustic systems, lighting management, fire alarm systems, building management systems, access technology and controls, as well as building and information technology for building security.

The entire value chain from the building investor to facility management is undergoing an enormous transformation process. Open and shared digital platforms are necessary to meet the growing demands of users. Ideally, digital facility management should include the complete automation of all operative building processes and services.

This enables facility managers to collect data on activities and building system performance, whose selection and analysis serve as a basis for effective decisions, planning, capital investment and optimal conditions for users and owners.

The change is not limited to the technology used per se, but also concerns the optimization of user behaviours in rooms and buildings. How will these buildings be used in the future and what flexibility is needed to make maximum use of the increasingly expensive space? Due to the size development of cities and the more flexible working behaviour of people due to mobile technologies, the use of office space has become more complicated. The efficient use of space under constantly changing conditions must be designed. Do employees need their own offices, meeting rooms or other facilities? There are countless variations here. The user data generated in facility management helps to qualitatively pre-plan and manage the changing requirements, to optimize the use of space and to set up efficient services for companies and employees (Jones Lang LaSalle IP 2016).

At the same time, the established FM companies are being joined by start-ups and new companies that are developing innovative digital services and bringing them to market. Parallel to this, manufacturers offer digital services for the use of their own products, which generate data and promise maximum benefit.

Some large corporations have adopted a holistic approach and have begun to digitally replicate the complete life cycle of buildings. Integral, open management platforms are used to generate and measure data in the building. Digital Smart Services evaluate, optimize and control these data and thus contribute to optimized usage and energy cost reductions.

In the area of the digital services described here, we will look at planning and architecture, air conditioning, heating, ventilation, plumbing, lighting, energy, elevators, and monitoring.

8.4   What are Digital and Smart Services and What Benefits Do They Have in the Value Chain?

Digital and smart services are present throughout the entire value chain and can be used by the building investor who places the order for the construction of a building, by all participants in the project planning sector, the producing building materials and components industry, the construction segment and, in an operational instance, the facility management responsible for the optimal use of the buildings.

The digital transformation affects the entire ecosystem, offers enormous possibilities in the areas of transparency (information), efficiency (speed), effectiveness (cost reductions) and value (quality) and has a high disruptive potential.

These digital technologies make processes completely transparent and connect technology with the user, because through networking the user gets the possibility of active influence and information in real time.

Digital services in facility management increase productivity, speed and availability of data and can also reduce energy and maintenance costs. To actually provide these services, companies often use software applications specified by suppliers or their digital platforms as well as networked computers and mobile equipment such as smartphones or tablets. Sensors attached to key building equipment collect data generated by the use of the facilities and technology. This data leads to consistent analyses for space requirement forecasts, energy consumption and the reliable operation of the technical building equipment (Jones Lang LaSalle IP 2016).

Consistently digitized services make it possible for every user of these processes to evaluate, compare, check and control optimizing comparisons based on performance data. Consistently automated processes in maintenance management replace paper and person-controlled processes.

Through possible, applied sensor technology in building equipment, computer-controlled processes that collect data are processed into usable formats. This provides a detailed overview and understanding of the object use and the consumption costs incurred.

The users and operators receive data and information that provide a sound basis for decision-making in investment planning, facility management and facility services.

If, for example, a craftsman is needed to maintain a heating system, the built-in sensors in the building heating system transmit a warning signal to the system. This information is then electronically displayed, recorded and forwarded to the management systems. The repair order is automatically forwarded directly to the service provider with whom a service or maintenance contract exists. These are all certified and qualified in advance and have agreed standard conditions for the performance of their services (Jones Lang 2016). By automating these processes, a lot of new data is collected and compared that was not available before: It is recorded when the service technicians arrived, how long they worked and when they left the object. The system also compares the invoice prices issued with the agreed contract prices. Benchmarking data from other objects is also used to compare how the costs of the repair are in line with other comparable services.

Digitalised services make processes consistent and completely transparent: in which phase the service is, when it started and has been completed, how much it costs, whether it is budgeted and how it compares to others.

Data on building utilization would be, for example, how many employees are present at any given time, how much energy is being used, how many and which consumables are being used. This usage data can be used to determine building occupancy and, ideally, even generate income from temporary rentals for unused rooms.

New business models, comparable to AirBnB, Inc. but for office space, will emerge and bring landlords and possible external users together.

Digitalised services will bring better results. The newly collected data and the use of the technology will determine the exact maintenance requirements, ensure optimal use, avoid interruptions and extend the service life of the building equipment.

Ineffective routine maintenance work, which involves servicing plant and machinery at fixed intervals and is still carried out regularly in many companies today, can be eliminated with real-time monitoring using digital technologies.

Digital services create transparency in real time, which the user can use optimally for himself and check at any time. Digital services optimize the user's use of time. Studies have shown that satisfied users reflect maximum customer loyalty. These services, which adapt to the user, fulfil the individualised desire for customer understanding: "They know exactly what I want and how I want it!"

The operational usability of digital smart services is extremely diverse and strongly dependent on the degree of cross-linking. In the first place, the following two questions keep coming up: What information do I get in what time and how can I use this information to optimize my costs and increase quality?

Digitisation and cross-linked networking in private residential buildings is called smart home technologies, with automation of lighting, air conditioning, heating, opening and networking of household appliances, entrance controls, alarm and surveillance systems and multimedia applications in the foreground (Botthof et al. 2016).

Office buildings, shopping centres, airports or other professionally operated buildings are described in the segment Smart Building Applications (Bramann and May 2015). Here the focus is on the cross-linked networking and automation of security, fire and intrusion detection, escape routes and energy optimisation potential in order to reduce operating costs.

Smart home technologies have the main motivation in lifestyle and smart building applications the optimisation of operating costs as a focal point.

8.5   Current Examples of Digital Smart Services

8.5.1   Cross-linked Networking of the Value Chain Through Building Information Modeling (BIM)

Digital services facilitate the cooperation of all network partners.

Digital Smart Services establish a close connection between the client or investor, the planning (architects, structural designer and specialists such as acousticians or energy planners), the construction side (general- and subcontractors), the supplying companies such as building material manufacturers or construction suppliers, and the subsequent operator (FM) of buildings.

These Smart Services ensure the best possible communication between all parties involved and reduce complexity to a manageable level. In the past, printed documents were used as the basis for communication. This form of collaboration allowed scope and interpretation when information was not properly presented and described. This meant that misunderstandings and misjudgements were preprogrammed, which usually only came to light during execution and often resulted in massive cost increases and time delays due to the need for changes.

In recent years, Building Information Modeling (BIM) has become established worldwide (see also: Baumanns et al. 2016). BIM is a holistic approach that structures the cooperation between all companies involved (Bramann and May 2015). BIM helps to link different qualities such as speed, reliability and cost savings in the construction process, transparent and efficient communication between all parties involved, energy savings in use and optimal ease of maintenance by means of a high degree of standardization.

Building Information Modeling technology digitally and virtually links the entire project and life cycle of a building object; from planning, construction, use and operation to possible demolition, all basic and necessary data is available.

The BIM object is a digital image (3-D) and comprehensible model, which is completely planned and recognizable before construction. This component or component model is accessible and known to all participants in the building creation chain. Only in this way it is possible to have a consistent, structured construction schedule be drawn up, on which up to 70 different involved companies have an influence.

The BIM software not only allows the creation and planning of three-dimensional building models, but also the simulation of the construction process, a cost plan and demonstrate the later use of the building.

> The BIM method is based on openness, trust and partnership. They form the foundation for successful realization and implementation. The process concept and the interaction between all individual components are the top priority. (Niedermaier and Bäck 2016)

What are the advantages for investors, building owners and building users in holistic project planning with BIM?

1. Transparency of construction planning
2. Sustainable management with all detailed costs for maintenance, cleaning and energy requirements
3. High quality documentation of the building
4. 3-D planning and modelling
5. Risk minimization and simple modification methodology before construction
6. Maximise use of capital
7. Professional, reliable time, project and cost planning
8. Template for future renovations, restructuring, conversions and extensions
9. Evacuation planning, fire and smoke generation planning
10. Comparison of finished buildings as a benchmark (construction costs, operating and energy costs)
11. High quality of execution
12. Long-term maintenance of value of the building

To be successful with BIM, it is crucial to make a contract with all parties involved from the very beginning and in advance that the BIM methods are the holistic basis and are used on a mandatory basis. Attempts to subsequently demand the BIM methods fail in many cases or are associated with enormous additional costs.

What are the advantages for planners such as architects, structural engineers, project execution supervision and special planners such as acousticians, energy or environmental planners in holistic project planning with BIM?

In the past, two-dimensional drawings were used in architecture. The basis of the Building Information Modeling approach is three-dimensional planning. Additional dimensions are added to the 3-D drawing model, such as the time schedule as project schedule, the construction costs and the detailed tender.

The outstanding advantage of the BIM system is that all companies involved in the planning process access the same database and thus have a common, coordinated basis. This concerted basis allows focused communication on the same information basis and with the same data formats.

Because all planning participants, such as architects, acousticians, structural engineers, energy, environmental, electrical, sanitary and heating planners and others access the same platform, communication errors are reduced to a minimum. Clear, coordinated construction models allow the best common, interdisciplinary functioning objects.

What are the advantages for executing companies such as general contractors, construction companies and craftsmen's companies when using BIM for integrated project planning?

The craftsmen carrying out the construction work have the great advantage that a detailed quantity survey is available for the individual products and construction production steps. Any changes can be easily tracked and determined. Today, many services still have to be performed manually on the construction site, which gives the person carrying out the construction work orientation for his own performance.

The building contractors and executing craftsmen have a construction schedule and a construction execution plan agreed with all parties involved and thus have the optimum prerequisite for providing the desired construction work on time and within budget.

The building materials and construction supply industry has understood that BIM is also an important opportunity to integrate their own products and systems. The software-based planning of construction objects can be professionally designed with BIM data sets. The manufacturers offer BIM models as system templates that can be easily and quickly integrated into existing planning. The provision of tested design models ensures that planning errors are minimized.

8.5.2 Examples from the Heating, Air Conditioning and Ventilation Industry

Digital services make the difference.

The holistic connected network of heating systems via the Internet makes services and mobile services possible, which not only help the specialist trades but also the user and the property owner (Gamperling 2017).

Viessmann, one of the leading international manufacturers of heating, industrial and cooling systems, provides its customers, their heating craftsmen and trade, with comprehensive digital services. These make their daily work much easier and enable a relationship with the end customer throughout the entire life cycle of a heating system—from initial contact to purchase and system services. Viessmann's Vitoguide, a toolbox for system control and monitoring, plays a central role. Vitoguide enables both the diagnosis and rectification of faults in connected heating systems, as well as the establishment of an early warning system for remote maintenance and the prevention of faults. In addition, the qualified installer can use Vitoguide to make recommendations for modernising or expanding the heating system.

Before buying a heating system, however, there is the offer. End customers today expect this in the shortest possible time. Fast responses to enquiries are crucial for sales success. For this reason, Viessmann's heating system calculator enables their heating craftsmen to create an offer automatically and ad hoc on their own website. For correct calculation, the basic data of the respective company can be stored, which are then combined in the heating system calculator with the interests of the potential customer to create a qualified quotation.

For the subsequent planning and implementation of the systems, Viessmann offers the specialist company additional online resources, including hydraulic diagrams, spare parts lists, functional descriptions, wiring diagrams, installation and service instructions.

For the end customer, the mobile Vaillant heating control system via app certainly offers great benefits. Another advantage and service for end customers is the heating configurator, which Vaillant installation partners can integrate on their own website. The configurator enables customers to quickly create their personal heating offer online.

With Vaillant products, end customers, housing associations and facility managers also benefit from the remote monitoring option with profiDIALOG. This tool puts the installation company in a position to check, analyse and parameterise its customers' heating systems completely remotely.

On site, the installer is supported by the Vaillant serviceDIALOG tool, which ensures the connection of his laptop to the local heating systems of his customers. This enables the heating engineer to analyse and adjust the connected systems and to call up data that, if necessary, help him to make a fault diagnosis.

Vaillant also offers many helpful tools and apps that support the heating engineer, for example in the planning and design of heating systems or the search for suitable spare parts.

Heating installers who install Buderus products use the Buderus "ProWork" app and the wide range of services offered by the mobile diagnostic tool "Smart Service Key": qualified installing companies can now fully commission customer systems via their smartphone or tablet (Android or iOS). In addition to the previous options—reading out data and adjusting the heating and hot water operation— trained partners can now also conveniently set the heating circuits, hot water preparation and solar heating in the app without the need for a cable connection to the boiler.

Junkers Bosch's digital services help end customers to make qualified purchasing decisions more quickly and to remotely control the heating system they have purchased from anywhere via smart home applications. In just a few minutes, an offer can be created on the Internet at www.heizungstausch.junkers.com, which is then checked and adjusted by the specialist company in a second step. For Junkers Bosch, efficient customer service is crucial. For this reason, homeowners can control the heating system via the Internet using a smartphone, tablet or PC, or allow their specialist technician online access. This also allows the heating system settings to be individually optimised, so that the systems have a longer service life and operate cost-effectively.

The networked single room controller EasyControl is the first smart room controller from Junkers Bosch that allows the temperature in each room to be set individually. Thanks to the new intelligent presence detection, the EasyControl learns when its users come home and can thus warm up the apartment or house in good time—even in the event of unplanned absence.

Summary: Heating Systems
In summary, digital Smart Services make it much easier for the end consumer to purchase and select a heating system. At the same time, the systems can be regulated and switched on and off remotely via a mobile app. This should enable energy cost savings of up to 25%. In the sales process, the individual offer for heating systems is created within minutes. During installation and maintenance of the systems, the installer has direct access to data of the heating system, thus enabling quick and competent initial installation, and during maintenance, fault detection can also be carried out online. In this way, waiting times can be avoided and quick reaction times can even solve some problems before they occur.

8.5.3   Examples from the Field of Energy Usage

Digital services optimize building performance and reduce energy costs.

The optimization of energy costs is one of the most important parts of building management. The costs for electricity, water and fuels (gas, oil) are becoming more and more expensive. The best possible, sustainable use of energy describes the building performance. It is important that other areas such as comfort and also the microclimate are positively influenced (the microclimate refers to the climate in the air layer up to about 2 m high in buildings).

The sustainable, efficient and continuous optimisation of energy building performance is at the forefront of digital and smart services. Here, the companies offer systems for optimising energy building performance that simultaneously control the technical systems and extend their service life. These services start with an analysis and evaluation of the energy consumption data, which then use energy flow analyses to provide an overview of the consumption distribution of the main consumers. Energy consumption reports, monitoring services, optimized data management and benchmarking create optimization proposals that reduce operating costs.

Smart thermostats for heating control in buildings with smartphone applications can be quickly set up and conveniently controlled. This thermostat with sensors for the indoor climate is connected to additional external outside temperature sensors that also control the window openings.

Symbols on the touch screen indicate whether the optimum indoor climate has been achieved. As soon as the room is entered or left, the climate is adapted to the conditions and optimised. Depending on how the room is occupied, the thermostat calculates the best heating strategy to save costs and keep energy consumption low. The operator can use the app to access this data and conveniently direct a large number of thermostats via his smartphone.

8.5.4 Examples from the Field of Building Security and Supervision (Monitoring)

Digital services make the building safe and secure.

Effective fire protection is essential in every building. Fire destroys lives of people and animals and causes great damage to property. There is a particular danger especially at night, as one is surprised by fire and poisonous gases cause severe toxicity without been noticed. Even when you are absent, you cannot react without real-time information. Intelligent electronic smoke alarm systems have become mandatory equipment in every building. Here, too, digital smart services help to permanently check and report air and room quality. Early detection through intelligent smoke detectors, which also measure the CO_2 content and trigger a networked alarm, are the solutions in demand.

8.5.5 Examples of Digital and Smart Services in the Elevator Industry

Digital services inform, create security and save time.

The elevator and escalator industries are structured in such a way that the main sources of income are in the after-market services sector. For this reason, most smart services of interest to users, customers and operators are found in predictive maintenance and digital monitoring.

Individual digital smart services are described here using examples from the global market leader Otis.

With the Otis customer portal "eService" depicted in Fig. 8.1, the elevator operator gets direct access to his elevators around the clock. With just one click, they can view all the performance data of their elevators, report a service interruption or check the current status of a malfunction. With this application it is possible to view the elevator history and thus the complete list of all incidents. Access to detailed

Fig. 8.1 eService. (Source: Otis Elevator Company)

Fig. 8.2 eCall. (Source: Otis Elevator Company)

operating data, status report and operating statistics describing the performance of the elevator is possible at any time.

Last but not least, there is also a direct telephone connection to the responsible Otis service centre/technician. If the customer/operator has an Otis maintenance contract, this application is provided free of charge.

Another Otis smart service is the "eCall" application depicted in Fig. 8.2, designed for lift users. With the "eCall" service, it is possible to order a lift from anywhere in the building without any problems. When entering the building, the app connects to the mobile network or to the internal WLAN. This saves the elevator user valuable time, as the "eCall" application allows him to call the elevator already on his way. The "eCall" app can also be used for several elevators in different

Fig. 8.3 eView. (Source: Otis Elevator Company)

buildings. Each lift can be registered separately. Individual user control allows, for example, the elevator door opening hours to be changed. In the case of a wheelchair user, an extended door opening time could make it much easier to get in. The application is available free of charge to every lift user. Registration is simple and intuitive. In advance, the elevator operator decides whether users register themselves or whether this is done only by the operator directly via the Otis "eService" customer portal.

Another Otis digital service is an information system in the form of a smart, interactive display in the elevator. The Otis-"eView" depicted in Fig. 8.3 combines user information, elevator cabin display, system monitoring and emergency call function in a smart and aesthetic design.

The display informs users about the direction of travel, location and floor destination, as well as the current date and time. At the same time, the user is kept up to date online with current and useful information from around the world while driving. Alternatively, individual information provided by the operator can be displayed, or offers from the immediate vicinity, such as the lunch menu of local restaurants. The design templates consist of modules and the content of the "eView" can be easily adapted by the elevator operator via the Otis "eService" customer portal. The integrated GSM module always maintains a constant connection to the Internet and the integrated remote monitoring system "REM" (Remote Elevator Monitoring), which currently and permanently monitors hundreds of elevator functions.

Summary: Elevator and Escalator Manufacturers

The digital platforms connect elevator operators, customers and ferry passengers with the individual elevators and also with the elevator manufacturer's service centres. Elevator data is evaluated in real time and possible faults are detected before they occur. All relevant data is available in a qualified form to every building operator with a maintenance contract. Furthermore, this data can be used to compare individual product types worldwide and to document and evaluate the susceptibility to faults. With these digital Smart Services, the products become better and safer and the maintenance costs become smaller and more manageable. Elevator users save time and are well informed.

The leading players in the elevator industry have cooperation with key digital partners such as Microsoft, AT&T, Vodafone, GE Digital and others to launch further innovative digital Smart Services in the future.

8.5.6 Digital and Smart Services from the Sanitary Industry

Digital services inform, protect and report dangers.

Water can bring us a lot of joy. Every day we wash our hands, take a shower or bath. We use water as food and water helps us in various activities every day. However, water can also be harmful. If water leaks in the wrong places, it destroys the surfaces and damages everything it comes in contact with. Water damages are the most common types of damages in buildings. The sources of danger are, for example, water pipes that are connected to kitchens, toilets and bathrooms. If these water pipes break or even flood basements, considerable damage is caused and the process of drying and restoring them to a usable state is long, complex and costly.

The plumbing industry has developed a sensor that is easily placed on floors or walls; it detects leaking water and when water touches the sensor, it flashes red, emits a sound and sends a signal to the user via an application on a smartphone. The sensors measure air temperature and humidity in real time and warn when they change critically.

Digital smart services are useful if they are able to provide reliable, rapid information about changes anywhere.

The sensors run on batteries but can also be connected to the power grid.

The owner of the house, investor or even facility management places the sensors in suitable locations and can easily connect them to the local WLAN and activate them with their smartphone app.

8.5.7   Digital Services as Smart Lighting

Digital services save energy, reduce costs and are environmentally friendly.

Smart Lighting is a digital, wireless lighting concept that controls the lighting time, lighting intensity and, of course, the power supply via the data network.

The Smart Lighting concept ensures that the lamps shine with the necessary brightness at the moment they are needed. This avoids permanent lighting.

The use of LED technology and the installation of intelligent sensor technology play a special role. Operators can expect significantly lower costs and a longer service life for the fluorescent materials used.

8.6   Which Digital and Smart Services Can We Expect and Count On in the Future?

Digitization, smart services and artificial intelligence support the holistically integrated concepts from individual planning and building construction steps and thus ensure that significantly better buildings can be designed at optimized costs and with minimized construction time. The beginnings for this are there and the start has been made. Large planning offices, construction companies and product producers have started to structure their own processes and to optimize them digitally. It will certainly be several decades before most of the participants in the value chain become an integrated part of the process and generate real networked process added value. The systems used and the sensor technology are still not coordinated with each other. A common platform that connects and controls all available data and systems is a necessary prerequisite for maximum individualization and optimization. This system platform could also be described as the brain of a building, which analyses the user data of the past and can propose intelligent solutions for future applications. This also makes maximized building utilization possible. Ventilation, heating and light adapt to the number of room users. The subsequent building cleaning and waste disposal depends on the actual use.

Smart services and digitalized networking will create added value for users and operators. The future will be determined by the individualization of products and personal user concepts that can be adapted, integrated and controlled to meet different needs. The customers shopping experience will be determined to a maximum extent by online product configurators and customers will receive immediate answers to their questions.

So far, most providers are still working on their own concepts for intelligent products and digital services. Over the next few years, these individual solutions will be linked together and evaluated as a unit. This will result in completely new service models for the entire value chain, the actual products and the possible after-sales services. It is no longer just a question of the hardware, but of the software and the compliant simultaneous connection of all units. User scenarios stage the entire picture, from access to buildings and rooms to the simultaneous integration of light, climate, heating, air, sound, information, security and entertainment. The trends in the smart home sector and the automation of applications in buildings support the need for joint user concepts (see also: Botthof et al. 2016 and also Carl and Lübcke 2016). Operations are made possible by smartphones and other personalized electronics and displays. In the first phase, the user wishes will have to be entered into the software applications. In the next phase, the user behaviour from the past will be used as a basis for future comfort, convenience and safety and will be proposed and activated automatically.

In the last 2–3 years digital open platforms have been established which will change ecosystems. By the year 2025, these digital platforms will be able to connect the entire value chain through Plug/Connect & Integrate (von Engelhardt et al. 2017). The complete life cycle, from the purchase of raw materials to the fully automated production of products, the planning of buildings to their later use, operation and maintenance as well as possible disposal, will be mapped digitally as an integrated network.

This technical sovereignty and digital economy produce massive changes in private and professional life for each and every one of us. Automation of processes, complete networking of the value-added chain, standards, performance and result control are permanently available. The former competitive advantages of individual companies will merge, as it will not be possible to further optimize individual business processes.

8.7 Conclusions

Digitization is still in its infancy and is the most important humanity revolution with global consequences for culture and all areas of life. Certainly, those companies that consistently and quickly develop and build the digital environment for themselves will have a temporary competitive advantage. In this time frame, it is essential to expand and secure their market position. When almost all organizations participating in the market have successfully implemented the digitization processes, it will be extremely difficult to differentiate themselves. Processes, systems, structures and automation will then be optimized across the board in such a way that there will no longer be any significant cost or performance advantages.

People and the corporate brands, i.e. the emotional relationships between market participants, will become even more the decisive component for a sustainable and trustworthy future.

References

Baumanns T, Freber P-S, Schober K-S, Kirchner F (2016) Bauwirtschaft im Wandel—trends und Potenziale bis 2020. Roland Berger GmbH, UniCredit Bank AG, München, Germany

Botthof A, Heimer T, Strese H (2016) SmartHome2Market. Marktperspektiven für die intelligente Heimvernetzung. Bundesministerium für Wirtschaft und Energie (BMWi), Öffentlichkeitsarbeit. www.bmwi.de, Berlin, Germany

Bramann H, May I (2015) Stufenplan Digitales Planen und Bauen Einführung moderner, IT-gestützter Prozesse und Technologien bei Planung, Bau und Betrieb von Bauwerken. Bundesministerium für Verkehr und digitale Infrastruktur (BMVdI), Berlin, Germany

Carl M, Lübcke M (2016) Das sichere Gebäude der Zukunft—Vertrauen als Schlüssel für Smart Home und Smart Building. Trendstudie des 2b AHEAD ThinkTanks, Leipzig, Germany

von Engelhardt S, Wangler L, Wischmann S (2017) Eigenschaften und Erfolgsfaktoren digitaler Plattformen. Begleitforschung AUTONOMIK für Industrie 4.0. iit-Institut für Innovation und Technik in der VDI/VDE Innovation + Technik GmbH Alfons Botthof, Berlin, Germany

Gamperling J (2017) Smart Home, Services, Digitale Heizung & Co. Heizungs-Journal Verlags-GmbH, Winnenden/Württemberg, Germany

Jones Lang LaSalle IP, Inc. (2016) Facility Management erfindet sich neu in der digitalen Welt. White Paper 2016, www.jll.com, Frankfurt, Germany

Niedermaier A, Bäck R (2016) Allplan BIM user guide, BIM: Worum es geht. Und was es bringt. Building Information Modeling verstehen: Methode Relevanz und Vorteile. Allplan GmbH, München, Germany

How to Radically Innovate While Utilizing a Firms' Capabilities: Practical Aspects of Corporate Entrepreneurship

9

Christof Siebert

9.1 Introduction—Theoretical Background

Firms that operate successfully in their markets sooner or later face the problem of saturation: growth rates in their established markets decline and thus they have to find ways to conquer new areas of business outside of the markets they are operating in—and furthermore in many cases using new technologies and applying new business models. The demands of digitalization put even more pressure on firms to innovate in unknown areas. Addressing new areas of business means that firms have to find ways to innovate radically while they are used to innovate incrementally—and doing both simultaneously. The question is why it seems so difficult for successful companies to follow this path.

9.1.1 Inertia

Tushman and O'Reilly (1996) describe structural and cultural inertia as roadblocks that hinder successful companies to radically innovate. Structural inertia is born from success—while companies get bigger, they introduce processes and structures to manage complexity. These structures and processes enable firms to operate efficiently in their established areas of expertise to fulfill customer needs in those markets they are successfully serving.

Cultural inertia refers to the unwritten rules, the believes and myths that develop over time in successful firms. There is a "this is how we do it" aspect that arises from success—because the belief is that success is the result of this doing.

C. Siebert (✉)
TRUMPF GmbH + Co. KG, Ditzingen, Germany
e-mail: christof.siebert@trumpf.com

© The Editor(s) (if applicable) and The Author(s), under exclusive license to Springer Nature Switzerland AG 2021
V. Nestle et al. (eds.), *Creating Innovation Spaces*, Management for Professionals, https://doi.org/10.1007/978-3-030-57642-4_9

So, firms learn what works best and implement these practices—either in formal ways through structures and processes or in informal ways through believes that form a firm's culture. This learning and adaption process is not a bad thing per se since it helps firms to stay successful in stable environment. But when customer demands change radically, new growth opportunities need to be pursued and thus high flexibility is needed, those very practices become a liability—inertia that prevents change.

9.1.2 Incremental and Radical Innovation

To be successful companies have to operate in two different modes simultaneously—they have to be operationally excellent in generating incremental innovation and they have to explore new opportunities to generate radical innovation at the same time.

Innovating incrementally is the straight-forward way of continuously serving your customers with better value: making machines faster odder more precise, adding features to software products, decreasing service reaction times. If you know your customers well you can anticipate their future needs and develop those products and features that serve those needs. Do this efficiently and you stay ahead of the curve. But it requires a stable business environment in which pursuing incremental innovation is sufficient to succeed. As Tushman, M.L. and O'Reilly III, C.A. (1996) emphasize you can find long periods of incremental change "punctuated by environmental shifts and revolutionary change".

Radical innovation is trickier—in unstable environments caused by technological changes, fundamental changes in the competitive landscape or regulatory changes a firm cannot react with incremental innovation alone. Serving customers with more of the same might not help when e.g. competitors from other industries enter your market with digital solutions that change the power structure and dynamic in the industry. The answer is radical innovation—products and services that generate big leaps in customer value and that potentially change dynamics of the market or the competitive situation within the market.

9.1.3 Corporate Entrepreneurship—Structure and Strategy

Corporate entrepreneurship can show a path out of inertia towards radical innovation. So, what is it?

The term *corporate entrepreneurship* describes the entrepreneurial efforts established firms can make to find new opportunities by utilizing the competencies they have gathered and recombining them (see Burgelman 1984). However, the actual implementation of corporate entrepreneurship is often compromised by a firm's established strategic and structural processes.

As discussed in Burgelman, R.A. (1983), two main ways of strategical approaches to innovation can be distinguished: "structure follows strategy" and "strategy follows structure". While the first describes a top-down approach in which top management defines the strategy and actions are derived from that, the latter can be considered as a bottom-up approach in which employees and middle managers create new business opportunities in "autonomous strategic initiatives". These initiatives have then to be defended and retrospectively been rationalized. Since these bottom-up corporate entrepreneurship activities are not derived from a pre-defined strategy decision criterion have to be found that allow corporate management to evaluate business opportunities that arise from these activities. Burgelman, R.A. (1984) proposes two main criteria: "strategic importance for corporate development" and "operational relatedness" which describes how an opportunity can be fostered by core capabilities of the company.

So top down strategic initiatives and bottom up entrepreneurial activities can co-exist if ways are found to evaluate entrepreneurial activities.

9.1.4   Corporate Entrepreneurship as a Dynamic Capability

When a firm is exposed to dynamic changes in markets and technologies it has to find ways to deal with it without ignoring competencies and assets it has acquired over years. But is it sufficient to rely on static competencies and assets? And shouldn't they be the source for competitive advantages?

The view on static competencies and assets of companies has evolved into the research of dynamic capabilities that help to be successful in dynamic markets. Eisenhardt and Martin (2000) describe dynamic capabilities as

> The firm's processes that use resources—specifically the processes to integrate, reconfigure, gain and release resources—to match and even create market change.

An example are product development processes in which developers from different disciplines are assigned to develop products and thus create value, so capabilities are dynamically used to be competitive.

As Teece (2007) mentions, entrepreneurial management is the prerequisite for maintaining dynamic capabilities and he describes entrepreneurship as the ability to sense, seize and reconfigure. Sensing opportunities, act on this perception and utilize capabilities to deal with it creates competitive advantage.

So corporate entrepreneurship can be seen as the capability of a firm's management to sense, seize and reconfigure which is especially important in dynamic business environments.

9.2   Practical Implementation of Corporate Entrepreneurship

A company finds itself in an unstable business environment. Incremental innovation processes are highly efficient but radical innovation is needed to stay competitive. Inertia is prevalent. Corporate Entrepreneurship as a dynamic capability can lead the way, you just have to sense and seize opportunity and reconfigure your competencies to stay competitive. How can this work in real life?

9.2.1 Sensing Opportunities—Finding Ideas for New Business

Sensing is all about identifying opportunities, be it the opportunity of a newly arising customer demand, the opportunity of a technological solution or the opportunities that a changing market environment is providing. Teece (2007) specifies sensing activities further:

> Sensing (and shaping) new opportunities is very much a scanning, creation, learning and interpretive activity.

Sensing activities can be characterized along different categories:

1. Central vs. decentral
2. Continuous vs. project/campaign based
3. To down vs. bottom up

Neither of the above-mentioned categories is per se better than the other but a careful orchestration of all the above is necessary. Central sensing (1) can e.g. be performed by specialized strategy or scouting departments that scan continuously (2) for new technologies and shifts in the market environment. Establishing a corporate venture capital unit to continuously scout for new opportunities in the startup ecosystem is another way to sense opportunities.

As part of an annual strategy process scouting can be performed campaign based (2) as a top down approach initiated by the top management (3). An often-underestimated way of sensing is the decentralized (1) bottom-up (3) approach in which employees are asked to share their ideas about opportunities, be it technological or market related ones.

Some companies establish idea management processes in which employees can continuously post ideas for new products and services. In doing this one can make sure that creative individuals have the possibility to place ideas that might otherwise remain unidentified. A careful system needs to be established, however, to make sure that those ideas can be utilized. There have to be criteria to evaluate the ideas, people dedicated to follow-up and defined ways of how to utilize those ideas and transform them into real products and services. In practice especially the last criterion is difficult to accomplish because either they compete with more established standard ways to gather ideas (e.g. product management processes in the core business that rely on information from sales departments) or ideas are related to business ideas for new products and services outside of the core business and there is no process nor structure to implement those ideas.

Another challenge is to keep attention high to fill the idea funnel. If idea management is a continuous process one has to make sure that the process has to be promoted internally. Addressing employees in campaigns can solve this issue.

But even then, there is one last question: Why shall you provide your business idea to a process if you are not the one who can follow up on it? This question goes beyond the question of an incentive scheme because the best business ideas come along with a person's aspiration to make it happen and not just seeing it being placed somewhere else. So just incentivizing to post ideas with material or immaterial benefits doesn't help. You have to find ways to let people participate in transforming ideas into new business.

9.2.2 Seizing Opportunities: How to Design an Internal Corporate Venturing Program

Internal corporate venturing (ICV) can be the vehicle that enables companies to utilize opportunities and generate new business while keeping employees engaged as "idea generators". So, what is internal corporate venturing?

Though there is almost fifty years of research on corporate entrepreneurship and internal corporate venturing as described by Hill and Georgoulas (2016), it is still difficult to clearly distinguish between the terms used. For this chapter, I refer to the definition of von Hippel (1977) that corporate venturing is

> an activity which seeks to generate new businesses for the corporation in which it resides.

So, in this sense it can be seen as one specific activity within the wider frame of corporate entrepreneurship. Burgelman (1984) emphasizes the role of the entrepreneur:

> Increasingly, there is an awareness that internal entrepreneurs are necessary for firms to achieve growth. The internal entrepreneur, like the external entrepreneur, enacts new opportunities and drives the development of new resource combinations or recombinations.

And with a reference to the organizational setting he claims:

> As a result, new forms of economic organization—a broader array of arrangements—are necessary.

Therefore, internal corporate venturing can be implemented in various arrangements. Burgelman (1984) describes special business units, new venture divisions and spin-offs among others as organization designs. In all that it is important to adapt the form to the company's way of working. An essential aspect is not only which organization design for internal corporate venturing is applied but also how it is designed and by whose initiative. In the following I will distinguish between two ways to design an internal corporate venturing setup that I have borrowed from software design approaches: big design upfront and emergent design.

Big Design Up Front

There are cases in which a company's top management realizes that there is the need to radically innovate to accomplish strategic targets and that this is difficult to accomplish within the given organization. This falls into Burgelman's

(1983) "structure-follows-strategy" category as described above. In this case top management might assign this task to their strategy department to come up with an internal corporate venturing program involving organization, processes and budgets: Design a program, define clear goals, create an organizational structure, calculate resources needed and hire experienced entrepreneurs to run the program. This top down approach can often be seen in large corporations and it has advantages: the organization is well staffed, the program has strong C-level support and it has the potential to gain traction rapidly. There are, however, threats associated with this approach, e.g. that established parts of the company do not have time to get used to the apparently alien ways of working in the new unit and so refuse to support it. These initiatives easily disturb a company's culture as claimed by Tushman and O'Reilly (1996):

> Cultural inertia, because it is so ephemeral and difficult to attack directly, is a key reason managers often fail to successfully introduce revolutionary change—even when they know that it is needed.

Another threat is the inherently insecure situation: since the organizational design of corporate entrepreneurship initiatives differs from how the biggest part of a company works an optimal design can hardly be found upfront. And when the organizational and processual design is as insecure as the innovation it seeks to generate it might be worth to think about experimentation and exploration in the design of such a program itself.

Emergent Design

Alternative seeds of internal corporate venturing are often initiatives by employees, comparable to what Burgelman (1983) describes as "autonomous strategic initiatives". They might not be embedded in a firm's strategy but based on ideas for new business that arise from creative engineers who see opportunities to use technology in a new way or by sales managers who identify customers' problems that are not yet addressed by any solution available in the market.

In this case an emergent design of internal corporate venturing might be a good approach: convince top management to support an experiment based on a few simple rules and adapt organization and processes as you go. A big advantage of this concept is that experience can grow while testing different concepts and organizational settings and processes can be adjusted to a company's culture much better than in a big design upfront approach.

But there are downsides: Since in an experimental setup not every step of a process and especially proceedings on the back end of a process (e.g. what to do with radical innovative ideas that have been successfully tested but cannot be pursued within the core organization) are well defined, there have to be the willingness to accept insecurity by all people involved especially by the internal entrepreneurs who you address.

Both ways of designing internal corporate venturing activities can work and often enough they are pursued simultaneously or one after the other by companies. Implementation of internal corporate venturing puts stress on a company's culture anyway and thus the process to design it has to fit to the company's (established) culture and decision processes otherwise it will never leave the design stage.

9.2.3   Reconfiguration—Internal Corporate Venturing between Relatedness and Autonomy

You have implemented processes to sense opportunities. You have decided to implement internal corporate venturing as a way to seize business and technological opportunities. There is still the challenge to design it in a way that a company's assets and competencies are utilized to gain a competitive advantage. Teece (2007) claims:

> A key to sustained profitable growth is the ability to recombine and to reconfigure assets and organizational structures as the enterprise grows, and as markets and technologies change, as they surely will.

This holds true on the level of implementation of internal corporate venturing as well: How to design it in a way that a company's assets can be used—selectively— and how to structure it so that it fits into the organization while having sufficient autonomy not to be slowed down by inertia? As Teece (2007) describes:

> In the end, it appears that in fast-paced environments organizational units must have considerable autonomy (to make decisions rapidly) but remain connected to activities that must be coordinated.

For the design of an ICV program these two contrasting aspects have to be balanced: *autonomy* from processes and structures to avoid a company's inertia and *relatedness* to the core business to utilize a company's competencies.

In a generic view an ICV program can be divided in two major phases as shown in Fig. 9.1:

Phase 1: From idea to problem-solution-fit.
Phase 2: from problem-solution-fit to scale-up.

The specific implementation of autonomy and relatedness can vary within the two phases and in the following I will provide a few thoughts and examples on this in respect to the two different phases.

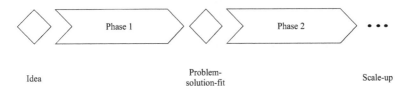

Fig. 9.1 Two main phases of an ICV program. (Source: author)

Phase 1: From Idea to Problem-Solution-Fit

This phase starts with ideas that can e.g. be collected from employees in a campaign or being generated in an ideation workshop. It ends with the problem-solution-fit which describes the state in which an entrepreneur has proved that a solution—the product—solves an actual problem. The first phase of an ICV program is therefore characterized by what Eric Ries described in his book The Lean Startup (2011) as

> Build-Measure-Learn. The fundamental activity of a startup is to turn ideas into products, measure how customers respond and then learn whether to pivot or persevere. All successful startup processes should be geared to accelerate that feedback look.

In companies with an engineering DNA—which can often be found in high-tech B2B companies—a solution rather than a problem often is the starting point for a business opportunity. A solution of this kind arises out of new technical possibilities—but if it can be transformed into customer value still have to be shown. That's why it is so important to validate solutions with potential customers in this first phase. However, when designing this first process step of an ICV program above mentioned balance between autonomy and relatedness to the core business have to be considered. A few examples show the difficulties that can arise:

- If you want to validate an idea for a product you might need access to existing customers of a business unit—but you have to approach them without having a product yet and your salespeople might not like to bother existing customers with new—immature—ideas.
- If you need to use components from existing products to design a minimum viable product you need access to your business units' R + D departments.
- Since typical ICV programs run for short terms between one and six months you need to be able to purchase fast—which could collide with your company's purchasing rules and processes.

These examples show that corporate entrepreneurs need access to company assets and competencies on one hand and having high autonomy on the other hand. This has to be considered when designing an ICV program: Evaluation of critical success factors in respect to relatedness and autonomy is important. Figure 9.2 lists three critical factors and their characteristics that lead to different levels of relatedness and autonomy:

1. Decision making within the program: This relates to decisions that entrepreneurial teams have to make within an ICV program and contains decisions about which markets to access, which customers to approach, which business models to aim for and how to design the product. Experience shows that high autonomy of entrepreneurial teams is needed to be fast within a given short program time frame but that coaching of entrepreneurial experts helps to make decisions better.
2. Budget: Within an ICV program entrepreneurial teams need to be fast, not only in decision making but especially in purchasing. Having a separate budget that

can be used to order anything from hardware to software ensures that the teams make fast progress. Simple governance principles such as dual control principle shall be applied within the teams. However, it is important to carefully decide the amount of money that entrepreneurial teams can spend. Scarcity of resources is needed for the teams to focus but the nature of the business idea needs to be considered—hardware products need more funding than software.

3. Decision making on program level: Within an ICV program decisions have to be made regarding the continuation of teams. Someone has to evaluate the ideas at the beginning of a program, within a program and at the end when problem-solution-fit has been reached. Higher autonomy might be reached by letting external experts evaluate the business ideas and decide about the continuation. However, when business ideas are sourced within a firm's business units and employees from those business units participate in an ICV program it can be wise to install a panel of business unit and corporate delegates. By this access to business unit resources can be established and commitment of the business unit management can be ensured. It has to be considered though that decisions of business unit delegates can be biased, especially when they do not want to lose high profile employees participating in the program.

It has to be noted that regarding relatedness I do not distinguish between the corporate's governance requirements and the entrepreneurial teams' needs to access the corporate's (and business units') resources. If the corporates' and the business units' management accept higher autonomy of the entrepreneurial teams—in other words: if they trust them—the need of the teams to get access to business units resources leads to a certain imbalance. So, in the beginning governance and access to resources might have to be coupled and later be loosened after trust has been built.

As Fig. 9.2 implies there is no right or wrong regarding the balance of relatedness and autonomy. When designing an ICV program one has to choose a certain set of characteristics and make sure that they fit to the corporate's processes and culture. And over time the set of characteristics can be adapted, e.g. after management got used to the alien way of doing things.

Phase 2: From Problem-Solution-Fit to Scale-up

Once problem-solution-fit have been proven by corporate entrepreneurs—which means: there are customers willing to pay for a certain solution—and management approves to proceed with the concept, ways have to be found to start the business and make sure it can scale. While phase 1 can be done in a relatively small, protected and low-key way phase 2 needs more resources and more funding to really get the business starting and this requires a thorough organizational design. The organization designs Burgelman (1984) mentions reach from direct integration over new venture divisions to complete spin offs. However, the practical implementation can be tricky because one has to analyze the corporates' processes and governance and define in detail which rules corporate entrepreneurs in phase 2 shall follow to maintain a certain level of control, which degree of freedom they need to be fast and

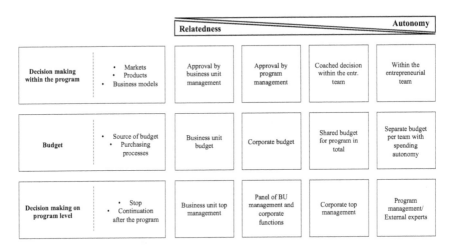

Fig. 9.2 Characteristics of the design of an ICV program in respect to relatedness and autonomy. (Source: author)

how they get access to some of the corporates' assets and competencies—in other words: how relatedness and autonomy can be balanced.

For the sake of practical applicability only one organizational setup shall be considered here, which is the *corporate startup*. The decision to establish a corporate startup at the end of phase 1 does not only depend on the quality and maturity of the problem-solution-fit reached in phase 1 but also on other aspects:

- *Strategic importance* (see also Burgelman 1984): Does it help to reach the firm's long-term goals? Does it generate future options that haven't been considered yet?
- *Commercial success*: Will the business be profitable in a foreseeable future? Do the numbers add up?
- *Team*: Is the entrepreneurial team able to scale the business? Do they have the skills needed in different disciplines?
- *Viability of the product*: Can the product being coded or manufactured within the boundary conditions of the customer demands?
- *Autonomy*: Does the business need autonomy from the corporate processes and structures to grow or can it be efficiently being integrated into the core business?
- *Relatedness*: Which capabilities and assets from the core organization are needed to successfully scale-up the business?

For the organizational setup of a corporate startup autonomy and relatedness are the most important aspects to consider. In contrast to phase 1 which can be run as a program with special rules (see Fig. 9.2) within an existing organization for a limited time a corporate startup needs to be established as a potentially longer lasting separate entity. The specific design shall be able to address the following issues:

- *Governance*: How does the corporate exercise control over the corporate startup? What is the minimum control that avoids potential damage on the corporate in case of failure or if liabilities are generated by the corporate startup? How to make sure that changes in the corporate governance (e.g. new rules issued by the top management) are applied automatically to corporate startups? How to specifically define exceptions from corporate governance rules?
- *Financing*: Where does the money come from? Who decides about financing rounds?
- *Shareholding*: Who owns a corporate startup if it is set up as a separate legal entity?

Different organizational designs can be found as shown in Table 9.1. While (1) is easy to establish and allows easy access to a company's capabilities it does not provide enough autonomy for an entrepreneurial team to scale-up a business that deals with radical rather than incremental innovation. Option (2) gives a certain degree of autonomy from established business units because a separate set of rules

Table 9.1 Main organization designs of corporate startups

	(1) Special project group within corporate structure	(2) Virtual startup in separate legal entity	(3) Separate legal entity
Description	Dedicated project group with higher degrees of freedom	Separate legal entity with special processes and rules that contains multiple project groups (virtual startups)	Corporate startup as separate legal entity with either the corporate as single shareholder or as one of multiple co-investors
Advantages	• Easy to set up within a given organization • Access to corporate assets and capabilities	• Easy to establish separate rules • Easy to found new virtual startups within the legal entity	• High autonomy • Entrepreneurial responsibility of founders • Success easy to measure
Disadvantages	• Autonomy very difficult to establish due to corporate rules • Entrepreneurial responsibility diffuses • Success difficult to measure • Difficult to establish separate brands • Risk of deprioritization	• Budget changes of legal entity affects all virtual startups • Autonomy of virtual startups • Entrepreneurial responsibility diffuses • Common overhead/shared services needed	• Potentially high efforts needed to establish and to maintain • Legal cost • Efforts in case of failure

can be defined that applies to all virtual startups within the legal entity. This setup can, however, lead to a diffusion of entrepreneurial responsibility if shared services (e.g. human resources, controlling, finance, etc.) are provided to the virtual startups. Option (3) allows for the highest autonomy for entrepreneurial teams combined with high responsibility because the founders have to take responsibility for every aspect of a company: from renting facilities over hiring employees to establishing sales channels. Relatedness to the mother company's capabilities can be ensured by carefully choosing the board members. If a corporate startup e.g. needs to address the mother company's customers high level sales representatives on the board can help to achieve this. The main disadvantage of option (3) is that in case of failure of the corporate startup the legal efforts can be high.

9.3   Conclusion

Corporate entrepreneurship and internal corporate venturing are easy to describe but difficult to implement. They want to unite what seem to be contradictions: autonomy from the very core processes and structures and relatedness to a company's capabilities at the same time. This can be perceived as unfair: picking only the advantages and avoiding the disadvantages. Burgelman describes internal corporate venturing (1984) as uncomfortable:

> ICV is likely to remain an uncomfortable process for the large complex organization. This is because ICV upsets carefully evolved routines and planning mechanisms, threatens the internal equilibrium of interests, and requires revising a firm's self-image.

But once a company acknowledge that radical innovation cannot be created from within it has to face the challenge and pick from the broad variety of tools: corporate venture capital, technology foresight, internal corporate venturing etc. In designing an internal corporate venturing program, it is helpful to consider autonomy and relatedness as the guiding principles that have to be carefully balanced. There is no best practice for this per se because company cultures are different, business models vary, and processes differ significantly—and the design of internal corporate venturing has to respect that. But if a company starts the journey towards internal corporate venturing it will surely realize that despite all hurdles and doubts radical innovation will evolve.

References

Burgelman RA (1983) A model of the interaction of strategic behavior, corporate context, and the concept of strategy. Acad Manag Rev 8(1983):61–70
Burgelman RA (1984) Designs for corporate entrepreneurship in established firms. Calif Manag Rev XXVI(3):154–166
Eisenhardt KM, Martin JA (2000) Dynamic capabilities: what are they? Strateg Manag J 21:1105–1121

Hill SA, Georgoulas S (2016) Internal corporate venturing: a review of (almost) five decades of literature. In: Zahra SA, Neubaum DO, Hayton JC (eds) Handbook of research on corporate entrepreneurship. Edward Elgar Publishing, pp 13–63

von Hippel E (1977) Successful and failing internal corporate ventures: an empirical analysis. Ind Mark Manag 6(3):163–174

Ries E (2011) The Lean startup: how today's entrepreneurs use continuous innovation to create radically successful businesses. Currency, New York

Teece DJ (2007) Explication dynamic capabilities: the nature and microfoundations of (sustainable) enterprise performance. Strateg Manag J 28:1319–1350

Tushman ML, O'Reilly CA III (1996) Ambidextrous organizations. Managing evolutionary and revolutionary change. Calif Manag Rev 38(4):8–30

Experience as an Architect in an Agile Environment

10

Annegret Junker

10.1 Introduction

Creating innovation spaces requires an overview about several levels of software architecture in an enterprise. Software architecture focuses from enterprise level and its business capabilities to the setup of load balancers and servers. But software design emerges from work of the development team. How can an architect or a group of people organize their work, that the software meets the requirements of their stakeholders and the software can constantly adapted to an ever-changing world?

10.1.1 Waterfall

In the good old time, the world was in good shape, at least for an architect. He or she got a task, a problem to solve. He or she could think about it and evaluate different solution approaches. In case one solution approach could be found, it was described in a more or less formal style. The according description would take over by the development and the architect could forget it. He or she could think about the next problem. The architect was the godlike, most important role in a software project. Obviously even at that point in time, there were such roles as project leads, business analysts, steering committee members etc. But he or she was the most important and were (almost) prayed to by his believers.

OK, even at that time, not everything was gold, what glittered. Even though our architect was our thinktank, our source of enlightenment, he or she never got what he or she had designed originally. Anyhow, when it worked, it was the design of

A. Junker (✉)
Adesso SE, Munich, Germany
e-mail: annegret.junker@adesso.de

© The Editor(s) (if applicable) and The Author(s), under exclusive license
to Springer Nature Switzerland AG 2021
V. Nestle et al. (eds.), *Creating Innovation Spaces*, Management for Professionals,
https://doi.org/10.1007/978-3-030-57642-4_10

the architect, when not, the others were to blame. It was a nice world, at least for an architect. The approach, as it was till the early 2000ers, was a pure "Top-down-approach". Everything should be thought over before the implementation starts.

Different implementation in comparison to the original design was not some kind of mischievous behavior of developers. Developers then and today need to develop something according to the current requirements and to the current technology. But requirements are not static. Requirements—especially in a technology environment—are highly dynamic. Requirements are changing, they are adapting to the current possibilities, technology is not static. New possibilities are evolving, which can solve the problem at hand better. Not to react to such possibilities would mean, to create software, which is obsolete with the first go-live.

Let us imagine how it could work using a sample project. The project is called "To Do List" and should provide the user a simple list, where he can manage his own task in an easy manner. The program would have the objects "Task", "List of Task", and "Owner", which means the owner of the task list. So far everything can be foreseen and formally described for implementation. But what happens if a manager wants to create tasks for his or her subordinates, if the user wants to access his or her tasks. One has to react on an ever-changing world.

10.1.2 Agile

Agility is covered in the four agile principles (Beck, et al., 2001):

- Individuals and interaction over processes and tools
- Working software over comprehensive documentation
- Customer collaboration over contract negotiations
- Responding to change over following a plan

Responding to change over following a plan contradicts the overall forethought design. To implement a software without a complete plan, would mean, to implement the software function by function, increment by increment. The according architecture emerges from the day by day work of the implementing team.

Today cross-functional teams develop software. They develop it, they test it, they bring it to productions, and they design it. To design software is architecting it. An emergent design is driven by the underlying requirements of the system, rather than a speculative planning of an architect. In our small sample, it would mean first we implement to manage small tasks by ourselves, then the task management by some manager. It works as long as somebody ask for a mobile access with certain offline functions. We haven't thought of that, the entire software only works with permanent online access. We need to rewrite the entire software.

Obviously, we can't define and implement a system without having all requirements. But in an ever-changing world, we can't have everything beforehand. We need to accept, that we have to react and can't define everything in advance.

The emergent design works for one team very nicely. The team can define self-responsible which tools, programming language, database technology etc. are used. But in more complex projects (as projects are usually are), several teams have to work together. There are topics which cannot be solved by one team alone. Topics such security, end-to-end monitoring, authentication, logging etc. are not in focus of feature-driven teams. Who takes care of such cross-cutting concerns? There must be some kind of structure, which takles those cross-cutting concerns on one hand and which ensures that the teams can work self-responsible on the other hand.

10.2 What Is Architecture?

In the chapter before we saw, that we have to solve several contradictions when developing software. We want to work in self-responsible teams, but we need to ensure that several teams can work independent from each other. We need to ensure that we create working software, but we need to document the interfaces in a way that someone else can use our function. We want to let the architecture emerge during implementation, but we need to synchronize several teams working on one application. All those questions refer to architecture. So, what is architecture?

According to ISO/IEC/IEEE 42010:2011 software architecture is the functional concepts or properties of a system in its environment embodied in its elements, relationships, and in the principles of its design and evolution (ISO/IEC/IEEE 2011).

The system can be only one simple application, a complex enterprise application or even a set of enterprise applications. It means, that architecture happens on several levels.

Figure 10.1 shows the different levels of architecture from enterprise architecture to the system architecture as base of a software ecosystem.

- Enterprise Architecture taking care of the enterprise applications and their collaboration,
- System Architecture taking care of systems hosting an enterprise application such as a purchase or a sales application, and
- Solution Architecture taking care of the strategic and tactical design of a more complex application.

10.2.1 Enterprise Architecture

Enterprise architecture is business-driven architecture. Business capabilities are broken down to functions. And functions are mapped to applications and components. Enterprise architecture provides blueprints to the teams, which help to solve common problem in a common way (we need to discuss later, how such a common way will accelerate or even slow down teams).

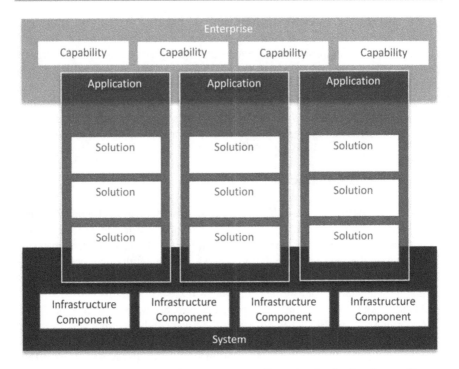

Fig. 10.1 Levels of architecture a software ecosystem—Enterprise, Application, System. (Source: author)

According to TOGAF—a wide-spread enterprise architecture framework, enterprise architecture is the structure of components, their inter-relationships, and the principles and guidelines governing their design and evolution over time (Josey et al. 2018).

It added to the creation of architecture the governance of architecture. The governance is quite focused in enterprise architecture, to ensure that the entire ecosystem of complex applications over the enterprise still works after several changings.

10.2.2 System Architecture

Usually system architecture is recognized as architectures of different infrastructure systems, such as load balancer, proxy server, event or message broker etc. Each of those play a role in the entire functionality of an application. But in the point of view of even that function, they are invisible. Obviously, a system architect has to take care of those architectural components, which ensure the non-functional requirements of the systems such as security or availability.

Usually those infrastructure components are shared components for several functions of an application. Therefore, they don't belong to one team. But each team working on the according application depends highly on all those shared components. The teams need someone who takes care that their specific requirements are taken into account among all others.

10.2.3 Solution Architecture

Because solution architecture takes care of directly of the solution, an architect has to ensure that the solution itself will work. Usually multiple teams are working on one solution. The architecture has to ensure, that the teams can work as independently as possible.

There is a need of some kind of complete end-to-end view. The solution at a whole should be visible to all. Where the solution is broken into team-suiting components, the teams involved focus on their according area of expertise (McSweeney 2019). Solution architecture is the tactical design of a software. It emerges from the team activities step by step. Implementing function by function creates an architecture, which is mostly unpredictable (Bloomberg 2013).

Agility give us the courage to accept such an unpredictability. But anyhow with that acceptance, we have to give developers and designers guidelines in which they are free to decide. A complete freedom of decisions in one team simply doesn't exist, because it interferes with the freedom of another team. Guidelines are necessary to ensure the freedom of one team without cut down the freedom of another team.

10.3   Organizational Challenges

Conway's Law is a wide-spread term. It predicts that you get a design how your organization communication is shaped (Conway 1968). Out of a software development point of view, it means that we have to tailor the teams in our application development according to the system, we want to have.

That requirement includes some principle contradiction, we have to face: Define some team structure which represents a communication structure of the system beforehand and avoid architecting up-front at the same time. Eric Evans gave us some ideas how we can tackle such a riddle. We need to distinguish between tactical and strategic design (Evans, 2004).

10.3.1 Tactical Design

The tactical design refers to the functions of a solution covered by one development team. The team develops its own ubiquitous language and model which represents the structure and behavior of their component. But that means that another team with another component develops its own specific language.

Both teams might use the term "Task". But the first team understood task as description, status and due date, means each single property of a task. Whereas the second team understands tasks as list given to a single person. Both meanings are well understood in their context but leaving the context might steer some discussions. Those boundaries as "bounded context" (Evans 2004) need to be defined.

10.3.2 Strategic Design

The strategic design refers to the definitions of bounded context. A bounded context might be the task management—referring to single tasks and their overviews. Another bounded context might refer to the process where the tasks are needed, e.g. some procurement with the task "check your supplier". Both domains contain a quite specific interpretation of task. To find those borders is part of strategic design.

As we saw before, we need to find a design which represents the communication of our desired system. When we have that, we need to assign the found bounded contexts to the teams to be established. Here we go for some pre-defined architecture. To define the teams upfront, we define the communication of a system. We have to be careful, to find the bounded context on one hand and we have to inspect and adapt our design constantly on the other hand. We need to be quite careful with our design. Team changes steer a lot of disturbances, which in the end slow down our project. But not to change the teams, when we see that our initial assumptions are not true anymore, is leaving to a not working system.

It is the duty of an architect to point out those contradictions and make proposals how to solve them.

10.4   Architectural Work

As we saw, architectural work is done on quite different levels and on quite different perspectives.

Figure 10.2 shows different type of architectural work which focus on different levels of architecture. Whereas on enterprise level business capabilities are mapped to applications using comprehensive models. On the other side of architecture levels, system architecture maps technology components like a loadbalancer or a server to business functions represented in applications.

System architecture focus on the base of each software ecosystem and its infrastructure components. Tactical design focus on the design of one solution and usually emerges from the teams and their work. Strategic design focuses on the definition of bounded context and the mapping of those bounded contexts to applications and solution architectures. Enterprise architecture focus on the mapping of business capabilities to applications.

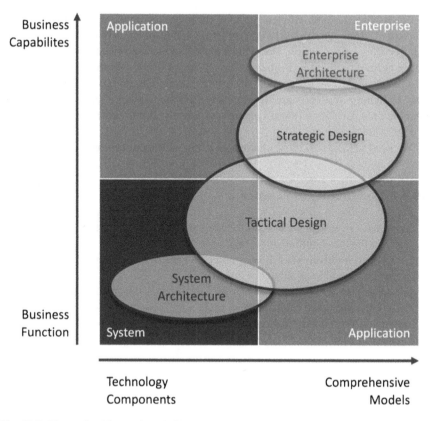

Fig. 10.2 Types of architectural work: Enterprise Architecture, Strategic Design, Tactical Design, System Architecture. (Source: author)

All those types of architectural work have to be addressed in the day by day work of an architect with respect to the agile values and the interest of stakeholders, like

- Self-responsibility of the teams
- Working software at now and in future
- Efficient work of teams
- Big Picture

Self-responsibility of teams allows teams to work independently, to create their own models, and to create in the end their own way of work. To do so they work efficiently and can react on changing requirements of their stakeholders.

Software needs to work not only at the moment, it needs to work over years. The software itself is changing and adapting over the time. It has to be ensured that the system can be understood and can be changed or enhanced to meet the requirements even in future.

Teams want to work efficiently and even the stakeholders want that teams work efficiently. When team A works on problem A and team B works on problem B, they can find their own solution. But what should happen if problem A is only slightly different from problem B. Probably team B can reuse the solution of team A.

The big picture of an application or the overarching targets are defined in the very beginning of a software development. But as everything else, it will change over the time. Usually it doesn't change completely. But it will change even though in a more subtle manner.

We need to tackle all those challenges in our architectural work.

10.4.1 Community of Practice

A community of practice can help to take care of overarching topics like the big-picture and the cross-cutting concerns.

In order to build up such a community of practice (or short CoP), the teams delegate team member as shown in Fig. 10.3.

Solutions created in one team can be brought to a larger audience. It requires that team members are able to leave their team context and can see the larger requirements of the application context. That requires a broader view to the

Fig. 10.3 Building a Community of Practice out of team member and architects. (Source: author)

application then the limited view of one solution and requires that teams allow their member to work for the community—and not 100% for the team.

The community itself can be supported by independent architects—e.g. some comprehensive architects, system-, and enterprise architects. The community can provide information about solutions created in the teams. There might be even some discussions about how to communicate between different components. The community can moderate those discussion and lead to a common understanding. And the community can document those decisions. The independent architects can take care of new technologies and according sample implementations. For them it is usually easier to take care of those, because they are not bound to the delivery pressure inside the teams.

In such a way the community can provide:

- Blueprints how solve common problems
- Guidelines how to integrate into the software ecosystem on application as well as on enterprise level
- Recommendations about usage of new technologies including sample implementations

It means that teams are able to work in freedom on one hand, but don't get lost in all those governance rules usually found in large enterprises.

10.4.2 Organizational Preconditions for a Community of Practice

A community of practice is great. But it can become quite frustrating in case all those created recommendations cannot be set into reality because the management doesn't allow it. We need a declaration from the management that architectural decisions made in the community are binding for the teams.

The management has to give some part of its decision competence to the community. Without such a decision competence the community will be some kind of a toothless tiger and that produces frustration.

Moreover, the architect who gave all those guidelines and rules needs to give his competence to the community as well. He or she doesn't lose his or her expertise. But to get a guideline, the community has to accept the recommendation of the architect and make it to such.

10.4.3 Work of an Architect

It seems at a first glance that in an agile team there is no architect anymore. But architectural work is everywhere. There are even people who don't belong to a team directly. Those comprehensive application, system, or even enterprise architects contribute still their work.

But the work is not the work of a command-and-control architect anymore who has all the answers before the work even starts.

Architectural work is to recommend and serve. Recommend technologies, structures, and communication protocols. Serve the teams as researcher and coach. The agile values

– Courage to contradict management and original approaches,
– Communication of valid solutions to teams and management,
– Give feedback to everyone, especially to oneself,
– And finding a simple solution to complex problems.

is part and challenge of the day by day work of an architect.

10.5   Conclusion

Agile practices form software development for over 20 years now since the publishing of the Agile Manifest in 2001 (Beck et al. 2001). Those agile practices have a deep influence on the work of a software architect. The architect cannot simply give some forethought design to someone else, he or she needs to be deeply involved in the development work.

Involvement of an architect into the day by day work of a team means that he or she might lose the big picture, and no one cares about cross-cutting concerns anymore. Therefore, such comprehensive work is needed. But one cannot do the work outside of the teams, because those rules and guidance wouldn't be accepted by the teams moreover the changing of requirements in business and technology wouldn't be met.

There a community is necessary which can organize the guidance and give the rules. If the community is created out of the directly affected people like team architects, system architects, enterprise architects etc. the decisions made are highly accepted by the teams and meet really the requirements and needs of a development team and even the expectations of the management. Architectural work changes from command and control to recommendation and service.

References

Beck K, Beedle M, van Bennekum A, Cockburn A, Cunningham W, Fowler M, Grenning J, Highsmith J, Hunt A, Jeffries R, Kern J, Marick B, Martin R, Mellor S, Schwaber K, Sutherland J, Thomas D (2001) Manifesto for Agile Software Development. Retrieved from Agile Manifesto: https://agilemanifesto.org/, June 14, 2020
Bloomberg J (2013) The Agile architecture revolution. Wiley, New Jersey
Conway ME (1968) How do committees invent? Datamation Magazin, p. 28–31.
Evans E (2004) Domain driven design: tackling complexity in the heart of software. Addison Wesley, San Francisco

ISO/IEC/IEEE (2011) Systems and software engineering—architecture description. ISO/IEC/IEEE 42010:2011.
Josey A, Harrison R, Homan P, Rouse M, van Sante T, Turner M, van der Merwe P (2018) The TOGAF(R) Standard, Version 9.2—a pocket guide. Van Haren Publishing, Zaltbommel
McSweeney A (2019) Introduction to solution architecture. Self published.

Why Emotional Intelligence Is the Key to Survival in an Ever-Changing Digital World

11

Franziska Stubbemann

11.1 Emotional Intelligence: Why These Life-Changing Abilities Should Not Simply Be Soft Skills

Most of us will have heard of the term "Emotional Intelligence (EQ)", which is often declared as "having soft skills" or silly and esoteric. It also comes up quite frequently in the gender discussion, which I will go into further detail later.

I remember having been part of a conference in Las Vegas with probably 20,000 attendants. When it came to the EQ talk, plenty of people left, because the topic is just mumbo-jumbo and people wanted to get back to "real business". Those who stayed however, had the revelation of a lifetime. In the following sections, I will give you a deeper insight in Emotional Intelligence, how to become better at being emotionally intelligent and what it will do with your success—in business and in private and why you need to aim for a higher EQ in order to survive and thrive in the digital times of change.

11.1.1 What Is Emotional Intelligence Really?

As already mentioned, many people have aversions to EQ or are sceptic about it, feeling it might be witchcraft or esoteric talk. But is it really?

What if I said: Emotional Intelligence beats classic human Intelligence known as IQ? Sounds harsh, but studies suggest (Goleman 2012), that people with a higher EQ rather than IQ will have longer lasting success and overall be happier. Who does not want to be more successful and happier? Well, point made.

F. Stubbemann (✉)
PTS Group AG and Adoptr, Bremen, Germany

Furthermore, Srivastava found, that individuals with a higher EQ have a stronger leadership potential (Srivastava 2013) compared to those with a lower EQ. This fact makes it crucial for managers, leaders or anyone with a responsibility to have.

Several areas in which having a high EQ makes a difference:

- Reduce stress and stressful situations: Stress is a common denominator for many of us. It results in mental and physical symptoms such as high blood pressure or anxiety. Stress is not always bad and makes us focus in crisis situations, but long-term stress may lead to chronic issues.
- Decision Making: When in stress or emotional situations, rationality is not part of our thinking. We act without considering long-term consequences, which may result in a negative outcome.
- Resilience: Failure is another common happening, especially, but not solely, in the start-up eco-system. Emotional intelligent individuals find it easier to draw inner strength and set new goals.

In short, Emotional Intelligence can be described as understanding ourselves and our reactions. This leads to understanding others around us and acting accordingly with them.

11.1.2 The Four Core Skills of Emotional Intelligence

The core of Emotional Intelligence can be split up into four skills in order to assist with understanding problems and training to become better at EQ.

As can be seen in Fig. 11.1 we tend to focus on the personal and the social skills. In the first step, we must recognize our emotions and secondly, we must regulate them.

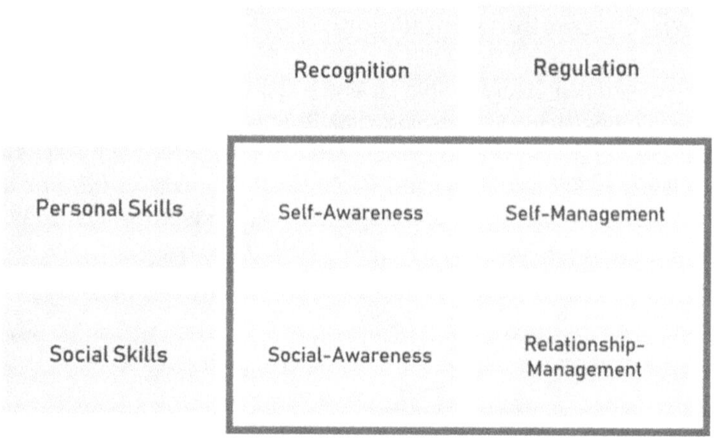

	Recognition	Regulation
Personal Skills	Self-Awareness	Self-Management
Social Skills	Social-Awareness	Relationship-Management

Fig. 11.1 Core of emotional intelligence. (Source: Author)

A practical example for the personal skills may be the following: an individual in a meeting recognizes, that he or she is bored or upset and has therefore practiced self-awareness. The second question is how he or she reacts and practices self-management: will the individual leave the meeting, risking appearing harsh or disrespectful to the remaining participants of the meeting, or will the individual choose to simply stay put and be as assertive as possible.

Social skills become even more important in the current times of social media, remote work and decentralized teams. In order to work together efficiently, our antennas must be extremely sensible, and ways need to be found, to connect with co-workers, partners or clients even when not sitting in the same meeting room.

In general, people tend to be strong in one or two of the core skills when beginning to train their Emotional Intelligence.

11.1.3 Can Emotional Intelligence Be Trained or Learned?

Other than the commonly referred to IQ, Emotional Intelligence can be trained, and one can become better at it. Not only can it be learned, but it must be taught and learned—especially in younger generations. It is a precursor to skill development for the future workforce and is best learned at a young age.

A simple task is one called "The good and the bad" and is best done with several people. Imagine a person from your professional life (no matter if current or previous) that brought out the best in you. Take 20 seconds and jot down what this person did to make you feel this way and how did this person make you feel.

Do the same for "The Bad": think of a person from your work-life, that managed to bring out the worst in you. What did this person do and how did he or she act to make you feel this way?

If you do this with others: take a look at their faces while they jot down notes and see how their facial expressions change. Smiling when asked about the good person, neutral or frowning when asked about the misliked person.

There is no need to go into detail when checking the answers. Common answers can be, that the good person was a great listener, a good supporter, honest and reliable. The bad person may have been a micro-manager, egoistic or arrogant.

The problem with emotions is, that they stick with us for a long time. The bad person may have worked with you more than ten years ago—the bad feeling will have lasted and may last for a long time to come.

There is a simple technique and lead questions that can help with managing EQ: RUM.

Recognize my emotions, understand my emotions and manage them accordingly.

Plenty of techniques are available to train your EQ and it can be measured by a large number of tests, but in short one has to manage personal competences and one's social competences—and act accordingly.

11.1.4 Why Does Gender and Diversity Matter for Emotional Intelligence?

On first impulse, many people will say, that women are more emotionally intelligent than men. But is that really the case? Or is this simply a stereotype, fed by former generations? Unfortunately, this cannot be answered easily or by simply quoting a study but there are different points of view:

A study by (Fernandez-Berrocal et al. 2012) concludes, that there are significant differences in several areas of the core skills and women tend to be more understanding and facilitating. Furthermore, the women in the study had higher results for the strategic area. In the areas of perceiving and experimenting both genders hat similar results.

But does this really result in one gender being more emotionally intelligent than the other?

When looking at the results, we are looking at two Bell Curves, that largely overlap. Which means, that the differences are only minor and Emotional Intelligence is not necessarily coherent with gender.

When speaking about diversity, not only gender plays a significant role, but also age. Fariselli et al. (2006) suggest, that there may be a slight correlation between a higher age and a higher EQ, however the sample group may have not been large enough to offer reliable results.

Do these results mean, that we can continue having all-male panels or teams consisting only of one gender, age group or ethnicity? Absolutely not. Apart from Emotional Intelligence, diversity is a key to perfecting soft skills of any sorts, and this requires a diverse group of individuals.

11.1.5 Is Emotional Intelligence Really a Soft Skill?

We tend to refer to skills such as time management, conflict management or resilience as soft skills. But the term "soft" implies, that these skills are something that are "nice to have" or easy to gain, but the opposite is the case.

For anyone working with clients or colleagues, these skills are not nice to have, but necessary and crucial. Therefore, some experts have started naming Emotional Intelligence "hard skills", which may sound to crass.

Undisputable though, all of these are critical, so critical skills may be the best term to choose in order to describe.

11.2 Digital Emotional Intelligence

The World Economic Forum states in their report "The Future of Jobs" (World Economic Forum 2018), that Emotional Intelligence is one of the most critical skills for the next generation in the workforce. Followed closely by "anything digital". So, it makes sense to connect both terms: Digital Emotional Intelligence.

Not only does this result in higher EQ scores within individuals, but also among companies, that use Digital Emotional Intelligence to build their brand.

11.2.1 What Is Digital Emotional Intelligence Exactly (DEQ)?

In short DEQ refers to the ability to transfer the skills from Emotional Intelligence to our connected and digitalized world.

As can be seen in (Bryant 2018), cultural resilience describes the ability to adapt and be resilient as our norms change. Digital Wellness describes, what was formerly known as Work-Life Balance, but with technology added in: being able to balance technology with emotional health and boundaries. This is especially hard considering we are available 24/7 and are always connected to the world around us using our smartphones and other devices.

11.2.2 Change Capacity and Change Management

Change Capacity is probably the most important task when setting up a new structure, project or workplace. Changes most likely result in individuals, who are stressed about the change and react by negativity and rejection, which in result may lead to the failure of the project and money wasted.

That efficient Change Management is a key to projects is—in most cases—well known but still often not deployed properly.

There are several change management methods, but the key to most efficient projects is being empathetic and noticing why employees are scared or rejecting changes.

A commonly known method is the ADKAR-Model (Prosci 2020). In this, but also in other models, the different levels of the change process are described and made measurable by using a series of strategies.

ADKAR splits the change process in five consecutive steps:

1. The Awareness for the need for change
2. The Desire to support the change
3. The Knowledge of how to change
4. The Ability to demonstrate skills and behaviors
5. The Reinforcement to make the changes stick

Project Management normally starts with the knowledge of how to change by teaching individuals how to use certain processes or products and ends with the ability to demonstrate skills and behaviors.

The most important steps however include raising awareness and creating a desire to change as well as reinforcing implemented changes, for a long-lasting success.

11.2.3 Should Companies Use DEQ More?

There are many companies, that use Emotional Intelligence or Emotional Marketing successfully—and this pays off. Some good examples are WWF with their
advertisements that trigger emotions such as being scared or afraid. The WWF
advertisement shows a human with the head of a fish and addresses climate change
by stating "Stop climate change before it changes you." (WWF 2011). The emotions
one feels while looking at the advertisement will more likely trigger change than a
simple advertisement without horrifying picture.

Another great example is Heineken's video advertisement "World's apart". In
this two-minute video, the company did a social experiment where two individuals
with totally different points of view on a specific topic were asked to share a drink
and discuss their views. All of the participants stated that this exchange truly opened
their minds and they continued talking with the person they would normally have
despised.

Apart from this bringing across a great message, this ad also resulted in a massive
engagement in social networks, reaching more than three million visits on YouTube
just a week after the launch.

This ad connects us with the company by using empathy, we feel for the
participants and are therefore triggered and emotionally captured.

All of the above examples are mainly based on marketing needs. However, it is
also crucial to have a company mindset which involves high levels of Emotional
Intelligence and is lived top-down. Some studies even suggest that the secret to a
successful company culture is a high level of Emotional Intelligence.

A great quote from Simon Sinek undermines this statement: "People don't buy
what you do; they buy why you do it. And what you do simply proves what you
believe" (Goodreads 2020).

It is not about the product one sells but about the emotions triggered by it.
Great customer service will result in happier customers, which will result in happier
employees and potentially better earnings overall for a company.

But how can a company build an emotionally intelligent company culture? The
answer is quite simple: by hiring emotional intelligent individuals and by letting
them act upon their intuitions.

Emotional intelligent managers will know their department inside out and will
be able to define the strengths and weaknesses of an individual and act accordingly.

Another benefit may also be an environment where errors and mistakes are
forgiven and learned from.

Any of the above given examples will result in changes to a company's culture
and will allow the creation of innovative spaces and ideas.

11.3 Conclusion

Why is all this so important when creating innovative spaces and when moving into a more digitalized world?

Digitalization is not only about Artificial Intelligence, the Internet of Things or other technologies—but about the people.

Jobs will change in the future, and they already massively have, but it remains a fact, that people are crucial and essential for the economy and the workforce.

Changes are occurring faster than ever before, and it is more important to stay ahead of things. This can only happen if we train our Emotional Intelligence, practice empathy and are aware of the people around us.

Easy ways to do this are to actively listen to colleagues and individuals in general and to practice self-awareness. Especially during times of social media and remote work, which is likely to gain even more popularity, we need to become more empathetic.

The critical skills (World Economic Forum 2016) for the upcoming generations will not be the same as they were five or even 10 years ago. The World Economic Forum suggest in their study "Future of Jobs Report" (World Economic Forum 2018), that skills such as critical thinking, Emotional Intelligence and coordinating with other individuals will be the most necessary and required.

Famous US-Author Maya Angelou once stated, "People forget what you said and what you did, but they will never forget how you made them feel." And this sums up Emotional Intelligence and the way we interact with others pretty well. Make sure to be at the "The Good list" mentioned above, and not on the bad one.

References

Bryant T (2018) Leaders need DEQ! Welcome to digital emotional intelligence. https://medium.com/@thomasfbryant/leaders-need-deq-welcome-to-digital-emotional-intelligence-f2bae5062dbf. Accessed June 24, 2020

Fariselli et al. (2006) Age and emotional intelligence; six seconds

Fernandez-Berrocal et al. (2012) Gender differences in emotional intelligence: the mediating effect of age; University of Malaga (Spain)

Goleman D (2012) Emotional intelligence: why it can matter more than IQ. Random House, New York

Goodreads (2020) Simon Sinek, start with why: how great leaders inspire everyone to take action, https://www.goodreads.com/quotes/668292-people-don-t-buy-what-you-do-they-buy-why-you. Accessed June 24, 2020

Prosci (2020) What is the ADKAR model?, https://www.prosci.com/adkar/adkar-model. Accessed June 24, 2020

Srivastava K (2013) Emotional intelligence and organizational effectiveness. Ind Psychiatry J 22(2):97–99. https://doi.org/10.4103/0972-6748.132912

World Economic Forum (2016) The 10 skills you need to thrive in the fourth industrial revolution.https://www.weforum.org/agenda/2016/01/the-10-skills-you-need-to-thrive-in-the-fourth-industrial-revolution/. Accessed June 24, 2020

World Economic Forum (2018). The future of jobs report

WWF (2011) Stop climate change before it changes you. https://media.treehugger.com/assets/images/2011/10/wwf-ad-fish-head.jpg. Accessed June 24, 2020

Professional Social Media and Innovation: How You Start Leveraging on Your Innovation through Strategic Content Creation on LinkedIn

12

Ilkay Özkisaoglu

12.1 Introduction

Have you ever considered what role professional social media could play in conjunction with your innovation?

My name is Ilkay Özkisaoglu and am a community architect on LinkedIn. Building communities that drive innovation for the good of society is what drives me, and I would like to take you to a bit of a private journey in this book through my action research (Harris in Thorpe and Holt 2008) approach. This chapter in this grand collection, will be different in that I will give you some personal insights as to why I wanted to become visible for the innovation community, how I built a personal brand and how I generate high ticket leads through content creation on LinkedIn.

If you believe professional social media comprises only of cat videos and other viral content, you will be surprised how LinkedIn in particular can help you implement your innovation on the marketplace. I registered with LinkedIn as early as August 2008, just shortly prior the Lehman Brothers collapse, because back then my US affiliates requested a profile for their US American customers and a presence of their German supplier on LinkedIn. My first impression was that LinkedIn is a job and recruiting portal and had nothing to do with business. So, I left my rudimentary profile unattended for a long period of time with only minor revisions reflecting my career steps until mid 2018, i.e. for ten years.

Even when I left my corporate job in October 2015 to pursue my dream of being a freelance Business Development Consultant, LinkedIn still did not resonate with me and I did not perceive it as an exception to the other even more known online career or social media (SoMe) platforms. Surprisingly, around autumn 2018

I. Özkisaoglu (✉)
IMBEO Passionate B2B Partnerships, Seybothenreuth, Germany
e-mail: ilkay.oezkisaoglu@imbeo.de

V. Nestle et al. (eds.), *Creating Innovation Spaces*, Management for Professionals, https://doi.org/10.1007/978-3-030-57642-4_12

I realized LinkedIn was changing, very fast. While browsing the feed I found a few peculiar content creators from the US and the UAE (United Arab Emirates) that were presenting content in a format that suddenly fully resonated with me. Rather than providing and giving dull information, the level of their attractive presentation appealed to me. There was native video that summed up professional learnings. Professional how-to videos were all over the place and I realized the international English-speaking community was clearly up-to-speed on LinkedIn.

The most important aspect that caught my attention was the level of personal branding that was sort of completely new to me. We know the classic one-way advertising and the building of a corporate brand, but personal brand? What was this for, was my immediate internal inquiry (Reason 1994 in Greenwood and Levin 2007)? Personal branding as I found during a 1:1 talk with a LinkedIn influencer out of Dubai and consuming subject online courses, was exciting, because it is more relatable to the person, rather than the corporate. With this approach I found that I could be better able to address one of the major issues any innovative undertaking has and that is the implementation of the innovation on the marketplace.

Why is it that I am so overly certain that innovation struggles more with the implementation rather the creative part? I am assigned among 1000 business innovation coaches by the EASME, the European Agency of Small and Medium-Sized Enterprises (Brussels, Belgium), that is an institution of the European Commission (Brussels, Belgium). Whereas most coaches have their focus on lean production, supply chain management, IT architecture and finance, my focus is on business development and I was frequently selected as a coach for more than a dozen beneficiaries that received grants from the 80 billion heavy "Horizon 2020" program (European Commission n.d.). This program is going to be replaced by the "European Innovation Council" (EIC) end of 2020 and I will continue coaching.

The pattern on hand is that beneficiaries' innovative CEOs, creatively live, learn and work on their innovation, but often fail both in understanding the market developmental side and gaining track on the innovation with their potential customers. Even though everyone thrives for innovation, it remains a struggle to develop markets with innovations. There are a variety of reasons that I have identified in my coaching praxis. Taking this further I would like to show you how these issues can be tackled by using professional SoMe, in particular LinkedIn.

12.2 Why Is Innovation Important?

Both in my innovation coaching praxis as well as my LinkedIn mentoring, I always start with a credo that I created

> Innovation is the only power disrupting the way we live, learn and work

and ask my coachees to tell me, which of these three are essentially disrupted by their innovation. While "disrupting" may sound a bit strong, it still resonates with many inventors, because that is what they were looking at, in the first place. Please ask yourself before you go on with this chapter on precisely this question and let

Fig. 12.1 "How growth champions create new value" (Gordon et al. 2016). (Source: author)

me know, what you came up with, by a separate email on this and the following questions that I piled up for you (for email address see appendices).

Q: What does your innovation disrupt, the way we live, learn or work?

12.2.1 Sources of Organic Growth

Besides the disrupting power and as the purpose of this book reveals, innovation helps strengthening international competitiveness with either launching a new product variant, a new product or even a new business model. Gordon et al. (2016) divided these three categories growth model with the "now, new & next" as depicted in Fig. 12.1. The beauty of the "next", which focus on business modelling rather than product/service, it is difficult to imitate.

I encourage my coachees not only to invent or develop an innovative product, but also create a competitive advantage by building-up barriers, like a unique business model, that is really difficult to overcome. Moreover, as soon as you start gaining visibility, and I see that frequently, imitators emerge all over the places. This is particularly true when gaining visibility on digital platforms. The danger is before your innovation has taken off you already have the first competitors on the feed claiming similar or identical features and product benefits.

In consequence, the more creative you now combine your resources and capabilities the less imitable you will become is my argument.

Q: What is your unique combination as a person or corporate?

Take me as an example:

I am disrupting the way the composite industry is communicating with their customers by exploiting LinkedIn in a professional way. With my innovation coaching, backed by the EASME, I have combined LinkedIn, innovation and industrial materials in a way that no single person can compete easily with my innovative marketing approach. There are thousands of composite marketers. Hundreds of SoMe consultants and countless innovation coaches, but the combination, with which I am able to monetize my services, is unique.

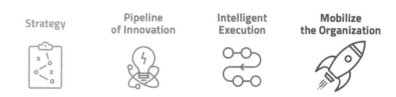

| Strategy | Pipeline of Innovation | Intelligent Execution | Mobilize the Organization |

Fig. 12.2 "Growth and Innovation" (McKinsey online n.d.). (Source: author)

12.2.2 Innovation Performance

Another model that I will lean on with McKinsey is their "Growth and Innovation" best practices online presentation, because it is a reminder on how important a pipeline of innovations can be. It is depicted in Fig. 12.2. During the coaching we always ensure that we end-up with a clear innovation marketing strategy. Yet, I always urge innovators to have a "pipeline of innovations" at hand, because you can test and see what initial response you can get on your ideas for example with your audience on LinkedIn at very reasonable cost. The typical LinkedIn member is literate, qualified and an experienced professional. It is very common that through adequate engagement you can tip your toe into the water and see what they think, provided you have managed this process "intelligently and mobilized your organization".

Q: In what shape is your innovation pipeline?

12.2.3 Eight Essentials of Innovation

I briefly touched already on McKinsey's Innovation models and one that I found particularly useful for my coaching practice are the "Eight Essentials of Innovation Performance" (De Jong et al. 2013). In Fig. 12.3 you can see the different stages and although they assume a linear process, I strongly advise to start extending your network early on by building a tribe or community of end-users through LinkedIn to achieve your targets much faster.

You may notice that I have slightly adapted this model to illustrate that within the scope of this chapter I am less concerned with the creative phase (upper level) and more with the implementation phase (lower level). Assuming the "next", i.e. the business model has already been identified and "evolved" as the last stage of the creative process chain, we now need to "accelerate" and to "beat the competition by developing and launching innovations quickly and effectively".

With your network on LinkedIn you can base your learning on the exchange with your end-users gain extremely useful insights. In the "Scale"-phase you could manage your product/service launch very effectively, by for example creating a dedicated group, company and respective showcase page or even an event run by you or through your pages. Networks are essential for innovations to be successfully

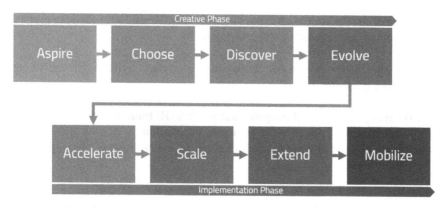

Fig. 12.3 Adapted from the "The Eight Essentials of innovation performance" (De Jong et al. 2013). (Source: author)

recognized. Through LinkedIn you could not only develop collaboration skills, but also choose your right business partners, which I have succeeded on numerous occasions. These could be end-users, resellers, or importers, if you would be looking into exports. At the time of writing this chapter we are in midst of a pan-European and global lockdown. The Covid-19 pandemic situation challenges us making face-to-face meetings almost impossible and in consequence digital platforms, including LinkedIn's main feed, online live events and webinars become very popular these days. A positive side effect is that the situation boosts my following immensely. Finally, creating a huge network does rarely suffice, you must be able to mobilize your network.

Q: How do you intend to mobilize your network?

12.3   The Role of Competitive Advantage and Where It Is Ideally Located

According Niraj Dawar (2013) the value is a product and illustrated in a formula like this

$$VALUE = WHAT + HOW$$

Describing the what is seldom an issue for innovators. The features, advantages and benefits can always easily be pinpointed, and I do recommend posting your innovation on LinkedIn detailing them from time to time. What is more difficult is the "how". Since we know "Business is people, people is business" you only start providing real and major value, once you let your personality as an innovator shine through. Of course, it is difficult to go online and talk about your personal values, but to create trust in your innovation begins with trust in you, the innovator. What also worked well is to start with explaining your why (Sinek 2009), i.e. your purpose before moving on to providing value on LinkedIn

My why?

Enabling SMEs to leverage on LinkedIn as a primary digital online marketing, PR and sales platform.

Q1: What is your why and purpose that made YOU innovate?

Q2: What value can you provide with your innovation?

Q3: What are your personal values that are in line with your innovation and target audience?

12.3.1 Differences in Up-/Downstream Competitive Advantage

Dawar (2013) coined this term and I would like to elaborate a bit on it, since I found that posting your innovation on LinkedIn is highly attractive once you exploit on a specific competitive advantage. Simply picture the Oil & Gas industry then the upstream becomes the oilfield exploration or oil refineries and petrochemical site.

Applying this picture on your own innovation, you would argue with competitive advantages that highlights your new product/service features, advertise your innovative technologies or even production processes. Now imagine the downright opposite, the downstream would be in the oil narrative petrol stations, where your customers fill-up their petrol in their vehicles and is considered as the last encounter in the whole value chain.

Downstream competitive advantages are now more concerned with the distribution and the end-user experience of your innovation. This is exactly the touchpoint that interests your audience more on LinkedIn. They would like to learn and hear more about what you know about what challenges them and how your innovation addresses this exact problem. Rather than featuring capital expenditures, grants, investments, patents or other know-how that may be internal to the innovator, what the LinkedIn network is more interested in is the innovation's capability to solve their unique problem.

Needless to say, that if you would brand yourself and/or your innovation appropriately with your digital tools on LinkedIn this becomes an outright downstream competitive advantage on its own.

If you are in an upstream mindset at this time of reading, you may be "finding yourself defending patents and products rather than your brand and market position" according Dawar. In contrast, "when you think of innovation and look at innovation more broadly in terms of new forms of value for customers" (Dawar 2013) then you created a mindset that is attractive to your audience and potential end-user on LinkedIn.

12.3.2 The Customer Behavior

There are over 690 million members on LinkedIn at the time of writing in June 2020 and according Jeff Weiner, the former CEO, who is now the Executive Chairman the aim of LinkedIn is to attract one billion members by "providing economic opportunity for every member of the workforce" (Weiner 2019). In 2020 my own German-speaking region comprises of 15 million members and it is unrealistic to believe that you will be known by all of them. Consequently, you need to address with your innovation, when entering the LinkedIn scene and become visible through content creation, these both questions:

Q1: Can I trust the innovative seller?
Q2: Will the innovation perform as expected?

Question one is best answered with before mentioned why concept (Sinek 2009) and the value formula, i.e. the what + how (Dawar 2013). Question two requires reporting on experiences made with the innovation's performance. Case studies posted on LinkedIn are appreciated a lot, and if you could add a result that is measurable, you could convince your audience to try your innovation out.

Please answer first these both questions, before you continue.

12.3.3 Cost and Risk

Alongside your downstream competitive advantage, it is advisable to elaborate and communicate as precise as possible which operational cost and risk your innovation reduces. Many of my industrial coachees have these in their mind and can tell me right away how their innovation mitigates risk. What is often a challenge admittedly, is that innovation implies a higher performance, and this is achieved by investing in the innovation, which is almost always more expensive than the current solution customers use.

If risk reduction alone does not outweigh the increased cost, the customer touch points shall be analyzed, and a case illustrated whereby the whole value chain is compared rather than the individual product/service cost. In my thermal insulation business for example waste at the end of the product use is a major cost. Some fibers are treated as special waste and cannot simply be dumped. Other products decrease downtime, like in the joints of a tilting furnace in an aluminum plant, where we reduced a three days downtime, due to metal joints leaking to 1 h, by replacing the metal by a textile and flanged bolted solution. Cases like this help balancing the increased price of your innovation with your consumer. Disseminating use cases like these through LinkedIn will ensure visibility, enhance personal or corporate branding plus will generate warm leads.

Q: How can you offset the higher price of your innovation by lowered cost and
risk in operation?

Fig. 12.4 Criteria of Purchase (Dawar 2013). (Source: author)

12.3.4 First to Market or First to Mind?

Extending the external network with your customers and being able to generate leads from your LinkedIn audience for your innovation assumes that you are not only visible to them, but also come first to their mind.

According Dawar (2013), it is not necessarily the first one, who enters the market, but those who managed to occupy a (blend of) criteria of purchase who succeed on the long run depicted in Fig. 12.4.

This poses a challenge to innovators' mindsets, since there is the belief that being the first may suffice. While it certainly gives an inventor a first mover advantage, still the selection of one or a blend of these criteria that is associated with your innovation will make you win (even more) in the competitive arena.

A real master in occupying all of these criteria is certainly Apple Inc. The touch or face ID stands for "safety". The icloud, one touch use and replacing heavy 4K resolution camera equipment by a simple smartphone is "convenient". The apps communicate through Siri's voice and apps operate with an intuitive "style". Last, but not least, you may agree that the "design" with the rounded corners and the slim corpus are eye-catching for consumers. Disclaimer: I am not affiliated to Apple Inc., nor do I advertise. I simply used the brand to demonstrate the criteria of purchase to ease learning for you.

LinkedIn is the place where you can occupy your individual criteria and resultingly become the first into the mind of your customers with your innovation.

Q: Which of the above-mentioned criteria do you intend to occupy with your innovation?

12.4 LinkedIn

At the time of writing there are 690 million members on LinkedIn. It transformed over the past 2 years from a pure job and recruiting portal to one that has networking and exchange in its core purpose. Me and my tribe use it for marketing and organic visibility in the first place. There is also the possibility to obtain sponsored content, which would fall into inorganic content dissemination on the platform. I am yet to be convinced that sales deals can be fully closed on LinkedIn and am therefore overly critical on the social selling theory. I view LinkedIn more as a personal/corporate branding, referral marketing and relationship management tool that enables members through content creation to be able to influence their industries.

Disclaimer: I am not an affiliate of or otherwise connected or paid by LinkedIn, but only a regular user with a LinkedIn Premium Account. LinkedIn is a trademark of LinkedIn Inc.

12.4.1 History and Mission

To put it into context LinkedIn was found 2002 in the Co-founder Reid Hoffman's living room (LinkedIn 2020). The website went officially online on 5. May 2003, just 2 years after Facebook. LinkedIn's current vision statement is "create economic opportunity for every member of the global workforce." and its mission statement to "connect the world's professionals to make them more productive and successful." At first sight, still the majority believes LinkedIn supports employers as well as employees to connect and grow. At a more closer look, LinkedIn has altered this and includes the active support of SMEs and SMBs and reflects this also in their core values that comprise of "being members first, relationships matter, be open-honest and constructive, demand excellence, take intelligent risks, and act like an owner." (Mission Statement Academy 2020).

12.4.2 The Magic LinkedIn Triangle

When I began to create and post content on 7 January 2019, I decided to use every form of content that LinkedIn is able to provide. As shown in Fig. 12.5 the video content form is salient. Although video has not the widest reach in terms of number of views, due to differences in counting the views, video for me is the #1 tool to drive and manifest a personal brand.

Video gives you the unique opportunity to give insights in you as a person. This does not mean that I rank pictures and articles lower in their branding effect, but for sure, in a video you simply cannot hide the way you speak, move and gesture. This makes you. Authentic, inimitable, and original in your approach. In Fig. 12.6 you can see that personal branding plays a major role in my "magic" LinkedIn triangle that illustrates that it is rarely possible to cover all three aspects with one single content form.

Video is also why I created a credo that is called

Video is the queen of content & Engagement is the king of content. (you can exchange the genders to your liking, of course).

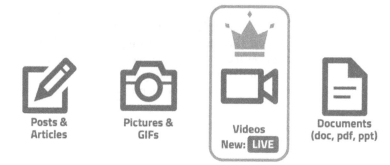

Fig. 12.5 Content forms of LinkedIn. (Source: author)

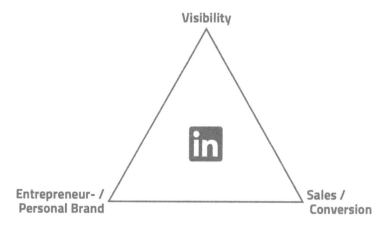

Fig. 12.6 The magic LinkedIn triangle. (Source: author)

In addition, this credo is shared by the legendary LinkedIn group members called DACH TV that I found in November 2019. The purpose was to give experienced video content creators from the German speaking countries Germany (D), Austria (A) and Switzerland (CH) and beginners alike a safe room to exercise their video skills. Through practicing they became more iterate in picture, light, audio and editing of videos that they progressively us to publish on the main LinkedIn(c) feed.

In essence, the group is a community or a tribe, as some of the SoMe gurus would call it. Having a community is important for the reach, support and being prioritized by LinkedIn in the feed through both viral actions, like likes, shares, comments and increased dwell time and lowered bounce rates (Dangi 2020).

Q: What is your primary goal on LinkedIn, visibility, creating a personal brand or sales/conversion?

12.4.3 LinkedIn philosophies

Since I took a constructionist (Easterby-Smith et al. 2012) view on my action research, I have tested all sorts of philosophies while posting on LinkedIn and observed the response to see what works best given my context. To introduce you to all of them in detail would go above and beyond the main aim of this chapter, so let me just bullet point some of them through these questions:

Q: Do you post to address a "Pain or Gain"?
Q: Are you inclined towards "Quality or Quantity" in posting?
Q: Do you provoke a simple viral reaction (a like for example) or are you promoting strategically dwell time on your post?
Q: Do you give the opportunity to "escape the enterprise & edutain" your following?
Q: How do you increase "digital credibility" with your "digital identity"?

If you would be interested to have a detailed chat about it, simply connect with me on LinkedIn.

12.4.4 Digital Credibility

Any individual, organization, service or object that is exposed digitally is assumed to possess a digital identity. Starting to create and post content on LinkedIn is similar to the feed prioritization of google. When do you rank on the first page of Google? If you are long enough on the internet with your website and have many backlinks to it, right? A similar concept seemingly applies on LinkedIn. The longer you are on the platform, the more people you engage with or they engage with you and the more dwell time your posts generate with your following, the higher your post gets ranked (Dangi 2020).

Through this vast amount of data, it seems you become "digitally credible". In Fig. 12.7 you can see what I recommend you should address on your posts to become more credible and rank higher by time.

12.4.5 Corporate Influencer and Brand Advocate

There are different ways to communicate with your target market on LinkedIn. In Fig. 12.8, I compiled them for you. At the core is your message (what you want to change), medium (the right contentform) and you the messenger. The messenger could be the corporate itself, as we know it from classical advertisements, PR or sales and marketing activities. The communication goes straight from the corporate to the target group. In social media it becomes increasingly difficult to gain visibility by the corporate, because people want to communicate rather with

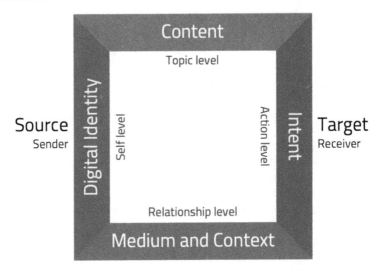

Fig. 12.7 Adapted Four-Side-Model of Communication (Friedemann Schulz von Thun in Hoepner 2017). (Source: author)

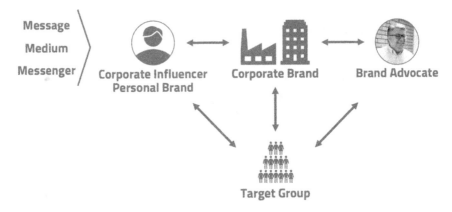

Fig. 12.8 Influencer and Brand Advocacy model. (Source: author)

people. Consequently, as a corporate you have the choice of appointing corporate influencers that are internal to the corporation or external brand advocates. Latter has the benefit, that it is a third person talking about the corporate's services and products. In addition, social media work can be a daunting task with many critical comments to deal with or time consuming with the shear amount of engagement a good post could trigger and brand advocates can ease your work.

12.4.6 LinkedIn Artificial Intelligence (AI) and Machine Learning (ML)

There is not much known about the LinkedIn algorithm since it is protected from the public in line with all the other known SoMe platforms. This clearly avoids gaming it and I am in favor of this general paradigm. From my thousands of posts, hundreds of videos, groups, events, company/showcase pages and events that I created, my take is, that each of the puzzle part helps gaining a credibility on LinkedIn that may boost reach significantly. I encourage you to use the tools depicted in Fig. 12.9 that are available and start feeding the machine so it can learn your preferences.

Whenever you see undesirable content on your feed, remember it is not the algorithm, but you that feeds the machine with undesired information by for example engaging on the apparently wrong content or not engaging enough with the desired content. The feed is only a mirror of your content consumption, good or bad.

12.4.7 Extending the network on LinkedIn

Extending your professional network is your net worth, as the saying goes. Figure 12.10 depicts various means for extending your network. Why not uploading your Gmail or Microsoft 365 Outlook contacts and let LinkedIn figure out, who of your contacts is already a LinkedIn member. You will be surprised, how many are already on the platform. They may be quiet consumers of content and not visible and that is why you did not stumble over them. Let LinkedIn invite those into your network. Chances are high, they will accept your invite since they know you already.

Fig. 12.9 LinkedIn tools. (Source: author)

Fig. 12.10 Extend your LinkedIn network. (Source: author)

In contrary, if LinkedIn finds that a good portion of your contacts is not yet on LinkedIn and asks you whether to invite them, click no. Unfortunately, at this stage, if you click yes, LinkedIn becomes a bit spammy and could annoy your otherwise friendly contact. Extending your network outside your existing one can be done by cold outreach, which means, whenever you stumble over an interesting contact why not invite her/him to your network with a friendly note. Other means to expanding your network is to comment on others' posts and make a connection request, once they respond back. By any means also connect with the people who invested time in responding in a constructive way on your own posts.

Beware of trolls and haters, though. There are always certain individuals that for whatever reason try to be disturbing. I would say these are still a tiny minority, may be one in a thousand. If negative comments do not stop with a friendly reminder you can always block this person.

12.5 Conclusion

In conclusion, what sets professional SoMe, and in particular LinkedIn apart from classical media is the fact, that you are now able to communicate directly with your ideal customer. Engaging through different forms of content, be it text, documents or even video resonates with your audience in an unprecedented way. Do not fall victim, though, that this is a self-entertaining medium. Using LinkedIn to its full potential requires time and effort, in both creating content and engaging with the community, but it pays of well. In my one and a half years where I am actively creating content and built a community architecture (with a handful sub-communities) I am generating constant warm leads for my own and my clients' businesses. I am frequently invited to campaigns and offered speaking gigs, since the work on LinkedIn has reinforced authority in the niche sectors. LinkedIn can assist you to gain momentum with your innovation roll-out with scaling, extending, and mobilizing your network.

Now you have all the necessary know-how, you may begin with your LinkedIn journey, right now. On LinkedIn please visit my profile and press the connect button, because I would love to learn more about you. If you like this chapter, it would finally mean the world to me, if you would hit the "recommend" button on my LinkedIn profile and let my audience know, what you thought of this book chapter.

Happy networking!

References

Dangi S (2020) Understanding dwell time to improve LinkedIn feed ranking, LinkedIn Engineering, Available online: https://engineering.linkedin.com/blog/2020/understanding-feed-dwell-time. Accessed 24 June 2020

Dawar N (2013) Tilt—shifting your strategy from products to customers. Harvard Business Review Press, Boston. ISBN: 978-1-4221-8717-3

De Jong M, Marston N, Roth E, van Biljon P (2013) The eight essentials of innovation performance. McKinsey and Company

Easterby-Smith M, Thorpe R, Jackson P (2012) Management research. Sage Publications. ISBN: 978-0-85702-117-5

European Commission (n.d.) What is Horizon 2020, European Commission. Available online https://ec.europa.eu/programmes/horizon2020/en/what-horizon-2020. Accessed 24 June 2020

Gordon J, Liedtke N, Timelin B (2016) NOW NEW NEXT: How growth champions create new value, marketing & sales. McKinsey and Company

Greenwood DJ, Levin M (2007) Introduction to action research-social research for social change. Sage Publications. ISBN: 978-1-4129-2597-6

Hoepner P (2017) Digitale Glaubwürdigkeit, Kompetenzzentrum Öffentliche IT (ÖFIT). ISBN: 978-3-9818892-1-5

LinkedIn (2020) About LinkedIn. Available online https://about.Linkedin.com/de-de. Accessed 24 June 2020

McKinsey (n.d.) Growth & Innovation. McKinsey, Available online https://www.mckinsey.com/business-functions/strategy-and-corporate-finance/how-we-help-clients/growth-and-innovation. Accessed 24 June 2020

Mission Statement Academy (2020) LinkedIn mission and vision statement analysis. Mission Statement Academy. Available online https://mission-statement.com/Linkedin/. Accessed 24 June 2020

Sinek S (2009) Start why—how great leaders inspire everyone to take action. Amazon. ISBN: 9782924412688

Thorpe R, Holt R (2008) The SAGE dictionary of qualitative management research. Sage Publications Ltd. ISBN: 978-1-4129-3528-9

Weiner, J. (2019) Watch CNBC's full interview with LinkedIn CEO Jeff Weiner. Available online https://www.youtube.com/watch?v=SvEHRcJcrcM. Accessed 24 June 2020

High Quality with Statistical Process Control 4.0 in Automation

13

Johannes Bernstein

13.1 Introduction

To generate high quality in most producing industries the process regulation and upcoming demands lead to a transformation of SPC (statistical process control) onto a new level (named here: SPC 4.0). Classical SPC and separating systems in "good" or "bad" (typically organized by selection) are not sufficient to compete with the best players on automated processes or products of tomorrow. Normally, 100% control—connected to a system which is able to validate the results in-line (no additional time, operators or processes are needed immediately)—is useful in a variety of modern applications (e.g. production of extruded profiles or measurement devices like rotatory encoders). The whole process-structures and data-systems have to be able to work very fast (in ms, very high speed), very stable (error safe, mainly network independent) including the whole post-processing structure (data fusion, validation, separation, statistical results etc.).

Therefore, the need of multi-sensor-systems with regard to any relevant parameters, e.g. defining the customer use of the product's properties have to be invented. Furthermore, reliable data formats have to be defined and the pre-processing of the data with overwhelmed system structures like data bases are necessary. Modern data-base technology collects the data then with main focus on a minimum of data size accordingly as well as to a maximum of data informative content and high robustness: a very challenging task. Additionally there is a layer (e.g. middle ware and an adapter to a central data system needed which is working mostly customer oriented between production machine and data base, on the other hand it must work as near as possible to a standard for flexibility in life-cycle-service and low costs for the initial installation. Stable processes with automated monitoring bring the trust

J. Bernstein (✉)
International Food Industry, Regensburg, Germany

V. Nestle et al. (eds.), *Creating Innovation Spaces*, Management for Professionals,
https://doi.org/10.1007/978-3-030-57642-4_13

on decisions which lead to efficiency and safety of products as they are the result of stable processes: the base for future successful enterprises.

13.2   Fundamentals and State of the Art According to Industry 4.0

In the next section there are presented basics, definitions and some main trends in digitalization in industry.

During the four industrial revolutions there was a rising amount of data. High amount of data in the fourth decade of industrial revolution data bases leads to the possibility of handling increasingly more Cyber Physical Systems. Therefore, the method of "Systems Engineering" can help to control functions over complex systems without the need of physical parts. Systems Engineering focusses on how to design, to integrate and to manage complex systems over their life cycles. It is an interdisciplinary way of working with the focus on functions and interactions. The system then uses this function to manage complexity. Often companies have to set a brownfield approach due to their existing systems and cannot build everything from scratch or completely new (greenfield approach).

Functional oriented handling of data is the future because the customer pays money for solutions and they can be directly connected to functions one of the products or services and to nothing else. In-line capability is one characteristic of modern production systems when they must be able to deal with whole production systems. They support it as a powerful part of the process control in production. Efficient and economic handling of mass data with the maximum of customer orientation is one guiding principle.

At all, it is helpful to divide the industry 4.0 activities in three groups, as Serban (2017) stated citing Unruh and Kiron (2017), see Fig. 13.1. Digitization and Digitalization are fundamental preconditions for the successful Digital Transformation.

The four steps of industrialization from eighteenth century to today are shown in Fig. 13.2, under citing Kachur (2018).

It is time for step 4 now. Different global players explain the first industrial revolution with the transition to mechanical manufacturing processes through water

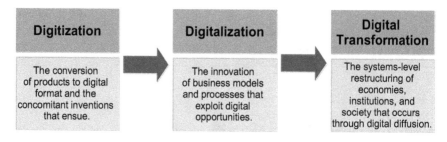

Fig. 13.1 A framework for understanding digitalization. (Source: Author)

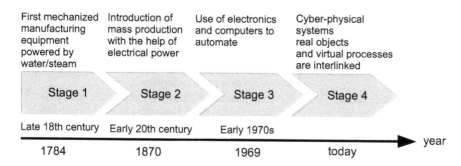

Fig. 13.2 Four stages of industrial revolution. (Source: Author)

and steam power, the second one with the mass production based on the division of labour electric energy. The third one explains the automation of production processes with electronics and IT. And now, the fourth one sets the basis of Cyber-Physical-Systems. Others say, the fourth stage includes "Internet of Things" and advanced network technology.

In Table 13.1 there are the nine main technologies listed to lead to the fourth industrial revolution according to Brunelli et al. (2017) who analyzed them.

As a matter of fact, a roadmap of ever enterprise has to be validated, which technologies in which period of time should be implemented to have maximum positive effects as well as an early Return on Investment (ROI).

Tomorrow's main fields of technologies are e.g. advanced robots, augmented reality, cloud computing, big data and analytics, horizontal and vertical system integration. To react quickly at the customer usually there is a need of IT-Systems which follow an architecture of flexibility and standard of automation and configuration like a kind of Standard Operating Procedure (SOP). Secondly, an Enterprise Resource Planning (ERP) tool is often used to ensure the Supply Chain Management (SCM). Third, Manufacturing Execution System (MES) are also needed to handle the high amount of data. Last but not least, to manage the requirements from the customer and the whole interaction and processes around, over a long period of time, systems for Customer Relationship Management (CRM) are installed.

To start the industry 4.0 journey there are six main steps to walk as Khurana et al. (2015), see Fig. 13.3.

The first step strategy work has to be done in every enterprise to know what the strategy is and where the capacity should be used. In the second step in initial proofs of concept should be shown what the benefits are and in which fields they act. Step 3 is needed to know how much capabilities are necessary for the digital transformation later. In fourth step there is the need to train data specialist. The kind of data obtained can vary but nearly every company will need deep knowledge about data handling. In step 5 transformation into a digital enterprise will be done and in step 6 economic optimization, daily done in every enterprise, can be achieved.

Table 13.1 Nine technologies are reshaping production and automated industry on the way to lean maturity and industry 4.0

Technology	Description
Advanced robots	Autonomous, cooperating industrial robots, with integrated sensors and standardized interfaces
Additive manufacturing	3D Printers, used predominantly to make spare parts and prototypes Decentralized 3D printing facilities, which reduce transport distance and inventory
Augmented reality	Digital enhancement, which facilitates maintenance, logistics, and SOPs Display devices, such as glasses
Simulation	Network simulation and optimization, which use real-time data from intelligent systems
Horizontal and vertical system integration	Data integration within and across companies using a standard data transfer protocol A fully integrated value chain from supplier to customer and organization structure
The industrial internet of things	A network of machines and products Multidirectional communication among network objects
Cloud computing	The management of huge volumes of data in open systems Real time communication for production systems
Cybersecurity	The management of heightened security risks due to a high level of networking Approach among intelligent machines, products and systems
Big data and analytics	The comprehensive evaluation of available data (from CRM, ERP and SCM systems), as well data from MES and machines Support for optimized real-time decision making

SOP: Standard Operating Procedure, CRM: Customer Relationship Management, ERP: Enterprise Resource Planning, SCM: Supply Chain Management, MES: Manufacturing Execution System

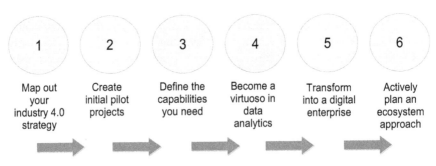

Fig. 13.3 Six steps to approach the industry 4.0 transformation in enterprises. (Source: Author)

In almost every company high amounts of data have to be handled building a gravity point of preparing the whole digital transformation, see Fig. 13.4, cited from Keller (2018). Therefore, data classification has to be organized and implemented, most times over a dozen of several systems in an international context and several languages. Specific data filtering methods have to be gained in order to process the high amount of data. Data fusion can become necessary e.g. for production data processing (e.g. see Sect. 4, here: Figs. 13.10 and 13.11).

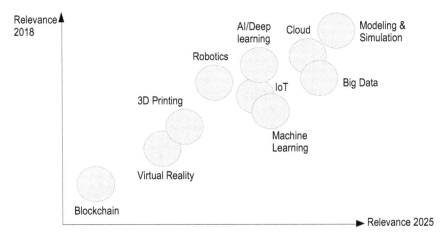

Fig. 13.4 Relevance of technologies today and in about 7 years. (IoT: internet of things, AI: Artificial Intelligence. Source: Author)

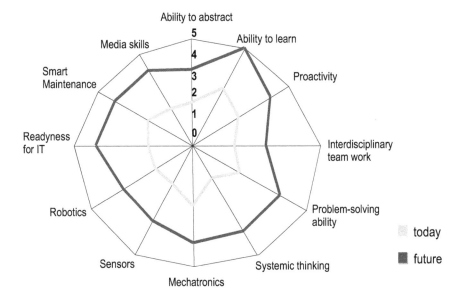

Fig. 13.5 Relevance of abilities today and in the future. (Source: Author)

Data analysis and process control in real-time are often helpful possibilities. Summarized it is a part of "Big Data", "Internet of things (IoT)" or "Cloud". The rising importance is shown consequently as Keller (2018) expects it.

It describes the relevance of abilities companies have today and in future to face the challenges of digitalization and industry 4.0, see here Fig. 13.5, cited from Festo Corp (2020). The ability to learn is very important as well as the readiness for

IT, systematic thinking, proactiveness as well as "Smart Maintenance" or "Media skills". Tomorrow's engineers ought to be prepared for all these fields. The ability to learn is much more important than today.

13.3   Digital and Automated Manufacturing of Tomorrow

So, smart factory for industry 4.0 means Machine, Human, Operation & Maintenance, Product Design and Planning & Control, see Fig. 13.6, content cited by Gorecky et al. (2019). To manage a smart factory, skills in all of these areas are necessary and have to be combined together.

A very exciting possibility of tomorrow e.g. are digital twins, because less companies neither their management nor their experts have knowledge about what it is. This is a big chance for being early adopter in that areas. Digital twins are non-physically realized products which are completely developed and understood (models with proof of concepts or better approved by test including validation and verification), see here as well Sect. 4.

The enormous advantages are generating expertise and earning money without all the efforts of traditional supply chain or production process. It is possible to be market leader and technological leader without being production leader. The business models are fast and internationally adaptable without the usual challenges of international production. Production can take place in the same company; but the know-how is not anymore mainly in the physical realization, it is more in a digital

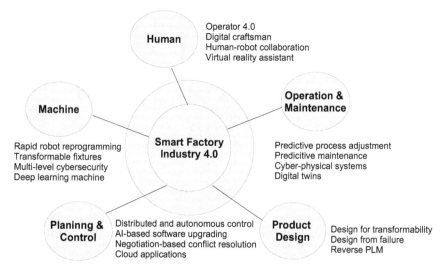

Fig. 13.6 Research challenges for smart factory. (PLM: Product Life-cycle-Management. AI: Artificial Intelligence. Source: Author)

twin. Therefore, it is not sufficient to have only mechanical or electronical drawings or components.

An integrative and comprehensive approach over all disciplines with a deep understanding of the whole product is still required. Typically models of the products and software knowledge are necessary. As a result, a system for handling is needed all that as well as processes a matter of fact processes and methods through the whole Product Life Cycle (PLM) to deal with it. Chances are high but the effort and the risk are as well high to be one of the first companies having digital twins in traditional industry sectors.

To install steps of digitalization and smart factory three typical agglomerated phases of generation and implementation on the journey of transformation can be determined: innovation, pilot and scale phases, see Table 13.2 content cited by Küpper et al. (2017).

Critical points of the innovation phase are transparency and the set of a gravity phase of the transformation. If the task is not clarified and with which main targets there is a high risk of a fail or disappointment because of the long need of time the challenge in the pilot phase is the realistically proof. Everybody, but especially the management, has to understand and believe in the pilot and its validation. In later steps there have to be gained effects and to scale the whole digital transformation on bigger even including internationalization. At all, the transformation has to go live, and it might occur that additional staff for the start is needed. Also, reducing fields within the company create sufficient capacities.

At this point there is the question to be answered which criteria for industry 4.0 in production are required to do it, cited by Caylar et al. (2016), see Fig. 13.7. Seven criteria are the main frame.

One very powerful criterion while installing industry 4.0 is the customer orientation. It is very important that in every stage of industry 4.0 the customer needs stay in focus. This might sound easier as it might be. On the one hand the customer will not pay for the transformation process and on the other hand expects a running business in the meanwhile.

Moreover, he expects the latest technologies as well as high quality with fast delivery. So, this is the highest demand on the transformation. It is not possible

Table 13.2 Three phases of a lean industry 4.0 journey

Innovate	Pilot	Scale
Gain transparency into business needs and challenges	Develop a minimum viable solution quickly and improve it through iterations	Scale up solutions along the supply chain and plant network
Assess pain points and how they can be addressed through Lean industry 4.0	Test and refine use case to validate them and demonstrate value	Deliver full potential through integrated solutions at full scale
Prioritize the highest-value use case by quantifying their potential	Deploy the enablers of Lean Industry 4.0	Track progress and manage change toward the target vision

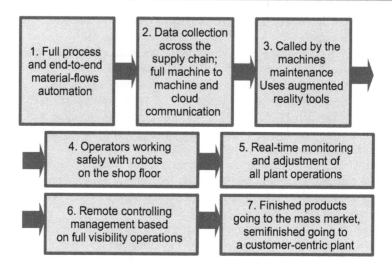

Fig. 13.7 Seven criteria for industry 4.0 ability in production. Very important in most cases is full automation and end-to-end processes. (Source: The author)

Table 13.3 Data-centric approach identifies the most valuable improvement levers

	Transparency	Predictability	Self-optimizing systems
Activities	Using data to understand performance of production lines	Analyzing big data (e.g. IT based in automation or production environment)	Automatically adjusting parameters to avoid incidents
	Gaining transparency into root causes of downtimes (e.g in automation)	Recognizing patterns (e.g. of products in the automation environment)	Self-controlled rerouting of products within the factory to allow for maintenance activities
	Benchmarking lines and factories (e.g according to KPI's)	Using machine learning to predict equipment breakdowns and poor-quality incidents	Technology based optimization in automation

KPI: key performance indicator. Important: production, automation

to drive greenfield approaches because there is no situation of starting new. It is a transformation. So, the approach needs to be fully transparent, predictable and self-optimizing, see Table 13.3, content cited by Küpper et al. (2017).

Nevertheless, the jobs of digital transformation have changed, the required shifts in job profiles are illustrated in Table 13.4, content cited by Caylar et al. (2016).

Independent of hiring new staff exclusively for the transformation process, employees of the company have to support the transition into great success. The people's flexibility rewards the change "from" the present "to" the future and is most important part of the process. It must be started as early as possible with a good plan for the change and supported all the time. Figure 13.8 shows the results of an analysis about the biggest challenges in industry by citing Geissbauer et al. (2015).

Table 13.4 Examples of required changes in job profiles for connected factory

	From …	… to
Worker (production)	Carries out production tasks, large share of manual tasks	Exception handler in production line, operator in automated environment
Maintenance expert	Troubleshooter and exception handler	Oversees of predictive maintenance, planning and steering based on data-driven analysis
Quality specialist	Inspects parts and controls quality standards after the fact	Smart engineer of process to online control for quality issues
Production planner	Top-down planning and steering of linear processes (50 percent build-to-stock)	Supply-chain planner Develops flexible self-steering value stream (100% build-to order)
Logistics planner	Plans supply in segmented approach (inbound, line delivery, outbound)	A planner on a full integrated supply chain from order to delivery
Team leader	Focus on leading people based on visible waste on shop floor	Leads team based on identified digital waste, brings insights to action

Here: focus on staff in the fields of production and automation

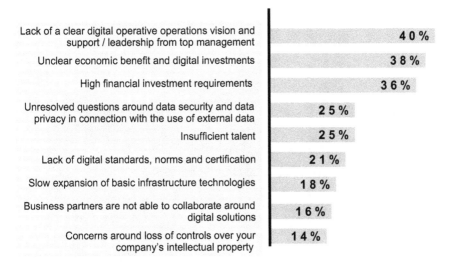

Fig. 13.8 Answer to the question: what are the biggest challenges or obstacles for building digital operation capabilities in your company? (Note: Included as one of three possible answers. Source: Author)

The highest reasons for showstopper are less transparency, unclear tasks and as a result too less investments in training and insufficiently unqualified people trying it. The often-existing fear about losing control of the company during the digital transformation phase is a non-reasonable thing not coming true most of the time.

In Fig. 13.9, content cited by Küpper et al. (2017), shows five aspects on how to gain the next level of operational excellence.

Flexibility, speed and quality as well as safety and productivity are significant factors (see as well Figs. 13.10 and 13.11). Industry 4.0 maturity is a topic as lean

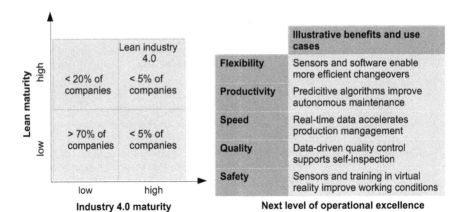

Industry 4.0 maturity   Next level of operational excellence

Fig. 13.9 Situation, benefits and use cases of the next level of operational excellence according to flexibility, productivity, speed, quality, safety. (Source: Author)

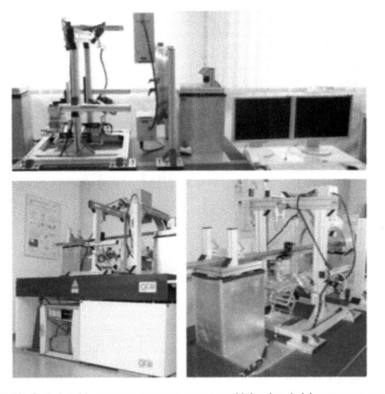

Fig. 13.10 Optical multi-sensor-measurement system combining data, in laboratory use, up: side view in laboratory mock-up; down left: isometric view, down right: near field. (Source: Author)

Fig. 13.11 Optical multi-sensor-measurement system combining data in the shop floor area, left: isometric side view, middle: side view, right: isometric top view. (Source: Author)

maturity is. Please see Fig. 13.9 to see the present state. There is shown the four fields of industry 4.0 and lean and the interaction of today's companies. Finally, about 70% are in the "low"/"low" area, only <5% are "high"/"high" and as a result ready for the transformation.

13.4   Example of Modern Process Control: Extruded Profiles

Optical Metrology is used in many industrial applications because of the advantages of non-contact and reliable measurement results especially for moving, damageable or flexible measurement objects. Unfortunately, in the shop there are many additional environmental influences affecting the measurement, which often have not occurred in the laboratory: dust, vibration, thermal drift of the ambient air, inconsistent part temperatures and high moving speeds of the objects. Furthermore, many measurement methods are predominantly set-up for laboratory conditions: offline-measurements with high-precision. Bringing the methods or furthermore multi-sensor-systems to the shop requires the abilities of resisting these constraints and still dealing precise.

As a result, there is often a total rework of the prototype and many expensive tests in the shop—with loss of production, waste or rework—necessary. In order to enlarge the range of the aptitude for these methods and to bring them faster to industry, simulations can be carried out preventively. So, the environmental influences could be categorized concerning their expected effect on the result.

There is potential of forecasting the maturity of a prototype with the objective: adequate dimensional measuring of real parts. The system combines the shadow method and several light-section systems to a compound of high accuracy and data density.

The idea of constitutive data quality was realized under the use of appropriate construction elements, data fusion, fast and robust algorithms in individual software and several robustness validations and cooling applications, see Fig. 13.10 from Bernstein (2011). By using provisions and compensating strategies the in-line measurements operate with acceptable uncertainties of <20 μm (measurement range ~ 100 mm, concave shapes). Classical systems achieve only uncertainties of 100 μm and cannot measure 360° contours.

The prototype calibrates itself in-line with 20 frames per second (fps), can measure brass materials and as well several others like e.g. fibre tapes. It resisted the shop floor environments for a long time period (>100 h). With respect to the space needed, installation time and costs in 24 h production the further research was partly made with simulations including the external influences. So, the test time after modeling and testing the digital twin was much shorter, more systematic and more efficient as Bernstein and Weckenmann (2011) stated.

After the successful validation on the digital twin, the verification in the shop was done, see Fig. 13.11 cited from Weckenmann and Bernstein (2013). The quality, the speed, the robustness was set on the first try over weeks. The whole system is a big advantage to save money, reduce scrap, rework and bad quality in later process steps of the extruding production.

The probability of avoiding waste in automated production by applying more accurate measurement technologies improves the quality of parts and of the whole processes. The here presented example showed, that optical multi-sensor measurement tasks can effectively be supported by simulative tests on a digital twin which respect the environmental influences in manufacturing process. So, the real test time can be reduced, and methods and prototypes can be improved. Furthermore, modern technologies in production help to reduce scrap and costs.

13.5 Conclusion

Automation, digitalization, statistical process control and similar fields are very important aspects of industry 4.0 with high potential in the next years. The mindset has to be changed on the main fields of technology, a very systematic approach including a straight strategy is necessary and as well very good and modern training concepts to transform the whole company to industry 4.0. Companies have to be focused to bring out the advantages of fast, intelligent data and processes for industry and their automation. Then there are many chances to win flexibility, transparency, high quality and speed in internal processes as well as new ways of managing products and services. New business models like digital products are more and more available and possible to implement. The handling of very complex product structures is better possible. Finally, there are great potentials for being faster, more economic and more precise as before.

References

Bernstein J (2011) Optisches Multi-Sensor-Messverfahren zur dimensionellen in-line Messung von Strangprofilen im Fertigungsprozess (Optical multi-sensor-method for the dimensional in-line measurement of extruded profiles in the shop floor). Dissertation, Berichte aus dem Lehrstuhl QFM, Shaker, Herzogenrath, ISBN: 978-3-8440-0345-1

Bernstein J, Weckenmann A (2011) Evaluation of an optical multi-sensor-measuring method for in-line measurement of extruded profiles. Metromeet, 7th International Conference on Industrial Dimensional Metrology, Bilbao

Brunelli J, Lukic V, Milton T, Tantardini M (2017) Five lessons from the frontlines of industry 4.0. The Boston Consulting Group (BCG). http://www.bcg.com. Accessed May 10, 2020

Caylar P-L, Naik K, Noterdaeme O (2016) Digital in industry: from buzzword to value creation. McKinsey & Company. http://www.mckinsey.com. Accessed June 14, 2020

Festo Corp (2020) Getting ready for digital transformation, competency development. https://www.festo.com/us/en/e/automation/training-and-consulting/digital-transformation-id_32846/. Accessed June 18, 2020

Geissbauer R, Vedso J, Schrauf S (2015) Industrie 4.0: building the digital enterprise. PwC, 2015 Global Digital IQ Survey

Gorecky D, Romer D, Kim DY (2019) Accelerating technological advancement and adoption of industry 4.0 technologies: smart-factory labs, digital capability centers and lighthouses networks. International Congress and Conferences on Computational Design and Engineering 2019 in Malaysia (Proceedings I3CDE 2019)

Kachur L (2018) Industry 4.0: the top 9 trends for 2018. DZone Community. https://dzone.com/articles/industry-40-the-top-9-trends-for-2018. Accessed June 18, 2020

Keller W (2018) Berufe 4.0—Wie Chemiker und Ingenieure in der digitalen Chemie arbeiten. Whitepaper, Initiative der Vereinigung für Chemie und Wirtschaft VCW (GDCh Fachgruppe, p. 69. https://www.gdch.de/fileadmin/downloads/Netzwerk_und_Strukturen/Fachgruppen/Vereinigung_fuer_Chemie_und_Wirtschaft/whitepaper_initiative_berufe_4.0_2018.pdf. Accessed June 18, 2020

Khurana A, Geissbauer R, Pillsbury S (2015) Defining the new DNA of industrial digital enterprises. PwC, 2015 Global Digital IQ Survey. http://www.pwc.com. Accessed June 14, 2020

Küpper D, Heidemann A, Ströhle J, Spindelndreier D, Knizek C (2017) When Lean meets industry 4.0—the next level of operational excellence. The Boston Consulting Group (BCG). http://www.bcg.com. Accessed May 16, 2020

Serban R (2017) The impact of big data, sustainability and digitalization on company performance. Studies in Business and Economics 12(3), Lucian Blaga University of Sibiu, Romania, De Gruyter (Open)

Unruh G, Kiron D (2017) Digital transformation on purpose. MIT Sloan Management Review, Big Idea: Leading sustainable organizations. https://sloanreview.mit.edu/article/digital-transformation-on-purpose/. Accessed June 18, 2020

Weckenmann A, Bernstein J (2013) Optical multi-sensor-measurements in the shop by compensating environmental influences, pp. 61–69, 12th CIRP Conference on Computer Aided Tolerancing, Procedia CIRP 10, Science Direct, Elsevier

Digital Platforms as Drivers of Innovation

14

Philip Meier

14.1 Introduction to Digital Platforms

Digital platforms possess technology-based business models that create value through the enablement of interactions, communication, co-creation, and exchange between two or more participating actors (Choudary 2015). These actions between the actors take place upon a pre-defined infrastructure obtaining a stable core and modular periphery. The framework for possible actions and interaction, the so-called platform governance, is determined by the platform operator (Constantinides et al. 2018). In order to present this theoretical definition in practical terms, a digital platform is presented and analyzed hereafter.

In 2007, a three-day design conference in San Francisco was the catalyst for the founding of one of the most successful start-ups of the past decade. The two young designers Brian Chesky and Joe Gebbia noticed that hotel prices had risen sharply as a result of the conference and other events in the corresponding period during which hotel capacity was in short supply. They decided without further ado to lay out some air mattresses on the floor of their three-room apartment and rent them out to fellow designers looking for accommodation. The idea for AirbedAndBreakfast, today AirBnB for short, was born (Parker et al. 2016). Ten years after the initial idea, Airbnb is the dominant digital platform for temporary private accommodation. The company employs over 3000 people (as of 2017), arranges more overnight stays for customers each month than the largest hotel chains, and is continuously expanding its portfolio of offers beyond overnight stays. How did Airbnb reach such size and market power in such a short time?

P. Meier (✉)
Alexander von Humboldt Institute for Internet and Society, University of the Arts Berlin, Berlin, Germany
e-mail: philip.meier@hiig.de

© The Editor(s) (if applicable) and The Author(s), under exclusive license to Springer Nature Switzerland AG 2021
V. Nestle et al. (eds.), *Creating Innovation Spaces*, Management for Professionals, https://doi.org/10.1007/978-3-030-57642-4_14

In addition to an enormously motivated and talented team of founders and education in one of the most successful incubation programs in the United States, the character of the digital platform represents a decisive success factor. Airbnb is not building new homes. The company does not create new travel needs among potential customers. It brings together the newly used but already existing spatial capacity with the existing need for temporary overnight accommodation. This use of existing capacity allows AirBnB to quickly scale over the years, as it is much easier and less capital-intensive to add a new housing offering to the platform than to build a new hotel building. Airbnb retains control over direct customer interaction and financial processing—two important factors for the company's success. Marketing activities can be controlled in a targeted manner via the customer interface and the value proposition can always be optimized in a customer-centric approach. In addition, the independent management of the financial operations creates trust with housing providers and travelers, enabling Airbnb to implement a monetization model by means of a commission fee. A professional photo service made it easier for early providers to present their own apartment attractively on the platform. Likewise, a clearly structured website with relevant selection options guaranteed travelers a good customer experience from the very beginning. By initiating targeted growth support for supply and demand, online platforms manage to continuously increase the value provided to the participants. With each new supplier and customer, the value for new and existing suppliers and customers increases. This phenomenon is called a positive network effect (Rochet and Tirole 2003; Parker and Van Alstyne 2005). In the case of Airbnb, every new housing offer attracts new customers, while more new customers make it more attractive for new suppliers to join the platform. Through a network-centric, i.e. supplier- and customer-focused strategy and the use of digital technologies, online platforms such as Airbnb are able to scale enormously quickly and efficiently with relatively low capital expenditure (Evans 2003). As a result, and in contrast to equal market competition, a monopolistic market position can potentially be established from which significant profit margins may be realized (Evans and Schmalensee 2016).

14.2 How Platforms Work

A digital platform is to be described as a (more or less) complex construct of rules, infrastructure, actors, and operations (Parker et al. 2016). To describe this construct, standardized and recurring components and principles exist. The business model of a platform has four basic components: the platform operator, the platform architecture, customers, and suppliers (Gawer and Cusumano 2014). A platform operator is a company that is visible to the public as the owner of the respective platform and has control over the customer and supplier interfaces. Furthermore, it is at the discretion of the platform operator to determine the platform governance mentioned above, in other words, to determine the rules of the game orchestrating the interaction between the individual actors. The operator is mostly also the one actor who took initiative and started to build up the whole platform ecosystem.

Common developments towards building a platform ecosystem start in either of two ways. It can begin with a physical product which achieves a high market penetration and later evolves into a platform after it gets connected, complemented with software capabilities and opened up for third pasties. The second common emergence pattern is embedded in an already connected innovation or supply chain ecosystem. Starting eye to eye, the platform building actor takes initiative to evolve into a central role between enabling key transactions with superior efficiency than before. Thus other involved actors in prior or later positions in the ecosystem gravitate around the newly created platform. The platform architecture is the underlying technical infrastructure that facilitates interaction between the various actors (Baldwin and Woodard 2008). The platform architecture is usually in the hands of the platform operator. A popular example is the technical foundation of the iOS operating system, which was developed, enhanced and operated by the platform owner Apple. The use cases of the emerging IoT platforms such as Siemens Mindsphere or GE's Predix show an example of the interaction between separate platforms and architecture operators. In terms of the underlying architecture, both platforms rely on established solutions such as SAP HANA, Microsoft Azure and/or Amazon Web Services, but still meet the characteristics of platform operators described above (Gawer and Cusumano 2014). Here, one could speak of meta platforms. Customers and suppliers act as actors on the platform and complete the list of components. In this context, customers are considered to be those actors who purchase the products or services offered on the platform. These products or services are created and offered by the suppliers or the platform operator. Taking up the example of Apple iOS, the external application developers in the App Store are the suppliers. In addition, Apple itself offers selected apps and services via the Store or other channels within the operating system and thus also acts as a supplier. This phenomenon whereby the platform operator offers its own products and services is often seen when the product or service in question either shows a high potential for success or, in addition, carries the risk of establishing itself as a platform of its own—potentially occupying the customer interface (Van Alstyne and Schrage 2016). The former can be illustrated by Apple's recently released proprietary music streaming service, which is largely motivated by the underlying potential for success and proof of concept for the model by providers such as Spotify and SoundCloud. Other proprietary services such as "Maps" and "Safari" are motivated by the argumentation regarding the independent platform and customer interface, as these services allow a wide range of complementary application development itself. The various technical systems through which customers and producers interact with the platform are referred to as interfaces in the following (Parker et al. 2016). While the interfaces for the customers of the Apple iOS platform are the respective applications on the smartphone, the primary producer interface has the character of a development environment upon which the respective applications are programmed. From the point of view of all actors, the activity on the platform is a constant give and take. These transactions refer to the exchange of goods, services, data, or units of value, for example. For example, the iOS user transfers money to the platform operator when purchasing an application. In return, the customer receives access to the respective application. The platform operator, in turn, pays the supplier or developer of the respective application and retains a standardized fee. The quality of the customer-oriented offer is considered to be a decisive competitive advantage among similar platforms. To ensure a high-quality offering despite rather loose ties between the actors and to present a relevant offer to the customer, access controls and filters provide the platform operator with the necessary tools (Libert et al. 2016). The relationships are loose in the sense that, in the case of the iOS platform, there are no individual contracts between Apple and the individual suppliers or customers. The interactions are based on generally established governing rules (Iansiti and Lakhani 2020). To ensure a high-quality application offering, Apple has defined certain technical standards that every application must satisfy. In addition, applications are manually checked for quality before release. Pleasant customer experience is ensured by the filter and suggestion functions in the iOS store. This enables the respective customer to navigate through the wide range of different applications. The greater the individuality of the platform operator's options for filtering the content for each customer, the more pleasant the customer experience (Boudreau 2010).

In general, digital platforms can be grouped in three categories. These categories are called innovation platform, transaction platform and integrated platform (Gawer 2014). On an innovation platform, the platform operator offers external suppliers the infrastructure to develop new products and services using the platform and offer them access to customers. Apple's iOS falls into this first category. The marketplace of the accommodation provider AirBnB described above is an example of the second category, the transaction platform. In this category, the platform operator creates a marketplace in which suppliers can address an existing offer specifically to a large customer group and use the existing infrastructure to conduct the associated transaction. Integration platforms combine the characteristics of the two categories mentioned above (Gawer 2011). In the case of Amazon, for example, existing supply and existing demand are brought together. In addition, Amazon's existing physical and virtual infrastructure offers suppliers a basis for developing entirely new product and service offerings. In addition to the three categories described, digital platforms can also be evaluated and classified according to their degree of openness (Van Alstyne and Schrage 2016). The more open a digital platform and the underlying infrastructure are towards suppliers and customers, the more influence and scope for action the respective actors have in their actions. In the open platform, the operator exercises less control, which favours growth. A closed approach can have a positive impact on the quality of the offer, as the operator exercises greater control. However, the example of mobile operating systems shows that both an open approach (Google/Android) and a more closed approach (Apple/iOS) can coexist very successfully.

14.3   Platform Success Factors

At this point, three significant success factors of digital platforms are to be emphasized namely high scalability, a moderate resource requirement, and a high increase in efficiency for both suppliers and customers. The success factors of scalability and moderate resource consumption are directly related to each other. An in-depth example of this is provided by the American Ride-Hailing provider Lyft. In competition with conventional taxi companies, Lyft offers an agency service for private driving service providers on a digital marketplace. The suppliers use already existing vehicles to offer their service, which makes it possible to quickly generate a large offering on the platform. Since Lyft is not forced to build up a cost-intensive in-house fleet, rapid growth is possible. By intelligently coordinating suppliers and buyers and taking care of administrative procedures such as payment and authentication, it is a tremendous time saver for both suppliers and customers to simply offer or book a car trip through Lyft. Tim Goodwyn is credited with the now inflationary used quote that Alibaba as the largest trading company does not have its own shops, AirBnB as a provider of overnight accommodation does not own hotels and Uber as a provider of mobility does not own cars. It is by no means quite that simple. Even in the conventional hotel industry, it is not unusual for hotel chains to rent buildings from real estate companies instead of building them themselves, and conventional taxi companies are also more likely to have ownership in taxi badges than to operate their own fleet. Nevertheless, both the rental contracts with real estate companies and the business relationship between taxi companies and drivers share an individual, long-term character. Business relationships between digital platform owners, such as Airbnb and Uber, and the respective service providers, on the other hand, have a much looser, standardized, and scalable form. This enables the platforms to grow rapidly. Another factor is the fact that the platform operators mentioned as examples have all been established and have grown to a relevant size within the last decade. This is accompanied by the fact that none of the companies has to bear "legacy burdens" from the pre-Internet era. On the contrary. All successful digital platforms are characterized by intensive and intelligent use of the latest technologies, algorithms, and organizational structures (Iansiti and Lakhani 2020).

When Amazon, for example, was unable to find an adequate cloud solution for handling the enormous amounts of data required to operate its own e-commerce platform efficiently, it quickly developed its own high-tech solution. Amazon Web Services now hosts a significant share of all online services on the American market and is responsible for a significant portion of the retail giant's revenues. The algorithms that Uber and Lyft use for route planning and demand-based pricing are highly sophisticated. In addition, the companies are working intensively on autonomous driving in order to remove the biggest cost factor in their business model, the driver, from the cost calculation in the medium term. Fast learning, lean processes, and flat hierarchies are of great importance in the organization and self-image of the platform companies (Cusumano et al. 2019). This often enables them to maintain the culture of a start-up despite the infrastructure and revenues of a large corporation.

14.4   Understanding Platform Potential in Different Industries

The market dominance of different platform owners like Apple or Airbnb demonstrates that the emergence of a digital platform in a market previously dominated by linear business models exhibits disruptive signs for incumbents in the respective market or industry. To assess digital disruption potential, Snjay Khosla and Mohan Sawhney (2014), Professor of Economics and Senior Fellow at the Kellog School of Management, introduced a model containing three different types of disruption. Sawhney distinguishes between the levels of product, market, and channel. Disruption at the product level is called "Servitization". Servitization means adding intelligence to a physical or virtual product through additional software Furthermore, there is no longer a one-time sale of the respective product. Instead, the service that the product in question fulfills is provided in a subscription or a usage-based compensation model. The example of Microsoft Office 365 is evidence of the current trend for vendors to move away from closed software products, moving towards software-as-a-service models.

Why is Servitization relevant in the context of digital platforms? To monetize a product or service based on usage, continuous data exchange with the respective service or product as well as a data architecture in which necessary analytical operations can take place to evaluate the usage is required. In addition, regular product improvements increase customer benefits. Solid technical data architecture and data-driven product or service optimization are fundamental steps from a linear to a platform-based business model.

Who is affected? Providers of non-connected products that can be offered in a usage-based commercial model through intelligent connectivity and a value-enhancing service offering. Examples are cars, sportswear, and watches.

Sawhney calls the disruption at the market level "Uberization". By this, he refers to the emergence of digital marketplaces whereby underutilized goods or labor can be brought together with corresponding demand in real-time. As the name already suggests, Uber fulfills the aforementioned criteria and thus has a potential for disrupting the mobility industry. With only a 4% utilization rate, privately owned cars definitely belong to the category of unused goods. Uber manages to create a supply of private drivers in its own marketplace thus increasing vehicle use. This offer is in turn brought together with passengers seeking mobility, resulting in a mobility service that was not available before.

Why is uberization relevant in the context of digital platforms? The intelligent orchestration of an existing or new offering addressing existing or new customer value is at the heart of any business model on digital platforms. In addition, in the case of the Uber example, an existing range of vehicles is used as far as possible. This procedure is also characteristic for digital platforms in terms of rapid scalability and can also be observed, for example, with AirBnB (existing living space), Lynjet (existing private jets) or Pager (existing medical staff).

Who is affected? Manufacturers and providers of goods and services with a low level of usage and a high level of standardization. Examples are machine tools, yachts and web design services.

Sawhney calls digital disruption at the distribution channel level "Amazonization". Amazonization describes the process of removing middlemen from a chain of transactions to create a more direct customer-to-product relationship. This third form of digital disruption can basically be summarized under keyword e-commerce. Even in industries traditionally organized through middlemen or direct sales, such as steel or automobile dealerships, the emergence of online sales platforms is evident. For example, the steel producer Klöckner recently launched Klöckner.i, a digital unit whose initial task is to develop and establish its own trading platform for industrial steel.

Why is Amazonization relevant in the context of digital platforms? Through the use of digital distribution platforms and direct online trading, it is possible to exclude physical dealer networks and middlemen and to collect valuable data through direct customer contact. To build an accurate sales platform and customer data, the characteristics of digital platforms described above must be taken into account.

Who is affected? Companies that act as intermediaries between producers and customers and provide limited additional value. Examples are Real estate agents, stockbrokers and car dealers.

In response to a potential disruption threat posed by a new digital platform, Sawhney provides four avenues of intervention:

1. building a proprietary platform. As an example, the American media company HBO, which, inspired by the video-on-demand services Netflix and Amazon Prime Video, recently launched its own streaming service HBO GO, using its existing network and partnerships to advance its own platform.
2. takeover of the potential disruptor. In this context, automotive manufacturer General Motors, for example, took over the software start-up Cruise in 2016, which is working on the development of an operating system for autonomous vehicles.
3. adaptation and transformation of the own value proposition. The expansion of its own product portfolio, the opening up of its own platform and interfaces and the building of an ecosystem around an existing product can be seen very clearly in the example of the first iPhone model, which was initially offered by Steve Jobs and Apple as a stand-alone product and was only expanded to include the iPhone developer platform after a few months.
4. digitalization of their own company. Video-On-Demand provider Netflix started the mail-order business for physical film carriers when the company lost the battle in the shop-based video rental business against the top dog of that time, Blockbuster. With the advent of the Internet and the digitalization of film carriers,

Netflix is changing to an Internet company and completely discontinues its mail-order business.

14.5   Conclusion

Due to the characteristics described in this section, individual digital platforms have developed into dominant market forces in recent years and it appears that competitors from traditional companies or new start-ups appear to struggle to catch up. In the past, however, there have been cases in which the emergence of a new technology or a superior customer understanding has led to the replacement of leading platforms. Especially the aspect of customer understanding associated with the network effects that are so relevant on platforms is an enormously important factor (Meyer and Lehnerd 2012). One example that illustrates this is eBay, the American retail platform, which attempted to enter the Chinese market. By taking over the eCommerce platform EachNet, which was dominant at the time, eBay apparently created optimal conditions for quickly conquering the Chinese market. It turned out, however, that eBay made a fatal mistake with regard to the customer group on the platform. While business growth in America was driven primarily by fashion products and consumer goods, high-tech and specialized products dominated trade on EachNet. Through strategic intervention, eBay attempted to expand the offering on EachNet to include fashion and consumer goods, but this had a negative impact. Both existing customers with an interest in technology and new suppliers of fashion items could not get along with each other, so the platform became uninteresting for both groups. Taobao, a start-up of the Alibaba Group, recognized the market potential of a trading platform for fashion and consumer goods at a time when the company could no longer compete with EachNet in the technical area. By initially focusing on the right customer and supplier groups, Taobao managed to replace EachNet and eBay as the dominant platform. In the context of innovation environments, digital platforms play an important role in that they can provide the basis for collaborative innovation processes. One example of this is the mobile operating systems iOS and Android. The software development environments and the respective connected marketplace offer innovators an excellent environment to implement, test and offer their own proposals. On the other hand, innovation platforms such as Jovoto can act as an innovation ecosystem in their own right. At Jovoto, partners invite tenders to solve specific problems, which are then addressed by the platform participants with concrete solution ideas. The reinforcement takes the form of a bonus for the winner or winners. In conclusion, given the current relevance of the topic for established companies and start-ups alike, a basic understanding of digital platforms is of equal importance when it comes to building a scalable and sustainably profitable business model around a service or product innovation.

The key lessons from this chapter are the following:

1. digital platforms, in their less capital-intensive and rapidly scalable character, are a powerful model for rapidly gaining market share in currently linearly organized markets.
2. in order to build and successfully operate a digital platform, it is important to know the key platform components and select them correctly. Furthermore, it is important to follow principles of success such as data-driven decision-making or focusing on core competencies.
3. in times of rapid technological change, the selection of the right customer group with the right value proposition is essential for success of any business model.

References

Alstyne MWV, Schrage M (2016, August 2) The best platforms are more than matchmakers. Harvard Business Review. https://hbr.org/2016/08/the-best-platforms-are-more-than-matchmakers

Baldwin CY, Woodard CJ (2008) The architecture of platforms: a unified view. Harvard Business School Finance Working Paper No. 09-034. https://doi.org/10.2139/ssrn.1265155

Boudreau K (2010) Open platform strategies and innovation: granting access vs. devolving control. Manag Sci 56(10):1849–1872. https://doi.org/10.1287/mnsc.1100.1215

Choudary SP (2015) Platform scale: How an emerging business model helps startups build large empires with minimum investment, 1st edn. Platform Thinking Labs Pte. Ltd

Constantinides P, Henfridsson O, Parker GG (2018) Introduction-platforms and infrastructures in the digital age. Inf Syst Res 29(2):381–400. https://doi.org/10.1287/isre.2018.0794

Cusumano MA, Gawer A, Yoffie DB (2019) The business of platforms: Strategy in the age of digital competition, innovation, and power, 1st edn. Harper Business, an imprint of HarperCollinsPublishers

Evans DS (2003) Some empirical aspects of multi-sided platform industries. SSRN Electronic Journal. https://doi.org/10.2139/ssrn.447981

Evans DS, Schmalensee R (2016) Matchmakers: the new economics of multisided platforms. Harvard Business Review Press

Gawer A (2011) Platforms, markets and innovation. Edward Elgar Publishing

Gawer A (2014) Bridging differing perspectives on technological platforms: toward an integrative framework. Res Policy 43(7):1239–1249. https://doi.org/10.1016/j.respol.2014.03.006

Gawer A, Cusumano MA (2014) Industry platforms and ecosystem innovation: platforms and innovation. J Prod Innov Manag 31(3):417–433. https://doi.org/10.1111/jpim.12105

Iansiti M, Lakhani KR (2020) Competing in the age of AI: strategy and leadership when algorithms and networks run the world. Harvard Business Review Press

Khosla S, Sawhney M (2014) Fewer, bigger, bolder: from mindless expansion to focused growth. Penguin

Libert B, Beck M, Wind J (2016) The network imperative: how to survive and grow in the age of digital business models. Harvard Business Review Press

Meyer MH, Lehnerd AP (2012) The power of product platforms: building value and cost leadership. The Free Press

Parker G, Van Alstyne M, Choudary SP (2016) Platform revolution: how networked markets are transforming the economy and how to make them work for you, 1st edn. W. W. NORTON & COMPANY

Parker GG, Van Alstyne MW (2005) Two-sided network effects: a theory of information product design. Manag Sci 51(10):1494–1504. https://doi.org/10.1287/mnsc.1050.0400

Rochet J-C, Tirole J (2003) Platform competition in two-sided markets. J Eur Econ Assoc 1(4):990–1029. https://doi.org/10.1162/154247603322493212

Expatriate and Expat-Preneur Ecosystems: Innovation Spaces Away from Home

15

Alexander Ruthemeier

15.1 Expatriates: Who They Are and Why They Matter

An expatriate is a person, who leaves their familiar environment in their home country behind, to live either temporarily or permanently in another country (Kraimer et al. 2001). Looking at closer differentiations, a distinction can be made into those expatriates that moved abroad because they were sent there by their employers on the one side and self-initiated expatriates on the other side (Doherty et al. 2011). The latter, research shows, do so for various reasons—for improving their general quality of life, for improving their economic situation, for studying abroad or for a wide variety of other, personal reasons. Actually, in many cases various combinations of these factors seem to interplay. In general, the research on expatriates in most cases focuses on people of above average education, thus, skilled individuals who can contribute to the economic development of their host-country (Roberts 2015).

The present book chapter aims at analyzing, how these highly skilled individuals can contribute to the emergence of so-called innovation spaces. As such, for the sake of this chapter, start-ups and their ecosystems are defined. This brings the focus of this chapter to a more narrow, distinctive term: The Expat-preneur ecosystem, a subset of both the ecosystem of entrepreneurs and the one of expatriates. Expat-preneurs, who are in the focus of interest here, are defined as typically self-initiated expatriates who found a company in their host-country, either immediately, thus after migrating with the founding intention, or after living there already (Vance et al. 2016). This group of individuals is considered to be strong innovators and successful start-up founders, however—they also face a certain set of challenges.

A. Ruthemeier (✉)
Expatrio, Berlin, Germany
e-mail: alex@ruthemeier.com

V. Nestle et al. (eds.), *Creating Innovation Spaces*, Management for Professionals, https://doi.org/10.1007/978-3-030-57642-4_15

If those challenges can be overcome or—optimally—reduced altogether, expat-preneurs should be able to not only boost their own economic success but also the one of their host countries.

15.2 Ecosystems

15.2.1 Ecosystems and Their Relevance: An Economic Observation

Jackson (2011) compares ecosystems in the economic context to those found in a biological setting: "The biological ecosystem is a system that includes all living organisms (biotic factors) in an area as well as its physical environments (abiotic factors) functioning together as a unit. It is characterized by one or more equilibrium states, where a relatively stable set of conditions exist to maintain a population or nutrient exchange at desirable levels." (p. 1). In a similar vein, the author argues an economic or societal ecosystem to work—it is shaped by the agents active in it and their relationship. In an optimal case, it can be argued, such an ecosystem reaches an equilibrium. Relevant actors therein are not all living organisms, but only those relevant for the particular system. On the topic of an *innovation ecosystem* or a so-called *innovation space*, human agents, thus, human capital, institutions and organizations can be named alongside other resources such as materials or infrastructure. The general structure and organization of the ecosystem in which an agent is active influences the strategy that should be chosen to succeed (Adner 2006). However, it has to be noted that one agent—be it an individual or an organization—is not limited to being active in one ecosystem but can be at the same time part of multiple—partially even overlapping—ecosystems.

When discussing the importance of ecosystems for expatriates, the term *social capital* cannot be omitted. Research shows, that social capital, thus the connections a person has and can use for their own success, tends to be an important predictor of entrepreneurial success in general (Anderson et al. 2007) and a factor closely linked to innovation (Thompson 2018). This seems especially true for expatriates, as the following section will explain in further detail.

15.2.2 Expatriate Ecosystem: Challenges and Chances

On the basis of numerous publications and research studies, the conditions that are cited as the cause of and contributing to the numerous migration thrusts or "migration waves" can be named as follows: general political and (world) economic conditions, new technologies, poverty, ethnic conflicts, global capitalism, racism, nation-building and (in some cases predominantly) the situation on the labour market (Pries 1996; Modood and Salt 2011).

Increasing cross-border migration is even seen as a natural consequence of a lack of attractive job opportunities in the migrants' countries of origin at a time when other economies are not sufficiently filling their skills gaps. The concept of

Skill Biased Technological Change is particularly relevant here (Card and DiNardo 2002).

This development will be favored by a number of other trends: Various factors, such as the ever-increasing digitalization, are giving rise to new and increasingly diverse forms of work, such as cloud collaboration, co-working spaces and home offices, both internationally and in heavily industrialized countries. The resulting changes in (customer) needs are also leading to a growing demand for new business models, which must guarantee high flexibility and spontaneous solution strategies and products (Balleer and Van Rens 2013; Jaumotte et al. 2013).

Expatriate ecosystems are also shaped by their relations to other ecosystems, such as the one of the host-countries. In the migration system approach, the dynamics of migration processes are seen in the context of economic, political, social and demographic factors, which can create a link between the nation of origin and the destination nation as a so-called *migration system*, that takes not only the host nation into consideration (Fawcett 1989). A specific feature of this theory is that migration is seen as a dynamic process in which both end points of the so-called migration flow are considered in terms of mutual differences but also dependencies. The approach is also based on different types and combinations of the already mentioned connection(s), which can be of the tangible, regulatory or relational type. These different types of connections in migration systems can also be assigned to different categories (state, mass cultural, within (family) networks and migrant agencies) (Fawcett 1989).

In contrast to the migration system approach, which makes an important contribution to the classification of the overall connections between different levels in the systems described, the so-called network approaches place the social emigration and immigration networks in the foreground of any considerations (Faist 1995). The influences of social networks, kinship relations and social capital on migration processes are undisputed and, precisely because of the social aspect of a personal relationship between migrants in the countries of origin and destination, lead to an increased probability of international labour migration and possibly to a chain migration. Social contacts are also among the factors that maintain migration flows.

In these regards, a connection can be seen to the idea of expatriate ecosystems, as proposed by Ruthemeier (2018). These ecosystems of tightly connected expats exist both in an online and an offline world—expatriates tend to be linked strongly to each other, forming their own community. This community, Ruthemeier (2018) was able to show, benefit not only the expatriates themselves, who by being part of such a group can gain social capital, a much-needed resource as Lee and Van Vorst (2010) show, but also the society itself (Ruthemeier 2018). Expatriates increase the number of employees in a society and thus have a positive influence on a rising gross domestic product (GDP). Furthermore, in many cases, expatriates bring with them a diverse repertoire of skills that often fit well with the skills of the local workforce and are able to supplement those existing skills. The human capital that grows in this way benefits the host country. An example of this development is the US, where expatriates have made a significant contribution to the growing research and development (Ruthemeier 2018).

Both these approaches and the pragmatic description of the advantages of expat ecosystems proposed by Ruthemeier (2018) highlight the importance of ecosystems, while subsequently pointing out, that ecosystems are not closed systems but rather connected ones, that are related to each other.

15.2.3 Expat-Preneur Ecosystem: At the Intersection of Entrepreneurs and Expatriates

The previous sections of this chapter described the role expatriates take on within their host economies and societies and the way the ecosystem can be linked to others. One of these roles of expatriates shall be described in further detail—the role they take on as entrepreneurs. While the description of the expatriate ecosystem put a strong focus on self-initiated and assigned expatriates and on the circumstances many expatriates are facing in their host companies and countries, expat-preneurs as defined by Vance, McNulty, Paik and D'Mello (2016) form a distinctive group and one of increasing relevance as research on the subject shows: They are described as *ideal migrants* and typically stem from higher educational backgrounds, often with experience in the fields of engineering or research (van Rooij and Margaryan 2019). Individuals like this immigrate into their host country, where they subsequently—either immediately or later on—found a company or become active as freelancers—and often do so with strong success, given their previous experiences and educational backgrounds (Vance et al. 2016).

In terms of ecosystems, expat-preneurs can be considered to be subset of not only one but two ecosystems—while this book chapter mostly focuses on the ecosystem of expatriates, for expat-preneurs a second ecosystem seems relevant: the one of entrepreneurs in general. Figure 15.1 shows the presumed relationship between those ecosystems and the expat-preneurs position within.

The expat-preneur ecosystem is therefore defined to be at the intersection of the Start-Up Ecosystem on the one hand and the Entrepreneur Ecosystem on the other hand. As expat-preneurs are entrepreneurs with an expatriate background, their ecosystem also stems from these two groups: The expat-preneur ecosystem is the overlap of the entrepreneur ecosystem and the expatriate ecosystem.

Thus, it can be assumed, that expat-preneurs should also gain their social capital from both these ecosystems. This claim is supported by research such as the one by Brixy, Sternberg and Vorderwülbecke (2011) who show, that expat-preneurs are a

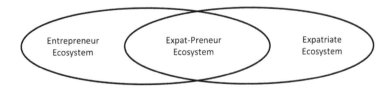

Fig. 15.1 The expat-preneur ecosystem. (Source: Author)

tightly knit group. While in general it can be argued that the lack of social capital can be a challenging factor for expatriates in general, especially in countries scoring not high on tolerance or openness, this does not seem to be completely true for this subset of expatriates: the group of expat-preneurs seems to be more interwoven and thus having stronger inter-relationships than the general group of entrepreneurs, which might pose an important success factor for this group of founders.

However, the social capital aspect also poses a great threat to expat-preneurs, as authors such as Suchkov (2018) point out: Immigrants—even highly skilled ones—tend to have difficulties connecting to the general ecosystem (thus other social and economic groups) of their host-country and thus often lack relevant connections that would benefit their entrepreneurial success and chances.

In this respect, reference is made on the one hand to the basic legal framework, which can be aggravating for immigration. Language barriers as well as potential cultural differences or a lack of openness of the host culture can also be challenging. This affects, for example, negotiations with customers, partners and suppliers, which are typically more difficult for expatriates than for other groups of entrepreneurs. Expat-preneurs in particular and expatriates in general also have difficulties in obtaining relevant information due to this lack of networking within the general entrepreneurial ecosystem, which in turn can be attributed to limited language skills in the host language or a lack of information in English (Suchkov 2018).

15.3 Innovation in the Expatriate Ecosystem

15.3.1 Innovation and Start-Ups: Requirements and Circumstances

Innovation is (not only but especially) important for start-ups. Schweer and Sahl (2017) accordingly describe start-ups as the core drivers of innovation in modern economies. Using their disruptive innovation approach is a strategy that can be used by other companies in order to foster their own innovation (Weiblen and Chesbrough 2015). Given this highly innovative atmosphere in which most start-ups exist, it comes as no surprise that many of them also stem from accordingly innovative branches with a high level of digitisation. Typical industries of successful start-ups are FinTech (Puschmann 2017), Social Media (Ghezzi et al. 2016) or CryptoCurrency (Cohen 2017). A study conducted by PWC (2016) confirms that young companies tend to be leaders in the field of digital transformation and, thus, are stronger digitalised than companies that are already older. With start-ups being the core drivers of innovation and digital transformation (Schweer and Sahl 2017), it becomes clear what an important role digital aspects play for start-ups. The successful focus on clients and their needs and the usage of digital means to fulfil these needs are described to be leading success factors in start-ups (Earley 2017).

One of the drivers of innovative output is the contemporary technological advancement itself, as can be argued with regards to services such as cloud-computing and an abundance of online available software. Labelled under the term *technology entrepreneurship,* these developments can be of special relevance for start-ups, as these approaches can significantly reduce hiring and fixed costs expenditures—thus addressing one of the core challenges many entrepreneurs and start-uppers face: the financial factor. By employing cloud technology and similar solutions, start-ups can approach new projects in a more flexible way. The example of As-A-Service-solutions clarify the way modern technologies and business models can strongly influence or even enable start-ups' success.

The term Infrastructure-as-a-Service (IAAP) covers a range of services that allow companies to rent computer infrastructure instead of buying it. Similar to other as-a-service approaches, the aim is to have corresponding services available on demand. This means that infrastructure no longer has to be purchased directly and correspondingly maintained, updated and secured internally, but can be rented as a service from external partners who specialize in precisely these solutions (Serrano et al. 2015).

This leads to a number of advantages especially for entrepreneurs, which are particularly reflected in the flexibility: Innovative approaches, new solutions, new products can be developed much more easily if new infrastructure does not have to be purchased for each new product or corresponding adaptations to the existing infrastructure have to be made. This results in increased scalability for entrepreneurs—both with regard to the new developments mentioned above and to changes in demand in existing areas (Ibrahim and Hemayed 2019). While these advantages seem to hold true for more establishes companies as well, it seems especially relevant for start-ups—as they typically lack financial resources as well as personal resources, ways to conduct lean innovation projects without the need for investments into infrastructure seem to be an important factor.

Such new ventures usually face one main challenge: finance (Audretsch et al. 2015). In the first phase after the foundation, in which in the best case the growth begins, such ventures are often mainly financed by the investors, known in the international context as the Three F's: Family, friends and fools. In this financially particularly difficult phase, it is a great added value for young entrepreneurs to be able to concentrate on their actual product or solution without having to focus on building their own server infrastructure. This is not just a financial distinction: Of course, own infrastructures are significantly more expensive than on-demand models, especially for start-ups, but the more serious issue here is the management and maintenance or control of such infrastructures. Personnel resources resulting from such processes also represent a potential burden for start-ups and other new businesses.

The time and energy seem to be better invested in the development of highly innovative products for which start-ups are known. Relevant studies show that the high flexibility and agility of start-ups seems to be their greatest advantage. Products and solutions are developed in an agile way and open innovation and collaboration are not foreign words. This makes start-ups the driving force in the development of new, innovative solutions. Start-ups are even described as the leading innovators, which can also inspire larger and more experienced companies. It is therefore all the more important, not only for the start-ups themselves but for the economic system as a whole, that start-ups and start-ups find the framework conditions that allow them precisely this flexibility and agility. On-demand or as-a-service solutions help start-ups to keep their costs not only low, but above all to plan them transparently.

Frugal innovation, in this context, as coined by Zeschky, Widenmayer and Gassmann (2011), concerns not only technological innovation but also institutional and social innovation. While it is, thereby, clearly distinct from sustainable development itself, authors such as Brem and Ivens (2013) still argue that the concept of frugal innovation is closely linked to sustainability, as it provides a framework in which the development of sustainable products and solutions can strive. The shift needed in order to put a stronger focus on sustainable development is described by Gladwin, Kennelly and Krause as an urgent one away from techno-centrism and towards a more socially focused development.

These approaches point out the role start-ups and entrepreneurs play when it comes to innovation and the challenges (and subsequent solutions) of relevance here. As lean approaches and a high-risk affinity are described to be general characteristics of start-ups and major resources when it comes to fostering innovation (Weiblen and Chesbrough 2015; Spender et al. 2017) it seems crucial to establish environments and circumstances in which they can foster. In order to so, it is important to identify the reasons, why start-ups tend to be so innovative—a closer look at the typical personality of entrepreneurs and of their approaches towards innovation is therefore heavily suggested. As start-ups more than other companies rely on collaborative approaches, often summarized under the term *open innovation* (Spender et al. 2017), and more often take risks in approaching new ideas, they tend to create more innovative outcomes than most (Carlson and Usher 2016).

15.3.2 The Expatriate and Expat-Preneur Personality: Prone to Innovation and Risk-Affine

Research on expatriates in general shows, that they typically possess a distinctive personality. Kreutzer (2006) explains in these regards, that expatriates are on average more open towards new experiences and more curious about them. Being an assertive, probably even dominant and above average extraverted personality also is described to be a defining factor for many expatriates. This is even more true, when analyzing the successfulness of integrating in the host society and shaping and creating one's own life environment there: Certain personality factors such as extraversion and openness are there again described to be strong predictors of success (Ones and Viswesvaran 1997). As helpful this is also described when it comes to creating social connections or—as a broader concept—the aforementioned social capital. Extraverted and open individuals tend to adapt faster to the host culture and are able to tie new connections faster than others.

The introduction to this section explained from a psychological perspective, which factors make the typical expatriate personality unique. Special attention therein can be put on the concept of openness—a personality trait closely related to innovation. Authors such as Jauk, Benedek and Neubauer (2014) argue, that openness can be considered to be one of the main predictors of innovative outcomes.

Individuals scoring high on openness tend to be more active in the fields of art, tend to be more innovative and in general seem to prefer activities that require creativity.

Also, the concept of assertiveness comes to mind—expatriates tend to be more assertive (Harari et al. 2018), which even seems to be an important requirement to become an expatriate in the first place. Even in places described to be welcoming towards expatriates and that offer positive experiences for them, a comparatively large number of various challenges needs to be overcome in order to build a successful and happy life (Kim and Tung 2013; Tahir and Ismail 2007).

Looking at these prototypical personality traits opens up a possible explanation for the aforementioned statement, that expatriates tend to become expat-preneurs more often that one might expect and that expat-preneurs tend to be successful innovators (Metzger 2016). Expat-preneurs therefore seem to differ in part from other entrepreneurs—an empirical study has shown that migrants are more likely to become active than other people and that they face more social challenges. However—as this discrepancy shows—they were less deterred by these (perceived) challenges from starting their own business (Metzger 2016).

As they typically possess certain personality traits that are not required but implied by their willful migration, they might also put them to use in other areas of life. It seems, that the personality traits needed to successfully and happily become an expatriate coincide with those that are needed to become a successful entrepreneur, as studies on entrepreneur personality show: Entrepreneurs are typically more open towards new experiences, more assertive and more risk-seeking or at least risk-tolerant than the average person (Nybakk and Hansen 2008). A similar observation can be made for expatriates themselves, as recent research shows (Selmer and Lauring 2010).

It is also argued that the tendency of migrants to found a company is also a consequence of a self-selection process. According to Brixy, Sternberg and Vorderwülbecke (2011) the individual decision of an Expatriate to move to Germany is a self-selective process. Most migrants leave their home country in the hope of finding better economic conditions in their host-country, of earning a higher income and achieving greater prosperity. Accordingly, expat-preneurs are characterized by a number of personality traits that should have a positive influence on the propensity to found a company. In particular, high performance, self-confidence and a low risk aversion are mentioned as important aspects in this respect. This observation from Germany also corresponds with the assessment in the international specialist literature: expat-preneurs are thus characterised by a higher degree of proactivity, more flexibility, higher expectations of self-efficacy and a conviction of internal control (Selmer et al. 2018).

Thus, it comes as no surprise to see statistics that indicate, that expatriates become entrepreneurs more often than other individuals (Efendic and Yetis 2013). It also does not seem to be a surprise, that regions with a strong expat-preneur ecosystem, such as Berlin or Singapore, also are becoming innovation hubs (see Sect. 15.4; Ruthemeier 2018). Environments influenced by the collaboration of entrepreneurs—typically highly innovative personalities themselves anyway—

stemming from different culture, thus combining different perspectives, seem to be excellent innovation spaces.

The positive influence expatriates (and subsequently expat-preneurs) can have on innovation outcomes is also highlighted by research on diversity in general. Based on this approach it seems that not only the expat-personality, that is shaped by openness and assertiveness, but also the diversity brought by expatriates itself can offer an important contribution. Diversity itself, authors such as Nathan and Lee (2013) argue, can on all levels positively influence innovation. Diversity and the different points of view it brings along, is considered to be a valuable source of creativity and innovation alike. However, diversity also needs the *right* management approaches and circumstances to flourish in regards to these positive outcomes— mismanagement and a lack of openness and tolerance can have hindering effects (Bassett-Jones 2005). Diversity can not only influence the innovativeness of companies or teams, but also the one of a whole ecosystem, such as a city or a region, Feldman and Audretsch (1999) show.

15.4 Examples of Expatriate Ecosystems

15.4.1 Singapore: Innovation and Expat Hub, an Easy Place to Do Business

"Singapore is widely known as one of the top hubs for business and culture in Asia. Part of its reputation stems from the city-state being rated both as the second best country to conduct business globally and as one of the most competitive places to do business." (Startup Genome 2019a, b). Thus, it comes as little surprise, that a recent study also sees Singapore to be one of the most outstanding regions for start-ups to flourish. Being strongly connected not only locally in Asia but globally, Singapore presents itself as an attractive place for expat-preneurs. This strong connectedness is described to be among the key success factors that brought Singapore to the 14th most successful start-up hub worldwide, as a 2019 study revealed. This key-trait is supplemented by a startup tax exemption schemes, that are aiming at reducing the financial struggles of start-ups in the early phases. As a result, other analyses such as one conducted by The Economist (2014) see Singapore as "the world's most tightly packed entrepreneurial ecosystem, and a perfect place to study the lengths to which a government can go to support startup colonies". Subsequently, Singapore is also considered to be one of the countries in the world, in which it is the easiest to do business—currently ranking on place number 2 in the world for the overall business conduction and number 4 when it comes to the easiness of starting a business (Straitstimes.com 2019). Singapore, therefore, so it seems, managed to create an environment that makes it easy for new start-ups to flourish—a challenge necessary for a country depending so strongly on innovation and new business as Singapore.

Typical start-ups in Singapore stem from the high-technology fields with a strong focus on Blockchain and Fintech. Start-up hubs such as *Block 71* and

JTC LanuchPad help making Singapore one of the most attractive locations for entrepreneurs and for investors alike. The strong focus on innovative start-ups is partially explained by the necessity to actually put exactly this focus: Singapore is considered to be a comparatively small country with a limited amount of natural resources. In order to build its wealth, thus, the country has to focus on creating an environment that attracts foreign investments and innovative solutions in order to thrive (Hospitalitynet 2019).

In order to fulfill this strategic necessity, a government agency was founded in 2018 with the core goal to identify key challenges and enable start-ups to flourish more and more easily: "Enterprise Singapore is the government agency championing enterprise development. We work with committed companies to build capabilities, innovate and internationalise" (Enterprise Singapore 2020).

A good example for German initiatives in Singapore is the German Accelerator Southeast-Asia, with tight bounds to the Singaporean Government, the German Chambers of Commerce abroad (AHK) and the German Embassy Singapore. It helps German start-ups to make a market entry to Southeast Asia with workshops and networking in the region.

In addition to these structural support systems for start-ups, Singapore also manages to be an attractive place for expatriates, again ranking among the top destinations worldwide (Onlinecitizenasia.com 2019). Singapore, being attractive in many regards to expatriates, manages to attract top-talents from all over the world, thus improving the employee market not only for start-ups but for established companies and corporations alike. Despite the relatively high cost of living, expatriates tend to enjoy the high quality of life in Singapore and, again, the easiness to settle and conduct business, highlighting a culture of openness and inclusiveness (Straitstimes.com 2019). A highlight of this focus on expatriate and expat-preneur culture is the yearly expat-preneur award presented by The Finder in Singapore to honor the most out-standing expat-preneurs.

15.5 Lessons Learned and Outlook

Research on social capital can be pointed out to be of strong relevance for expat-preneurs, a group of potential innovators. Social capital is relevant for entrepreneurs in general and seems to be of a very particular relevance to expat-preneurs: While it can be shown that they in general *lack* social capital and are less integrated in national business networks, their ecosystem (the expat-preneur ecosystem as described throughout this chapter) itself provides them with a vast amount of social capital—expat-preneurs are throughout research and practical observations described to be a group well connected both on a regional and on an international level. A high level of support within this group can be observed which also allows for international mobility—given a high level of digitalization of start-ups in this group, international connectivity and mobility seem to be one of the major success factors.

One of the reasons why the ecosystem of expat-preneurs is described to be as of such high relevance to the general economic development was shown throughout this chapter—expat-preneurs seem to be a group of highly innovative individuals. Expat-preneur hubs such as Singapore, a place widely known and respected for being attractive regions for founders and expatriates alike, are also innovation hubs, responsible for big amounts of creative outputs, new solutions and innovative business models.

From the author's point of view, this can be explained by two main reasons: First, the typical expat-preneur personality seems to be a strong match for innovative output: Assertive, open, extraverted individuals who tend to have made a wide variety of different life experiences seem well fitted to be active in highly innovative environments and to accordingly generate innovative outcomes. These outcomes can be seen as general drivers of economic innovation (Freeman and Engel 2007; Weiblen and Chesbrough 2015).

Second, the concept of diversity can be mentioned in regard to innovative outcomes: Innovation seems to happen easier in diverse settings that inspire the sharing of different experiences, approaches and philosophies. This can be shown from different perspectives even outside the realms of entrepreneurship, where team compositions driven by diversity in regard to personality or culture can be seen as important drivers of innovation and creativity (Bassett-Jones 2005; McLeod et al. 1996).

However, for both these explanations it seems relevant, that certain circumstances and environments are needed, for innovation to strive instead of conflicts to arise. Research on diversity in teams, for example (Shachaf 2008) is able to show, that it can also lead to communication problems, conflicts and general performance issues. Whether innovative and in general successful outcomes or problematic scenarios arise from diversity-shaped collaborations seems to depend strongly on the management of such collaborations and on the circumstances (Bassett-Jones 2005). Again, the role of openness cannot be over-estimated: Openness towards new experiences and new cultures is an important factor for successful collaborations in this field. Also, openness in general is an important factor for innovation, research shows.

Concludingly, throughout this chapter a number of challenges and chances for the expat-preneur ecosystem and the individuals within it could be observed. These are depicted in Fig. 15.2. While this list does not claim comprehensiveness, it gives an overview over some of the subjects relevant to the question, whether the ecosystem described throughout this work will live up to its high expectations or be shaped by challenges and problems.

This again points out the importance of creating the right circumstances for expat-preneurs to strive in: While they seem to do well in creating and shaping their own ecosystem, a country, a society, or a region has to be open enough to allow for the growth of such an ecosystem and to allow this ecosystem to integrate itself into the overall ecosystem of entrepreneurs. Doing so allows for increased economic growth—especially due to the highly innovative nature of many start-ups in general and those of expat-preneurs in general.

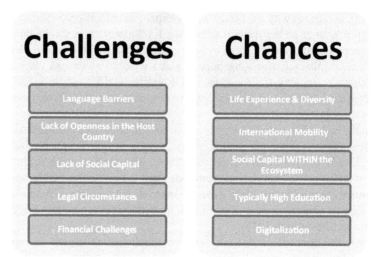

Fig. 15.2 Chances and challenges. (Source: Author)

A gaze towards Singapore, as it was described within this book chapter, clearly shows, that this strategy seems to be viable: Singapore founded a government agency with the clear purpose to foster innovation and internationalization, thus, acknowledging the relatedness between those two concepts. A country that relies economically so strongly on innovative business models and start-ups is clearly dependent on expat-preneurs, who contribute sustainably to creating an innovation space.

The present work discussed three different, though overlapping groups—expatriates, entrepreneurs and expat-preneurs. What seems true after this analysis is, that these groups seem to be able to strongly contribute to innovation spaces and to innovative outcomes. However, it can also be summarized, that the right circumstances do play an important role. The present work discussed this from two different perspectives—a technological one and a societal one. The societal perspective was described on the example of innovation and start-up hub Singapore. More than most countries, Singapore manages to create the right institutional and societal circumstances for innovation to flourish. The second perspective chosen to highlight the importance of circumstantial factors was the technological one. This book chapter described how modern, digital approaches like as-a-service-solutions can help start-ups create more innovative output. Fostering such approaches both on a company and a society level seems therefore imperative in order to help entrepreneurs to accelerate and innovation spaces to succeed.

References

Adner R (2006) Match your innovation strategy to your innovation ecosystem. Harv Bus Rev 84(4):98

Anderson A, Park J, Jack S (2007) Entrepreneurial social capital: conceptualizing social capital in new high-tech firms. Int Small Bus J 25(3):245–272

Audretsch DB, Heger D, Veith T (2015) Infrastructure and entrepreneurship. Small Bus Econ 44(2):219–230

Balleer A, Van Rens T (2013) Skill-biased technological change and the business cycle. Rev Econ Stat 95(4):1222–1237

Bassett-Jones N (2005) The paradox of diversity management, creativity and innovation. Creat Innov Manag 14(2):169–175

Brem A, Ivens B (2013) Do frugal and reverse innovation foster sustainability? Introduction of a conceptual framework. J Technol Manag Grow Econ 4(2):31–50

Brixy U, Sternberg R, Vorderwülbecke A (2011) Unternehmensgründungen von Migranten: Ein Weg zur ökonomischen und sozialen Integration (No. 8/2011). IAB-Kurzbericht

Card D, DiNardo JE (2002) Skill-biased technological change and rising wage inequality: some problems and puzzles. J Labor Econ 20(4):733–783

Carlson M, Usher N (2016) News startups as agents of innovation: for-profit digital news startup manifestos as metajournalistic discourse. Digit Journal 4(5):563–581

Cohen B (2017) Post-capitalist entrepreneurship: startups for the 99%. Productivity Press

Doherty N, Dickmann M, Mills T (2011) Exploring the motives of company-backed and self-initiated expatriates. Int J Hum Resour Manag 22(03):595–611

Earley S (2017) The evolving role of the CDO. IT Prof 19(1):64–69. https://doi.org/10.1109/mitp.2017.4

Economist (2014) All together now. https://www.economist.com/special-report/2014/01/16/all-together-now. Accessed 24 June 2020

Efendic N, Yetis Z (2013) Exploring expatriate entrepreneurship (summary). Front Entrepreneurship Res 33(15):3

Enterprise Singapore (2020) About enterprise Singapore. https://www.enterprisesg.gov.sg/about-us/overview. Accessed 24 June 2020

Faist T (1995) A preliminary analysis of political-institutional aspects of international migration: internationalization, transnationalization, and internal globalization. ZeS arbeitspapier, 10/19

Fawcett JT (1989) Networks, linkages, and migration systems. Int Migr Rev 23(3):671–680

Feldman MP, Audretsch DB (1999) Innovation in cities:: science-based diversity, specialization and localized competition. Eur Econ Rev 43(2):409–429

Freeman J, Engel JS (2007) Models of innovation: startups and mature corporations. Calif Manag Rev 50(1):94–119

German Accelerator, Our Southeast Asia Program. https://www.germanaccelerator.com/our-programs/southeast-asia/. Accessed 30 June 2020

Ghezzi A, Gastaldi L, Lettieri E, Martini A, Corso M (2016) A role for startups in unleashing the disruptive power of social media. Int J Inf Manag 36(6):1152–1159

Harari MB, Reaves AC, Beane DA, Laginess AJ, Viswesvaran C (2018) Personality and expatriate adjustment: a meta-analysis. J Occup Organ Psychol 91(3):486–517

Hospitalitynet (2019) Singapore startup ecosystem: an entrepreneur's paradise? https://www.hospitalitynet.org/news/4095363.html. Accessed 22 June 2020

Ibrahim FA, Hemayed EE (2019) Trusted cloud computing architectures for infrastructure as a service: survey and systematic literature review. Comput Secur 82:196–226

Jackson DJ (2011) What is an innovation ecosystem. Natl Sci Found 1(2)

Jauk E, Benedek M, Neubauer AC (2014) The road to creative achievement: a latent variable model of ability and personality predictors. Eur J Personal 28(1):95–105

Jaumotte F, Lall S, Papageorgiou C (2013) Rising income inequality: technology, or trade and financial globalization? IMF Econ Rev 61(2):271–309

Kim HD, Tung RL (2013) Opportunities and challenges for expatriates in emerging markets: an exploratory study of Korean expatriates in India. Int J Hum Resour Manag 24(5):1029–1050

Kraimer ML, Wayne SJ, Jaworski RAA (2001) Sources of support and expatriate performance: the mediating role of expatriate adjustment. Pers Psychol 54(1):71–99

Kreutzer F (2006) Becoming an expatriate: die transnationale Karriere eines dual-career couple. In: Transnationale Karrieren. VS Verlag für Sozialwissenschaften, pp 34–63

Lee LY, Van Vorst D (2010) The influences of social capital and social support on expatriates' cultural adjustment: an empirical validation in Taiwan. Int J Manag 27(3):628

McLeod PL, Lobel SA, Cox TH Jr (1996) Ethnic diversity and creativity in small groups. Small Group Res 27(2):248–264

Metzger G (2016) Migranten überdurchschnittlich gründungsaktiv–Arbeitsmarkt spielt große Rolle. KfW Research, Fokus Volkswirtschaft

Modood T, Salt J (2011) Global migration, ethnicity and Britishness. In: Global migration, ethnicity and Britishness. Palgrave Macmillan, London, pp 248–268

Nathan M, Lee N (2013) Cultural diversity, innovation, and entrepreneurship: firm-level evidence from London. Econ Geogr 89(4):367–394

Nybakk E, Hansen E (2008) Entrepreneurial attitude, innovation and performance among Norwegian nature-based tourism enterprises. Forest Policy Econ 10(7–8):473–479

Ones DS, Viswesvaran C (1997) Personality determinants in the prediction of aspects of expatriate job success. In: Aycan Z (ed) New approaches to employee management, Vol. 4. Expatriate management: theory and research. Elsevier Science/JAI Press, pp 63–92

Onlinecitizenasia.com (2019) Expat-insider survey Singapore. https://www.onlinecitizenasia.com/2019/09/06/expat-insider-survey-singapore-ranks-6th-out-of-64-destinations-worldwide/. Accessed 24 June 2020

Pries L (1996) Transnationale Soziale Räume. Theoretisch-empirische Skizze am Beispiel der Arbeitswanderung Mexiko-USA. Z Soziol 25:437–453

Puschmann T (2017) Fintech. Bus Inf Syst Eng 59(1):69–76

Roberts DC (2015) Expatriate workers in international higher education. J Coll Charact 16(1):37–43

PWC (2016) Industry 4.0: Building the digital enterprise. Retrieved

van Rooij N, Margaryan L (2019) Integration of "ideal migrants": Dutch lifestyle expat-preneurs in Swedish campgrounds. Rural Soc 28(3):183–197

Ruthemeier A (2018) Expatriates – im Ökosystem zu Hause in der Ferne. In: Plugmann P (ed) Innovationsumgebungen gestalten. Springer Gabler, Wiesbaden

Schweer D, Sahl JC (2017) The digital transformation of industry–the benefit for Germany. In: The drivers of digital transformation. Springer, Cham, pp 23–31

Selmer J, Lauring J (2010) Self-initiated academic expatriates: inherent demographics and reasons to expatriate. Eur Manag Rev 7(3):169–179

Selmer J, McNulty Y, Lauring J, Vance C (2018) Who is an expat-preneur? Toward a better understanding of a key talent sector supporting international entrepreneurship. J Int Entrep 16(2):134–149

Serrano N, Gallardo G, Hernantes J (2015) Infrastructure as a service and cloud technologies. IEEE Softw 32(2):30–36

Shachaf P (2008) Cultural diversity and information and communication technology impacts on global virtual teams: an exploratory study. Inf Manag 45(2):131–142

Spender JC, Corvello V, Grimaldi M, Rippa P (2017) Startups and open innovation: a review of the literature. Eur J Innov Manag 20(1):4–30

Startup Genome (2019a) Global ecosystem report. https://startupgenome.com/reports/global-startup-ecosystem-report-2019. Accessed 24 June 2020

Startup Genome (2019b) Singapore. https://startupgenome.com/ecosystems/singapore. Accessed 22 June 2020

Straitstimes.com (2019) Singapore dethroned by Switzerland as overall best place for expats but stays top for families: survey. https://www.straitstimes.com/business/economy/top-pay-sees-switzerland-dethrone-singapore-as-no-1-country-for-expats-hsbc-survey. Accessed 22 June 2020

Suchkov A (2018) New land of opportunity: premises and constraints for immigrant entrepreneur-ship in Sweden

Tahir AHM, Ismail M (2007) Cross-cultural challenges and adjustments of expatriates: a case study in Malaysia. Altern: Turk J Int Relat 6:72–99

Thompson M (2018) Social capital, innovation and economic growth. J Behav Exp Econ 73:46–52

Vance CM, McNulty Y, Paik Y, D'Mello J (2016) The expat-preneur: conceptualizing a growing international career phenomenon. J Global Mobility 4(2):202–224

Weiblen T, Chesbrough HW (2015) Engaging with startups to enhance corporate innovation. Calif Manag Rev 57(2):66–90

Zeschky M, Widenmayer B, Gassmann O (2011) Frugal innovation in emerging markets. Res Technol Manag 54(4):38–45

The Role of Law in Creating Space for
Innovation: An Example from the Healthcare
Sector in Germany

16

Roman Grinblat

16.1 Introduction

16.1.1 Current Relevance and Context

The urge for innovation is omnipresent and tangible. The relevance of the topic is clearly reflected in political programs at all levels. The EU Commission emphasizes the importance of innovation and promotes the "Innovation Union" as a flagship initiative for Europe (European Commission 2013). The TRIPS Agreement of the WTO mentions the "promotion of technological innovation" as a regulatory objective (Art. 7), and the OECD also repeatedly emphasises innovation as an objective (OECD 2020). The national government of Germany also targets the promotion of innovation (Bundesregierung 2018).

Innovation has long been the subject of various scientific disciplines. Independent disciplines of innovation research have been developed in economics, sociology, political science, psychology and the natural sciences (Engel and Morlok 1988; Towfigh and Petersen 2017). New disciplines such as neuroscience and creativity research are also adding new insights to the matter. However, the subject of "Innovation and Law" is not an independent or even in-depth subject of innovation research in Germany.

One of the few legal scholars in Germany dealing with innovation and law is the former Federal Constitutional Court judge Wolfgang Hoffman-Riem. He was the first in the German legal community to systematise legal innovation research (Hoffman-Riem 1997). His analyses cover a wide range of areas of law, including environmental law, telecommunications law, public procurement law and contract

R. Grinblat (✉)
Baden-Wuerttemberg Cooperative State University (DHBW), Heidenheim, Germany
e-mail: roman.grinbla@dhbw-heidenheim.de

law, in which the question of promoting innovation is discussed. However, a sector specific analysis of the type conducted in this chapter for the healthcare sector has not yet been conducted, leaving room for further research.

16.1.2 Definition of "Law" "Space" and "Innovation"

In order to discuss the role of law in creating space for innovation the terms "law", "space" and "innovation" must be defined.

16.1.2.1 Law

For the purposes of this chapter law includes not only national, international and European legal norms, but also sub-legislative regulations such as administrative regulations, case law and soft law.

16.1.2.2 Space

"Space" in this context is neither a physical or spatial concept nor a specific business area. Rather "space" is an environment allowing the creation, grow and spreading of innovations. It can include a multitude of different actors, such as consumers/patients, business stakeholders, political and other institutions such as research and educational institutions.

In literature the term "innovation ecosystem" is used (Glauner 2018; Grandstand and Holgerson 2020). This term is close to the understanding of "space" used in this chapter because an innovation ecosystem is characterised by a larger number of actors, where the actors are interconnected by exerting a mutual effect on each other. The members of an innovation ecosystem work cooperatively and competitively to support new products and services, to satisfy customer needs and to initiate the next round of innovation.

However, the understanding of "innovation spaces" used in this chapter differs from the "innovation ecosystem" in several respects. An innovation space is not necessarily product-driven or fixed on product innovation. It is not necessarily result driven and its evolution can affect social attitudes to a topic, which is not the primary goal of an innovation ecosystem. The normative incentive e.g. in the environmental law to introduce innovation can change a whole industry or even the point of view of a whole society. An innovation ecosystem in contrast does not contain millions of stakeholders or even the society as a whole.

16.1.2.3 Innovation

Depending on the discipline and its focus, the term innovation is defined differently (Hauschildt et al. 2016; Hoffman-Riem 1997; Mai 2014). This can perhaps serve as an explanation for the fact that, although innovation research has a long conceptual history (Godin 2015), to date there is neither a self-contained innovation theory nor a generally accepted definition of the concept of innovation (Hensel and Wirsam 2008). Based on the Latin word "innovatio", innovation means something new, renewal or novelty. Most contemporary definitions of 'innovation', seen as an outcome of a process, rest on two defining characteristics, a degree of newness or change and a degree of usefulness or success in application of the newness. 'New' could mean new to the world, a particular nation, a group or even one firm.

The degree of usefulness or success in application of the newness are very important as these aspects distinguish innovation from invention. In the context of legal innovation research, the degree of usefulness or success in application equate with significance (Hornung 2015). Significance can be based for example on the following criteria (Hoffman-Riem 2016):

- Importance for the development of the legal system
- Legally effective solution of problems
- Scope in terms of content and time
- Recognition by courts
- Value in the scientific discourse and legal practice

Finally, Hoffman-Riem's legal innovation theory distinguishes between innovation through law and innovation in law (Hoffman-Riem 2016). A good example is environmental law, where innovative environmental protection measures have also been stimulated by legal requirements and where novel legal instruments such as environmental certificates and tradable rights for emissions are used. These two types of innovation—external and internal legal innovation—influence and complement each other (Hoffman-Riem 2010).

16.1.3 The Importance of Law in Innovation Research

Before discussing the role of law in creating space for innovation on the example of the healthcare sector, it is worth analysing the status quo.

According to Hoffman-Riem it can be observed in practically all studies from non-legal disciplines that law does not become the subject of closer analysis or part of theory formation even in disciplines intensively influenced by law (Hoffman-Riem 2016). The situation is made more difficult by the fact that, as already mentioned, innovation research is not yet able to carry out a decidedly differentiated and in-depth analysis of the use and possibilities of law. This may be due to the fact that in non-legal innovation research the law is seen more as an obstacle or a "Black-Box" rather than an accelerator.

Often other disciplines overlook the fact that law bears responsibility for innovation. This responsibility is embedded in the constitutional framework and is concretized by principles such as freedom of competition and science, equal opportunities, health protection and the guarantee of human dignity (Eifert and Hoffmann-Riem 2009). In essence, legal innovation research is also concerned with enhancing the common welfare—consisting of individual, group and societal interests.

Despite the common core scholars on legal innovation argue that in order to deal with the specific function of law in or as an object of innovation processes, jurisprudential innovation research is largely dependent on itself (Hoffman-Riem 1997; Hoffman-Riem and Schneider 1998).

The situation in practice is different from that in academic discourse. In the healthcare sector large corporations, medium-sized companies as well as start-ups often need legal support for the introduction of innovation. It actually already starts in the development stage, during which, for example, IP law often plays a role, continues throughout the sales stage with drafting of contracts and ends with the diffusion of innovation (Rogers 2003). For the latter, amongst others data protection law, administrative law and liability law play an important role. Thus, there is a discrepancy between the stage of development of legal innovation research and the actual demand for legal advice and control of innovations. It would be advantageous if this gap were to be closed or at least narrowed.

This is particularly the case with innovations control, because not every innovation is automatically advantageous, as vividly illustrated by the example of the atomic bomb. In this respect, legal innovation management and responsibility as shown above has an extremely important role to play in the legal consultancy as well, e.g. regulation and advice on Genome-Editing such as CRISP/CAS 9 or TALEN technology (Transcription activator-like effector nuclease) (Deuring 2019; Bern 2020; Forum Bio-und Gentechnologie e.V. 2019).

16.2 German Healthcare System: A Normative Permanent Building Site for Innovation

The German healthcare system is a good example for illustrating the role of law in creating innovation spaces. Healthcare represents a highly socially relevant sector in which a wide range of companies and numerous groups of people are employed, much more than, for example, in the car industry (Statistisches Bundesamt 2020). Since 2017 healthcare expenditure in Germany has exceeded 1 billion euro per day (Statistisches Bundesamt 2020). It is an innovation-driven sector in which, for example, medical devices, in-vitro diagnostics, pharmaceuticals and bio-technology are subject to constant innovation pressure with partially average innovation cycles of 3 years (Medtech Europe 2018; BVmed 2007; VfA 2019; critical Glaeske and Ludwig 2018). The healthcare system is complex and has many sources of law, such as the German Social Security Code Book V (SGB V), the German Drug Law (AMG), German Medical Device Law (MPG) and European directives. This normative framework is subject to constant additions, deletions and revisions. Since its introduction in 1988 until the Medicines Restructuring Act (AMNOG of 22.12.2010), i.e. within 22 years, the SGB V has been amended more than 144 times. Thus, on average there has been a new amendment to the law every two months. The healthcare system can without hesitation be described as a permanent normative building site (Grinblat 2011). The amount of regulations allows an in-depth analysis of effects and consequences of the law on innovation spaces.

First, we need to note that when we talk about health care, we primarily mean the German statutory health insurance (SHI; Gesetzliche Krankenversicherung), which covers about 90 percent of the insured population an where health services and medical products are reimbursed. Already because of the quantitative reasons innovation for patients plays an important role in this area. Private health insurance is of secondary importance in this context, although it naturally forms also part of the dual health care system in Germany.

The German SHI "market" is geared towards a benefit-oriented and at the same time economical provision of care, as expressed in the provisions of the SGB V. Thus, the benefits made available to the insured must be sufficient, appropriate and economical and may not exceed what is necessary; the quality and effectiveness of the benefits must correspond to the generally recognised state of medical knowledge and take medical progress into account (§§ 2, 12 SGB V).

Although the German social security market can certainly be described as robust, it did not exactly shine with its excessive implementation of innovations in the statutory benefits catalogue (Bundesrechnungshof 2019). The best example is the development of electronic health records (EHRs). The electronic patient file (ePA) will not be able to store important diagnosis and treatment data until January 1, 2021, in order to make health data available to practitioners across disciplines and sectors. Same issue applies for the electronic medical chip cards which are used nationwide by all the SHI-insured and were until recently not able to store even a drug medication plan.

There are different reasons for this fact. Firstly, it is related to the historical development, as the SHI in Germany and the corresponding law is based on the nineteenth century Bismarckian system and the Reichsversicherungsordnung (RVO). Thus, until recently, the word "digital" was not even mentioned once in the SGB V.

Secondly the German health care is based on a "neo-corporatistic" system with numerous special interests consisting of doctors, hospitals and sickness funds. Together with the National Association of Statutory Health Insurance Physicians, the National Association of Statutory Health Insurance Dentists and the German Hospital Federation, the National Association of Statutory Health Insurance Funds forms the Federal Joint Committee (Gemeinsamer Bundesausschuss/G-BA) which decides on the specific benefits to be included in the statutory health insurance catalogue.

Thirdly the introduction of innovations is made more difficult by the fact that in Germany we have completely different access routes for innovations in the outpatient and the inpatient sectors. In the German outpatient sector, new types of services and products (so called Neue Untersuchungs- und Behandlungsmethode/NUB) in the SHI system are generally prohibited and subject to permission, i.e. everything new is prohibited until it has been expressly permitted (§ 135 para. 1 sen. 1 SGB V). The G-BA is responsible for granting permission (§ 91 SGB V). It decides, in the form of guidelines, which new method may be used under which conditions at the expense of the SHI system in order to ensure sufficient, appropriate and economical care for the insured (§ 92 SGB V). Until recently, the evaluation procedure leading up to the decision of the G-BA could still take many years (Deutscher Bundestag 2018).

For services provided in the inpatient sector, permission is generally granted (BSG v. 06.05.2009—B 6 A 1/08 R). This means that new services and products may be provided in hospitals without prior examination as long as the G-BA has not explicitly excluded them (§ 137c SGB V). The legislator's guiding principle is to ensure that patients have rapid access to innovations (Deutscher Bundestag 2015). In this respect, parts of the literature argue that the normative framework in the inpatient sector favours the introduction and dissemination of innovations in the SHI system more than in the outpatient sector (Arnold et al. 2000; Vera and Salge 2008; Häckl 2010). However, this does not correspond to practice, as there are currently only a few ways to perpetuate innovations in the inpatient sector. The reason for this is the remuneration modalities for the provision of services in hospitals.

16.3   Law Promoting Digitalisation in Healthcare: The New DGV

So how can it be that under the above-mentioned circumstances law can promote innovation in the social health insurance? Some authors believe that innovations in the health care system can hardly be shaped by law (Knieps 1996). The Digital Care Act (Digitale-Versorgungs-Gesetz/DGV) which came in to force on December 18, 2019 shows the opposite (Federal Ministry of Healthcare 2019).

Already on the first page under the heading "Problems and Goals", the draft stated that under the current legal framework, the German health care system is only adaptive and agile to a limited extent in implementing digital solutions and new innovative forms of cooperation (Deutscher Bundestag 2019). Therefore, continued legislative adjustments are necessary in order to adapt the structures of the health care system to the dynamics of digital transformation and the speed of innovation processes. A remarkably open self-criticism of the German legislator.

16.3.1 Reimbursement of Digital Health Innovations and Fast-Track Procedure

To achieve this goal, the law aims, among other things, to bring digital health applications rapidly into supply. According to §27 para 1 S. 2 Nr. 3 Var. 5, §33a para 1 S. 1 SGB V the medical treatment includes the provision of digital health applications. In addition, a new evaluation procedure was created by further regulation (Digitale-Gesundheitsanwendungen-Verordnung/DiGA; Federal Ministry of Healthcare 2020). The procedure is designed as a fast track and takes three months. In this time frame the manufacturer must prove safety, functional capability, quality, data protection and data security and in particular a positive benefit effects of the health application. If it is not possible to prove positive effects on health care provision within three-month, digital health applications can initially be included in health care provision for a limited period of twelve months. During this time, the positive effects of the supply must be proven. However, this 12-month period could be extended up to another 12 months under the circumstances of § 139e IV 7 SGB V.

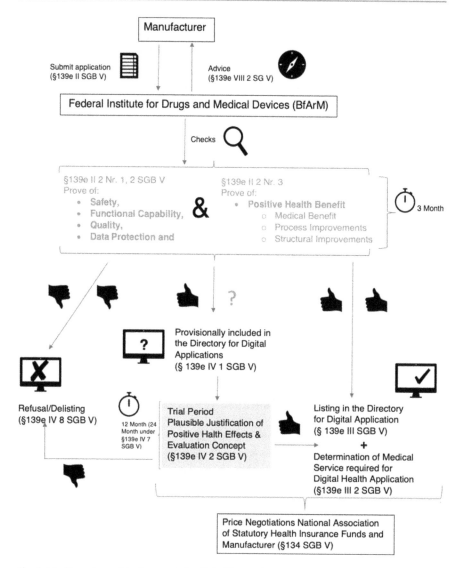

Fig. 16.1 Procedure of the fast-track for digital innovation. (Source: Author)

The responsible body for the approval procedure is the Federal Institute for Drugs and Medical Devices (BfArM). It also maintains an index of reimbursable digital health applications according to § 139e SGB V (BfArM 2020). For the overview and the relevant provisions of the fast-track procedure see Fig. 16.1.

The example of digital health apps illustrates at least three effects that law might have on innovation spaces.

- It has a direct steering effect on the innovative power of companies. With the prospect of cost reimbursement by health insurance companies and access to a potential 76 million insured people, start-ups in particular can receive venture capital and develop new products and/or develop existing products further.
- It accelerates network effects and cluster formation. Small, medium and large companies can join forces to penetrate the health care market. Especially as the financial risk is reduced by the bridging of 12 months.
- After all, the law contributes to a positive basic attitude or at least a rethinking of innovation among some stakeholders. Insured persons, doctors, health insurances and companies have to deal with the topic for various reasons. Irrespective of the outcome of this engagement process, the normative framework thus lowers the hurdles for a discourse on the topic.

In addition, the fast-track procedure shows very clear an internal legal innovation. This procedure has been newly anchored in the law and accelerates the introduction but also the dissemination of digital innovations. Because the regulation is very new and the index of reimbursable digital health applications is not available to the public yet, it remains to be seen, whether this innovation within the law will prove its worth or whether it requires further modification. The virtual DiGA summit with more than 1600 stakeholders from the health care sector and a planned English Summit can be seen as indications that innovative legal provisions can have an effect on innovation spaces and/or trigger innovation (Health Innovation Hub 2020).

16.3.2 SHI-Funds: The New Venture Capitalists?

Another innovative legal instrument is the possibility for health insurance funds to actively promote digital health innovations and also design the digital healthcare processes. They can develop digital health applications in cooperation with third parties or having them develop the application (§68a III SGB V). Furthermore, statutory health insurance funds can use up to 2 percent of their financial reserves to acquire shares in investment funds in the EU, EEA or Switzerland (§§68a IV Alt. 2, 263a SGB V). With 21 billion Euros of financial reserves (1.Q. 2019; Federal Ministry of Healthcare 2020a), this represents 420 million in venture capital.

These instruments represent an absolute novelty and have the potential to act as a catalyst for innovations in the German health care system.

16.4　Conclusion

As a result of this book chapter the following theses can be noted:

1. The topic of innovation through law and innovation in law is still underrepresented in legal research, especially in the field of healthcare.

2. The law is often regarded as an obstacle to innovation. However, the non-legal sciences fail to recognise that the law has a high degree of responsibility for innovation which is derived from the constitution.
3. In contrast to the more rudimentary legal innovation research, there is a high demand for legal advice on the introduction, implementation and dissemination of innovation.
4. Although some authors claim that law cannot directly influence innovation in healthcare, the DVG introduced in 2019 shows the opposite.
5. The introduction of digital health applications into the statutory health sector has a direct impact on innovation. It creates and strengthens the innovative power of companies, generates network and cluster effects and finally it can positively influence the attitude of many stakeholders in the health care sector towards digitisation.
6. The fast track procedure of the BfArM is a prime example of innovation in law, because it has anchored a new type of procedure in a legal system. The same applies to the legal possibility of venture capital of statutory health insurance funds.

References

Arnold M, Litsch M, Schnellschmidt H, Ackermann T (2000) Krankenhausreport 2000—Schwerpunkt Vergütungsreform mit DRGs 2001, 159 p
Bern CG (2020) Genome Editing in Zeiten Von CRISPR/Cas: Eine Rechtliche Analyse, 222 p
Bundesinstitut für Arzneimittel und Medizinprodukte (2020) Das Fast-Track-Verfahren für digitale Gesundheitsanwendungen (DiGA) nach § 139e SGB V. Ein Leitfaden für Hersteller, Leistungserbringer und Anwender, pp 1–138. https://www.bfarm.de/DE/Medizinprodukte/DVG/_node.html. Accessed June 30, 2020
Bundesrechnungshof (2019) Bericht an den Haushaltsausschuss des Deutschen Bundestages nach § 88 Abs. 2 BHO über die Einführung der elektronischen Gesundheitskarte und der Telematikinfrastruktur, pp 1–41. https://www.bundesrechnungshof.de/de/presse-service/abonnements/berichte-rss. Accessed June 30, 2020
Bundesregierung (2018) Forschung und Innovationen. High Hightech-Strategie für Deutschland 2025. https://www.hightech-strategie.de/de/hightech-strategie-2025-1726.html
BVMed—The German Medical Technology Association, Cepton Consulting (2007) Nutzen durch Innovationen. Eine Studie zum Beitrag der medizintechnologischen Industrie zur Verbesserung der Gesundheitsversorgung in Deutschland. 1–60. https://www.bvmed.de/de/branche/innovationskraft/nutzen-durch-innovation. Accessed June 30, 2020
Deuring S (2019) Rechtliche Herausforderungen moderner Verfahren der Intervention in die menschliche Keimbahn. CRISPR/Cas9, hiPS-Zellen und Mitochondrientransfer im deutsch—französischen Rechtsvergleich, 505 p
Deutscher Bundestag (2015) Beschlussempfehlung und Bericht des Ausschusses für Gesundheit, BT-Drs. 18/5123 vom 10.6.2020. https://www.bundestag.de/drs. Accessed June 30, 2020
Deutscher Bundestag (2018) Report of the Chairman of the G-BA on compliance with deadlines in G-BA advisory procedures—German Parliament, Committee on Health, Committee printed matter 19(14)0009 vom 17.4.2018. https://www.bundestag.de/drs. Accessed June 30, 2020
Deutscher Bundestag (2019) Entwurf eines Gesetzes für eine bessere Versorgung durch Digitalisierung und Innovation (Digitale-Versorgung-Gesetz—DVG), BT-Drs. 19/13438 vom 23.9.2019. https://www.bundestag.de/drs. Accessed June 30, 2020
Eifert M, Hoffmann-Riem W (2009) Innovationsve rantwortung. Innovation und Recht III, 312 p

Engel C, Morlok M (1988) *Öffentliches Recht als ein Gegenstand ökonomischer Forschung*. Die Begegnung der deutschen Staatsrechtslehre mit der Konstitutionellen Politischen Ökonomie

European Commission (2013) Innovation union. A pocket guide on a Europe 2020 initiative, Luxembourg, https://doi.org/10.2777/59336

Federal Ministry of Healthcare (2019) Entwurf eines Gesetzes für eine bessere Versorgung durch Digitalisierung und Innovation (Digitale-Versorgung-Gesetz—DVG), BGBl. I Nr. 48, pp 2562–2584

Federal Ministry of Healthcare (2020) Verordnung über das Verfahren und die Anforderungen zur Prüfung der Erstattungsfähigkeit digitaler Gesundheitsanwendungen in der gesetzlichen Krankenversicheurng (Digitale-Gesundheitsanwendungen-Verordnung—DiGAV), BGBl. I Nr. 18, pp 768–798

Federal Ministry of Healthcare (2020a) Finanzreserven der Krankenkassen im 1. Quartal 2019 weiter bei rund 21 Milliarden Euro. DPA Meldung v. 20.6.2019. https://www.bundesgesundheitsministerium.de/presse/pressemitteilungen/2019/2-quartal/finanzergebnisse-gkv-1q-2019.html. Accessed June 30, 2020

Form Bio-und Gentechnologie e.V (2019.) Das große Dilemma: Genome Editing—verboten, aber nicht nachweisbar, https://www.transgen.de/aktuell/2742.genome-editing-nachweisverfahren.html. Accessed June 30, 2020

Glaeske G, Ludwig WD (2018) Innovationsreport 2018. Auswertungsergebnisse von Routinedaten der Techniker Krankenkasse aus den Jahren 2015 bis 2017. https://www.tk.de. Accessed June 30, 2020

Glauner P (2018) The artificial intelligence revolution, pp 67–78. In Innovationsumgebungen gestalten. Impulse für Start-ups und etablierte Unternehmen im globalen Wettbewerb, 277 p

Godin B (2015) Innovation contested: the idea of innovation over the centuries, 354 p

Grandstand O, Holgerson M (2020) Innovation ecosystems: a conceptual review and a new definition, Technovation, 90–91, 102098, pp 1–12. https://doi.org/10.1016/j.technovation.2019.102098

Grinblat, R. (2011) Rechtsfragen der Ausschreibung von Hilfsmitteln, 314 p

Häckl D (2010) Neue Technologien im Gesundheitswesen, p 162

Hauschildt J, Salomo S, Schultz C, Kock A (2016) Innovationsmangagement, 6. Edt. 479 p

Health Innovation Hub of the Federal Ministry of Health/hih (2020) DiGA Summit—Summary, Video, Docs, next steps. https://hih-2025.de/diga-summit-summary-video-docs-next-steps/. Accessed June 30, 2020

Hensel M, Wirsam J (2008) Diffusion von Innovationen. Das Beispiel Voice over IP, 120 p

Hoffman-Riem W (1997) Innovationen durch Recht und im Recht, pp 2–32. In Schulte M (Eds.) Technische Innovationen und Recht—Antrieb oder Hemmnis

Hoffman-Riem W (2010) Offene Rechtswissenschaft, pp 177–273

Hoffman-Riem W (2016) Innovationen im Recht, pp 11–31

Hoffman-Riem W, Schneider J-P (1998) Rechtswissenschaftliche Innovationsforschung. Grundlagen, Forschungsansätze, Gegenstandbereiche, 412 p

Hornung G (2015) Grundrechtsinnovationen, 674 p

Knieps F (1996) Arzneimittelinnovationen aus der Perspektive der Krankenkassen, pp 52–58. In Albring M, Wille E (Eds.), Innovationen in der Arzneimitteltherapie: Definition, medizinische Umsetzung und Finanzierung. https://doi.org/10.3726/b14079

Mai M (2014) Handbuch Innovationen. Interdisziplinäre Grundlagen und Anwendungsfelder. 369 p

Medtech Europe (2018) The European medical technology industry in figures, pp 1–44

OECD (2020) Science, technology and innovation outlook 2020, https://www.oecd.org/sti/science-technology-innovation-outlook/. Accessed June 30, 2020

Rogers EM (2003) Diffusion of innovations, 3rd ed, p 11

Statistisches Bundesamt (2020). https://www.destatis.de/DE/Themen/Gesellschaft-Umwelt/Gesundheit/_inhalt.html. Accessed June 30, 2020

Towfigh EV, Petersen N (2017) Ökonomische Methoden im Recht. Eine Einführung für Juristen, p 291

Vera A, Salge TO (2008) Innovationen im Krankenhaus—das Beispiel England. Das Krankenhaus 100(11):1184–1189

VfA/German Association of Research-Based Pharmaceutical Companies (2019) Positionspapier Pharma/Biotech und Innovationen, https://www.vfa.de/download/pos-pharma-biotech-innovationen.pdf. Accessed June 30, 2020

Start-Ups Meet SMEs 17

Michael Krause

17.1 Start-Ups Meet SMEs

17.1.1 Overcoming Obstacles to Innovation by Collaborating

Since 2015, we have met numerous SMEs through our "Innovation offensive for SMEs and founders"—for example, Ille Papier Service GmbH in Altenstadt with 500 employees, and Heggemann AG in Büren, which has 200. These are two highly innovative companies; both regularly develop new products and services. Ille Papier Service GmbH focuses on hygiene products (ILLE Papier Service GmbH 2018), while Heggemann AG's main business is producing parts for the aerospace industry (Heggemann 2018).

The objective of the "Innovation offensive" is to network enterprises—particularly SMEs—, start-ups, research institutes and multipliers, positioning them to work together on new joint projects and products. Unlike corporations, neither of the two SMEs mentioned above has a large in-house R&D department; these enterprises are dependent on collaboration to develop new products and services. The same is true for most small and medium enterprises (SMEs). Only around 80.000 people (BMBF 2014, p. 99) work in research and development at SMEs (Institut für Mittelstandsforschung Bonn 2018). These enterprises often lack financial resources and find themselves "mired" in their operative business, making it simply impossible for the typical SME to develop an in-house R&D department.

M. Krause (✉)
Kunststoff-Institut Lüdenscheid, Lüdenscheid, Germany

KIMW-Qualifizierungs gGmbH, KIMW-Forschungs gGmbH, Lüdenscheid/Nordrhein Westfalen, Germany
e-mail: krause@kunststoff-institut.de

V. Nestle et al. (eds.), *Creating Innovation Spaces*, Management for Professionals, https://doi.org/10.1007/978-3-030-57642-4_17

At the launch of this year's "Innovation offensive" in Paderborn, the managing director of aircraft part producer Heggemann AG described the situation as follows: as a traditional German SME, his company only has a small R&D department and therefore depends on collaboration with research institutes, such as the University of Paderborn, and involvement in research projects, e.g. as part of the cooperative industrial research programme (Industrielle Gemeinschaftsforschung, or IGF). These close collaborations are essential for his company, as they open up access to business-related networks and scientific experts. For example, he has employed a number of PhD graduates from the University of Paderborn following completion of their research projects.

The managing director's statement is backed up by a study carried out by the North Rhine-Westphalia Chamber of Commerce and Industry (IHK NRW 2014). In the study, SMEs were asked to identify obstacles to innovation in their enterprises. The key reasons listed by the representatives of the various SMEs were: lack of capital, lack of experts, lack of infrastructure and potential risk exposure.

However, innovating is essential to survival in the digital transformation age—and that doesn't just mean new products and services, but also new business models: a "business model innovation".

How can these innovation processes be driven forward and obstacles to innovation surmounted? The key, as described by the managing director of the aerospace parts producer, may lie in collaboration.

The main drivers of collaboration are to be found in partnerships with research institutes, multipliers, other enterprises—and, in particular, with start-ups. Although it is true that new start-ups have been declining in number for some years (Baharian and Wallisch 2016), some interesting start-up scenes have nevertheless developed—in Berlin, for example. Partnerships are useful to both sides, as they establish a win-win situation: while start-ups benefit from the wealth of experience built up in established businesses, the experienced entrepreneurs gain new momentum from motivated young enterprises with a fresh view of the market and valuable contributions for the new digital world.

Figure 17.1 shows some results from a study commissioned by the German Federal Ministry for Economic Affairs and Energy (Bundesministerium für

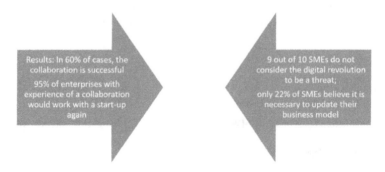

Fig. 17.1 SMEs meet start-ups (Baharian and Wallisch 2017). (Source: Author)

Wirtschaft und Energie, BMWi) and carried out by the centre of excellence RKW Kompetenzzentrum (Baharian and Wallisch 2017). The study surveyed SMEs and start-ups with experience of working in partnership. In total, 60% of the enterprises surveyed considered the collaboration with a start-up successful. It is also interesting to note that 95% of the SMEs surveyed would work with a start-up again (Baharian and Wallisch 2017, p. 14).

The studies are supported by concrete examples, such as a tea product provider collaborating with a start-up. The managing director of this company reported on their partnership with the start-up at an industrial dialogue. The start-up has built an online shop where customers can create personalised tea blends based on their requirements, i.e. each customer can blend their own individual tea.

17.2 Benefits for Start-Ups

It is easier than ever nowadays to distribute and market new products using digital opportunities. Consequently, the modern start-up is in a much better position, at least in B2C segments (business-to-consumer). Through my roles as a mentor and expert for various start-up competitions, my personal consulting role at various start-ups and my involvement with a number of coworking spaces and university business incubators, I have gained insights into the reality of their situations and identified a number of phenomena. Studies show that as a general rule, many start-ups fail.

First, though, we need to define what a start-up actually is. Start-ups are young enterprises that develop innovative (new) products and services and make them scalable (Hüsing 2018). That is, not every new business is a start-up. Start-ups aim for rapid growth, and this typically makes them dependent on venture capital.

One common reason that start-ups fail is that they do not have an interdisciplinary team: perhaps they have no engineers or IT specialists, or perhaps they are lacking sales representatives, business developers or economists. Essentially: the right people are key to success. One way to put together an interdisciplinary team relatively quickly is to make use of coworking spaces. These new spaces for start-ups, enterprises and multipliers are ideal for teambuilding—Factory Berlin is one example.

People work together in large shared spaces, where start-ups, enterprises and other multipliers can hold discussions, exchange ideas and launch joint projects.

I have also found that the customer focus is often missing, for example when it comes to more complex products in the B2B sector (business-to-business). These are often developed through spin-offs, perhaps created by universities as the results of research projects. However, the projects frequently suffer from a lack of ongoing communication with the customer. In other words, constant feedback from the target group, be that an enterprise or the end customer, is a vital element.

After all, innovating is about solving problems—that is, problems experienced by some number of customers, who are prepared to pay an appropriate price for an effective solution. In order to maintain this feedback loop, enterprises and start-ups must regularly survey their customers and implement iterative adaptations as necessary, continuously improving their product (Maura 2013, p. 23). There is a good reason that creative techniques such as "Design Thinking" are steadily becoming more popular. The need to rapidly develop a structured business model applies equally to start-ups; this can be done by e.g. using the "Business Model Canvas" to analyse relevant parameters and key factors (e.g. USPs, customer channels, revenues, etc.).

Another common issue for start-ups is a lack of essential capital. This makes identifying suitable investors crucial to their survival. Venture capital structures in Germany are not yet sufficiently well developed, unlike in the USA or Israel, and currently stand at approx. € 700 m (Richters 2015). The Federal Government is actively working on promoting investment activities through "Business Angels", e.g. with the "Invest—Venture capital grant" programme, in which the BMWi returns equity investors 20% of their investment (BMWi 2018).

It is also crucial for start-ups to make use of sales networks and infrastructures. In my discussions with start-ups, I frequently encounter an assumption that sales and marketing can be achieved simply through online marketing. I do consider online marketing to be absolutely essential, and with the right content marketing, it can achieve very good results. However, the enterprise must also have an overall sales and marketing strategy—and that means that an expert in this field is a key element of a successful start-up team. Another element of this strategy is to develop a network of collaboration partners, particularly in the B2B sector. Initial pilot projects with customers can be useful in this sense, and the start-up team may be able to exploit personal connections in order to gradually build up a customer base. If a start-up needs a particular infrastructure, e.g. machines, materials or IT, collaboration with a university or enterprise may again play a vital role.

The success factors outlined here indicate that a key to success may be found in collaboration—with other large or medium-sized enterprises, start-ups, multipliers, associations and research institutes or other institutes. I believe that collaboration with SMEs can be particularly interesting here, as these are often family-run companies with short decision routes and decentralised organisational structures. By contrast, the complex structures or larger corporations often results in slower decision-making processes, and it can take some time to set up a collaboration— also partly due to processing in the corporation's legal department and extensive regulations. Working with SMEs can therefore give a young start-up the advantage of speed. On the other hand, larger corporations do of course have greater financial resources.

Ultimately, the right choice of partner must always depend on the project itself. A prerequisite when searching for the right collaboration partner or approaching a potential partner is to have the target customer clearly defined. Ideally, the start-up product will be complemented by relevant products from the cooperation partner.

One way start-ups might win added value through collaborating with enterprises is by exploiting the company's infrastructure and established processes and structures, which can make testing and optimising processes more efficient (Fig. 17.2). Another benefit of collaborating with SMEs is that the start-up may be able to tap into the established company's networks. Companies typically collaborate with

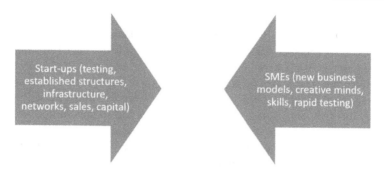

Fig. 17.2 Collaborative benefits for SMEs and start-ups (Baharian and Wallisch 2017). (Source: Author)

other companies, are organised into associations and may also work with research institutes.

Furthermore, established businesses have well-developed and effective sales structures, something a start-up normally would not have access to. Forming a partnership can open doors—and sales is a decisive factor for the success of a start-up. For example, one enterprise from the AiF sphere, whose 3000 employees included a large number of sales representatives, gave a start-up access to its sales network and thereby created a unique scaling effect.

Another potential benefit of collaborating is that the enterprise may itself invest money into the scheme, resulting in a long-term joint project.

Intermediate summary:

> Working with enterprises can be highly beneficial for start-ups. Many of the potential obstacles that start-ups struggle to overcome as they launch their business activity can be reduced through collaboration. Smaller companies can generally act more quickly and flexibly; on the other hand, larger corporations have more financial resources. When start-ups carry out a market analysis, this should include defining partnership models and outlining which collaboration partners are relevant to them. Potential partners can then be approached directly. Existing contacts from the private sphere may be useful at this stage. Start-ups should also involve themselves in networks relevant to their field and participate in events and groups that yield opportunities to meet potential collaboration partners—for example, trade fairs, conferences, association activities.

17.3 Benefits for SMEs

During regular discussions with numerous SMEs, both during individual meetings on site and as part of campaigns, I have opportunities to see how SME innovation projects play out in reality, and to observe where "the shoe pinches". First, though, we need to define what is meant by an SME. While the European Commission defines SMEs as enterprises with fewer than 250 employees and revenues below € 50 m, the German SME research institute (Institut für Mittelstandsforschung, IfM), describes "Mittelstand" companies (SMEs) as enterprises with fewer than

500 employees and revenues under € 50 m, and the German Federal Ministry of Education and Research (Bundesministerium für Bildung und Forschung, BMBF 2018) makes its schemes available to enterprises with fewer than 1000 employees and revenues below € 100 m.

It is therefore clear that there is no one definition of SME, or of what is meant by Mittelstand—indeed, family-run companies that do not fall within these limits will often say that they nonetheless consider themselves part of the "Mittelstand". One thing that is clear, however, is that the German "Mittelstand" has a unique structure, and numerous employment relationships depend on the "German Mittelstand".

SMEs have highly diverse approaches to innovation. The example above of the aircraft part producer shows that small and medium-sized enterprises (using the IfM definition) are particularly dependent on collaboration: the smaller the enterprise, the greater its need for collaboration. By contrast, larger companies and particularly corporations are able to maintain their own R&D and innovation departments and may employ technology scouts to keep up to date with research results, current trends and start-up activities.

The study carried out by the RKW Kompetenzzentrum indicates that collaborations between start-ups and SMEs are effective. Another interesting observation from this study is that nine out of ten SMEs do not consider the digital revolution to be an existential threat (Fig. 17.1) (Baharian and Wallisch 2017, p. 4). During my discussions with SMEs, it was evident that they often do not have much interest in tackling buzzwords such as Industry 4.0 or the "Internet of Things". Typically, specialist service providers, research institutes and even start-ups fail to communicate the key elements of digital matters; they are simply not speaking the same language as the entrepreneurs and do not address their needs. It's also the case that different enterprises, with their wildly differing structures, need different levels of "catching up on" the various issues. General approaches are not appropriate for enterprises with very specific products who occupy particular niches, particularly in the B2B sector.

Instead, an individual digital strategy is needed for every business. For example, one enterprise in the medical sector explained that they only have a very few customers, who are themselves business customers. Developing a social media strategy would be unlikely to benefit this enterprise.

Start-ups also need to be aware that the B2C sector is highly competitive and the future potential for digital business models lies particularly in the B2B sector. With these new digital models, the problems and challenges faced by enterprises could be solved by start-ups, and then in turn lead to new products and services. Over time, highly solution-oriented strategies could yield long-term success.

Another interesting result from the RKW study is that only 22% of the enterprises surveyed consider it necessary to update their business model regularly (Fig. 17.1) (Baharian and Wallisch 2017, p. 16). I believe, however, that it is essential to regularly look at one's own business model in order to meet the constant challenges of a fast-moving world.

What actually is a business model, though, and how should you structure one for your enterprise?

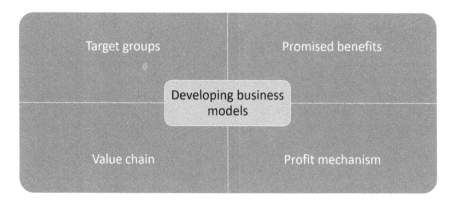

Fig. 17.3 Developing business models (Gassmann et al. 2017). (Source: Author)

There are various options and tools that can be used to structure a company's business model and update it as necessary. One is the "Business Model Canvas" method; another alternative is the Business Model Navigator developed by the University of St. Gallen (Gassmann et al. 2017). In this latter model, you start by defining your target group (see Fig. 17.3): who are my customers? What are the target groups, and how can I define them? Which market segments am I targeting?

Another aspect deals with the question: what benefits do I promise my customers? For example, do I offer a particularly good price or make particular quality claims regarding my product or excellent service? How do I stand out from my competitors?

The next stage is to define your value chain: which resources do I use to deliver the promised benefits? What human resources and infrastructure do I need?

Finally, you analyse your profit mechanism: how does the enterprise earn money? What is our pricing strategy?

Once these four areas of the business model have been defined, you are ready to update your existing business model. The University of St. Gallen has established through a number of studies that 90% of business models can be categorised into 55 patterns.

One such pattern is the "add-on" business model. In this model, the customer receives the basic service at a very low price. This basic service is reduced to the bare minimum, and additional services can then be purchased at a higher price. This is the model used, for example, by various airlines: a customer might book a basic package that does not include a seat reservation, only allows limited luggage, and does not cover food or drinks in-flight. These services can be purchased for an additional cost (Gassmann et al. 2017, p. 94).

Another business model is "cross-selling". In this model, customers of the company's basic product are offered other services adapted to the target group. A good example of this model is petrol stations, which may have shops selling sandwiches and pastries, newspapers, etc. alongside the basic fuel purchase (Gassmann et al. 2017, p. 124).

Another interesting business model is "crowdsourcing". In this model, the "crowd", i.e. internet users, is asked how particular problems could be solved, or asked to give their opinion of particular products. Clothing manufacturers use this kind of model to try and analyse future trends and update their collections accordingly at regular intervals (Gassmann et al. 2017, p. 132). Using this model gives the entrepreneurs the freedom to solve their problems differently in the future, but does also leave some elements open.

Another model in which the "crowd" is called on to help is the "crowdfunding" business model. Projects often fail when they are unable to secure the necessary financing. "Crowdfunding" gives an enterprise the chance to realise a project that conventional banks have refused funding to. Anyone who is interested can contribute a small amount of money to the project. Sustainable projects, in particular, have a good chance of being financed. Crowdfunding is generally sourced through a suitable platform (Gassmann et al. 2017, p. 128).

Regardless of the choice of model, it is crucial that the enterprise understands that continuous improvement of their products may be necessary, but is not sufficient—a successful business model is also essential to generating long-term success. The company's products must be anchored in a good business model in which the factors mentioned above are carefully tuned and coordinated (Gassmann et al. 2017).

To achieve this effectively, the enterprise must consider its products in terms of their functionality and as part of a whole. For example, rail providers cannot limit their analysis to ticket sales; they need to consider a customer journey in its entirety—say from Berlin to Cologne—, taking into account all the customer's requirements and needs (punctuality, service, drinks, etc.). The patterns described above can be used and adapted to by each specific enterprise to fit their framework and products, creating completely new configurations each time.

Another phenomenon that frequently comes up when talking to enterprises is the balance between the importance of collaboration and the need this entails to disclose business secrets. There is no off-the-shelf solution to managing this balancing act. As already discussed, SMEs in particular are often not in a position to handle everything themselves, particularly during early research stages. Partnerships and collaboration can be the key they need to resolve this deadlock.

Working with start-ups can bring many benefits for SMEs (see Table 2.1). For example, start-ups can help with digital projects that have perhaps presented significant obstacles for the enterprise in the past.

Agile approaches and a fresh perspective from the start-ups can also help enterprises to integrate new ideas into the company.

Another issue SMEs often face is a lack of creative minds. Working with start-ups can help them overcome this obstacle to innovation, and perhaps even to inspire employees from the enterprise to get actively involved in product design. It is also helpful for the management to provide incentives that motivate innovation and encourage employees to become an active part of the creative processes. Simply employing "innovation managers" is not sufficient; innovative approaches must be integrated into every sector and department.

Another useful approach involves outsourcing risks and making use of external capacity. An SME's workforce is usually engaged at full capacity with their operative tasks. Partnering with a start-up can make it possible for the SME to implement projects they could not otherwise tackle due to a lack of capacity—and to achieve them faster.

17.3.1 Intermediate Summary

SMEs must be open to cooperation in order to secure long-term success. While collaborations with research institutes are certainly helpful, start-ups can also make interesting partners for SMEs, as they bring fresh perspectives and can help to surmount various obstacles hindering innovation—such as a lack of experts, increased risk exposure, and perhaps also insufficient capital. Smaller enterprises struggle in particular with developing new business models and digital products and services. The issue is often not limited to adapting existing products; it's about the need for a broader, more interdisciplinary perspective. For example, it might make sense to venture into entirely new market segments, which has the added benefit of diversifying the enterprise's risk exposure. Start-ups can be helpful for this kind of venture.

17.4 Collaboration in Practice: The Pilot Programme

Individual successful examples drawn from our network highlight simultaneously both the interest in and the need for a concrete programme aimed at promoting collaboration between SMEs and start-ups. An initial call for interest in our network attracted a very positive response from both sides.

It is not easy for an individual enterprise and a start-up to find each other initially—tracking down the right collaboration partner can be difficult to do. The AiF has a unique network including 100 research associations (all in the industrial sector), 1200 research institutes and 50,000 enterprises. The network also has contacts with transfer centres, business incubators, start-up competition organisers and coworking spaces. By searching this comprehensive network, the AiF can identify perfect fits for both sides. These kinds of partnerships do not generally emerge naturally: some of them are only developed thanks to personal contacts. The programme counters this issue by creating a way to initiate partnerships on a more targeted basis, looking at potential profitability, and establishing a transparent system.

In the first phase, "Matching" (Fig. 17.4), an analysis identifies the needs of the enterprises and start-ups. The requirements that emerge from this are then used as a basis to bring together the right partners with pinpoint accuracy.

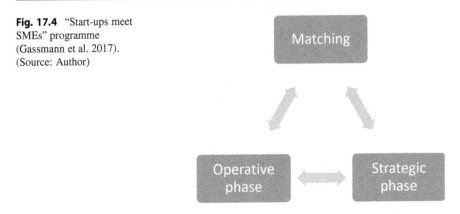

During the next stage, "Support through the operative phase", the AiF helps
manage the partnerships between the start-ups and established SMEs. This operative
phase involves discussions regarding joint projects, potential issues and new ideas.
Teams are set up comprising employees from the established enterprise and
representatives from the start-up; new ideas are developed during "Hackathons"
and "Design Thinking" models. Ideally, this stage yields an initial approach to a
joint project.

The operative phase is followed by the third, "Strategic" phase, in which this
initial approach is refined. First decisions are made by the collaboration partners
and long-term projects are discussed. The established enterprise may be able to
use its own customer networks to implement iterative processes, collecting rapid
customer feedback on potential new products and services. Once the products
are ready to market, the established enterprise can exploit its own sales network.
The entrepreneur may also be able to provide infrastructure and capital. Another
option is to found a company. A basic principle is that the approach should be
designed flexibly at each stage, since every partnership has a unique configuration
and requires a customised approach.

The "Start-ups meet SMEs" programme was launched in spring 2017, in
partnership with the BMWi. The BMWi also established a Steering Committee for
the programme.

By analysing existing projects and studies within the network and introducing
new pilot projects, some initial findings have been established. It turns out that many
of the start-ups studied are pursuing interdisciplinary projects—for example, digital
platforms, e-commerce, apps and products in the B2C sector are very popular. The
interdisciplinary nature of these projects means that start-ups developing digital
products and services of this type can slot into every sector of industry. These
start-ups are also engaged in targeted searches for collaboration partners to work
on potential joint projects. For example, the start-up Foxbase in our network has
been working with the company Henkel ever since its foundation. The partnership
helps boost the start-up's reputation. Foxbase offers a solution that makes B2B sales

easier for enterprises, for example, through simplified, customer-friendly product descriptions (Foxbase GmbH 2018).

Equally, however, some start-ups develop products targeted to a specific sector. One of the start-ups we are supporting—currently in the process of preparing a spin-off from a university—develops measurement systems for the steel industry that can be used to significantly reduce production waste in steelworks. This is a classic B2B solution designed with enterprises in the steel industry in mind, both as a source of partners for potential pilot projects and as the target customer.

Turning back to established enterprises, we find that they are looking for both sector-specific and interdisciplinary start-ups as partners. It is clear, based on the early project launches, that it is considerably more difficult to find the right sector-specific start-ups.

We work through various channels to bring together suitable partners—for example, in collaboration with Mécénat Merode e. V. via the AiF F·T·K GmbH Advisory Board, which was founded partly for this programme. We also offer workshops on the topic "Start-ups meet SMEs", as a part of our "Innovation offensive for SMEs and founders".

In one of these workshops, Niklas Schwichtenberg, founder of Actus GmbH, described the forms and advantages of the collaboration (Actus One GmbH 2018):

"From the initial idea, through financing the enterprise, to implementation, we were supported and helped by SMEs." The idea of carrying out a project in partnership with a company like this has several simultaneous advantages for us. For example, we can develop practical solutions that work as "proof of concept" while still in the design phase. Particularly by working with small enterprises, we can test and validate new ideas, and then produce a "lean" implementation.

We were also delighted by the personal relationships that are quickly established when working together. Working with an SME, your contact person is often part of the management and also in a position to be intensively involved in the collaboration. That establishes an excellent basis for trust and creates a foundation for rapid development of your own enterprise. This in turn helps our partners: they can feed their own ideas, suggestions and requirements into our product development, and ultimately receive what is essentially a tailored product. We also found that the close collaboration and discussion at all levels opened up new potential. For example, some fantastic ideas emerged from our employees, which then in turn gave the management the opportunity to focus more on encouraging personnel and staff development. Another positive effect was the reflective process that we sparked off. For example, various questions emerged: Is my enterprise well-positioned for digitalisation in other domains? How does my corporate culture need to change to remain attractive to future talent? How could we think more innovatively, including in other domains?

We believe that this kind of food for thought is an important 'by-product' or 'waste product' of close collaborations between start-ups and SMEs."

Actus GmbH offers digital products that help to optimise communication in the enterprise across all company levels. The application also includes ways to identify the skills of individual employees and help promote ideas from creative employees. (Actus One GmbH 2018)

The AiF also networks partners together directly. The enterprises in the AiF network and the AiF research associations receive regular updates and are introduced to promising start-ups. The intention for the future is to integrate start-ups more tightly into research projects being carried out through the cooperative industrial research programme (IGF).

The objective of this one-year pilot phase is to launch three to five pilot projects and draw further conclusions from these projects.

17.5   Conclusion

The unique structure of the German "Mittelstand" (SMEs) represents an international competitive advantage. The smaller an SME is, the more it depends on collaboration for its innovative activities, as many SMEs do not have their own R&D department. SMEs also find it harder to identify, support, and integrate creative minds into their enterprises. People with these kinds of skills typically focus on larger enterprises when seeking work. The SMEs also lack the financial resources to push forward with risky projects. In addition, the digital transformation and new business model approaches are not yet part of the general consciousness. Collaborating with start-ups might be the key to compensating for these bottlenecks. Openness to this kind of collaboration is essential.

In return, start-ups can win considerable added value by working with SMEs—the start-ups do not have established structures and networks; they also lack financial resources. However, SMEs have exactly these structures.

In the ideal case, a successful "matching" procedure results in close collaboration between the two partners. As part of a joint project, the SME might e.g. open up its sales network so that the start-up can benefit from the infrastructure; the start-up might also receive financial support from the SME.

Close collaboration on an equal basis is essential to this process, since the difference in perspectives can also lead to conflicts.

Another element associated with collaborations between start-ups and SMEs is an opportunity to resolve certain problems experienced by the enterprise, allowing the start-up to focus on pilot projects. In these pilot projects, existing prototypes and products that have not yet reached maturity can be tested and adjustments can be made based on feedback from the enterprise. This could be a decisive advantage, turning around the current nine out of ten failure rate for start-ups.

Initial pilot projects have indicated that a tailored approach is required for each project. The structure of the activities, as described above, must remain flexible—it is not necessary for every project to trace the same course through the three phases described. The first projects launched at the impetus of the AiF certainly seem extremely promising and have been received very well by both sides.

17.5.1 New Example from the Plastics Industry

In 2019, I moved into the plastics industry, an industry sector that is currently undergoing a transformation. Both the automotive industry and the packaging industry are key segments of the plastics sector, and these two industries are under considerable pressure—innovation is vital to their survival. Recycled materials, in particular, are growing in importance, as the trend to assess products on their sustainability aspects grows. This is another situation where collaboration between start-ups and SMEs can have an important role to play. The Lüdenscheid plastics institute has been working with a promising start-up (Cirplus) since 2020. The objective is to develop a digital business model. Two sectors are to be united on a platform: on one side, the plastics processors looking for recycled materials to manufacture their products, and on the other side, the providers of recycled materials. The start-up has access to networks via the institute. This example is another interesting collaboration variant.

References

Actus One (2018) Vorteile der Zusammenarbeit [Advantages of cooperation] http://www.actusone.com/. Accessed April 5, 2018

Baharian A, Wallisch M (2016) Gründungen in Deutschland 2016 [Start-ups in Germany 2016], RKW Rationalisierungs- und Innovationszentrum der Deutschen Wirtschaft e.V. Kompetenzzentrum https://www.rkw-kompetenzzentrum.de/gruendung/faktenblatt/gruendungen-in-deutschland-2016/. Accessed April 5, 2018

Baharian A, Wallisch M (2017) Mittelstand meets Startup: Potenziale der Zusammenarbeit [SME meets Start-up: the potential of cooperation], RKW Rationalisierungs- und Innovationszentrum der Deutschen Wirtschaft e.V. Kompetenzzentrum https://www.rkw-kompetenzzentrum.de/gruendung/studie/mittelstand-meets-startup-potenziale-der-zusammenarbeit/. Accessed April 5, 2018

Bundesministerium für Bildung und Forschung (BMBF) (2014) Bundesbericht Forschung und Innovation 2014 [Federal report on research and innovation 2014]. http://www.bundesbericht-forschung-innovation.de/files/BuFI_2014_barrierefrei.pdf. Accessed April 5, 2018

Bundesministerium für Bildung und Forschung (BMBF) (2018) Innovativer mittelstand [Innovative SMEs] https://www.bmbf.de/de/mittelstand-3133.html. Accessed April 5, 2018

Bundesministerium für Wirtschaft und Energie (BMWi) (2018) INvest-Zuschuss und Wagniskapital [INvest grant and venture capital] https://www.bmwi.de/Redaktion/DE/Dossier/invest.html. Accessed April 5, 2018

Foxbase GmbH (2018) Über uns [About us]. https://www.foxbase.de/. Accessed April 5, 2018

Gassmann O, Frankenberger K, Csik M (2017) Geschäftsmodelle entwickeln: 55 innovative Konzepte mit dem St. Galler Business Model Navigator. [Developing business models: 55 innovative concepts with the St. Gallen Business Model Navigator] 2nd ed. Hanser, München

Heggemann AG (2018) About. http://www.heggemann.com/. Accessed April 5, 2018

Hüsing A (2018) Was verdammt noch mal ist eigentlich ein Start-up? [What on earth is a start-up, anyway?] https://www.deutsche-startups.de/2015/04/22/was-ist-eigentlich-ein-startup/. Accessed April 5, 2018

ILLE Papier Service GmbH (2018) Einsatzgebiete [Applications] http://www.ille.de/produkte/einsatzgebiete/. Accessed April 5, 2018

Industrie und Handelskammer Nordrhein-Westfalen (2014) Industrie- und Innovationsreport [Industry and Innovation report]

Institut für Mittelstandsforschung Bonn (2018) Mittelstandsdefinition des IfM [IfM definition of Mittelstand (SMEs)]. https://www.ifm-bonn.org/definitionen/mittelstandsdefinition-des-ifm-bonn/. Accessed: April 5, 2018

Maura A (2013) Running lean. Das how-to für erfolgreiche innovation. [The how-to for successful innovation] O'Reilly, Cologne

Richters K (2015) So viel wurde 2014 in Deutschland investiert [Investment in Germany in 2014] https://www.gruenderszene.de/allgemein/bvk-venture-capital-2014. Accessed April 5, 2018

The Five Elements of AI to Leverage Data and Dominate Your Industry

18

Alexander Thamm

18.1 Introduction

Artificial intelligence, big/fast/smart data, machine learning, deep learning, data lakes, pattern recognition, data science, predictive analytics . . . I am sure you have heard many of those terms and buzzwords, but do you really know what they mean and how they relate to each other? During the last two decades, together with my team, we had the opportunity to work with more than 100 companies in more than 700 projects coined with one of the many buzzwords above (Alexander Thamm GmbH 2020a). While the terminology and nuances evolved over time, all of those initiatives shared one common goal:

Principle 1: "Turn Data into Value leveraging technology like AI".

As **data**, we understand a symbolic representation of observations, so in our business context mostly measurement of processes in your business. In order to use the data it needs to be digital, meaning interpretable by machines and not on paper. Many insurers, for example, have tons of data on paper or magnetic tape drives. This data has to be digitalized and stored in order to be processed with AI.

With **value** we mostly mean economic value as in saving costs, increasing profit or tapping into new revenue streams. But it can also mean a prerequisite of economic success, for example reaching strategic goals like marketing to a new type of customer or achieving new capabilities. Last but certainly not least it will in most cases considerably increase working conditions within your company, boosting employee satisfaction. It frees workers from dull jobs, leaving them more time to deal with customers—or, in a medical environment, with patients. Gaining new insights or conducting fundamental research that does not create measurable value

A. Thamm (✉)
Alexander Thamm GmbH, Munich, Germany
e-mail: at@alexanderthamm.com

© The Editor(s) (if applicable) and The Author(s), under exclusive license to Springer Nature Switzerland AG 2021
V. Nestle et al. (eds.), *Creating Innovation Spaces*, Management for Professionals, https://doi.org/10.1007/978-3-030-57642-4_18

235

to us is consequently not what we want to invest our resources in as a company—we leave this to scientific facilities.[1]

And what now is **AI**? With many existing definitions as pointed out by Patrick Glauner, let's define artificial intelligence as the ability of a machine to perform tasks normally requiring human intelligence (Glauner 2020). See also the famous test by Alan Turing where people had to guess whether they are interaction with a machine or a real human (Turing 1950). The tricky part is that not all AI is the same and here is where most people get confused.

18.2   What Is AI and Why that Matters for Business?

We distinguish between three categories of AI—**traditional AI**, **weak/narrow AI** and **strong/general AI (AGI)**, which are depicted in Fig. 18.1. Briefly, traditional AI is considered old school and often undervalued. Narrow AI is where the current hype comes from and general or strong AI is what freaks people out.

What sets **traditional AI**, depicted in Fig. 18.2, apart from the other two is that algorithms are expert systems that take input data and generate output based on "hard-coded" rules. All of those rules are predefined by humans like for example the IBM chess computer Deep Blue, which set an important milestone for AI by winning against chess grandmaster Garry Kasparov in 1997 (Kasparov et al. 1995; Hsu 2002).

The reason for AI being so relevant today is the rise of **machine learning**, depicted in Fig. 18.2, and further its most advanced sub-field of deep learning. Therefore, what most people think of when they hear AI is machines that can learn from historic data to solve problems like humans. The rules that define the machines' decisions are not programmed by humans, but by the machine itself. The machines learn from historic inputs and outputs to derive the rules.

Today, humans need to clearly define the problem, the input data, the type of algorithm and the complete environment in order to make machine learning work. That is what we call **narrow AI** or **weak AI**, because the machine can just learn to solve a narrowly defined task. Please note when building AI products in your business:

> The use case needs to be clearly defined and operationalized by you in order get actionable results from AI.

Still today, we encounter executives whose expectations towards AI are too high. I sometimes listen to conversations in the board where AI sounds like a golden donkey that you feed data then magic happens and you just collect the money. This is a fairy tale.[2] To be fair, with recent hypes like data mining and Big Data there was

---

[1]If in alignment with your long term strategic goals or if patenting a certain core algorithm or machine learning model (for example as an automotive company for autonomous driving) conducting fundamental research might deliver value in the long term and therefore be reasonable.

[2]See Brothers Grimm's fairy tale about the "Gold Donkey" that drops gold coins for its owner.

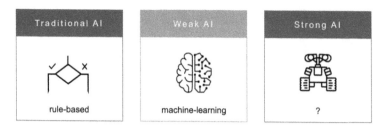

Fig. 18.1 Three categories of AI. (Source: Author)

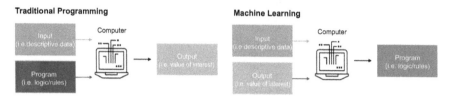

Fig. 18.2 Traditional programming vs. machine learning. (Source: Author)

hope that algorithms would find patterns relevant to one's business just by crawling through huge amounts of data—we now know that didn't work (Thamm 2017). Andrew Ng, former head of Google Brain and the Baidu AI Group, formulates it nicely:

> There are a lot of tools that AI people like me have. But it turns out that 99% of their recent wave of economic value driven by AI is through one idea. The technical term is supervised learning." All that means is an AI that is very good at figuring out input to output or A to B mappings such as input an email and output whether it is spam or not. That's your spam filter. (Ng 2019)

Research institutes and companies like Deepmind are working on what we call Artificial General Intelligence (AGI) or **strong AI** (Shu 2014). This means that an AI could solve any problem a human can and for some researchers this includes having a consciousness. We see interesting development especially with AI dominating video and board games (Schrittwieser et al. 2020) but a robot that says "I love you" based on its feelings like a human would do is still a fantasy. In 2016, researchers from Oxford and Yale universities conducted a survey of 352 leading AI researchers to collect their estimates of whether and when we will see AGI—the results show that experts are rather optimistic and see a real chance for AGI to evolve but rather within the next 100 vs. 10 years (Grace et al. 2018).

Having clarified what we understand of generating value from data by leveraging AI, why is now the time for you to do so (or do more if you are already doing)?

AI technology is transforming every industry, just like electricity a century ago. By 2030, AI will generate an estimated GDP growth of $13 trillion (Ng 2018). At the moment, "Chimerica" is globally dominating with Europe and the rest of the world lacking behind. As for now leading tech-companies have generated most of the value, see Fig. 18.3, but the next wave will be generated by originally non-

Rank	2010	2020
1	Exxon (US$ 369 billion)	Apple (US$ 1315 billion)
2	PetroChina (US$ 303 billion)	Microsoft (US$ 1213 billion)
3	Apple (US$ 295 billion)	Alphabet (US$ 928 billion)
4	BHP Billiton (US$ 244 billion)	Amazon (US$ 926 billion)
5	Microsoft (US$ 369 billion)	Facebook (US$ 590 billion)
6	ICBC (US$ 233 billion)	Alibaba (US$ 580 billion)
7	Petrobras (US$ 229 billion)	Berkshire Hathaway (US$ 554 billion)
8	China Construction Bank (US$ 222 billion)	Tencent (US$ 461 billion)
9	Royal Dutch Shell (US$ 209 billion)	JPMorgan Chase (US$ 439 billion)
10	Nestle (US$ 204 billion)	Visa (US$ 420 billion)

Fig. 18.3 Publicly traded companies with highest market value in 2010 and 2020. (Source: Author)

software companies. The question only is if your company will be on the winning or losing side.

Principle 2: "If you miss the AI train you will be out of business within the next 10 years." (Thamm et al. 2020).

Working with 100+ enterprises at alexanderthamm.com during the last decade, we distilled five elements that are key to separate winners from losers in the AI era. We were excited to find a pattern of those five elements within each individual company across different markets and industries. We use the term elements because all five need to be orchestrated for success. Most companies we work for are not evenly mature within the five elements, depending on their culture and business model they are ahead in one or two of the five. So what are the five to thrive?

1. Effective AI product portfolio & development
2. Engaging AI culture & organizational structure
3. Professional AI training & hiring
4. Hands-on Data & AI governance
5. Solid Data & AI platform

Whereas in the end all five need to be mastered and aligned, it is possible for any organization to follow the order of focus from one to five and become a strong AI company.

Figure 18.4 depicts a real example from a project with a large German enterprise, where we defined three work streams including the five AI elements. As illustrated the five elements are interwoven within a coherent framework we call the data &

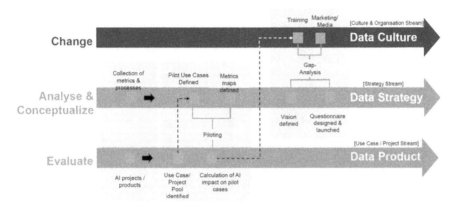

Fig. 18.4 AI transformation roadmap example. (Source: Author)

AI journey (Alexander Thamm GmbH 2020b). In contrast to traditional strategy projects or transformational initiatives, your AI adoption program does not follow a linear structure like concept phase, implementation phase and evaluation phase. Due to the complexity and uncertainty of AI, all workstreams are integrated and it is better you start with implementation, not strategy or concept.

> Some executives will think that developing an AI strategy should be the first step. In my experience, most companies will not be able to develop a thoughtful AI strategy until it has had some basic experience with AI (. . .). (Ng 2018)

18.3   AI Product Portfolio & Development

18.3.1 Building Your AI Product Portfolio

For your first AI projects, it is important to proof value rather than trying to solve the companies most difficult problems with AI. It is natural, that some people in your organization are sceptic about AI and need to be convinced to invest in further AI projects. The best way to market AI is by succeeding—seeing is believing. This may sound contradictory to the "fail-fast" principle, but in the beginning one out of three use cases should be successful with regards to the goals you were setting (McGrath Gunther 2011). Those first wins will help you get momentum and share your insights across the organization to ensure sponsorship and funding.

Remember our definition of value, your AI project will either help you become more effective in your current business like targeting your customers more precisely, help to reduce costs like for example by automation of labor or enable your team to venture into new business models like offering an uptime guarantee for your machines for a monthly subscription fee powered by predictive maintenance. An exciting example is the RIO Platform (https://rio.cloud/de/)—a spin-off from truck and bus manufacturer MAN where they offer predictive maintenance based on AI.

Furthermore, the use case should be feasible. We distinguish between three different dimensions of feasibility: data, predictability and actionability. In order to assess feasibility, we evaluate the following criteria:

- *Data*: Is relevant data available? Are we allowed to use the data for our purpose (e.g. GDPR)? What quality does the data have? Etc.
- *Predictability*: Do we expect to find a signal in the data? Has anyone ever predicted something similar? What do we know about root cause in our business domain? Etc.
- *Actionability*: After successfully predicting the output, can we influence the input[3] ? Can we address the use case within the organization or are there internal politics/conflicts? Etc.

After assessing your potential use cases, you can assort them within a nice portfolio matrix—value on the y-axis and feasibility on the x-axis, depicted in Fig. 18.5. Now build a first set of candidate use cases from the upper right of your matrix and get started.

18.3.2 AI Product Development: Getting Started with Your Use Cases

For classical IT products with low uncertainty you can follow a linear project management process like plan, build and run. However, due to the high uncertainty of AI use cases an agile process with three phases helps you to mitigate risk and optimize your return on investment, see Fig. 18.6.

To give you some very practical advice, a good size of your first project to build an AI product should be around 100k for the prototype, which should be running within 2–3 months. With projects sprints of 2 weeks lengths, this would give you around five to six implementation sprints—about 20k € per sprint.

Principle 3: "After building your use case portfolio, build prototypes in the Lab, scale to more users and robust products within the Factory and run your product as a service in Operations."

Lab Phase
Within the Lab phase, your goal is to proof that your AI use case problem is solvable by building a running prototype. The best way to start your use case is to bring all stakeholders together into one (virtual) room and specify the use case concept. This

---

[3]For example, an ice cream truck owner might find a positive impact of more hours of sun per day to their daily revenue, but can he make the sun shine more? No, so their use case outcome is not actionable for him.

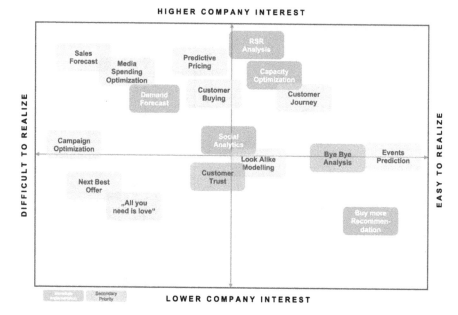

HIGHER COMPANY INTEREST

Fig. 18.5 Use case portfolio matrix. (Source: Author)

helps to align on the detailed business value, key results and definition of done for the use case. We like to use aspects of agile and design thinking to define the solution space and collect as much domain knowledge and hypotheses from the business experts as possible (Alexander Thamm GmbH 2020c). Also, a joined workshop helps to get everybody engaged and motivated into supporting the project. During the first lab implementation the team of business analysts, data engineers and data scientists works in short sprints of 1–2 weeks. They iterate from business understanding to data intelligence to predictive analytics to insights visualization to generate first a proof of concept and ultimately a prototype running on real data (Thamm et al. 2020).

Factory Phase

After the prototype is built and running on real data, the goal of the factory phase is to actually realize the expected value and bring the AI product to life. Unfortunately, still today most AI products die during that phase. There are so many reasons for this with the main one being unrealistic expectations. In the Lab phase you built dirty work around for complex issues and everybody had high tolerance for bugs of your product. Now in the Factory Phase your AI product is expected to constantly deliver robust predictions, scale to a much larger user base and work on different input data (more markets, more products, more brands, etc.). Naturally, you need a higher budget (often +500k €) and you need to be generous with your timeline towards a first release (6–12 months). You also need to be smart about the selection

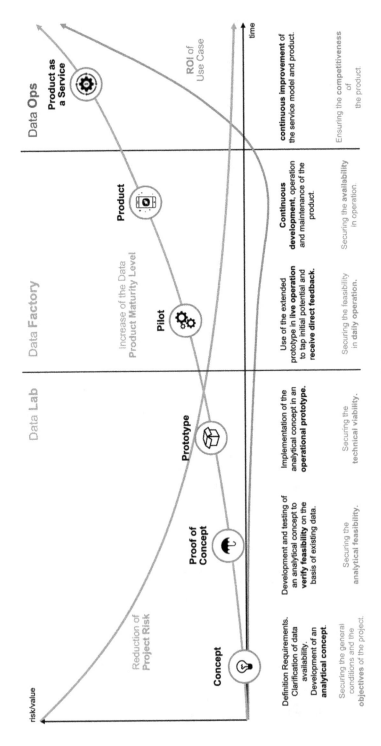

Fig. 18.6 Agile AI product development process with three phases. (Source: Author)

of features that will be part of the first release—with the hardest part being the selection of features that will NOT be part of the release. This comes with the need for sophisticated expectation management skills towards the stakeholders involved. Also during this phase an agile approach as for example suggested by the SCRUM framework is a good one to follow. Go step by step, e.g. sprint by sprint, constantly collect user feedback until you reach the pilot status (like a ß-version in software development) and finally your AI product 1.0 is released.

Operations Phase

In the operations phase your product is in use and customers (whether internal or external) are working with your data product. They will expect stable performance, meaning not only that uptime and sufficient computing resources need to be ensured (which in and of itself is a challenge, since sophisticated AI products are typically very compute intensive), but also that models continue to perform well over time. AI models if not frequently retrained tend to "drift", so as part of the operations phase you should put in place processes to monitor how your model is performing and include adjustment mechanisms for the model if necessary.

Unlike traditional software products, operating an AI product also comes with the additional burden of managing *data dependencies* (i.e. ensuring that changes in input data or updates to pipeline code do not negatively impact your product), *model dependencies* (i.e. ensuring that the models that your data scientists come up with are versioned, packaged and that the correct models are deployed) and *application dependencies* (i.e. ensuring that whatever application uses your models also knows how to interpret its results).

In addition, during the operations phase you need to put processes in place for monitoring and controlling who has access to your product. While we encourage opening AI products for broad use within companies, we do not recommend doing so without also identifying users (both human and technical) and understanding their use cases. Even small changes to any of your product's data, model or application dependencies could have a huge detrimental effect if an unknown business-critical service is unaware of the change.

18.4   AI Culture and Organizational Structure

AI is here to stay. Like the internet or electricity, it can be compared to a fabric that will pervade your whole organization—a meta-technology leveraged to some extent anywhere by your employees. While you are making your first hands on experiences implementing AI prototypes you will encounter resistance and fear within your staff. Today the vast majority inside and outside of your company does not understand how AI works and is influenced by media and science fiction movies. In addition, many of your staff are apprehensive with respect to the new technology or even fearful, especially if they think that a machine is taking over their job. You need to address these feelings for the AI-journey of your company to be successful. To the other extreme, some fellow executives might have been on a showcase roadshow to one of the world's AI hot spots and came back "brainwashed" that AI can solve all problems with the snap of a finger. Both is not true. To build a strong AI culture throughout your entire organization (engaging literally everybody on the payroll) you need to balance expectations and motivation constantly.

Furthermore, it is crucial to understand that AI needs a much more interdisciplinary approach and teamwork within the company than for example your digitization initiative, like including mutual understanding of different stakeholders. Most attempts to turn an enterprise into an AI-company fail, because the data scientists do not know the specific pain points of the business—and the management does not know what AI is able or unable to do. In addition, the development of an AI model involves a lot of domain knowledge from experts who know little or nothing about AI—but all about the relevant data and processes that are at the base of a certain use case.

I believe that the best way to do build a strong AI culture is to be passionate and authentic about AI. Help people understand that humankind is on the verge of a radical change in productivity through AI and now is the time to be part of it within your company. For a deeper dive into the evolutional character of AI for mankind, I can recommend the following two books: "The Second Machine Age: Work, Progress, and Prosperity in a Time of Brilliant Technologies" (Brynjolfsson and McAffee 2014) and "The Zero Marginal Cost Society" (Rifkin 2014). Be passionate and market your results, but don't get mislead into overpromising what's possible.[4]

18.4.1 Vision and Mission

An engaging and specific vision and mission are critical to bring the staff of your company behind the goals you aim to achieve with AI. Let's have a look at how Google does this:

Google's AI vision is: "Bringing the benefits of AI to everyone—At Google AI, we're conducting research that advances the state-of-the-art in the field, applying AI to products and to new domains, and developing tools to ensure that everyone can access AI." (Google AI 2020).

Their AI mission statement is a logical consequence of Google's overall mission: "Google's mission is to organize the world's information and make it universally accessible and useful. AI is helping us do that in exciting new ways, solving problems for our users, our customers, and the world." (Google AI 2020).

With Google deriving their AI vision and mission from the overall company purpose, they align everybody to a coherent goal which builds the foundation of a strong AI culture. Furthermore, this helps in hard investment decisions when for

---

[4]See for example how IBM Watson overpromised and underdelivered—https://spectrum.ieee.org/biomedical/diagnostics/how-ibm-watson-overpromised-and-underdelivered-on-ai-health-care.

example, two AI product candidates may yield a similar return, but there's just funding for one. In this case, the decision for the one which is most consistent with your vision, is easy.

Principle 4: "Leverage your legacy and domain expertise within your industry in order to build unique IP and become the dominant leader of AI products relevant to your internal and external customer base."

18.4.2 Building an In-House AI Team

Following principle no. 4 it makes sense for you to build your own AI capacities. As AI capabilities are crucial to build competitive advantage within your industry it is too risky to solely rely on consulting or software suppliers on the long run. However, for commodity AI cases (sales forecasting, invoicing prediction, web traffic scoring, process mining, etc.) where you are not planning to generate a competitive advantage yourself better buy not make. Furthermore, consulting and service providers can help you gain momentum quickly and prevent typical pitfalls.

One of those pitfalls is to separate your AI business innovation (also called AI strategy), data science and data/AI engineering teams from another into separate pillars. Rather build small interdisciplinary teams for implementing AI use cases—following the two pizza team paradigm by Amazon's CEO, Jeff Bezos (Cain 2017) meaning that a tech team should not have more members than two family pizzas can feed This will also reflect into your culture, as interdisciplinary teams will solve issues on a daily basis before they become big ones. Patrick Glauner discusses different best practices where in the reporting line to set up your in-house AI team (Glauner 2020). Most companies start with a central unit within their IT, finance or most relevant business function. What most successful companies have in common is the maturity evolution illustrated in Fig. 18.7.

Stage 1: After starting first proof of concepts (PoCs) during a first Lab Phase, a community forms around AI enthusiasts. They struggle with standards, budgets and leveraging synergies.

Stage 2: A project organization or strategic initiative is formed with a smaller (usually one to five mio. €) dedicated budget and 2–3 FTE of internal staff in order to build solid prototypes and bring first use cases to production

Stage 3: After first successful prototypes but struggles to get AI use cases productive, an in-house AI team is formed with the objective to bringing AI use cases to production, setting up blueprints for Data & AI governance and raising awareness for AI within the organization.

Stage 4: After further success and first productive AI applications that start generating value, AI is leveraged across the organization and used universally like Microsoft Excel. Costs are relatively high, since AI operations are difficult and a lot of different technologies are used.

Stage 5: The organization can be considered an industry AI champion where an "AI first" strategy is lived day by day, all products are prioritized regarding AI

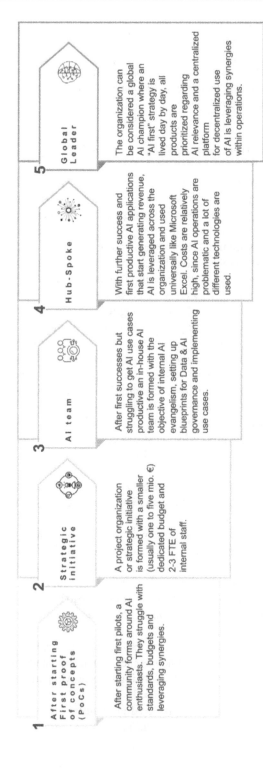

Fig. 18.7 Maturity evolution of organizations in terms of AI capabilities. (Source: Author)

relevance and a centralized platform for decentralized use of AI is leveraging synergies within operations.

18.5   AI Training & Hiring

We are still in the situation of lacking AI talent worldwide. Fortunately, also universities in Europe have started Data Science and AI education programs during the last years. For an overview on German universities please have a look at the article "Studium Künstliche Intelligenz: Diese Universitäten lehren und forschen zu KI" (Lojkasek 2020). Moreover, there is plenty of self-training material and massive open online courses (MOOCs) available as well as dedicated data academies who offer trainings from beginner to expert level. Those developments make it easier and less costly to educate your existing employees on AI. As more and more jobs will be augmented and automated by AI in the future, employers feel the responsibility to develop existing employees into new AI driven roles (Scott 2020). Ultimately, it is often more efficient to train a veteran in your company with a lot of domain understanding basic data science skills instead of hiring an person with a PhD in math and having her/him understand how your business works. In order to setup an effective AI team you need a mix of domain and AI expertise. New roles have risen within the area of AI as depicted in Fig. 18.8. Note that there is a recent trend of replacing "data" or "machine learning" with "ai" as a prefix for the job titles—however, their jobs remain the same.

1. *Business Analyst*: acts as an interface between data team and business unit, has deep domain understanding to translate business requirements into analytical

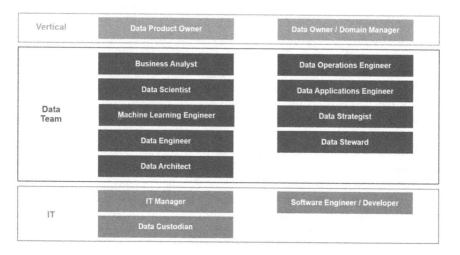

Fig. 18.8 Overview of AI-relevant roles. (Source: Author)

challenges. She/he can be considered as an AI generalist or citizen data scientist with strong communication and visualization skills. Note: the term "citizen data scientist" was coined by the analyst company Gartner in 2018 describing someone with basic skills in data science (Idoine 2018).

2. *Data Scientist*: considered to have the sexiest job of the twenty-first century, they were supposed to be the unicorns of data and AI (Davenport and Patil 2012). She/he knows how to derive input variables from business hypotheses, collect and prepare the data, choose and train machine learning models and deliver the results in a concise visualization. Like a "jack of all trades", she/he can deliver a proof of concept or even prototype within the lab phase (see p. 8), but needs help from engineers as a "master of none" in factory and operations phases.

3. *ML Engineer*: maybe the hottest new role—she/he develops productive software for machine learning (as opposed to prototypical code from Data Scientists), builds pipelines for the development and evaluation of ML models and transfers ML models into productive environment. She/he also creates systems that monitor model quality.

4. *Data Engineer*: also a hot newer role—she/he focuses on data provision for analytics roles, data modelling and data preparation. She/he is also responsible for the design, implementation and documentation of data pipelines to provide productive code that is quality assured following data governance guidelines. Nicknamed "data plumber" she/he builds continuous integration and continuous delivery (CI/CD) pipelines.

5. *Data Architect*: as the name suggests, she/he is responsible for the whole architecture of data platforms and AI products. She/he also analyses existing IT architectures and advises on a technical level for system architectures and processes, also according to DevOps criteria. With experience in classic data warehouse and modern data lake architectures she/he defines concepts how data from different entities and IT systems is stored, used, integrated and managed.

6. *Data Ops Engineer:* similar to an IT operations engineer, she/he is responsible for the smooth operation of the technical data architecture in live operation, ensures that the hardware and infrastructure are working and orchestrates the different technologies and versioning concepts. She/he also manages the pipelines and clusters for the data product and monitoring according to operational concepts, such as service level agreements (SLA) including response times and tickets.

7. *Data Apps Engineer*: analogue and in close coordination with the data ops engineer, she/he is responsible for the smooth operation of the application (AI product) in live operation.

8. *Data Strategist*: often with a background in consulting, she/he designs and executes data strategies, identifies relevant use cases and associated opportunities in the departments and drafts use case roadmaps as well as business cases. Capable of methods like design thinking she/he conducts interviews and workshops for requirements gathering to develop AI-driven business models. She/he sets

guidelines for the legal and ethical handling of data (data governance) with her/his great communication and presentation skills.

9. *IT Manager*: in a classic IT role—she/he is responsible for the IT source systems and operates them from a technical point of view, acting as interface between Data Team and IT.

10. *Software Developer*: still a very relevant role because software developers basically build everything "around" the core AI product like backends and frontends.

Principle 5: "Staff your AI products as diverse as possible with veterans from inside your organization, tech-gurus that you hire from outside and shooting starts among your staff that fancy numbers and algorithms."

Besides training and hiring those specialized data and AI roles into your organization, educate everybody about AI in order to help them adapt to their new roles in the AI era and set your basis for a strong AI culture. It makes sense to distinguish your trainings into three different target groups and educate on the following topics:

1. *C-Level and top executives*: Explain basic buzzwords about data and AI. Show status-quo of most successful AI use cases within and outside industry. Start with use case ideation and define first lighthouse projects. Convey sense of urgency using plausible best practices.

2. *Middle management and division leaders*: Educate on their "sandwich-position" between top executives' expectations to deliver AI return on investment (ROI) and AI expert employees' expectations to play with leading edge technology. Focus on short to middle term AI use cases and necessary capabilities regarding their specific business functions to lower entry barriers.

3. *All operative employees*: Communicate and motivate the companies AI vision and strategy. Educate on basic AI terminology and relief fears of far future dystopia and threat of losing their jobs. Motivate for deeper AI training and applying for AI roles.

18.6   Data & AI Governance

If data is the new oil/electricity/fabric it should be treated like a valuable company asset. Let's imagine the following formula:

Principle 6: Value $=$ Data $\times$ AI $+$ X.

Following principle no. 1, we generate value from data by leveraging AI. The "X" in the formula above represents the actual business application—the specific problem we solve. Which of those components can we successfully protect against competition in the long run?

The X $=$ Application/business domain? No because business applications and business models are being copied every day. Hard to successfully protect longterm.

Fig. 18.9 Key aspects of data governance. (Source: Author)

The AI = algorithm? This is harder to answer. Of course, you can patent your algorithm and try hard to keep your key employees or partners who invented the algorithm and model structure. But also, here in the long run, similar algorithms will be invented by your competition—that is also the reason why leading tech companies are open sourcing their IP instead of protecting it (Google Open Source 2020).

The Data = your own data generated within your business processes? We have a winner. Your data is what makes your AI products unique. No one else can train machine learning models from your data and come up with exact the same models— if you protect your own data and treat it like the precious asset it is.

According to Dr. Carsten Dittmar and Christian Fürber "Data Governance is the management system for data and comprises all measures to orchestrate people, processes and technology in such a way that operational data is assigned the status of a company-wide asset, the value of the data is efficiently maximized in compliance with a legal and ethical framework and the availability of semantically uniform, content-consistent, accurate and timely data can be ensured at all times" (Dittmar and Fürber 2020). See Fig. 18.9 for further details on Data Governance.

18.6.1 Motivation and Objectives of Data Governance

Treating data as a company asset and giving it high importance is a prerequisite for following principle no. 4 "Building unique IP"—to be more specific in Fig. 18.10 there are the six motivators for data governance along with examples for how they create value for you and what measures you can take in order to achieve this.

18.6.2 Central Roles Within Data Governance

Similar to existing roles within your business functions like finance and human resources, new roles are emerging within the area of data governance:

Data Governance Goal	Example Value Creation	Exemplary Measures
Data Transparency	◆ Reduction of search costs/development times ◆ Development of new potential/business areas ◆ Reduction of procurement costs of external data ◆ Reduction of data and system redundancies	◆ Introduction of a central data catalogue ◆ Establishment of data responsibilities ◆ Definition and implementation of processes for publishing and enrichment of metadata
Data Quality / Data Integrity	◆ Increase in process efficiency ◆ Basis for automation/AI ◆ More turnover, satisfaction and service quality through 360° customer view ◆ Lower procurement/production costs through 360° product view	◆ Development of data monitoring and data cleansing systems and services ◆ Establishment of quality gates in data production ◆ Establishment of a standardized data quality management ◆ Monitoring of data quality with data quality reports
Data Availability	◆ Reduction of development times in information supply and digitization ◆ Increase employee satisfaction and productivity ◆ Identification of inefficiencies	◆ Building a central raw data layer ◆ Development of self-service analytics platforms ◆ Establishment of a standard process for data access authorizations ◆ Establishment of a data owner to release data
Data Protection / Data Compliance	◆ Avoidance of fines ◆ Strengthening customer loyalty by increasing trust ◆ Strengthening corporate image ◆ Maintaining the business model/licenses	◆ Basic creation of legal certainty and security of action in data exchange through guidelines ◆ Classification of data according to protection needs, confidentiality and divisibility
Data Security	◆ Avoidance of financial losses/image damage ◆ Protection against industrial espionage/securing your own competitive advantage	◆ Definition of structural measures for access control ◆ Definition of security measures for electronic transmission
Data Monetization	◆ Additional business area through data services for external customers ◆ New customers/partners/skills ◆ Additional revenue	◆ Supplementation of physical core products by digital services ◆ Provision of analysis results ◆ Development of new data-based business models

Fig. 18.10 Overview of data governance goals. (Source: Author)

1. *Data Governance Director*[5] is responsible for all data governance activities, owns the budget and acts as central escalation authority. As leader of the data governance organization, she/he is member of the senior management with a deep understanding of core processes and functions.
2. *Data Custodian*: is in charge of the IT implementation for technical specifications like data quality measures, monitoring data management processes and correct connection of data sources as well as the database structure. She/he works within or very close to the IT department.
3. *Data Steward*: organizes domain-oriented data objects (key performance indicators (KPIs), master data structures). She/he works within the line of business, has deep understanding of the data generating process and the actual meaning and interpretation of the data. Thus, she/he designs and executes logical and semantic data quality measures.
4. *Data Owner*: organizes data areas (data domains). She/he is the more senior role compared to Data Stewards and has coherent understanding of the overall domain landscape. She/he is accountable for metadata enrichment policies and decides upon who can access the data.
5. *Data/AI Product Owner*: is responsible for an AI product or a data-driven business application. She/he is part of the respective business function and as a senior manager possesses great understanding of the overall business process landscape. Thus, she/he defines and prioritizes user requirements/product features.

18.6.3 Best Practice Data Catalog Processes

During the last years the data catalog has become best practice for implementing data governance. Figure 18.11 illustrates the process how a data catalog orchestrates knowledge and data sharing within a larger enterprise. For further details on the topic see this article: https://www.alexanderthamm.com/de/blog/datenkatalog-grundlage-datengetriebene-use-cases/

18.7 Data & AI Platform

In order to leverage data and AI across your whole organization you need technology: hardware and software to store, process and analyze your data, build machine learning algorithms and build intuitive interfaces for humans to interact with AI. Once your first prototypes of AI products are up and running and diving deeper into your data looking for hidden patterns in your business, you encounter three mayor challenges:

---

[5]In some companies this role is covered by the Chief Data Officer.

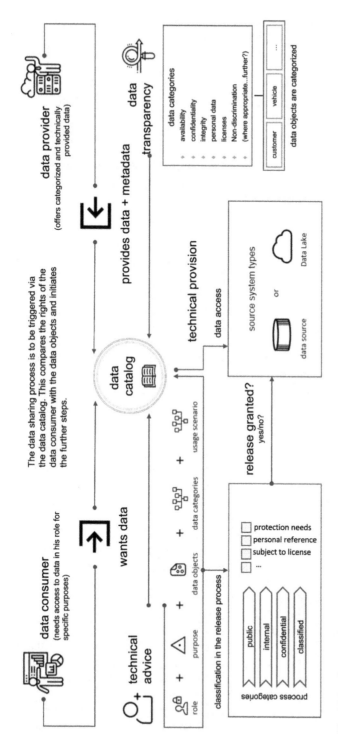

Fig. 18.11 Data catalog as core for data governance. (Source: Author)

1. You realize scaling your prototype is much harder than expected
2. You don't know how IT can operate your AI product
3. You get confused with all the different software tools everybody uses

What you need is an AI platform that balances synergies and scalability with state-of the art flexibility and versatility. You can never have both to 100 percent, but best practices exist to find the right balance:

Principle 7: "Build an AI reference architecture and adjust it to user personas and use cases."

Figure 18.12 below illustrates a possible reference architecture for data and AI. Don't worry if this looks somehow overwhelming and complex to you—we will describe it bit by bit. Also, our goal is not to make you an expert on AI architecture but to explain key elements and core terminology.

1. *Data Hub:* includes all storages of raw data, e.g. several different data lakes that have to be separated for example due to legal reasons where data may not be blended.
2. *Data Lake*: a centralized repository that stores and processes company-wide data in its raw format. Like a data warehouse, it is an architectural blueprint, i.e. a logical concept rather than a tangible entity. Unlike a data warehouse, the data lake can include all different types of data like structured data (rows and columns), semi-structured data (CSV, logs, XML, JSON) and unstructured data (text, images, audio) (Thamm et al. 2020).
3. *Data Transformation Layer*: here, the data gets prepared for machine learning and further analytical purposes. Following predefined user scenarios, data is prepared into data products (microservices) to optimize performance for later stages.
4. *Data Warehouse (DWH)*: as a classic way to store structured data, the DWH is still used in modern architectures to quickly answer predefined questions and for periodical reporting. So, the data warehouse is a centralized data storage system that integrates company-wide data. Like the data lake it is a logical concept and realized with several relational database systems.
5. *Stream Processing*: here we process every single datapoint as soon as it is generated and do something with it in real-time. Consider for example a repair-facility fitted camera at an entrance where trains are driven into. Instead of taking pictures of the whole train and then processing them all in one batch, each individual picture is sent into the cloud as soon as it is taken, where an AI algorithm then detects damage and sends a result back so that facility operators can immediately start working on any detected damage.
6. *Batch Processing*: here we typically deal with historical data that has been collected over time. If we stay with the example of the repair-facility we have above, then once a month we might process all pictures that were taken in that month and use them to retrain our models.
7. *Computation Layer*: this stage is where most of the magic happens. Machine learning models are trained, tested and used for predictions (scoring).

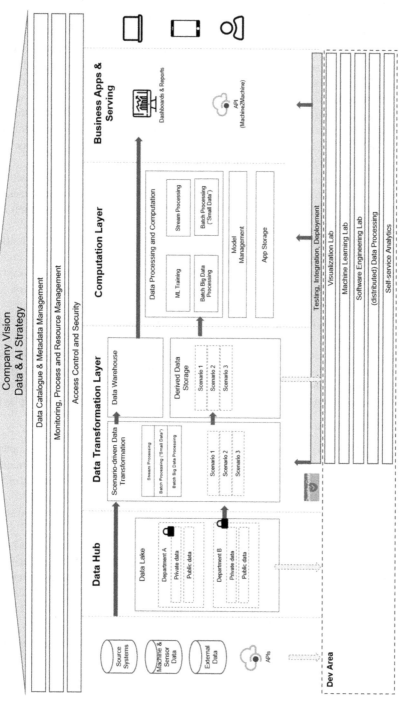

Fig. 18.12 Possible reference architecture for data and AI. (Source: Author)

8. *ML Training*: within the ML training process, machine learning models are learning to predict outcomes or represent patterns from historic data.

9. *Model Management*: the process of developing an AI Product is iterative and results in various candidate models. The creation of these models needs to be tracked in such a way that it is clear which models were created using which input datasets, model architectures, hyperparameters, etc.—and such that performance metrics are comparable across all candidates. The purpose of a model management system is to perform such tracking and to present the tracked information in a manner that allows data scientists to select a model to put into production. In addition, Model Management systems are responsible for monitoring AI Models in production.

10. *App Storage*: acts as a store unit for running an AI app. Can be used for temporary app-specific data or in combination with in-memory databases for fast ad hoc calculations. Often used in combination with data exploration and data discovery tools.

11. *Dev Area*: within the development area, business analysts and data scientists can play and explore the data. Also known as a "sandbox" experiments are conducted and most of the development work within the lab phase is conducted. Usually, you have different lab environments depending on the users' preferences for software and use cases.

12. *Business Apps and Serving*: this layer represents interface for all business users. Optimally, they can consume AI products across different devices with beautiful and easy to understand visualizations. Moreover, this layer should enable users to collaborate—discuss predictions, annotate known anomalies detected by AI, investigate rising issues, simulate financial forecasts. In other words, interact with data and AI to become more efficient and effective on a daily and playful basis.

A model such as the one above can be implemented in one of three manners: on-premise, meaning that the hardware that your platforms run on is maintained by you directly; in the cloud, meaning that you outsource the management of the infrastructure to a dedicated provider; or a hybrid-cloud, meaning that some of the infrastructure that your platform runs on remains under your management and some of it is managed by a cloud provider.

The trend in recent years is very much to move to an entirely cloud-based infrastructure. Major cloud providers such as Amazon Web Services, Microsoft Azure and Google Cloud Platform can provide not only hardware infrastructure but also additional layers of managed services at huge economies of scale. Of course, the cost of using cloud providers is still significant, but in the long run companies benefit significantly from reduced cost and maintenance complexity, can scale usage up and down almost at will, and gain access to sophisticated best-in-class tools and services.

18.8   Conclusion

The first part of this chapter explains what AI is and that your mission should be "To turn Data into Value leveraging technology like AI" (principle no. 1). There is no doubt, that AI will change our lives like the invention of the internet did for the last three decades. "If you miss the AI train you will be out of business within the next 10 years." (principle no. 2). In order to achieve this, I suggest the following step-by-step approach: "After building your use case portfolio, build prototypes in the Lab, scale to more users and robust products within the Factory and run your product as a service in Operations." (principle no. 3) As a prerequisite for success, build your AI vision based on your company's principles and core values and keep in mind to "leverage your legacy and domain expertise within your industry to build unique IP and become the dominant leader of AI products relevant to your internal and external customer base." (principle no. 4) Your success will highly depend on the right people and team set up. I recommend you to "staff your AI products as diverse as possible with veterans from inside your organization, tech-gurus that you hire from outside and shooting starts among your staff that fancy numbers and algorithms." (principle no. 5). Be aware that "data" is the most important part in the equation of principle no. 6 "Value = Data × AI + X" and thus invest in a thorough data governance setup along with dedicated roles who take care of setup and implementation. Last but not least, in order to leverage synergies and create AI products faster, "build an AI reference architecture and adjust it to user personas and use cases." (principle no. 7).

References

Alexander Thamm GmbH (2020a) Case studies. Sehen Sie sich unsere spannenden data science Projekte an. Alexander Thamm GmbH. https://www.alexanderthamm.com/de/usecases/. Accessed 19 June 2020

Alexander Thamm GmbH (2020b) Data journey. Start your journey from the Data Strategy to the finished Data Product. Alexander Thamm GmbH. https://www.alexanderthamm.com/en/data-journey/. Accessed 27 June 2020

Alexander Thamm GmbH (2020c) Use case workshop. Starten Sie noch heute Ihre data journey. Alexander Thamm GmbH. https://www.alexanderthamm.com/de/data-science-use-case-workshop/. Accessed 27 June 2020

Brynjolfsson E, McAffee A (2014) The second machine age: work, progress, and prosperity in a time of brilliant technologies. W. W. Norton & Company

Cain A (2017) Jeff Bezos's productivity tip? the '2 pizza rule' – this trick helps amazon's founder keep his meetings productive and useful. Inc. https://www.inc.com/business-insider/jeff-bezos-productivity-tip-two-pizza-rule.html. Accessed 28 June 2020

Davenport H, Patil DJ (2012) Data scientists: The Sexiest Job of the 21st century. Harvard Business Review. https://hbr.org/2012/10/data-scientist-the-sexiest-job-of-the-21st-century. Accessed 29 June 2020

Dittmar C, Fürber C (2020) Data governance als Wegbereiter der Digitalisierung. In: Gluchowski P (ed) Data governance – Grundlagen, Konzepte und Anwendungen. dpunkt.verlag, pp 13–33

Glauner P (2020) Unlocking the power of artificial intelligence for your business. In: Glauner P, Plugmann P (eds) Innovative technologies for market leadership: investing in the future (future of business and finance). Springer, pp 45–59

Google AI (2020) About Google AI. Google AI. https://ai.google/about/. Accessed 28 June 2020

Google Open Source (2020) Why open source?. Google Open Source. opensource.google/docs/why/. Accessed 28 June 2020

Grace K, Salvatier J, Dafoe A, Zhang B, Evans O (2018) Viewpoint: when will AI exceed human performance? Evidence from AI experts. J Artif Intell Res. https://www.jair.org/index.php/jair/article/view/11222/26431. Accessed 30 June 2020

Hsu F (2002) Behind deep blue: building the computer that defeated the world chess champion. Princeton University Press

Idoine C (2018) Citizen data scientists and why they matter. Gartner. https://blogs.gartner.com/carlie-idoine/2018/05/13/citizen-data-scientists-and-why-they-matter/. Accessed 29 June 2020

Kasparov G, Speelman J, Wade B (1995) Garry Kasparov's fighting chess. Henry Holt & Co

Lojkasek J (2020) Studium Künstliche Intelligenz: Diese Universitäten lehren und forschen zu KI. Alexander Thamm GmbH. https://www.alexanderthamm.com/de/blog/studium-kuenstliche-intelligenz/. Accessed 30 June 2020

McGrath Gunther R (2011) Failing by design. Harvard Business Review. https://hbr.org/2011/04/failing-by-design%20or%20The%20lean%20startup. Accessed 27 June 2020

Ng A (2018) AI transformation playbook. How to lead your company into the AI era. Landing AI. https://landing.ai/wp-content/uploads/2020/05/LandingAI_Transformation_Playbook_11-19.pdf. Accessed 27 June 2020

Ng A (2019) Andrew Ng explains enterprise ai strategy. CXOTALK. https://www.cxotalk.com/episode/andrew-ng-explains-enterprise-ai-strategy. Accessed 19 June 2020

Rifkin J (2014) The zero marginal cost society: the internet of things, the collaborative commons, and the eclipse of capitalism. St. Martin's Press

Schrittwieser J, Antonoglou I, Hubert T, Simonyan K, Sifret L, Schmitt S, Guez A, Lockhart E, Hassabis E, Graepel T, Lillicrap T, Silver D (2020) Mastering atari, go, chess and shogi by planning with a learned model. ArXiv.org. https://arxiv.org/pdf/1911.08265.pdf. Accessed 30 June 2020

Scott K (2020) Reprogramming the American dream: from rural America to Silicon Valley – making AI service us all. Harper Business

Shu C (2014) Google acquires artificial intelligence startup DeepMind for more than $500M. Techcrunch. https://techcrunch.com/2014/01/26/google-deepmind/?guccounter=1. Accessed 27 June 2020

Thamm A (2017) Big Data is dead. Data is "Just Data", regardless of quantity, structure or speed. LinkedIn. https://www.linkedin.com/pulse/big-data-dead-just-regardless-quantity-structure-speed-thamm/. Accessed 19 June 2020

Thamm A, Gramlich M, Borek A (2020) The ultimate data and AI guide: 150 FAQs about artificial intelligence, machine learning and data. Data AI Press

Turing, A (1950) Computing Machinery and Intelligence. Mind, New Series, 59(236):433–460

Leveraging the Human Factor through Holarchy: A Case Study

Habib Lesevic

19.1 Introduction

In an increasingly complex and volatile business environment, an organisation's ability to not only execute operationally but devise innovation that is meaningful and relevant for its markets and employees alike is becoming the seminal strategic capability to cultivate. In addition, rapid advancements in robotics and artificial intelligence as well as their growing implementation in organisations' operating models are challenging the human's role in our productive processes. Where previously analytical thinking, rational decision making and operational execution were high value tasks performed by predominately humans, robotics and AI have made such inroads, that human superiority over these tasks is in doubt—and in some places has already been surpassed. As AI-powered organisations grow evermore capable of complex problem solving and efficient execution, humans' ability to empathise, envision, innovate, create value and make meaning even in volatile environments will become the foremost value-add of a human workforce and the key driver of sustainable competitive advantage. We have coined this profoundly human capability the "Human Factor."

Yet, most organisations today still function on operating models that place emphasis on hiring, cultivating and progressing analytical and executional competencies while limiting degrees of freedom for experimentation, discovery and innovation in the name of control. In other words, if the Human Factor will become the foremost driver of competitive advantage in a hyper-dynamic, automated society, organisations today are not structured and operated in a manner that allows them to fully cultivate and leverage their Human Factor.

H. Lesevic (✉)
Journey 2 Creation GmbH, Berlin, Germany
e-mail: habib@j2c.de

V. Nestle et al. (eds.), *Creating Innovation Spaces*, Management for Professionals,
https://doi.org/10.1007/978-3-030-57642-4_19

259

The answer to this dilemma is not a new method or a new management fad—rather it is a thorough rethink of the very organisational principles that have guided businesses to growth and success since the Industrial Revolution.

In this chapter, I would like to explore the opportunity that lies in an operational rethink and highlight the human potential that can be unlocked by embracing a different approach—namely a "holarchic" one—to operating a business.

19.1.1 What Is a Holarchy and Why Does it Matter?

The word holarchy is derived from the Greek word "holon" which describes the principle of something being part of a whole while at the same time also being whole in itself (Koestler 1967). Thus, a holarchy is an organisational ideal in which all parts within an organisation integrate into a meaningful whole yet can simultaneously function individually as wholes as well. In applied terms, we take this to mean that each individual within an organisation ought to be equipped to autonomously and intrinsically act in the best interest of the organisation, make meaningful strategic and tactical decisions for the organisation, and contribute towards its purpose all while adhering to the organisation's ethos and behavioural principles at all times.

This is quite different to a traditional hierarchy—derived from the Greek *hier + arkhes*, meaning "sacred leader"—where strategic decision making and operational execution tend to be divided across hierarchical lines, usually travelling from top to bottom respectively.

Where hierarchies are excellent at providing control, coordination, and predictability across large organisational structures, holarchies tend to emphasise responsiveness, adaptability and dynamism over control and predictability.

Our premise is that operating models that aspire towards the holarchic ideal provide the best structural foundation upon which to design environments that drive innovation, cultivate purposeful value creation and leverage the Human Factor in highly volatile and fast-changing business contexts.

19.1.2 How to Design a Holarchy?

It would be my pleasure to present a blueprint on how to implement a holarchy in any organisation—and in fact such attempts indeed exist (Robertson 2015). However, we have come to recognise that a sustainable operating model needs to be designed along the particular contextual circumstances that surround it. As such, it would be counterproductive to proclaim a new operating model on these pages for the reader to implement. Instead, I would like to propose three factors to consider when designing a holarchic operating model. We will then follow this section up with a case discussion of our company's own holarchic operating model to illustrate and translate these factors into a real-life example.

19.1.2.1 Factor 1: Surface & Challenge Assumptions

Shifting an organisation from a hierarchical to a holarchic operating model is not merely a shift in method or process—it is foremost a shift in paradigm. Figure 19.1 depicts the anatomy of a paradigm using the WPA model. Therefore, the first step in any such transformation project should be the surfacing and challenging of consciously and unconsciously held assumptions on the topic (Mason and Mitroff 1981). Why is this important? The worldview we hold with its underlying beliefs, experiences, values and assumptions affects the radius of possibilities that we perceive which in turn affects the choices and actions that we believe to be available to us. If we do not make such assumptions explicit and challenge them in the process, we risk limiting our radius of possibilities to the known and thus risk enacting changes that are merely cosmetic in nature—if even that. To put it differently: An organisation's operating model is informed by the assumptions it holds about effective organisation, human nature and motivation, the purpose of an organisation, leadership, as well as its process of value creation.

In order to achieve radical transformation of an operating model, the operating model must be challenged radically—that is at its very root (radical from Latin *radix* meaning "root"). This is done by answering questions such as the following and surfacing from their respective answers any explicit or implicit values, assumptions and beliefs that may be held:

- What makes an organisation successful?
- What makes a good employee?

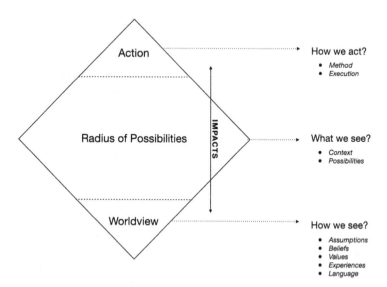

Fig. 19.1 The WPA Model visualises the anatomy of a paradigm and how its elements influence one another. (Source: author)

- What are the five to ten most important expectations that the organisation holds towards its employees and why?
- What are the five to ten most important expectations that the organisation holds towards its leadership and why?
- If there were no leadership, the organisation would ...
- If there were no leadership, the staff would ...
- An employee is most motivated when ...
- The purpose of this organisation is .... in order to ...

Surfaced beliefs, values, and assumptions must then be challenged in their *trueness* (is this true?), *usefulness* (does this empower or disempower the organisation and its staff?), and *desirability* (shall these values, beliefs and assumptions be guiding principles for the organisation's operating model?), which in turn provides the basis for engagement with the next factor.

19.1.2.2 Factor 2: Design a Purposeful, Productive Environment

An organisation's productive environment emerges from the physical, processual, and methodological structures put in place within which employees collaborate and perform their productive activities. Processes in particular are often not recognised as constituting a productive environment, when in fact they are crucial! The processes by which information is managed and shared, decisions are made, resources are managed across the organisation, communication is practiced, direction is coordinated and enforced, behaviour is incentivised and performance is managed as well as the tools with which all of this is achieved agglomerate into one of the most important and most defining aspects of the productive environment to affect employees' willingness and ability to perform, contribute, and innovate. Therefore, it is essential to design processes and employ tools and methods that are *genuinely* in tune with the values, intentions and purpose that an organisation wants to embody and cultivate. This is of course a highly individual undertaking as no two organisations are alike and processes and tools *must be* fit for and adapted to purpose, people, product and ethos (see Fig. 19.2).

What is more, all elements of a productive environment must be purposeful— that is, it must be clear what their purpose is and how they contribute towards the overarching goal of the organisation and its creation of value. Note that here *"reasonable"* is often equated to *"purposeful"*, however reason and purpose are hardly the same thing at all! The former describes *the circumstances that have led to something* whereas the latter describes the *aim that something is supposed to achieve.*

In order to devise an operating model that drives innovation and leverages the Human Factor, it is essential to deliberately design a productive environment that embodies an organisation's values, is explicitly purposeful throughout, and is adapted to its specific context including its purpose, people, product, and ethos.

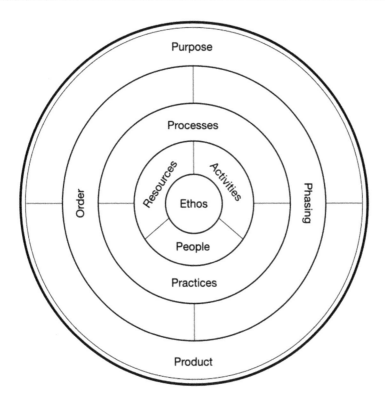

Fig. 19.2 The IVM Framework highlights elements to consider when designing for a purposeful, productive environment. (Source: author)

19.1.2.3 Factor 3: Continuously Cultivate Mindset and Culture

When it comes to designing and employing a holarchic operating model that can leverage an organisation's Human Factor, one of the core ingredients of success is the continuous cultivation of mindset and culture. Given that in a holarchy all parts are supposed to be able to function autonomously as wholes at any given time, its unique challenge—next to ensuring that the environmental conditions enable staff to enact this expectation—is to ensure that employees are emancipated and empowered to a degree that allows for relevant, purposeful, and meaningful autonomous decision making and action to occur.

This is often as much a matter of psychological structure, self-image, self-belief, contextual awareness and assertion of ownership within each employee as it is a matter of structure, orientation, and degrees of freedom in their environment. These components of mindset cannot just be anticipated to manifest purely by *expecting* them from employees—they must be actively and continuously cultivated to come to fruition. (Fromm 1942)

At the same time, feelings of belonging and psychological safety can support and accelerate the cultivation of empowerment and emancipation in the individual (see

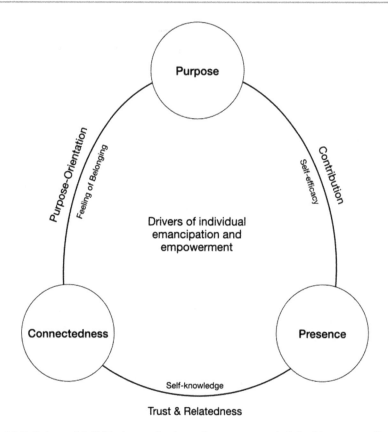

Fig. 19.3 Drivers of individual emancipation and empowerment in holarchic systems. (Source: author)

Fig. 19.3). This is why the continuous cultivation of mindset should be accompanied by efforts to establish and nurture a culture of trust where the predominate coordinates of belonging are relatedness and purposeful contribution (Zak 2017).

19.2 Case Study

On the following pages, I want to enliven the theory discussed thus far by laying out a practical, real-life example of a holarchic operating model that is successfully in daily use at an established organisation.

The case at hand is our company, J2C—Journey 2 Creation GmbH. J2C is an innovation and consulting company based in Berlin, Germany and was established in 2014. Our focus is on generating entrepreneurial growth, driving radical collaboration, and cultivating human potential in our clients. We founded J2C with the intention to build a company that would not only deliver meaningful, innovative and sustainable value to its clients, but do so in a manner that would transcend the established operating models that are commonplace in our industry. Consequently, J2C has been exploring, developing and operating a holarchic model since its very inception. In this process, we discovered early on that, as of yet, no blueprint for a functional, transferable holarchic operating model exists and that we would have to design a suitable model ourselves. In that sense, the following pages are not to be understood as a blueprint for holarchy, but rather as a snapshot and experience report that is meant to provide inspiration, insight, and orientation to anyone who intends to develop a holarchic operating model for their organisation—be that a corporation, a government agency, or a startup.

The case is mapped out along the three factors introduced in the previous sections in order to facilitate the link between the choices made in the case and the theory that inspired them—and in fact emerged from them. What is more, due to the inevitable constraints that come with the format of a book chapter, not all minute details or iterations of our journey to developing our current holarchic operating model can be presented here as that would go beyond the scope of this book. Nevertheless, everything that is presented here is in daily operation and integral to the running of our company.

19.2.1 Factor 1: Surfacing & Challenging Assumptions

When we set out to found J2C, we made a conscious choice to embrace and develop an operating model that would place great emphasis on leveraging the Human Factor to the best of our ability. This also meant that we actively decided against operating the company in one of the established models that are commonplace in our industry as those tend to build on assumptions that we deemed incompatible with the objectives we had set out for ourselves.

19.2.1.1 Assumptions on Strategic Control

Most common operating models in our industry (and beyond) are at heart based on a hierarchical foundation and adhere to the organisational principles of the "Machine" (Morgan 1986). This means that they emphasise the concentration of strategic decision making power and control predominately at the top of the hierarchy. Metaphorically speaking, such operating models assume that "one brain" ought to direct "many limbs." The assumption is that, in order to ensure strategic coherence and meaningful production, a centralised controller is needed to organise and coordinate all productive efforts, thereby prioritising control, planning and execution in their operational logic over participation and discovery (Laloux and Wilber 2014).

These perspectives are wholly incompatible with a holarchic approach, as they restrict the "part" from being a whole in its own right by restricting access to information and strategic decision-making power.

We realised that in a holarchic operating model, the metaphor of an "Organism" or "Network" is more appropriate, where "many brains" direct "many limbs" (often their own) and strategic decision-making power is—for the most part—decentralised and localised. The assumption is that through contribution, conflict and discovery a meaningful strategic direction and, in consequence, productive coherence will *emerge* from within the collective intelligence of the organisation (Eberhart et al. 2001). Thus, a holarchic operating model will emphasise self-organisation over hierarchical domination and will aim to encourage contribution, conflict and discovery in order to accelerate emergence rather than insisting on long-term planning and linear execution of such plans.

19.2.1.2 Assumptions on Self-Organisation

One major mistake we made at the beginning of our process was that we approached the idea of self-organisation indiscriminately. In other words, we did not distinguish between the different reasons and purposes of self-organisation. Only with time did we discover that there seem to be in fact two major motivations to self-organise: self-organisation for participation and self-organisation for contribution. Both motivations are born out of a perceived under-utilisation of the available human potential in hierarchical operating models, but the assumptions as to *why* such potential is under-utilised differ. In the first perspective, hierarchical operating models under-utilise human potential because participation in decision making processes is strictly (and hierarchically) regulated. In the second perspective, hierarchical operating models under-utilise human potential because their structures do not allow for meaningful contributions to be made easily as they restrict their "travel upward" to the strategic decision makers who could actually enforce them. At first sight this may seem like a trivial detail, but in fact the implications for the design of a holarchic operating model are significant.

If an operating model is designed to enable self-organisation for participation, participation in decision making processes is elevated to a *right* and the aim of the model becomes that as many participate in decision making processes as possible. This is akin to democratic or sociocratic models.

If an operating model is designed to enable self-organisation for contribution however, the aim of the model becomes to enable and foster meaningful contribution across the organisation and to ensure that the most relevant and purposeful contributions make it to market. In this approach, participation in decision making processes is not a right but rather a *privilege* that is earned through repeated purposeful, impactful contribution and that can be lost again accordingly. This is akin to evolutionary or meritocratic models.

We discovered that an operating model based on self-organisation for contribution is more likely to produce purposeful and impactful autonomous contributions that emerge into strategic coherence. We also discovered that decision making processes produce better, faster and more purposeful results and that they are less susceptible to rogue influences when participation in decision making processes is "gated" by repeatedly relevant proof of contribution.

19.2.1.3 Assumptions on Process Design

As discussed previously, processes are integral to operating models. However, we discovered that the concept of a "process" can in fact be inadequate for holarchic operating models as a process implies linear execution of a string of tasks arranged in a particular order. The key issue here is not the linearity, but rather that a process doesn't leave much room to interpret the environment it takes place in and make adaptations in accordance to its environmental conditions. This stands in direct opposition to the principles of a holarchic operating model, where employees are encouraged and expected to autonomously make purposeful and relevant decisions and take impactful actions in dynamic, volatile environments. The alternative is to conceptualise processes as *heuristics* instead. A heuristic is a set of guidelines, methods or approaches that aims to produce immediate results while encouraging and even requiring engagement and discovery with the immediate environment at hand. While this can seem a mere matter of semantics at first glance, we noticed a shift in our design decisions as well as our staff's felt empowerment and emancipation, when we started formulating heuristics instead of processes for our company's workflows. Examples of this will be presented in a later section.

19.2.1.4 Assumptions on Human Motivation

A commonly held assumption in hierarchical operating models is that human nature is such that any given individual will tend towards the minimum necessary effort unless incentivised. In addition, the most effective incentive mechanisms are assumed to be external—renumeration, promotion, status, or even threat. What is more, it is often assumed that the majority of people lack the strategic and ana-lytical acumen to autonomously make purposeful and impactful decisions without hierarchical guidance. This preconception on human motivation and capability is irreconcilable with a holarchic operating model, as such a model depends to a significant degree on the self-motivated contribution of its participants. Luckily, experience has given us ample evidence that as long as an individual feels empowered and is provided with at least a minimum of orientation, they are likely to act in a self-motivated, purpose-orientated and proactive manner. What is more, we have discovered that a holarchic operating model can inspire employees to embrace their employment as a mean to formulate, embody and propagate meaning in their lives and in the environments they serve.

19.2.1.5 Assumptions on Organisational Purpose

In hierarchical operating models the assumption tends to be that the primary purpose of an organisation is to generate profit and satisfy the growth expectations of its shareholders and investors. We discovered that this is entirely insufficient to inspire intrinsic motivation, purpose-orientation, and intrinsic ownership across a broad section of an organisation's staff. To operate a holarchic model, an organisation needs to define its purpose on the basis of the meaningful value it wants to create and deliver to its markets and the positive impact it intends to have on the lives of its customers and its broader environment. In fact, this can be taken even further: Laloux and Wilber (2014) for example argues that a meaningful purpose alone is not enough; the purpose needs to have an evolutionary quality to it—that is, be relevant not just in its immediate business context but in a larger planetarian, evolutionary context as well—in order to achieve the motivational pull in staff. I would like to add that, whatever the purpose of the organisation may be, it is essential that this is an authentic and genuine purpose rather than a mere marketing statement.

19.2.2 Factor 2: Designing a Purposeful Productive Environment

In designing our company's productive environment, we went through several iterations and experimented with different conceptualisations of the company over its six years of existence. It is worthwhile to note that this process of experimentation, discovery and iteration is still ongoing. Thus, what is presented on the following pages should be understood as a snapshot of the current state of affairs rather than the final version of our holarchic operating model. That said, the current operating model has been in place for a few years now and so far has withstood the test of time in the sense that no major changes to the design have been necessary since its emergence. It is also important to consider the elements presented in this section not in isolation but as interwoven elements which together constitute a (hopefully) coherent productive environment. I should add that, while an attempt was made to present a complete picture, not all subtleties to all elements of the environment will have made it into this chapter, as such an endeavour would go beyond the scope of this book.

19.2.2.1 Conceptualising the Productive Environment

Given that the experience with holarchic operating models is still comparatively sparse amongst entrepreneurs (system designers) and employees (system participants) alike, we have discovered that it is beneficial to provide a visual conceptualisation of the holarchic productive environment akin to an organisational chart. After several experimental iterations, we settled and currently conceptualise our productive environment with what we call the 40° Degrees Model (see Fig. 19.4).

The 40° Degrees Model suggests that our productive environment is designed on the basis of a shared ethos which at once represents the foundation as well as the rules of engagement of this environment. The latter aspect is further represented by the shared boundaries emerging from the shared ethos. Note that it is an ongoing discussion within our organisation, whether the shared ethos should be institutionalised through the creation of a policy document. So far we have decided against that, as we are convinced that a shared ethos and its corresponding values and beliefs must be lived and embodied by all staff to have any genuine weight and relevance. The risk of institutionalising such an ethos through the creation of an authoritative document (e.g. a "code of ethics") risks to externalise the burden of embodiment from the individual to the document itself, thereby losing its function as the regulating principles of action and interaction within the operating model. What is more, capturing the ethos in a policy document risks rendering it static so that

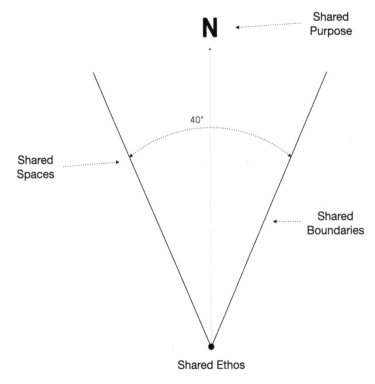

Fig. 19.4 Our 40° Degrees Model conceptualises J2C's productive environment as a bounded shared space with inherent degrees of freedom orientated towards the delivery of a shared purpose. (Source: author)

it may not evolve with the organisation as its staff, purpose, and maturity evolves. Ethos in our organisation is therefore lived, shared and evolved in a manner that is akin to an oral tradition rather than a written tradition (Davis 2009).

Elements that make up this shared ethos are the paradigmatic assumptions discussed in the sections above, as well as values and beliefs on mindset, behaviour, conflict culture and collaboration outlined in the text below.

Next up, the 40° Degrees Model demands the existence of a shared purpose and represents this shared purpose as a cardinal direction towards which the entire productive environment is configured. This implies that the purpose has enough clarity, meaning, and relevance to serve as an orientating factor at all times while also alluding to the importance of the metaphorical magnetism and universal relevance a purpose should exude to serve as cardinal direction for all employees. Similar as with the ethos, so far we have resisted capturing the organisation's purpose formally and definitely with such classical tools as e.g. a mission statement for the same reasons as outlined above. That said, part of the purpose of an organisation usually gets formally transported through its value propositions to its market. So in a way, our organisation's purpose does at least in part exist in some written form, though great care is taken to ensure that this does not lead to a deterioration of the purpose to a marketing or employer branding ploy.

Next, the 40° Degrees Model emphasises the importance of shared boundaries to a productive environment. Boundaries are important for two reasons: First, they give orientation and direction to employees to ensure that all actions and interactions within the environment are in accordance with the organisation's shared ethos and directed towards its shared purpose. Second, shared boundaries are important to the emergence of a distinct identity and thus feelings of belonging, ownership and ultimately an organisational culture. Therefore, defining what is *not* within the bounds of a productive environment is as important as defining what *is* within that environment.

In the 40° Degrees Model a shared space emerges from the previously discussed elements, within which employees are given full degrees of freedom to conceptualise, negotiate, embody and deliver the organisation's purpose. These shared spaces can be facilitated through heuristics that guide local interaction and decision making between employees. Some of the most important heuristics within J2C will be outlined further below.

The 40° Degrees Model suggests that, while the shared ethos at its foundation is non-negotiable, degrees of freedom open up quickly and radically in regard to the manner in which the organisation's ethos and purpose are embodied and delivered. In other words, a standardised foundation provides the basis from which the *maximum amount of purposeful diversity* in embodiment, expression, and delivery of an organisation's purpose can emerge. To our understanding, this is the very essence of the ideas and benefits of a holarchic operating model and at the heart of leveraging an organisation's Human Factor truly and sustainably.

So what then constitutes the "maximum amount of purposeful diversity" within a productive environment? This is where the "40°" of the 40° Degrees Model come into play. The idea here is that, up to a metaphorical 40° divergence in embodiment and expression, all contributions will still continue to tend towards the cardinal direction that is the organisation's shared purpose. Any wider than that and productive efforts risk to disintegrate into a degree of diversity that becomes incoherent to the market. At this point, the productive environment is also at risk of being disjointed and discerped into separate sub-environments of competing purposes, ethics and identities. What *exactly* constitutes the full 40° of a productive environment is a matter of continuous negotiation, reflection, and adaptation of an organisation's ethos, purpose, boundaries, and organising heuristics.

Therefore, it makes sense to devise some form of "immunology" for a holarchic operating model, which ensures that the integrity and coherence of the organisation and its productive environment is maintained.

19.2.2.2 Devising an Immunology for the Holarchy

As discussed in the previous paragraph, we believe that it is paramount for a holarchic operating model to establish an "immunological function" that works towards ensuring infrastructural integrity and strategic coherence across all productive efforts in the organisation.

At J2C we have done this through the instalment of a "System Function" (which ought to ensure infrastructural integrity) and a "Strategy Function" (which ought to ensure strategic coherence across the organisation).

In hierarchical operating models, these functions are traditionally fulfilled by management, which—through the concentration of strategic decision making power and denominated authority—dictate and enforce a singular, coherent vision and according operational execution (Laloux and Wilber 2014).

This is where our functions differ though. Firstly, the job of both functions is not to *dictate and enforce* a coherent standard across the company but rather to *harmonise and integrate* productive efforts that are ongoing within the organisation. Only where harmonisation and integration proves to be impossible due to too high a degree of divergence or due to rogue intentions from a contributing party, can the System and Strategy Functions enter into confrontation to challenge and resolve such situations. But even in those moments, hierarchical power is severely restricted for both functions and only becomes applicable and enforceable in the most system critical of cases (e.g. potentially existentially threatening or malicious situations).

It should also be mentioned that both functions are enacted by teams not individuals, and that participation in either function is never denominated but *emergent*. This means that participation in the System and Strategy Functions is based on continuous purposeful contribution towards, and proactive ownership of, immunological challenges in a manner that is recognised as purposeful and valuable by the majority of the organisation.

What also follows from this, is that participation in an immunological function can never be considered permanent. So, the composition of both teams is dynamic and changes as proactive ownership of, engagement with, and contribution towards immunological challenges emerge and shift across employees.

19.2.2.3 Guiding Heuristics within J2C

As mentioned before, J2C employs guiding heuristics to regulate interactions and facilitate ownership, decision making, contribution and collaboration within its productive environment.

J2C does not operate a denominated hierarchy or fixed titles. Instead, there are only four roles that pertain exclusively to client engagements: Strategic Partner, Project Lead, Coach, and Support.

Employees slip "in and out" of these roles on the basis of the particular context of a client engagement. This means that an employee can be a Strategic Partner in one engagement and at the same time function as Support in another engagement, sometimes even while working with the same colleagues in both engagements.

Employees have the right to refuse participation in a client engagement on the basis of their availability and interest in the work at hand. This is to make sure that all project teams enter an engagement with primarily intrinsic motivation while also serving as a mechanism to ensure that the temporary hierarchical power afforded to Strategic Partners within engagements is used in a respectful, considerate and purposeful manner.

In terms of regulating work outside of client engagements, employees decide autonomously when and from where to work. In other words, there is no central time-tracking, no minimum work contingent, nor any compulsory attendance during office times. Employees also autonomously decide when and for how long they go on vacation. Here as well there are no maximum contingents, however, employees are asked to practice mindfulness in regard to their commitments to colleagues and client engagements.

In order to provide a balancing factor to these degrees of freedom, all engagements, availability and absence data as well as performance metrics are completely transparent and available on a per day basis to anyone inside the organisation.

One of the biggest challenges in self-organising teams is to regulate decision making. At J2C, anyone can in principle participate in any decision-making process across the organisation. Local decisions on the job as well as decisions that affect only the employee themselves can be made without involving anyone else. Decisions that have a broader organisational impact can also be picked up and advanced by anyone in the organisation but the activation of such "decision spaces" must be announced and made transparent within the organisation to make participation in them possible.

In accordance with our value to self-organise for contribution, the weighting of anyone's participation and decision-making power in decision spaces is dependent on the person's continuous, purposeful contribution and recognised meaningful impact as well as their recognised expertise in that decision space.

The aim in all decision making is to have the best idea make it—so open, purposeful conflict is a key ingredient here and will be further expanded upon in the section below.

In the event that a shared perspective and solution cannot be established, decisions can be "branched" over a predetermined timeframe in order to test the competing ideas in real-life conditions and use the resulting evidence as basis for harmonisation at the end of the determined timeframe.

In general, the expectation is that decision makers own decisions and respective results, thereby explicitly challenging participation without the necessary dedication to also execute and deliver a decision.

In regard to expense and investment decisions, all employees have direct access to company resources for on-the-job expenditures (travel, accommodation, materials etc.) without the need for any further approval. Purposeful investments of up to €2,000 Euros per month equally can be made by anyone without the need for any further approval (liquidity permitting). Purposeful investments of up to €10,000 Euros must be supported by at least four employees and must be approved by the System Function (i.e. necessary resources are available and disposable). For any investments above €10,000 Euros, the System Function must confirm and approve availability of funds and the Strategy Function must confirm and approve the strategic purposefulness and contextual relevance of such an investment.

Here again as a balancing factor, all financial data of the organisation as well as individual and collective spending and investments are transparently available in real-time to all staff and regular updates on financial performance and investment decisions are prepared weekly by the System Function.

Financial renumeration and incentivisation is handled via salaries exclusively, which are set and decided by the employees themselves. That means that each employee at J2C chooses their own salary. They do so in an annual company-wide salary setting process that requires each individual to self-reflect holistically on their contribution and value-added to the organisation. A chosen salary then gets multiplied by a fixed factor from which individual performance goals are derived. Salaries are not approved individually but rather in a collective go/no-go decision made by the System Function based on whether the company projects to be able to afford the total over the coming 12 months.

Once again, all salary data and performance goals are made transparently available to all staff within the organisation. In case of changed individual circumstances or sustained underperformance, employees are expected to correct their salaries proactively and can be confronted and challenged by anyone inside the company to do so if deemed appropriate.

In general, all information at J2C is transparently and openly available to all staff unless otherwise requested or required (e.g. by clients).

J2C operates push-pull heuristics when it comes to information sharing. This means that all employees are expected to continuously consider whether they hold any information that could be necessary or beneficial to others in the organisation and, if that is the case, proactively share it with them. Equally, if an employee requires information, they have the right to approach anyone within the organisation with such a request at which point the approached person or team is obliged to provide the requested information to the best of their knowledge and ability.

Lastly, anyone at J2C has the right to hire new staff. Three types of hires exist: project-based hires, competence-based hires, and systemic hires. Depending on which type of hire it is, the decision to do so and the choice of candidate need to be supported by a predetermined number of employees within J2C. If this "gate" is achieved, the hire can be made. In any case, J2C insists on hiring people, not roles. That means that a person's life experience, way of being, mindset, and motivations are to be considered above mere skill- and competence-matches.

These represent some of the most important heuristics that guide and facilitate the productive environment at J2C. It is important to consider these heuristics in combination rather than in isolation as they are designed to regulate one another.

I should add that these heuristics too can be challenged and changed by the team if enough momentum can be gathered or the company's context or circumstances change. So, the productive environment laid out here should be interpreted as a living, breathing, continuously adapting and evolving organism rather than a fixed and rigid mechanical structure.

In general, we strive to cultivate a productive environment that emphasises effectiveness over efficiency, progress and learning over perfection, evidence over assumptions, and collaboration over silos.

We use company-wide tools to facilitate contribution and collaboration across the organisation. Our tool choices are predominately guided by the needs arising from our productive environment and the determination to enable our staff to work and collaborate from anywhere, anytime.

Evidently, this productive environment differs significantly from more traditional, hierarchical operating models. However, we are convinced that a holarchic operating model such as our own provides the best conditions to leverage the Human Factor and its innovation power inside any given organisation.

19.2.3 Factor 3: Continuously Cultivating Mindset and Culture

As mentioned earlier, we have come to realise that this third factor is one of the most critical elements to the success of a holarchic operating model. Often the significantly increased degrees of freedom afforded to staff in a holarchic operating model are treated by onlookers as some form of "Employee Eldorado" that is all benefit and no difficulty to the employee. However, the reduced determinism and significantly increased degrees of freedom in holarchic operating models— especially compared to traditional hierarchical models—can be very challenging indeed.

In holarchic organisations, employees are much more frequently and intensively expected to take ownership and initiative, cultivate contextual awareness and repeatedly make strategic decisions, all while dealing with higher levels of uncertainty than in traditional models. Therefore, employees' ability and willingness to self-generate, self-reflect, and self-correct is paramount to both, the functioning of a holarchic operating model, as well as their individual success within such a model (Flaherty 2010). This is why the psycho-spiritual qualities of self-knowledge, self-efficacy, and feeling of belonging are so crucial to develop individually and collectively alike—they constitute the key drivers to the cultivation of an emancipated and empowered workforce (Krishnamurti 1975).

19.2.3.1 Cultivating an Emancipated, Empowered Mindset

A significant challenge, especially for new hires in our organisation, is to sustainably shift from a passive mindset so often cultivated in traditional hierarchical operating models to an emancipated, empowered mindset required to thrive in a holarchic operating model. The latter is defined by the fact that it recognises and affirms one's creative and productive power, thus enabling them to embody this power through *self-generation* (the ability to generate a direction and purposeful contributions autonomously), *self-reflection* (the ability to purposefully reflect a direction or path of action autonomously), and *self-correction* (the ability to adapt a direction or path of action autonomously) (Flaherty 2010).

We have found that the ability to embrace and embody such a mindset is dependent on a person's inherent psychological structure, their self-image, their feelings of self-efficacy and their willingness to affirm certain attitudes and engage with certain environmental factors. Whereas an individual's psychological structure constitutes their personal foundation from which such a mindset can be pursued,

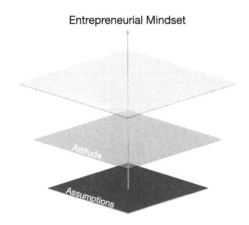

Entrepreneurial Mindset

COMPETENCE
- Ability to self-generate
- Ability to self-reflect
- Ability to self-correct

ATTITUDE
- Willingness to experiment
- Willingness to act purpose-orientated
- Willingness to embrace learning opportunities
- Willingness to handle uncertainty

ASSUMPTIONS
- Reality is malleable
- The shaping of reality is a social process
- "I have the power to participate in this process"
- The shaping of reality is continuous

Fig. 19.5 The Entrepreneurial Mindset highlights the assumptions, attitude and competences that constitute an emancipated and empowered mindset. (Source: author)

all other aspects mentioned above can be actively cultivated through a process of *insight, intention, and practice* (Fromm 1976).

In order to facilitate insight on the underlying factors that enable the cultivation of an emancipated and empowered mindset, we have formulated a concept we call "The Entrepreneurial Mindset," which lays out the assumptions, attitudes and competences that constitute an emancipated and empowered mindset (see Fig. 19.5).

We chose the terminology "entrepreneurial" in reference to the French root of the word, which implies the ability to take the space between how something is and how something could be in order to deliver this new way of being. In addition, the word is commonly associated with autonomous, purposeful initiative in the pursuit of value creation which further links this mindset to the purpose and context for which it is desirable.

The Entrepreneurial Mindset defines the explicit paradigmatic and behavioural standard that each individual in our organisation is expected to aspire towards and is upheld as such in any and all interactions within the company's productive environment.

Employees accordingly are encouraged and challenged to continuously work on developing and strengthening an entrepreneurial mindset. Support for this in the form of peer based as well as professional mentorship and coaching accompaniment is made available to anyone upon request.

19.2.3.2 Dealing with Self-Limiting, Disempowering Mental Habits

In encouraging, facilitating and challenging the company-wide cultivation of an emancipated and empowered mindset, we have come to identify seemingly universal, recurring mental habits that have self-limiting, disempowering effects and therefore can significantly aggravate purposeful participation and sustainable well-being in a holarchic operating model. If unchecked, these mental habits can evolve

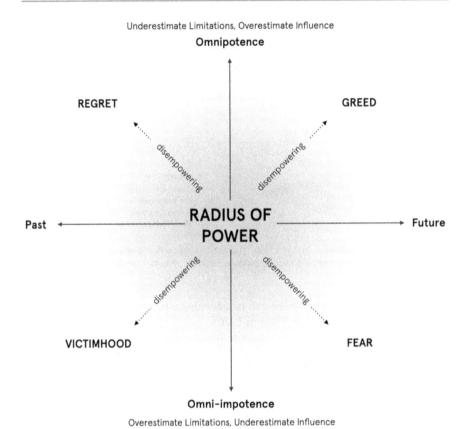

Fig. 19.6 The Mental Traps Framework builds on two axes (self-knowledge and temporal position) along which mental habits related to emancipation and empowerment tend to play out. It further visualises the four most common mental traps and the disempowering mental habits that lead to them. (Source: author)

from individual patterns to cultural patterns, thereby significantly impairing the holarchic operating model and the Human Factor it aims to leverage. In order to help our staff recognise, confront and deal with these mental habits within themselves as well as in their team environment, we have formulated the four most commonly occurring "mental traps" and their corresponding mental habits in a framework we call the "Mental Traps Framework", depicted in Fig. 19.6.

The Mental Traps Framework not only serves employees as tool to recognise and counter disempowering mental habits within themselves and in their team environment, but also establishes a shared understanding and shared language that enables our staff to uncover, confront and deal with disempowering patterns on a cultural level as well.

19.2.3.3 Cultivating a Positive Conflict Culture

As implied in previous sections, cultivating an open, direct and positive conflict culture is absolutely crucial for a holarchic operating model to function and an organisation's Human Factor to be leveraged. Here it is important to first distinguish between positive and negative conflict.

Positive conflict describes conflict where all parties engage with the intention and aim to work out the best course of purposeful action and actively practice trust towards the opposing party. Negative conflict, on the other hand, describes conflict where one or more parties engage with the intention and aim to dominate and subordinate the other party and do so with active distrust towards them.

To our mind, negative conflict is entirely undesirable in a holarchic operating model or any other operating model for that matter. Positive conflict, however, is not only desirable but an absolute necessity for a holarchic operating model to function appropriately and sustainably.

But positive conflict does not necessarily come naturally to everyone. What is more, it often gets convoluted with appeasement or conflict avoidance strategies, where attempts are made to deal with conflict indirectly or to harmonise tension prematurely in order to avoid any confrontation arising openly in the first place.

We have therefore devised a framework we call the "Positive Conflict Framework" (see Fig. 19.7) with the aim to encourage, enable and challenge our staff to continuously practice and cultivate the willingness and competence for positive conflict within themselves and the organisation as a whole.

The Positive Conflict Framework suggests that there are three "dimensions of influence" impacting simultaneously on any conflict situation and that these dimensions together with their respective subtleties must be actively managed by all parties in order to conduct a positive conflict and cultivate a corresponding culture down the line.

19.2.3.4 Cultivating Relatedness and Belonging

In order to encourage and facilitate the cultivation of relatedness between individuals in the organisation and feelings of belonging to the organisation, its staff, and its purpose, we employ several devices. For one, we have established "Home Base Circles," which are non-work-related teams of up to six members, whose purpose it is to provide relational, emotional, and cultural support to one another. A small monthly budget is made available to each Home Base Circle in order to enable them to create and enjoy shared, non-work-related experiences together on a regular basis. Home Base Circles are reshuffled randomly every 8–12 months in order to increase the interpersonal touchpoints across all staff. In addition, every two months our organisation conducts an "Internal Day," which is shorthand for a day-long, peer-organised company gathering that can consist of a series of work sessions, reflective sessions, open discussions, various experiential formats, as well as informal activities. Last but not least, anyone inside the organisation can organise or host extracurricular activities for our workforce and diverse recurring wellness offerings are made available to all staff regularly. Whereas these elements could

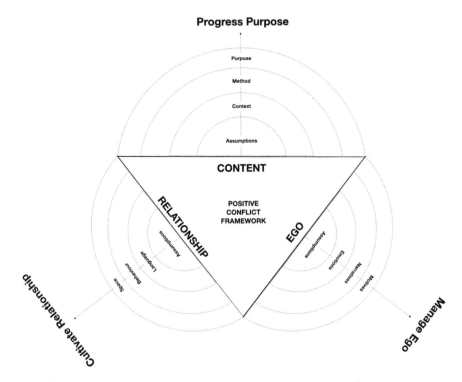

Fig. 19.7 The Positive Conflict Framework provides a guide to the most important aspects to consider when engaging in a positive conflict. (Source: author)

appear as unnecessary or decadent to a bystander, to our mind, they are integral for the cultivation of relatedness, feelings of belonging, well-being and assertion of ownership of the company's identity, purpose, and evolutionary trajectory across our staff.

19.3   Conclusion

Designing or shifting an organisation's operating model along the principles of a holarchy is no trivial task. Conscious and unconscious assumptions, beliefs and values must be surfaced and potentially challenged in order to "liberate" an organisation from the bias of traditional hierarchical operating models and create the conditions upon which a holarchic operating model can be constructed. Then a productive environment must be designed that is purposeful throughout, reflects and embodies the organisation's values, beliefs and aspirations consistently throughout, while also being adapted to the organisation's particular context of purpose, people, product, and ethos. Furthermore, measures must be taken continuously to encourage and facilitate the cultivation and sustainable embodiment of an emancipated and empowered mindset and culture across the entire workforce.

For us, embarking on this admittedly challenging journey so far has been worthwhile. J2C has grown consistently throughout its inauguration and in recent years has managed to attract interdisciplinary talent that we are proud of and excited about. Our team has won the trust of the majority of Germany's DAX30 companies and has successfully delivered innovation and transformation projects in the private and public sector across Europe, Asia, the Americas and the Middle East—all while employing a self-organising holarchy to do so. What is more, despite our comparatively expensive operating model and emphasis on purpose before profit, J2C has consistently performed in at least the top quartile in terms of profitability in comparison to our inner-European competitors—testament to the phenomenal productive and innovative potential that resides in human workforces all over the world but may currently be stifled by operating models that treat them as a resources rather than the emancipated, empowered and profoundly creative forces they can be.

Since a viable blueprint for a holarchic operating model that can be transferred to any and all organisations does as of yet not exist, the case study presented in this chapter aims to share experience and insight with the reader and highlight idiosyncrasies and potential solutions to challenges that can emerge in holarchic operating models from a practitioner's point of view.

I hope that this chapter will provide inspiration and a possible starting point from which readers can embark on their very own journey towards a holarchically operated organisation that is not only capable of thriving and surviving in an increasingly complex, uncertain and hyper-dynamic environment, but also achieves a sustainable creative and competitive advantage by leveraging their Human Factor and its innovation power in the emergent twenty-first century.

References

Davis W (2009) The Wayfinders: why ancient wisdom matters in the modern world. House of Anansi Press, Toronto

Eberhart R, Shi Y, Kennedy J (2001) Swarm intelligence. Morgan Kaufmann, San Francisco

Flaherty J (2010) Coaching: evoking excellence in others, 3rd edn. Butterworth-Heinemann, Oxford

Fromm E (1942) The fear of freedom. Routledge & Kegan Paul, London

Fromm E (1976) To have or to be? Harper & Row, New York

Koestler A (1967) The ghost in the machine. Hutchinson, London

Krishnamurti J (1975) Freedom from the known. Harper & Row, New York

Laloux F, Wilber K (2014) Reinventing organizations: a guide to creating organizations inspired by the next stage in human consciousness. Nelson Parker, Brussels

Mason RO, Mitroff II (1981) Challenging strategic planning assumptions: theory, cases and techniques. Wiley, New York

Morgan G (1986) Images of organization. Sage Publications, Beverly Hills

Robertson B (2015) Holacracy: the new management system for a rapidly changing world. Henry Holt & Co., New York

Zak P (2017) The trust factor. AMACOM Books, New York

Designing a Corporate Accelerator: Enabling the Collaboration of Incumbent Companies and Start-ups to Foster Innovation

20

Marcel Engelmann

20.1 Introduction

The interest of companies to collaborate with start-ups has been growing in the recent years (De Groote and Backmann 2020). There is hardly a day that goes by where the press does not report on partnerships of start-ups with established companies. Many articles illustrate that established companies benefit from collaboration with start-us. Start-up companies on the other hand seem to benefit from collaboration with incumbent corporates as well. As illustrated by Pauwels et al., the collaboration with a renowned corporate enhances the reputation of the start-up company and thereby increases the chances of survival (Pauwels et al. 2016). The exchange with start-ups also gains importance for existing companies as many innovations originate outside the corporates own research and development department (Chesbrough and Crowther 2006; Chesbrough 2003) and the pressure to test innovative technologies as well as new business models is increasing. This increase in pressure on incumbent companies to constantly offer new and better products and services can be traced back to globalization and technological progress (McFarlane 1984). These developments also led to reduced barriers of entry, technological advantages becoming obsolete more quickly and customers having more transparency about markets (Hora et al. 2018). New start-up companies with better products and/or services for the customers are pushing existing companies out of the market or reducing their market share as they grow faster than the market itself (Sedláček and Sterk 2017). In order to stay competitive existing companies, amongst other things, collaborate with start-up companies to maintain or even extend their

M. Engelmann (✉)
MENUX GmbH, Wolfsburg, Germany
e-mail: marcel.engelmann@menux.de

V. Nestle et al. (eds.), *Creating Innovation Spaces*, Management for Professionals, https://doi.org/10.1007/978-3-030-57642-4_20

position in the market. However, the activities to collaborate differ for each company (Peter 2019).

These collaborative activities of corporates can be located within the academic theory of the open innovation phenomenon (Chesbrough 2003). The term open innovation refers to the opening of the innovation process of organizations and thus the active strategic use of the outside world to increase the innovation potential of the company (Lichtenthaler 2008). Chesbrough defines open innovation as "[...] the use of purposive inflows and outflows of knowledge to accelerate internal innovation, and expand the markets for external use of innovation, respectively [...]" (Chesbrough and Appleyard 2007). For large corporations it has become increasingly common to innovate through an open innovation process. Opening up the innovation process to external organizations has been recognized by both researchers and managers as being key to successful innovation (Chesbrough and Bogers 2014). Commonly used approaches for open innovation in incumbent companies are the joint development of products and services (Weiblen and Chesbrough 2015), the inclusion of start-up companies in corporate accelerator programs (Gutmann et al. 2019) or the direct investments through corporate venture capital funds (Chesbrough 2002). Open Innovation is utilized to transfer new technologies, working methods and knowledge into existing companies and thereby benefit from the developments that happened within start-up companies (Spender et al. 2017). In particular, large companies are keen to learn from the agility of young and fast-growing start-up companies to reenergize the companies own innovation strength and improve their innovation performance (Weiblen and Chesbrough 2015). Collaboration with start-up companies is also aimed to recruit new talents and rejuvenating the work culture of the current workforce of the company (Cohen 2013; Dempwolf et al. 2014; Hochberg 2016).

A phenomenon in the context of corporate entrepreneurship and open innovation, which can be found in practice for ten years (Cohen and Hochberg 2014) and in research for the past six years (Jackson et al. 2015) is the corporate accelerator (Kanbach and Stubner 2016; Urbaniec and Žur 2020). This phenomenon has a growing research interest of scholars around the world and seems to be relevant for practical application in medium as well as large companies (Kanbach and Stubner 2016).

For this reason, this book article examines the corporate accelerator phenomenon in more detail and sheds light on the different design configurations and typologies. Finally, a conclusion is provided. The presented insights should enable executives, founders, managers, students as well as interested readers to understand the corporate accelerator phenomenon, empower them to draw their own conclusions as well as imagine the implication of design choices for their business strategy.

20.2   Design Consideration of a Corporate Accelerator

Corporate accelerators are time-limited, selective, cohort-based programs for start-up companies sponsored by one or multiple corporates that may provide various services and finical resources to accelerate the development of the venture and end with a demo day (Cohen 2013; Kanbach and Stubner 2016; Kohler 2016). However, there is currently no uniform definition of this phenomenon. This chapter therefore draws on the existing literature to provide an overview of the various design consideration of corporate accelerator programs and organizes them into a well-structured framework extending the research of Kohler (Kohler 2016). This framework consists of proposition (what), process (how), people (who) and presence (where) (Kohler 2016). In addition, the strategy (why) behind the corporate accelerator is examined in detail (Kanbach and Stubner 2016).

20.2.1 Strategy: Why Does a Company Need a Corporate Accelerator?

There are several reasons why a corporate accelerator should be used by corporates for collaborating with start-up companies. Derived from the overall strategy of the company, conclusions are drawn on if, why and how a corporate accelerator program might help to achieve the selected strategic objectives (Kanbach and Stubner 2016). As already discussed in the previous chapter, companies are facing strong global competition and innovations are increasingly coming from outside the company's boundaries (Hora et al. 2018). Collaboration with start-up companies offers, among other things, the possibility to try out innovative technologies and gain new knowledge in order to enter new markets, become more productive or save costs (Kohler 2016). If the management comes to the conclusion that the company is not able to work on all relevant topics itself, a collaboration with start-up companies using a corporate accelerator is often considered. Once it has been decided that a corporate accelerator should be used to execute the company's strategy, the objectives must be defined. A non-exhaustive list of objectives for a corporate accelerator is given in the following.

Finical objectives could be the creation of new revenue streams with a certain minimum finical target. The revenues can be generated through a planned exit event, which includes the sale to another company or an initial public offering on the stock market. There is also the option to participate on revenues generated by the start-ups after the corporate accelerator program through participation on sales or other reward systems. Reduced cost due to efficiency gains or the more efficient use of resources are additional finical objectives, which can be pursued. However, it is much more difficult to measure reduced cost than additional revenue for an incumbent company (Kohler 2016; Kanbach and Stubner 2016).

Strategic objectives, that are used in current corporate accelerator programs are the improvement of the work culture, improved hiring, better retention of employees, increase in brand value, better evaluation and faster expansion to new markets, development of new and more innovative suppliers, evaluation of technologies and methods or even the transfer of technological as well as methodical knowledge into the companies practice (Kohler 2016; Kanbach and Stubner 2016).

Social objectives are rarely pursued from a corporate accelerator. However, they aim to improve the start-up ecosystem, enable better education for entrepreneurs, create well-paying jobs or improve environmental conditions (Kohler 2016; Jackson and Richter 2017).

The company's executives interested in operating a corporate accelerator must make strategic decisions regarding the importance of the different finical, strategic and/or social objectives in order to create the guidelines for the set-up and operations of the corporate accelerator. The objectives defined in the strategy significantly influence the design configurations described in the following.

20.2.2 Propositions: How Does the Corporate Accelerator Operate?

Depending on the strategy for the corporate accelerator, it must be defined how the objectives might be achieved. For this purpose, the following is a non-exhaustive elaboration of the possible design configurations for a corporate accelerator program regarding the operations.

One main defining design decision for a corporate accelerator program is the possible obligation of the start-up to transfer shares of the company to the incumbent company to attend the corporate accelerator program. This design consideration determines whether the accelerator has mainly financial goals or whether other goals also may have a high priority. Once it has been decided that a participation in the equity capital is necessary, it must be determined how many shares need to be transferred by the start-up company and under what conditions. In the past, start-ups often had to give up five to ten percent of their shares in the company's equity and received 25,000 to 150,000 Euro in addition to the possibility to participate in the corporate accelerator program in return (Kanbach and Stubner 2016). Today most corporate accelerator doesn't take any equity as it creates more conflicts than benefits for the start-up as well as for the corporate. Start-ups do not want to give up any shares in such an early phase and most corporates, on the other hand, cannot do much with the shares either, as they usually have no plans for active portfolio management and/or no or limited knowledge about the financing of start-up companies through venture capital. In addition, it creates a high degree of dependency on each other without knowing whether a collaboration will create a mutual benefit (Kupp et al. 2017).

The industry or topic focus is another important design consideration of a corporate accelerator. Most corporate accelerators have an industry focus or at least one focus topic, as this allows them to create synergies and build the right contacts and networks both within the company and with external partners (Kanbach and Stubner 2016). Only the corporate accelerators with primarily financial or social objectives have a rather undefined, broad or no industry or topic focus. The number of start-up companies within a cohort is another design choice that is decisive for the design of the corporate accelerator. Most corporate accelerators include five to ten start-up companies in a cohort. If the cohorts are too large, the organizers of the corporate accelerator are unable to provide tailored support for the start-up's needs and thus waste potential for growth. Cohorts that are too small usually do not generate the (financial) value to justify the costs. Within a corporate accelerator, many start-up companies work together with a specialist department within the incumbent company to test their technology or try out new methods (Moschner et al. 2019).

Especially crucial and one of the main characteristics for the differentiation of corporate accelerators is the organization that operates the corporate accelerator. Different models for the organization have evolved over the past years. The corporate accelerator can be part of a department, become an own department or turn into an independent subsidiary. Also, an external third company can be used as the main organizer of the corporate accelerator (Kanbach and Stubner 2016). To sustainable operate the corporate accelerator it must be financially viable. In many cases, the corporate accelerator can be sustainably financed through internal contracting with the specialist departments. The departments pay for a pilot project and in return receive an implementation of a concrete project as well as the knowledge in working with new technologies, methods and start-up companies in general. However, it is also possible that a corporate accelerator does not need to earn money because of the focus on social objectives. On the other hand, there are also corporate accelerators, which exclusively have to finance themselves by selling shares or participating in the revenues of the start-up they accelerated. The management of the corporate accelerator only receives pre-financing for the initial setup and must then survive from its own revenues.

20.2.3 Process: What Does the Corporate Accelerator Do?

Various processes within the corporate accelerator must be executed. These processes are the general program design, the search for start-up companies, the selection of start-up companies, the on-boarding, the program design in detail with focus on course offerings, mentoring, co-creation and exchange possibilities, as well as the final event (demo day). Also, the post-program relationship as well as the portfolio management and the change management for the corporate accelerator are the processes of the corporate accelerator that need to be designed.

For the program the main design consideration is the duration. Most corporate accelerators last over three to six months. However, the greater proportion of corporate accelerators tend to run for three months. A defining design choice is the stage of the start-up. This parameter is particularly important for the search process. Many corporate accelerators used to concentrate on young start-ups with hardly more than a minimum viable product in order to obtain equity in these companies as early as possible. This concept was adopted mainly due to the successful classic business accelerator examples Y Combinator, Plug&Play or 500 Startups. The investment successes of these accelerators with successful and high-paying exits of companies like Stripe, AirBnB or DropBox seemed to be attractive for many corporate at first glance. In the life cycle of the corporate accelerator, more and more companies have found out that they benefit more from collaboration with later-stage start-up companies than from exits as these cases are rare. Later-stage start-ups are also better equipped to deal with the needs and processes of large established companies, enabling innovations to be implemented into the incumbent's value chain. The selection of the start-ups accepted into the corporate accelerator is also influenced by the team. Especially in the case of young companies there is hardly any better indicator, because it is not possible to predict the future success of the company by looking at past turnover numbers or other achievements as they don't exist yet or are not conclusive.

During the development in the recent years of the corporate accelerator program contents it has become clear that it is advantageous to customize them according to the individual needs of the company and thereby offer the necessary flexibility to provide tailored support for the venture. Depending on the program, the demo day offers the possibility to invite investors or other companies with similar technological problems to establish relationships with interesting partners for the start-up. So far, processes for the post-program relationship with start-up companies have been largely overlooked both in research and in practice. In order to convince new start-ups through recommendations as applicants for the program as well as to follow the development of the start-up companies, the organization of alumni events seems to be beneficial and should be considered in the design (Kanbach and Stubner 2016).

20.2.4 People: Who is Involved in the Corporate Accelerator?

In order to implement the processes for a corporate accelerator, people with the appropriate skills are needed to accomplish the objectives from the corporate strategy with the available resources. In order to operate a corporate accelerator, it has been proven that the support of top management, especially the CEO, is a key factor for the success (Kanbach and Stubner 2016). Next, at least one person must be found who is or likes to be well networked within the start-up ecosystem and is able to communicate effectively with young and rapidly growing start-ups. So far, employees who are already working in the company, but are currently on the verge of taking on a new position seem to be the most suitable candidates. Newly hired employees with experience in corporate and start-up setting seem also to be suitable but might have to work on the corporate network internally.

Once the right person or group of people has been found to execute the corporate accelerator program, the development of relationships in the start-up ecosystem must be initiated. This is mainly due to the fact that corporate accelerator, as well as other organizations and programs that support start-ups, have grown in size and numbers in recent years. This is why many programs today compete for the application of interesting start-up companies. After the right start-up has been found, the appropriate mentors for the program must be identified. These mentors are there to support the start-up during its development in the corporate accelerator and to help with strategic decision-making during the program. The mentors should be tailored to the needs of the start-ups. Many corporate accelerators also offer a curriculum for the founders. This knowledge from areas such as marketing, sales, product management, human resources, law and finance is designed to prepare the start-up companies to apply the right processes and techniques as growth continues. To convey this learning content, experts are needed who can shed light on the subject area and have a high affinity with the special cases of young and rapidly growing companies. These experts can either come from within the company itself or be external.

In order to transfer knowledge from the start-up to the incumbent company, an exchange between these two parties must take place. This exchange can happen for example with a pilot project together with a specialist department. This exchange should be organized in such a way that the high level of bureaucracy, which is usually prevalent in existing companies, is absorbed by the management team of the corporate accelerator. The collaboration between the founders and the employees of the specialist department should be optimized in order to run as smoothly as possible. The people from the specialist department must be open to new processes, products and services and at the same time have a problem or a task to solve so that the added value for the start-up and department is evident (Kohler 2016).

20.2.5 Place: Where Does the Corporate Accelerator Take Place?

Participation in the corporate accelerator program can be carried out remotely via the internet or with physical presence of the start-up company. Most corporate accelerator programs require at least a partial physical presence of its participants. A virtual corporate accelerator has the advantage that start-up companies from all over the world can participate and thus a high number of start-ups can be addressed. However, local corporate accelerators lead to a higher level of interaction and knowledge exchange. Depending on the objectives of the program, the design should be adapted. Regarding the physical presence it can be chosen whether the corporate accelerator is carried out at the headquarters of the corporate, a place close to the corporate or a place in an existing start-up eco-system, which might have a higher distance to the headquarters of the sponsoring company. In case of integration into a local start-up ecosystem, co-working space are particularly popular, as they can be rented for a short period of time and an existing network of start-ups already exists. However, the greater distance between the specialist departments of the incumbent company and the location of the corporate accelerator may lead to inadequate results for both the specialist department and the start-up company. In addition, the design of the office space within the location must also be taken into account. The space must be designed in such a way that the collaboration between the people from the corporate and the start-up company is encouraged (Kohler 2016).

20.3 Typologies of Corporate Accelerator Programs

Over the last ten years different typologies of corporate accelerator emerged. Through the work of Pauwels et al., Kanbach and Stubner six different types of corporate accelerator have been discovered so far (Kanbach and Stubner 2016; Pauwels et al. 2016). The different types of corporate accelerator are the welfare simulator, the ecosystem builder, the listening post, the value chain investor, the test laboratory and the unicorn hunter. These different types of corporate accelerator are presented below to show when which type of corporate accelerator should be used.

20.3.1 Welfare Simulator

The welfare simulator has the primary goal to benefit the society. There is no participation in the equity of the start-up company. In some cases, however, a pilot project will be financially rewarded, or a scholarship will be paid to cover living expenses of the founders. Financial goals are not in the focus of the program. It provides the most extensive curriculum of all corporate accelerator. Serial entrepreneurs or executives of the sponsoring company are mentors of the start-ups and do this usually gratuitously. Mostly young and early-stage start-up companies are accepted into this type of corporate accelerator. The corporate accelerator is usually based at the company's headquarters and the start-ups come from university spin-offs or the local area. Many of these corporate accelerators are dependent on a good economic situation. As soon as an unfavorable economic situation emerges, these programs are likely to be discontinued as no other funding is available (Pauwels et al. 2016).

20.3.2 Ecosystem Builder

The ecosystem builder is similar to the welfare simulator. However, the focus of this type of corporate accelerator is primarily on the integration of start-ups with the local and international start-up ecosystem. The ecosystem builder usually only includes companies that already have a track record and are at least testing the product together with one or more customers. The ecosystem builder is also often financed by several companies. The operation of the corporate accelerator is often carried out together with several companies or is outsourced to a third-party service provider. Major providers in this area are Plug&Play and Techstars. The mentors usually come from the involved companies or the service partner. Start-up companies do not have to give up their equity to the corporate accelerator. However, financial support is usually not provided either. In some cases, there is the possibility of a paid pilot project with a partner company of the corporate accelerator (Pauwels et al. 2016).

20.3.3 Listening Post

The listening post has purely strategic without any financial objectives. The main task of this type of corporate accelerator is to understand recent trends and developments in a respective market and initiate relationships with startups. Accelerators of this type are exploration oriented and don't take any equity. The focus of the listening post corporate accelerator is mainly connected to the interest of the parent company. Startups that are selected to be part of this corporate accelerator passed the idea stage and are able to show promising ideas in the incumbent's field of interest. The listening post accelerator is most of the times run by the corporate alone without external partners, which differentiates this type from the ecosystem builder (Kanbach and Stubner 2016).

20.3.4 Test Laboratory

The test laboratory creates a protected environment to test promising internal and external business ideas. The inclusion of internal companies and departments is a special feature of this type of corporate accelerator. The focus of the selection of start-up companies for this corporate accelerator is on early-stage start-ups that are currently looking to improve their idea. Most of the time the corporate accelerator is located outside the headquarters. In some cases, it is necessary for the start-up company to give up equity to the corporate accelerator organization (Kanbach and Stubner 2016).

20.3.5 Value Chain Investor

The value chain investor is currently the most popular type of corporate accelerator and has mostly strategic objectives. The main objectives are the identification, development and integration of new products and services into parent company's value chain through startups within the same customer group. Startups provide new innovative products or services, while the corporate provides access to customers. There is a strong industry focus related to parent company sponsoring the corporate accelerator. This type of corporate accelerator focuses on later-stage start-ups, which are able to cope with the processes of large firms. It can be run together with a professional third-party provider or organized as an own internal department (Kanbach and Stubner 2016).

20.3.6 Unicorn Hunter

The unicorn hunter has purely financial objectives. This corporate accelerator tries to generate financial benefits by making numerous investments in promising startups and sell their shares at a higher price. It is mostly an own subsidiary of the sponsoring company and has its own location inside a startup ecosystem. Their name "Unicorn hunter" comes from the search to find a company that might be valued over one billion Euro in the future. This type of accelerator program is agnostic to the stage of the start-up and takes five to ten percent equity in the start-up company. In exchange the start-up gets assets in form of technologies, networks, competences, media coverage and knowledge as well as financial resources with a sum of 25,000 to 150,000 Euro (Kanbach and Stubner 2016).

20.4 Conclusion

The purpose of this paper was to provide insights into the various design considerations and the resulting typologies of corporate accelerators in practice. By examining current research and practice, a comprehensive overview was created. Five design categories with more than 30 design considerations where presented. Six typologies were introduced. With this comprehensive overview, executives are enabled to develop better strategies for their corporate accelerator program. Managers of corporate accelerators have the opportunity to improve their operations and students gain an insight into a fast-growing topic that is relevant to start-ups and corporations alike. In the near future, the topic seems to remain relevant both in research and practice. This can be confirmed by the increase in the number of accelerators in recent years as well as the growing number of publications on this phenomenon. Of particular interest for the future of corporate accelerators is the question of whether the corporate accelerator is sustainable in an increasing dynamic market environment and how the exchange between start-ups and incumbent companies can be improved further.

References

Chesbrough H, Bogers M (2014) Explicating open innovation: clarifying an emerging paradigm for understanding innovation. In: New Frontiers in open innovation. Oxford University Press, Oxford, pp 3–28

Chesbrough H, Crowther AK (2006) Beyond high tech: early adopters of open innovation in other industries. R&D Manag 36(3):229–236

Chesbrough HW (2002) Making sense of corporate venture capital. Harv Bus Rev 80(3):90–99

Chesbrough HW (2003) Open innovation: the new imperative for creating and profiting from technology. Harvard Business Press

Chesbrough HW, Appleyard MM (2007) Open innovation and strategy. Calif Manag Rev 50(1):57–76

Cohen S (2013) What do accelerators do? Insights from incubators and angels. Innovations: Technol., Governance, Globalization 8(3–4):19–25

Cohen S, Hochberg YV (2014) Accelerating startups: the seed accelerator phenomenon. (March 30, 2014). Available at SSRN: https://ssrn.com/abstract=2418000 or https://doi.org/10.2139/ssrn.2418000

De Groote JK, Backmann J (2020) Initiating open innovation collaborations between incumbents and startups: how can David and Goliath get along? Int J Innov Manag 24(2):2050011

Dempwolf CS, Auer J, D'Ippolito M (2014) Innovation accelerators: defining characteristics among startup assistance organizations. Small Bus Adm:1–44. https://doi.org/10.13140/RG.2.2.36244.09602

Gutmann T, Kanbach D, Seltman S (2019) Exploring the benefits of corporate accelerators: investigating the SAP Industry 4.0 Startup Program. Probl Perspect Manag 17(3):218

Hochberg YV (2016) Accelerating entrepreneurs and ecosystems: the seed accelerator model. Innov Policy Econ 16(1):25–51

Hora W, Gast J, Kailer N, Rey-Marti A, Mas-Tur A (2018) David and Goliath: causes and effects of coopetition between start-ups and corporates. Rev Manag Sci 12(2):411–439

Jackson P, Richter N (2017) Situational logic: an analysis of open innovation using corporate accelerators. Int J Innov Manag 21(7):1750062

Jackson P, Richter N, Schildhauer T (2015) Open Innovation with digital startups using corporate accelerators—a review of the current state of research. Z Politikberatung (ZPB)/Policy Advice Political Consult 7(4):152–159

Kanbach DK, Stubner S (2016) Corporate accelerators as recent form of startup engagement: The what, the why, and the how. J Appl Bus Res (JABR) 32(6):1761–1776

Kohler T (2016) Corporate accelerators: building bridges between corporations and startups. Business Horizons 59(3):347–357

Kupp M, Marval M, Borchers P (2017) Corporate accelerators: fostering innovation while bringing together startups and large firms. J Bus Strateg 38:47–53

Lichtenthaler U (2008) Open innovation in practice: an analysis of strategic approaches to technology transactions. IEEE Trans Eng Manag 55(1):148–157

McFarlane FW (1984) Information technology changes the way you compete. Harvard Business Review, Reprint Service, pp 98–103.

Moschner SL, Fink AA, Kurpjuweit S, Wagner SM, Herstatt C (2019) Toward a better understanding of corporate accelerator models. Business Horizons 62(5):637–647

Pauwels C, Clarysse B, Wright M, Van Hove J (2016) Understanding a new generation incubation model: the accelerator. Technovation 50:13–24

Peter L (2019) Gestaltungsbereiche für Grossunternehmen zur Kollaboration mit Startups: Das Startup-Collaboration-Model. Die Unternehmung 73(3):193–212

Sedláček P, Sterk V (2017) The growth potential of startups over the business cycle. Am Econ Rev 107(10):3182–3210

Spender JC, Corvello V, Grimaldi M, Rippa P (2017) Startups and open innovation: a review of the literature. Eur J Innov Manag 20:4–30

Urbaniec M, Żur A (2020) Business model innovation in corporate entrepreneurship: exploratory insights from corporate accelerators. Int Entrep Manag J:1–24. https://doi.org/10.1007/s11365-020-00646-1

Weiblen T, Chesbrough HW (2015) Engaging with startups to enhance corporate innovation. Calif Manag Rev 57(2):66–90

Leadership in Transformation: How to Lead in the Digital Era?

21

Dana Goldhammer

21.1 Introduction

What does digitalization actually mean? New technologies promise us new innovative business models. New technologies and the associated lower use of assets allow for greater scaling. This, in turn, hides either the danger or the opportunity of a greater impact on our current business model, depending on whether our own model is attacked, or we attack it ourselves. In addition, new technologies create completely new value chains and thus internal processes. Existing processes can be redesigned and automated or even completely eliminated. The goals in each case are cost reduction, optimized assets and/or the reduction of human intervention through automation, in short: increasing effectiveness and efficiency.

The changes can create new job profiles. Existing roles change or are completely eliminated. Digitalization is changing the way people work together within and between companies. New working models must be in line with existing models. Employees ask for individual solutions and change their demands on their managers. Do these employees still need a manager or more leadership?

New technologies enable new mechanisms. Innovative business models scale quickly and mostly globally. They operate in ecosystems and the creation of ecosystems enables them. The development and impact of technologies and new business model types are difficult for most managers to assess. Are they a threat or an opportunity? How must and can I react? Which skills and capabilities do I need? How do I lead my company or my division into a digital era?

D. Goldhammer (✉)
TÜV Rheinland AG, Cologne, Germany

© The Editor(s) (if applicable) and The Author(s), under exclusive license
to Springer Nature Switzerland AG 2021
V. Nestle et al. (eds.), *Creating Innovation Spaces*, Management for Professionals,
https://doi.org/10.1007/978-3-030-57642-4_21

21.2   Finding Strategic Orientation

The new digital era is complex and the effects are difficult to foresee for many companies. Too many managers are still wondering which impact this trend could have on them and whether they might be able to wait out the so-called digital transformation until their retirement. This is a comprehensible question if we take the human desire for as little change as possible as a basis. However, hope is in vain. The title of this chapter lulls us into a sense of security, because we are already in the middle of digital times and have to face the consequences. At the latest since Covid-19 and its effects on the economy and the working environments this issue has become very visible. This should not be frightening. Because, as with all change, what counts is how we deal with it.

For many people, digitalization, especially in the context of innovation, means the question of how to handle data and information. People are quick to talk about big data, data analytics and making money with data-driven business models. New digital innovation units are set-up, all available data are collected and evaluated, a lot of money is invested in technology and managers await promising answers from all the analyses. Usually, impatience sets in at some point, because somehow, there is no money made yet, no products worthy of demonstration follow the big marketing announcements, and the plan is not yet apparent. Thus, the first innovation labs, digital hubs or similarly good sounding units are already being closed or their resources cut back.

Please do not get me wrong. Even if there is still no significant success in many activities, it is still better to try than to have done nothing at all. The golden path may lie somewhere in between.

There are most likely a small number of executives in traditional companies who developed the great vision more than five years ago and are now very successfully implementing the digital transformation. For all others, the digital world initially seems overwhelming and unimaginable. The question is now: where do we start? Countless numbers of consultants have entered the market. Every consultancy has its focus and cannot bring the salutary answer from outside into the company.

It has always been good advice to think in terms of business development from the customer's perspective. The same with digitalization, but usually it is even more difficult. What do customers want in the future? Developing strategies behind the curtain will not have a real impact and help achieving specific goals. We need information on the customer needs, expectations, issues, compelling events, problems and pain. This is the first challenge for managers. The classic strategy development department or the chief of strategy himself is not enough to predict and plan the next five years. Moreover, does this planning for such a long time period still work at all?

Leaders have to develop a vision for their company or field. One of the main questions can be: where do we want to go and which role do we want to claim for ourselves in the future? There is a need for a framework or so-called guiding principles to provide and ensure orientation for strategy development and subsequent implementation measures in order to be able to assume this role. This can be a clear demarcation: for example, if a service company determines that it wants to continue to focus on service and on information-based business models and therefore will in future rely on partnerships for operating platforms instead of developing them itself. There is no need to discuss this question any longer in the later strategy development process for each individual service development. This guidance will not only accelerate the process, but also increase the autonomy of the responsible employees and thus the likelihood of innovation.

During the strategy development process, it is important to talk to customers, to involve them in the process. The same applies to the employees: The experts in the company, who work with the customers on a daily basis have to be involved. In the best-case scenario, we already have additional customer data that allows us to derive conclusions regarding their needs. If we do not start with the customer to derive our future services and strategy, we might base major developments on pure assumptions and miss the target. Instead of comprehensive systems, we had better analyze the right data from the right data sources. It is well invested time to identify these based on our conclusions.

In order to create the target picture of one's own company, one has two essential questions. Which technologies have an impact on my business/performance? What is the market situation? Do I have to adapt, supplement, adjust or completely redevelop my services? What does this mean for my services, as depicted in Fig. 21.1? Can partners or existing solutions help me with this?

The viewpoint of external experts as well as that of our employees can support us in these questions. Many managers believe they have to provide all the answers by themselves. In times of rapidly changing markets, many opportunities and specializations, this is a claim that is difficult to meet. It is a balancing act between the courage to question the status quo and, if necessary, to change it. The same applies to the involvement of employees, with the supposed danger that the so-called urge to protect the status quo will prevent too much change from being tackled. This is the second important task of managers: to communicate their own vision and gain the trust of employees through transparency. Particularly in companies that are more traditional, uncertainty quickly arises as to whether digitalization is not just an excuse for job cuts. In some areas, technologies can certainly contribute to job reduction through automation. This is a part of increasing efficiency, too. On the other hand, many companies have enough vacancies due to shortages of skilled workers and thus orders that they cannot accept due to lack of capacity. In the course of presenting the vision and future corporate goal, management should explain the reduction of non-value-adding activities and the growth of value-adding shares to the employees in a transparent and comprehensible way. In addition, digitalization not only affects processes and works through automation. Digital technologies also open up opportunities for new markets or even new (innovative) business models. The vision and the many new opportunities should inspire current and potential employees to contribute to the best of their abilities.

Once the essential questions of the impact of digital technologies and require-ments on current and potential new services are clear, one can derive the strategic

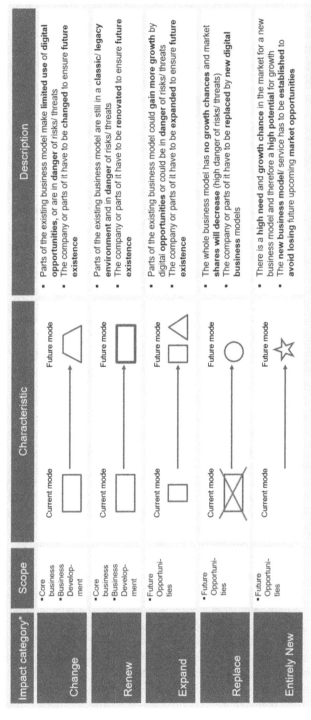

Fig. 21.1 Characteristics of the business impact categories. (Source: author)

Impact category*	Scope	Characteristic		Description
		Current mode	Future mode	
Change	•Core business •Business Development			▪ Parts of the existing business model make **limited use of digital opportunities**, or are in **danger** of risks/ threats ▪ The company or parts of it have to be **changed** to ensure **future existence**
Renew	•Core business •Business Development			▪ Parts of the existing business model are still in a **classic/ legacy environment** and in **danger** of risks/ threats ▪ The company or parts of it have to be **renovated** to ensure **future existence**
Expand	•Future Opportunities			▪ Parts of the existing business model could **gain more growth** by digital **opportunities** or could be in **danger** of risks/ threats ▪ The company or parts of it have to be **expanded** to ensure **future existence**
Replace	•Future Opportunities			▪ The whole business model has **no growth chances** and market **shares will decrease** (high danger of risks/ threats) ▪ The company or parts of it have to be **replaced** by **new digital business models**
Entirely New	•Future Opportunities			▪ There is a **high need** and **growth chance** in the market for a new business model and therefore a **high potential** for growth ▪ The **new business model**/ service has to be **established** to **avoid losing** future upcoming **market opportunities**

* Classic tasks of the corporate and/ or portfolio Strategy like **divest, defend or watch!** should also be applied

roadmap. This includes, among other things, the necessary digital skills "that a company needs to design, create and communicate digital value creation to customers. Always relating to the organization, people & skills, processes and technologies" (Hentrich and Pachmajer 2016). Superordinate digital skills include Smart Manufacturing, Sales & Customer Analytics, IoT, Agile Collaboration and many more. You can either provide these trainings yourself or by external partners.

21.3 Achieving Operationalization

Once we have established the vision and strategic roadmap for our digital future, we can move on to the implementation. How do we implement strategies in the rapidly changing times of the digital world? Are classic approaches for strategic projects or operational decisions within hierarchies still suitable for everyday use and target-oriented? At this point, managers must answer crucial questions again: Which environment do I have to create for excellent operational processes? On which information can I base my decisions on a daily basis that minimizes risk?

Let us turn once again to the Big Data discussion. We may believe that we get good decision support if we only have as much data as possible from many data sources and preferably ad hoc "at the push of a button". It is common for managers to want to collect data before they know what questions they want answered—Big Data as the Holy Grail, answering questions we do not even know. It may sound crazy, but this is common practice in companies, which has resulted in large data analysis projects. At the other extreme, it is preferable to measure only the financial ratios that form the basis for the annual performance assessment. For effective operational management, it is essential to identify the key performance indicators and make them measurable. It is not a question of the figures, but rather of their reasonableness. Instead of being driven by the big-data and key performance indicator obsession, we can think about "how to get the right data to the right decision-makers, according to basic logistical principles".

Who are the best decision makers in the digital era? Now we have the next challenge for managers. While market conditions keep changing rapidly and complexity keeps increasing, can a single manager still personally make all decisions in a company/area? Who makes decisions on the customer side? How quickly do we have to make decisions on our side and derive and implement results accordingly? There is no longer a tendency to have just one contact person on the customer side. Through networking and change of process chains, different responsibilities are emerging at different levels in companies. For example, the IT department is no longer solely responsible for digital solutions. More and more specialist departments are taking an active role and working together with solution providers. This increases the number of contacts on the customer side. Eventually we have to serve them all. On the other hand, overarching processes mean that individual departments no longer decide for themselves, but value-adding offers must be addressed at management or purchasing level. Only a company that adapts to these new structures and transforms itself can react and, above all, act quickly.

In this situation traditional companies like to react with new account managers, new divisions and new area managers who like to establish a new hierarchical level. This does not always have anything to do with process acceleration. In order to make decisions where they arise and generate direct action, employees facing to the customer must be able to act autonomously and agilely. Who could do this better than the existing team? For managers this means, creating an appropriate environment and framework. Often the first thought is "I should delegate responsibility to my employees? But they are not capable of doing that." Well, certainly not overnight: Transformation is a process. This also applies to the transfer of responsibility and new ways of working. This requires trust, which must grow on both sides. On the one hand, managers learn to trust that employees will make the right decisions and deliver results to the customer in the desired quality. On the other hand, the employees learn that they will be trusted in the long run. They take responsibility for their decisions and learn to deal with unexpected results and failures. This environment of trust requires communication, transparency, agile methods and above all patience. There will be setbacks on this development path. The decisions will not be the same as those the manager would have made. Dealing with a complaint may have been too accommodating. Ideas were tried out that no customer bought. Not all this is easy to bear as a manager who is used to making his or her own decisions.

Handing over responsibility is not an easy job. However, this is essential if we want to attract and retain the best matching employees in the future. New generations demand responsibility and freedom. They are more used to work with the customer and are connected through new technologies. As managers, we must promote these employees and try to clear the path for them. They will refer to the guiding principles and gain experience through trial and error. They can serve as role models for current employees in the company. Without thinking patterns trained for years in the company, new employees will act in an unbiased way and exemplify new values and methods. Existing employees will find it much easier to adopt new approaches when they experience them live, rather than hearing a lot about change programs in meetings and conferences. Doing instead of talking. Lengthy plans and discussions about possible obstacles do not help. One cannot perfectly plan and roll out agile working methods in the company. It is easier to start in one area, learn and adapt the approach if necessary. Therefore, every single manager can give the starting signal and get into action. Those responsible for innovation should be thrilled about these developments. After all, these types of cooperation are nothing new to them. The digital transformation spreads the mechanisms of the innovation world throughout the entire company.

21.4   Creating New Working Environments

New technologies have led to a big discussion about new workplaces or New Work. For me, digital environments also mean agile environments. We are keen to find solutions to create new standardized offers for new workplaces and new working models to meet the needs of our employees. This is particularly difficult for managers who are used to control and presence. Micromanagement is difficult to do remotely.

Frequently, we use black and white thinking at this point. When we talk about new work, we often think of home office. Immediately we discuss requirements based on laws and works councils and assume that all this is difficult to realize. Moreover, does the communication within the team not miss out then? However, very few employees would like to be 100% in their home office. What about co-working spaces, cafés or other company locations? It would also be too easy to talk only about Generation Y or Z in this context. Depending on character and life situation, a different way of working is convenient.

In the future workplace we might work with guiding principles rather than fixed models. Working models will have to be individually designed, especially for so-called knowledge workers. Will new and modified job profiles have to meet the same conditions as the old ones? Based on the strategy and the required skills, we can derive which requirements the working models have to meet, for example in terms of time and physical availability. In this way, we create the foundation and at the same time have a good degree of flexibility in which managers can respond to the individual needs of their employees. This requires a lot of open-mindedness from people.

For most managers, the figures come first and we tend to focus on the head count. Preferably full-time, because that fits better into traditional budget planning. Based on-site, because then we can check not only the results but also the actions of each individual employee in detail. Ideally, no special requests such as sabbaticals, further studies, parental leave, home office, personal development and so on are mentioned. The only dilemma is that employees today are much more willing to leave companies that are not able to fulfil their wishes. Not to mention inner resignation, which, as we know, is not helping our goals either. Making special agreements is more economical in the medium and long term.

When working models are designed and adapted individually, we keep employees in the company. This makes it more attractive for new employees and promotes diversified teams and reduced recruiting efforts. Work in networks, virtual teams, different working hours can be controlled, but require some rules in the team. There are manifold opportunities every team can determine for itself. If the goals are clear to everyone, agreed rules help in day-to-day, self-directed work. Essential points are, amongst others, areas of responsibility and decision-making powers. It must be clear, for example, in which cases the superior is required to decide, when he or she wishes to contribute to the decision-making process and when he or she should simply be informed. Once determined, the team members can safely decide how to proceed in all situations. The supervisor transparently communicates all essential information and the context in which the team works and which it needs to perform its tasks. The team itself determines and carries out the control of the necessary tasks and activities to achieve the goals. To make the activities in the team visible to everyone at all times, tools such as Kanban boards support this process. On these boards, the tasks written on individual cards are assigned the status "in planning", "in process" and "completed". This allows current progress and critical points to be transparently tracked. Remote teams like to use digital alternatives, such as Slack or Jira.

Does the entire team still need regular exchange? In team meetings, project statuses are often reported, commented on, excessive background information is shared and perhaps even explanations and excuses are given. The supervisor passes on unfiltered information about current decisions made by his or her superiors and developments within the company, possibly enriched somewhat with his or her own comments on the perceived sense of these. For the entire team, neither one nor the other is really of value. Lars Vollmer, entrepreneur and co-founder of intrinsify.me, speaks out against regulated team meetings (Vollmer 2017): "In a nutshell, this means that if you want to get rid of time-consuming meetings and energy-sapping regulations, you should not work on the meetings themselves, but create a corresponding structure in the company. A structure that makes ritualized meetings obsolete. Of course, the employees would then continue to talk and discuss with each other. Maybe even more than before, but no longer within the rigid framework of a team meetings or project status meeting, because they no longer need them."

Easier said than done. Those who do not want to miss regular exchange within the team should manage the valuable time in which the team comes together. The exchange of current experiences as well as the need for support by the supervisor or the team should be a priority. Important contextual information is reported, discussions are held. Status reports and general information belong in the (online) tools.

In order to develop and maintain the team culture, in addition to regular exchange during work, team meetings and team events, it is also useful to regularly take time to look back on the experiences gained and learn from them. In so-called retrospectives, the team looks back on a certain period together with the manager. A frequency of one month is especially recommended at the beginning of change processes. For more variety, teams can chose different methods, depending on the goal or preference of the team. A selection offers for example Fun Retrospectives (2018) online.

In addition to learning together as a team, the development of the individual employee in the course of digitalization also requires a different perspective. When markets, customers, technologies and the working environment change at shorter intervals, how should we plan and design human resources development for the future? Which role can the HR department play and which role must the manager take on? How can we identify necessary measures? An interesting approach is taken by Netflix. The company is committed to hiring only the best experts in their respective fields. Based on the assumption that they are the best and therefore no training or instruction can be better than their own knowledge, they offer no seminars or training. Probably an extreme example. However, will standardized further training courses be the means of choice in the future in times of new job profiles, where there are sometimes no standardized vocational training schemes? Can we assume that everyone, including career changers, has the same level of knowledge to be able to attend the same training? Are parts of a seminar already familiar to one person, while the other is still lacking basic requirements? Yet individual contents can be exciting for both. The future of learning becomes more individual. Managers will work together with the individual employee in a dialogue to determine what he or she would like to do and what skills they need for future tasks. New knowledge is generated ad hoc in projects, through online learning units, at subject-specific meetings, in (cross-company) networks. There are numerous learning opportunities, online and physically on-site.

For many managers the question of their own role arises. If I no longer lead and control the way and in the future my employees decide what to do and how, what is my raison d'être?

21.5 Develop Your Own Leadership Role

New focuses, new environments go hand in hand with a new personal direction. Is it possible for every manager to adapt himself and his own capabilities? Not every management style fits into new digital and faster environments. We no longer operate exclusively within our own company, but in ecosystems that are evolving within an innovation and digitalization process. As a result, managers face changes that they cannot cope with in the worst case. This causes anxiety. Now each of us can decide whether we surrender to fear, deny all changes and hold on to the here and now or whether we deal intensively with our environment and how we can adapt to it. Employees do not necessarily expect the perfect supervisor, but honor the authentic boss who is open to his or her fears and tries to approach change and learn together with the team.

Characteristics that have been desired by companies for decades and have been trained in management development programs are not easy to change. They have been successful for a long time. It cannot all be worthless all at once, can it? Employees in new (cooperation-oriented) working models expect new leadership. They demand more leadership than management from a leader. In conversations with employees, they often referred to two pictures: the lighthouse and tower of strength. Both are equally applicable.

The lighthouse shows the way, i.e. sets the targets. It provides orientation during the journey, without having to take the steering wheel. The orientation can be the context of the team's work environment, which is always presented transparently. This may include answers to the following questions: What do stakeholders want? Why do we have to adjust? What is the background of certain top-down decisions? It not only lights up the destination, so to speak, but also draws obstacles on the map on the way there. This allows the team to decide whether they can enter the port directly or whether course corrections are necessary because rocks have to be bypassed.

At the same time, the manager was described as a tower of strength. The image is more likely to be used by employees who are not yet completely confident in independent navigation. They need the feeling that someone is providing for calmer waters. That someone is there when mistakes happen. In addition to the lighthouse, they also need more "crash barriers" to guide them. Just like their managers, employees struggle with fears. They might feel insecure in times of digital change. Their range of tasks and the expectations of their own capabilities also change. Here the supervisor is called for as a coach. He should, as described above, individually shape and actively accompany the development of the employee. To do this, he or she needs to show empathy and see the individual in every single employee. Perhaps that does not fit any longer to traditional procedures like the performance review once a year. Further examples would be the large training and development catalog, which is arranged in intensive work by the human resources development department or the manager who can still give the employee professional support or ask "difficult" practice questions in job interviews. If we want to hire the best experts, this means, in turn, that they have greater expertise than their supervisor does. Accepting this is one side of the coin. Understanding it is the prerequisite for being able to successfully answer the strategic, operative working model and management questions—as described in this chapter—at all. This requires an open approach to your own fears and demands. The other side of the coin is the practical handling. What skills am I looking for and do I have to design the position? How does the cooperation with the recruiting department work? Does it find the experts via classic job advertisement? What questions can we ask in the interview? If we want to work in self-controlled teams in the future, what role does the team play in the recruiting process? When technology is developing so fast and permanent learning is the norm, the knowledge required at the time of recruitment may no longer play a major role. In addition to the matching basic requirements for our potential employees, we will in future pay more attention to values, adaptability, personal networks, and individual approach in order to gain up-to-date knowledge, the opinion of further team members and so forth. "Hire great people" (Management 3.0 BV 2018), a Management 3.0 module by author Jürgen Appelo, describes precisely this process of finding the right people and, among other things, gives concrete practical tips in the form of the behavioral interview on how we can learn more about actual competencies instead of asking hypothetical questions.

Whether employees correspond to the values of a company is a crucial point for the selection and for the success of the joint effort. Companies work intensively on defining their corporate and leadership values. Unfortunately, the values written down rarely match the values applied and experienced in the company. How can we reach consistency? Nico Rose, Professor of Business Psychology, describes in an article the Leadership Value Chain of the management professor Robert Quinn, as depicted in Fig. 21.2. 'In this model, everything depends on the values and beliefs of the management level, for example: "If people make enough effort and the framework conditions are right, they can learn almost anything" (or not). Another rationale of the model: "The higher levels are conditioned by the lower levels and can therefore also be blocked by them in terms of (positive) changes" (Rose 2018).

In order for managers to accept that their team members have a higher level of expertise, they must not only understand their role as coach, lighthouse or tower of strength in terms of the necessary tasks, but should rather understand the attitude

Fig. 21.2 Leadership Value Chain—Radical change from the roots (Rose 2018). (Source: author)

and values behind them. By living and demonstrating these values, we pave the way for the success of the company and can thus authentically convey the target image and the Guiding Principles and thus develop a motivating environment. Netflix also offers us a good example of a written, applied and extremely pragmatic corporate culture. The core statement is that people always face processes. As few rules as possible and at the same time as much creativity as possible: this is to achieve a high degree of flexibility and effectiveness (Netflix 2018). The values are described very precisely to make clear what the company expects. This makes it theoretically very easy for employees and managers to live by them. The prerequisite is that everyone has the same personal values. Not every value fits everyone. In this respect, it is important that every manager also strictly scrutinizes whether he or she can really internalize and exemplify the necessary values.

Collaboration, creativity and entrepreneurship have become important values in many companies. However, especially in many larger companies, managers are so involved in internal processes and coordination that there is often not enough time for external networking and inspiration. Managers may not be the experts for all topics, but they should still take the time to find out about current developments and innovative trends. If we want to make up our minds how the market is developing and how our division/company has to position itself, external networking is an essential task for managers. The challenge is to identify the right mix of formal and informal networks. Which conferences do I attend specifically and where do I engage in meaningful ecosystems of representatives of my industry and my customers, thought leaders, potential partners and key stakeholders? The creation of a stakeholder map can provide a good basis for the selection process. I am not only talking about traditional networks but also about meetups, intrinsic and informal meetings of innovation enthusiasts, demodays and similar events.

I talked about the fact that managers from every business unit can start to change. However, middle managers in particular can face the challenge of their own traditional superiors in the course of the digital transformation. Along with customers and employees, they are an essential part of the stakeholder map. The commitment of the CEO or senior management is often cited as the key factor for the success of digital transformation and innovation. While this makes the initiative much easier, it is not a criterion for exclusion or even an excuse for oversleeping the digital era. At this point, managers assume the role of the necessary translator between the demands of the market and those of the employees as well as the evolution of management.

21.6 Conclusion

We need digital, creative and solution-oriented leaders. All mentioned targets require leaders who combine in-depth business knowledge and experience with the ability to develop digital strategies fully aligned with and supported by the agreed business objectives. Leaders with creative skills to envision a digital future. Last but not least, leaders with the personal skills and confidence to drive organizational transformation.

This is what we should be looking for, regardless of hierarchy, to lead our teams and companies. Because using solution-oriented thinking, creating meaning and the leadership that supports it is the key to finding what is new, what is better, what comes next and—most importantly—what gets us there.

References

Fun Retrospectives (2018). http://www.funretrospectives.com/category/retrospective/, Accessed 24 June 2020
Hentrich C, Pachmajer M (2016) d.quarks—Der Weg zum digitalen Unternehmen. Murmann Publishers, Hamburg
Management 3.0 BV (2018) Management 3.0 Plus Module: hiring great people. https://management30.com/modules/hire-great-people/. Accessed 24 June 2020
Netflix (2018) Netflix culture. https://jobs.netflix.com/culture. Accessed 24 June 2020
Rose N (2018) Von Krawatten im Kopf und radikalem Wandel. https://www.xing.com/news/insiders/articles/von-krawatten-im-kopf-und-radikalem-wandel-1098581?sc_p=da863_bning_share=news. Accessed 24 June 2020
Vollmer L (2017) Theater deluxe. Reglements—für wen eigentlich? https://www.foerderland.de/organisieren/news/artikel/reglements-fuer-wen-eigentlich/?utm_content=bufferc70d9tm_medium=socialtm_source=twitter.comtm_campaign=buffer. Accessed 24 June 2020

How to Exploit Me as Much as Possible

22

Tamim Al-Marie

22.1 Introduction

As in my mid-twenties, surrounded by several people with great leadership experience I would like to offer you a view from the other side. I prefer to write about real world experiences than about things I have only read in theory. While I have no experience in making right decisions to furniture the office of my company, I do have a lot of experience working in various offices.

When it comes to changing your company culture and office space, I assume you do it to change how your employee work, work together. One might even say that you change it for your employees. Therefore, I believe it could be a valuable perspective to understand how an office "feels" like for your employees.

To get to the point where you can call your projects somewhat innovative you need to think about the problem in a different way and finally come up with a new solution. I mean if it would not be new it would be the same as before and hence not innovative—that is probably not a big surprise it is even rather obvious.

Here is what I have not only observed over and over again in practice but also have learned in theory as part of my training as a pharmacist, when we discussed the human nervous system: In the face of great danger we tend to fall into old patterns. Do not get me wrong, that is really good because when we have to act as fast as possible, we should not "waste" our time thinking of new ways. What worked great for our ancestors to escape from wild animals who were trying to eat them unfortunately does not work good at all if you want to innovate your Business.

T. Al-Marie (✉)
2B AHEAD Ventures GmbH, Leipzig, Germany
e-mail: tamim@2bahead-ventures.com

© The Editor(s) (if applicable) and The Author(s), under exclusive license to Springer Nature Switzerland AG 2021
V. Nestle et al. (eds.), *Creating Innovation Spaces*, Management for Professionals, https://doi.org/10.1007/978-3-030-57642-4_22

If you want to be able to think of new ways you need different kinds of let us call them freedom of thought.

We have to accept that this takes some time. You have to take the time to really focus on this one problem, also as an employee you have to take the time, it has to be possible to take the time. I am firmly convinced that we are not free in our minds if all day long we think of our closing time at 5 pm. Although it is theoretically possible to simply force your employees to stay in the office longer, there is a better way. At least a better way from the employees' point of view: You could actually make me want to stay in your office. To make a long story short: You need people who like your company, who enjoy their work and who are willing to spend a lot of time in the office.

There are a lot of approaches to drive innovation through radically erasing all rules and restrictions, but we will come to that later.

When you have people, who love to work in your company and I hope you do have them, with exploiting them I mean enabling your employees to work as hard, passionate and creative as they desire to do by themselves. They are happy because they achieve what they want resulting in your company achieving what you want hence you are happy, too. Exploiting could not be more positive. Although, please do not take that phrase to seriously.

22.2   Everything I Need

Obviously, it takes more than a nice office to hire people like that. Nevertheless, as this book is not about human resources and hiring the right people let's assume you already did a great job on that. Now you have a bunch of people who enjoy working for you or let us call it working with you. And who likes to spend a lot of time crunching your problems, they take ownership, they think of your problems as if they were theirs and are willing to find creative solutions.

22.2.1 Take a Seat on the Sofa

When it comes to organizing your office space, you want to enable them as much as possible to follow their path to new solutions and not restrict them with the framework of a common office which is associated to common solutions. It's not about turning your office into a pure amusement zone therefore we have amusement parks, it doesn't necessarily have to be a living room either, well, maybe a little bit, but the right reason makes all the difference. It should not be the reason that your employees hate working in your company so much and would rather be hang out in a living room. It should be because they love the work so much that they want to work even when they are not in the office—even if they are in the living room. You have less of the usual office constraints when working in a different place, but you also want to keep an eye on productivity. In my experience, the best way for an employee to work is to combine an office with a living room, or rather to integrate them into one another. I have never felt the advantage of a living room next to an office as I have experienced it especially in modern offices of larger corporations.

So when you have integrated a living area into your somehow office-like area where it's fun to spend time with your colleagues, also because you have not only hired antisocial fools, where you don't feel the urge to leave the ugly office as soon as possible, people stay longer. They stay and discuss their problems with your colleagues and because it is so much fun to stay there, they even take the time to listen to their colleagues' problems—maybe they are working in completely different teams and areas—and so a team assigned to a project gets input from people who have nothing to do with that project and the associated problems. But not in a way that an external consultant is imposed on the team and now gives his clever comments, but that someone, comparable to a friend, offers his perspective on their problem.

How can you get more diverse people working on a project when people are working on a project who are not even working on that project?

Yes, one condition is of course that you have at least hired people with different backgrounds. As I said before, a new office will not solve all your problems, it is just one piece of a wonderful puzzle. If everyone in your office/company is the same, cross-team collaboration will not be of much use.

22.2.2 Time to Eat

If they have no reason to leave the office as soon as possible and they stay longer, it is only a matter of time before they get hungry. A reason to leave the office and go home? Or a reason to cook together with colleagues and talk about the projects they are working on in a friendly atmosphere?

It's not about free food at the office. Weekly fruit baskets are obviously a nice gesture. But what I really care about is that if the office is not in the city centre and there are no snack bars just around the corner, and I have no kitchen or storage space for food in the office, then of course I have to go home as soon as I get hungry. In theory, there is nothing wrong with bringing a pre-cooked meal or a few slices of bread to work. But, as I have observed, this tends to lead to a culture where everyone eats their own meal for themselves and plays on their smartphones, so they do not have to talk to anyone.

My experience is also that in companies, no matter what size (but of course, the bigger the company, the more the problem grows), people tend to work on the same topics in the same company without even knowing it. Maybe, just maybe, your company could benefit from some synergies. And maybe it just needs to start with the people in the company communicating more. The kitchen could be a further step to enhance the natural conversation between your employees.

As with the living room, the communicative character has a greater impact if it is integrated and the kitchen is not simply placed next to the office as a break room, as is the case with a coffee kitchen in classic office buildings.

Of course, nobody wants to be the guy who hangs around the break room all the time, but the guy who works hard. If instead the kitchen is integrated into the work areas, you can work at a high table in the kitchen, and if someone is waiting for the coffee machine, you have a short chat about what you are working on. I think there are a lot of cases where that can be very helpful. I do not mean that there must be a hot plate on every desk, but an open kitchen works just fine.

Yes, of course you do not sit down at the kitchen table if you want to work in a concentrated way. But there is this kind of work where you look for creative ways to solve your problem. In my experience, a little break here and there, combined with fresh input from your colleague, is incredibly useful when you are doing this kind of work. And then there are the cases where you have a really quick but very important question to someone who is very busy today. Instead of scheduling a meeting and waiting for days for a free time slot: when you see him go to the coffee machine, just spontaneously join him. I stopped counting the times when this kind of conversations tremendously increased the speed in which I could get things done.

22.2.3 Working Material

Here is the last thing I really appreciate as an employee in offices where I really enjoy working: The infrastructure to try new things, or in other words, to work without constraints. I am talking about whiteboards, flipcharts, mobile desks, different types of desks and seating—a dream for creative minds who don't like restrictions when it comes to work.

I am deeply convinced that there is no such thing as the optimal tool for working, neither the perfect table nor the perfect office. There are different requirements and preferences for every single type of task and every single type of person. So, the only way to get as close to perfection as possible is to offer a wide range of working environments. For example, I travel a lot, so in most situations a laptop is perfect for me because it saves space and is suitable for many different tasks at the same time. But every now and then there comes a point where I get stuck. Then I often reach for a flipchart (assuming I am in the office, of course) to visualize the problem, most of the time that is how I find a way to continue. Or I print out the sources I am looking at and arrange them on a large whiteboard. It's the same with organizing tasks while I usually structure my life in a note program on my laptop, when I'm at home, I like to structure everything on my whiteboard, and when I'm overwhelmed, I write down the steps on paper.

So, it seems to be a great opportunity to simply offer your employees as many different ways of working as possible. Also, if you want to encourage your employees to think in new ways and try new methods, why stop at work materials? I think this is a very simple and easy, but also tremendously effective way.

22.3   Fundamentals Touched On

If you have successfully brought your employees to the point where they talk to each other—what do you want them to talk about? Just brag about their successes, maybe create bubbles and walls so as not to be the one that makes mistakes? Or do you want them to talk about the things that really bother them, about mistakes and about problems with projects, so that they can really help each other?

22.3.1 Failure Culture

Then start to make it possible for them to talk about mistakes and the things that are not going well. Although the chapter is mainly about the office structure, I would like to briefly mention a few points about a healthy failure culture and the kind of leadership I enjoy as an employee, because it is immensely important to me and furthermore, without it, even the greatest office is quite useless.

In my opinion, it is plausible that in order to be willing to talk about the problems you are dealing with, you need a culture in which mistakes are usually not a bad thing. Or rather, to try something that, to exaggerate, you have no idea about, you need a company culture that allows you to have the courage to be a beginner, rather than a culture where it is considered stupid not to know everything. Then you start talking openly about it, openly about what you tried, what didn't work and also about what you learned, what works well, instead of pretending to know everything—which, as we all know, nobody does.

Maybe this is the first step towards learning from each other. Since you have a company that hires smart people who work a lot, who therefore have a lot of experience and knowledge—it is even more valuable if they share their thoughts with each other.

22.3.2 Follow Your Passion

If you want your employees to try new things—let them try new things. One Phrase that was said by my boss Stefan Jenzowsky in a team meeting shortly after I started working for him and which I will never forget was something like this: 'We have a lot of work to do. Now more work than ever is coming in, which is a good sign that we are good. We should be happy about that. But we need to focus now! We have to make a clear distinction between the things that are part of our business model, those that move us forward, and on the other hand there are a lot of things that people would like us to do, but we don't have to do them because they are not part of what we are actually doing. If you want to do something because you are interested in it, then do it! I will never stop you from doing something you want to do. But don't do things that we don't have to do and that you don't even want to do.' Not only did he make it clear to us how important it is to prioritize radically what

I really like, because I appreciate the idea that at the end of the day my hard work shows results, but above all, and this was even more important to me, he allows us, romantically speaking, to follow our passion. At that moment I knew that I was in the right company. In my opinion, when people have the opportunity to work on things they are really interested in, they flourish on these projects. So when you distribute tasks in your team, you must of course pay attention to who can do the tasks well, or at least is able to do them, but if at the same time you manage to include who wants to do the task, then in my experience as a team member, the team members are especially happy.

22.3.3 Own Experiences

Another way to let people try new ways of approaching a problem is to let them try it even if you have doubts about that solution yourself. If your employee has an idea about how to solve a certain problem, especially if he is young and unexperienced like me, it happens that you, as a much more experienced person, already know that it won't work that way. Maybe you even know why. I am not saying you should not instruct your employees at all. Of course, you should. But I have seen it from time to time that my supervisor knew that there was a better way to solve the problem, and he had told me about his experience too, but when I really believed in my idea of how to solve it, he let me try. Of course, later I usually concluded that his way was better, and then we changed the strategy, but still.

How effective that is for a company is another question and I don't see myself in the position to provide an answer to that, but as an employee I can tell you that it is perceived as a fantastic way of leadership. I think that I learn a lot more and develop better as an employee in this way than if I just followed instructions. I also learn to appreciate his experience and way of thinking much more, because I see that my idea did not work, but his did. This makes me believe in his way much more next time, and then I work much more passionately to realize his idea than if I only follow because I have to. Finally, it just feels really good to have the freedom to persue your ideas and encourages you to keep coming up with new ideas even if you're not sure if they will work out. I mean, how can you ever be 100% sure that your idea will work? Never, right? That is why it is so important to try it. I think that is why a culture that encourages trying out new ideas and where you are not condemned if you fail sometimes is crucial.

Offer your team help, but let them experiment, even if you know it is the wrong way. I have made the experience that doing something in my own way automatically creates ownership and responsibility. The responsibility makes it much easier for me to go the extra mile. If you go one step further for your own projects and give everything to show that your own idea works, then that is something completely different than working late into the night to conduct a micro-managed process for someone who knew how to do it, but is too important and busy to do it himself. I am not saying that this is not the more productive way. But if you want your employees to come up with new ideas, good new ideas, which I think is more likely if they like what they're doing, then allowing mistakes might be the right way to follow.

22.4   How Did You Get Me Hooked?

When I realized how much I enjoyed working in this office, I became more and more curious why. More than that, although I enjoyed working on the projects I was working on, I still had unproductive and even more importantly, uncreative phases in other places and in other offices. I was writing my first book at the time, about studying pharmacy, and I had moments when I sat in front of my laptop and just could not think of anything meaningful. Spontaneously driving to the office even on a Saturday evening was often the solution. Something about this place helped me to be creative but at the same time to really get things done.

I had often heard that this was no coincidence, but that Sven had designed the concept that way. So, I decided to finally talk to Sven Gabor Janzky, the founder of 2B AHEAD ThinkTank, a trend institute, 2B AHEAD Ventures, the company where I work is located in the same office. Now I wanted to know exactly how my special relationship with this office came about. He said to me that in order for me to understand, we first have to talk about corporate culture basics and football.

22.4.1 Rules Versus Routines

Put simply, he said that culture is the sum of the rules and routines of each team member. The rules form a framework in which the routines can be lived out and which justifies the routines. We all bring certain routines and thought patterns to the company, routines we learned in our school system, at university or in previous jobs. If we were to enter a company without any rules, we would simply continue with our usual routines (Jánszky 2015).

In this way I learned that what I experienced as freedom does not arise from the absence of rules, not at all. That said, in order to give your employees the opportunity to think freely, you don't have to avoid rules, you have to set the right rules. And Sven explained why: If you enter a room with your learned routines without any rules at all, it is only a matter of time until you establish the rules that form a fixed framework around your routines and thus justify your old routines. Whether they make sense or not is irrelevant. With the new rules you set up around your routines, you give them a meaning (Jánszky 2015).

"You can't break routines, but you can break rules," (Jánszky 2015, p. 3) and now he started talking about football, frankly a subject I don't know anything about, but that should not bother us now, let us just trust him on this: every time there is a new coach, the team has to change its routines to the new coach's playing methods.

In particular, Sven spoke about Thomas Tuchel (Borussia Dortmund). When he came to Mainz 05, his team was obsessed with playing along the side lines of the field. These longline passes had to be abolished. If you want to know why it makes

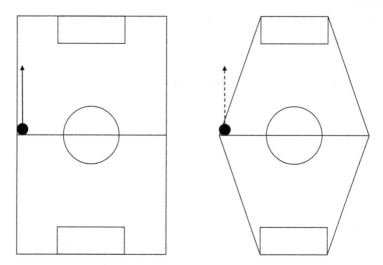

Fig. 22.1 Modified football field. (Source: author)

sense to change this, you would have to read a book about football. The only thing that should interest us here is how he managed to change this strongly established routine. Simply banning this playing method would be as effective as asking your staff to communicate more. Have you ever tried that? Or have you heard of anyone who has? How successful was this approach? If success was limited, it could be because you can't break routines. What did Thomas Tuchel do then? He broke the rules that formed the justifiable framework for this routine. For half a year the team had to train on a modified football field as depicted in Fig. 22.1 (Jánszky 2015).

He cut off the corners of the football field. Players who wanted to follow their old routines thus broke the rule. A longline pass would unavoidably lead to an out. Therefore, the team had no other option than to change their routine. That was exactly what Tuchel wanted to achieve. Notice that he had not said it once. The team changed its routine all by itself, simply because the justifying frame of rules was no longer there (Jánszky 2015).

22.4.2 Erase All Office Characteristics

When I heard the following, I was shocked in a way, even a little disappointed in myself. I thought I was the kind of person who loves to stay in the office for hours and works hard. What I am going to tell you now casts a whole new light on the time I had spent in this office.

As Sven describes what he learned from Tuchel's tactic is: "Neither of us can change the thought patterns of the other. Only you can do that yourself. But we can take away people's ability to continue following their old routines if we consistently

and uncompromisingly break those rules that set the framework for the routines."
(Jánszky 2015, S. 3).

As I said, I do not know anything about football, so let's talk about our playing
field: the office. Here is what Sven did in our office: to bring more dynamics, agility
and creativity into the team, he simply took the opportunity to sit in the same seat
all the time and thus be on his own. To improve communication, he introduced the
rule that nobody has his own seat. Nobody had the possibility to hide in his own
corner. And it went even further: to forget the usual, dusty office rules, he banned
all typical office elements that are visually associated with offices (Jánszky 2015).

Not a single chair recognizable as an office chair (Jánszky 2015). To be honest,
I have always wondered why we have so many gaming chairs, I thought it was a
desire of our tech guys who simply love computer games.

Not one typical sterile office wall (Jánszky 2015). I must admit that I really like
sterile walls. But it has worked out that it does not feel like a typical office. We have
so-called theme walls, simply everything that makes it look less like an office. It is
not that I like the way it looks (to be honest, I would never furnish my apartment
this way). It is just that I really enjoy being there, even if it completely contradicts
my ideas of aesthetics. I appreciate it so much that I meet friends/colleagues there
also on weekends to work together. But if I had been asked for my opinion when
they furnished it, I would probably have just raised my nose. That was the point that
fascinated me so much.

On the other hand, it really hit me because I saw myself as the ambitious type
of young person who loves to stay in the office all day and even on weekends. But
there he was, and he said to me: 'Well, I tried to delete everything that is office-like.
That's why you are there all the time.'—So, does that mean that I do not want to
stay in the office all the time? Does it mean that I am normal, like all the other guys,
and maybe I will not stay all weekend in something that really looks like an office.
But at this point enough about my personality and back to the office.

We have project areas where teams sit together at kitchen tables (Jánszky 2015).
I love the meetings there, and yet I hated sitting in the kitchen at my parents'
house—isn't that crazy? When I tell people about working in the office, I am often
asked whether it was not too loud when almost everyone is sitting in one big open
office, and whether I could even focus there. Is it louder there than when I sit alone
in a room? Yes. Is it therefore more difficult for me to concentrate? No, on the
contrary, it is difficult to describe, but it is more a busy backdrop than a distracting
sound. Of course, you need your quiet place for some activities, that is why we
have communication rooms. But when I use these rooms for conference calls, for
example, I always look forward to when the conference call is over and I can return
to the living area of our office where life is happening and I feel so comfortable.

As Sven explained it, not everyone was happy when these things changed
(Jánszky 2015). But when all these changes happened, I was not yet in the company.
So unfortunately, I have no personal experience of how I would react to these kinds
of changes myself. When I joined, I unknowingly entered a room with completely
different rules that forced me to follow new routines that I have come to appreciate
very much. And I didn't even realize why it all happened the way it did.

22.5   One Concept as an Example

I am not saying that this is the perfect office, not at all. Maybe, as we have learned, it's not even an office. Nor am I saying that this is the perfect and only good concept for creating an environment in which creative people can thrive. Maybe there is no such thing as the perfect office concept because companies and employees can be so different. I am just saying that of all the things I have experienced in terms of work environments, this is the concept that has made me the happiest as an employee. I think it is a great example of how you can create a space where you can exploit your employees. By that I don't really mean exploitation in a bad way, of course not, I know that's not your goal at all, because you're a great CEO, otherwise you wouldn't worry so much about the office that you would read a book about it, but what I do mean is that this could be a way to give your employees as much opportunity as possible to make the most of their day, enjoy their time in your company and thus improve the innovative success of your company.

And again, I am not saying that I know it is a great management decision that will increase revenues, although I think it could be such a decision. But I am not an experienced manager, I am an employee who tells you what he likes about working in innovative spaces.

I appreciate it very much that you think about how you can offer your employees the best possible working environment, and that you even read a book about it. On the contrary, you are willing to listen to a voice of the employees, and I think that is a really beautiful and important step. Maybe you have found at least one point that you find interesting enough to try it out in your company, maybe it will even make your employees happy and benefit your business in general—that would make me very happy too.

22.6   Conclusion

What I learned from the conversation with Sven and from Tuchel's concept, after I could already feel the effect an office can have on an employee. Not only do you give the team what they want by giving them areas to work in that are more relaxed than in the common office and a kitchen for cooking together, but you also take away the things and rules they need to continue with their routines that you want them to change.

We also talked about cases that have shown us that only a new office furnishing does not heal all wounds: I think it has become quite clear that just setting up a start-up-like office will not change much in a company where people want to go home as quickly as possible, because not only do they not like their job, but they don't have anything to talk about with their colleagues.

What I am convinced of, however, is that the right office for your company is a very important element in getting the best out of all your valuable employees. When you think about how high the personnel costs in a company are, it seems to be a worthwhile investment to get more out of expensive employees by restructuring the office space.

Reference

Jánszky SG (2015) Trendanalyse: Wie verändert man eine Unternehmenskultur. 2b AHEAD ThinkTank, Leipzig, Deutschland

An Entrepreneurial Approach to Designing Innovation Space

Jamshid Alamuti

23.1 Introduction

Reading this book, you've certainly been exposed to the definition of "Innovation", so I'm not going to bore you with that. However, in this chapter, we will establish a few additional definitions to ensure we have a fully aligned understanding of the subject.

Also, allow me to assume that you, as a reader, have your own idea of where the concept of innovation space comes from. Some of you have surely experienced the typical consultative approach to implementing innovation within an organization, where a physical environment is set up to make innovation "happen". Others may be familiar with factory shop floors, R&D departments and other organizational infrastructure that, up until today, we understood to be where Innovation was happening. What I'm asking here is to free yourself from a rigid definition of what an innovation space is. Within this chapter, I'm proposing that you consider new components to help you understand and define what an innovation space is.

This chapter aims to explore why there is a need for a specific physical space to drive innovation. It also aims to investigate where innovation is born, what it needs to flourish and at what stage of a process does the physical space become part of the innovation eco-system. Here, I am not looking only at the eco-system of innovation, but at its core characteristics and I am diving deeper into the question of whether innovation is experienced naturally or if it is forced or developed by design. Can you manipulate innovation to happen or it is generated within a natural, or even partially instinctive, environment?

J. Alamuti (✉)
House of Creative Entrepreneurship, Berlin, Germany
e-mail: jamshid@houseofce.com

© The Editor(s) (if applicable) and The Author(s), under exclusive license
to Springer Nature Switzerland AG 2021
V. Nestle et al. (eds.), *Creating Innovation Spaces*, Management for Professionals,
https://doi.org/10.1007/978-3-030-57642-4_23

If a position is to be taken, this chapter promotes a scenario where innovation is born out of creative interaction with the eco-system. This occurs mostly in response to a challenge or with the desire to optimize a situation to find a better solution for an existing approach. If this scenario has a valid root, not only does the approach becomes unique (depending on the problem and the individual who is trying to solve it) but the "process" also becomes purely an over-rated part of the game. The more important elements then become the attributes that might unleash or limit creativity, and therefore innovation.

In this case, the question of whether tools, space or processes will save the day and become enabling or even indispensable elements, is to be explored and will come after discussing the characteristics and the human-centric approach.

23.2 Cornerstones

When implementing innovation, organizations have to consider a few inevitable investments, including a dedicated budget, dedicated resources, a clear mission and focus, as well as education and tools to enable processes. If we compare the eco-system of innovation to a building, I look at these investments as the floors of the building, the doors and windows, the rooms and elevators. But where and how did this all get started? Before the first walls were erected? I pursue this comparison as a way to challenge the validity of the ecosystem as such.

I am arguing that it all starts with the individual and their attitude towards innovation. The right personality, the right personal attributes to be precise. Leaders within organizations that have a culture of innovation will never question what's needed to enable the process of innovation, they welcome mistakes out of which one can learn, they dare to take risks and they don't limit themselves to the three to five years of their managerial contracts. What I am trying to say is that you can have all that's needed to build an eco-system of innovation, but without a vision and a "doing" mentality there is a high chance you will fail to successfully introduce innovation into your organization, regardless of the setting. Don't go the simple route, signing contracts that tell you what you need to be more innovative. Start with the cornerstones, start with your people, with yourself and by connecting with your customers.

Let me use an example to expand on this a little: the Sony Walkman. If I'm not mistaken, this was the very first portable media player. I had a few of them. The first in 1980, just a year after it was released. Now, we are talking about Sony, one of the most technologically advanced companies at that time. A business with a strong brand reputation, a huge customer base, a proper budget and basically everything you can think of that defines success. So why was Sony not able to maintain its leading position within the market segment it had very much created? Remember, their claim was:

allowing people to listen to music of their choice on the move.

Why did Sony fail? And how did Apple manage to take over this vision not that many years later? I am not comfortable believing that Sony lacked the ecosystem needed for innovation. So, whatever went wrong must relate to the human factor. Did the company not read the needs of their customers? Were there greater risks to be taken and Sony was not ready or willing to do so? Were they too comfortable with the success they had and did not dare or want to disrupt their own business? Were they not willing to transform? No matter how I look at these questions, I end up realizing that what Sony lacked was the right attitude. The attitude of an entrepreneur: taking risks, listening to customers' needs and anticipating their preferences, daring to disrupt, and being willing to fail in order to succeed.

Let's look at another example: Nokia! It's no surprise that Nokia's failure is regularly used as a case study in disruptive innovation sessions. I mean, we are talking about the best-selling mobile phone brand in the world as of winter 1998. Their profit margins quadrupled between 1995 and 1999. But in 2007, the iPhone was introduced, and the giant of the mobile phone business lost out to market newcomer Apple. How does this happen?

Remember, we are talking about a company that was the market leader in mobile technology. Are we going to suggest that the reason they failed at innovating was because of the process? Or was it a lack of innovation space and innovation budget? Or was it the absence of culture and attitude?

It's funny that in both the cases of Sony and Nokia, it was Apple that entered as the game-changing competitor. What was Apple doing differently? I can't stop myself from jumping to the conclusion that it came down to two words: creativity and entrepreneurship. It was definitely not about technology. The technology was accessible to all these players at that time. And so, it is apparent that the human factor matters, in this case, in the context of transformation. People evolve, society and technology progress and organizations are accordingly affected.

As an organization, you know transformation is critical to stay ahead of your competition. And you know you will have to re-think your products and services to remain innovative. This is where you can go wrong or be spot on!

What needs to be changed? Processes? Tools? Is it a technological trans-formation, as in rebooting the production line with robotics? Is it optimizing administrative tasks with new tools, software or systems? Can these types of efforts be categorized as innovation at all? Or does innovation start psychologically, in the head of each individual, by adopting a new culture? A different culture of product and service design? If we take the latter as valid, is innovation then not something that you plant as a seed and slowly but surely it becomes a sustainable part of your organization? A long-term, ongoing and never-ending innovation journey?

Allow me to explain my logic. What I am after is the culture of innovation and the concept that innovation is an inevitable creative act used to engage with challenges. I am aware that we can describe different categories or types of innovation and that accordingly, the requirements might vary. However, I do believe that the starting point for innovation is the right attitude and culture. And it is the culture that organically suggests the setting for innovation therefore it makes sense to explore the fundamental cornerstones.

23.2.1 Entrepreneurship

As mentioned, I am following the thesis that innovation needs culture, much more than a specific space, certain tools, a budget or processes. Don't get me wrong, all of those are needed as well. Some more than others, but none are of any use if the culture for innovation is not there. What I am trying to say is that if you and your team have the right attitude towards innovation, you can be innovative in any room you pick within your office. I have seen agencies and consulting companies selling the magic of some great looking, playful environment, such as the innovation lab or the innovation hub. But I have to admit I am sorry to see that money gets spent on these spaces. While they might tick off the boxes on the strategic agenda and support the claim that the infrastructure for innovation has been provided, they often remain empty.

Let me connect the dots between "Culture" and "Entrepreneurship". What do these two words have in common? And how do they relate to innovation?

Culture, as we understand it, is a set of values and beliefs. These values and beliefs are translated into action by a set of attitudes and behaviors. Culture develops and manifests gradually. At the societal level, it takes generations for behaviors to turn into norms and habits. Norms and habits make us comfortable. At some stage, we don't question them anymore and might even develop a blind spot for the necessity of improving, changing or replacing them, or even introduce new norms and habits as circumstances might have been changing. Translating it into a corporate organization, there are many similarities. Companies become the cities and countries, departments become household and families and tribes, and colleagues around you are comparable to your friends and families, with all emotional ups and downs. The difference is in corporate formal distancing, the battle to keep the balance between emotions and rational. Now interestingly and contrary to a cultural organ, the corporate is not necessarily built upon their or any values. I am not generalizing. But I hope you agree, there are enough companies where values or purpose is just some lines in some documents. It is a matter of living and breathing the values until they become a natural part of the company's personality, culture, the authentic face of the organization. I therefore follow the hypothesis that the sustainably leading organizations are usually those who defined their values and managed to not only communicate them, but to transport them to all levels of the company and with that managed to establish a visible and believable culture.

When I look at the definition of Entrepreneurship, I end up with a similar scenario. The set of attitudes and behaviors of entrepreneurs are so typical that you can identify an entrepreneur based on the validation of those behaviors. Even if each individual is different and approaches the business differently, we can still describe entrepreneurial behavior and even go so far as to consider training our teams and companies in Entrepreneurial behaviors and attitudes. With that, we can even provide an approach and a process of engagement between our corporate interaction with society and the market.

Interestingly, when you look at the typical attributes of an entrepreneur, you find them absolutely useful for describing the culture of innovation. It is perhaps very daring of me to try to sum up the characteristics of an entrepreneur in few bullet points, so I cautiously boil it down. Above all, an entrepreneur wants to make things happen. It's not just the big dream, but it goes all the way down to seeing it, feeling it, using it, as mentioned: "making it happen"! This already is one of the most valuable attributes for innovation. No matter what risk or how much failure, let's dare to make it become reality. Taking risks, permitting failure, thinking outside the box, not giving up, getting your hands dirty, avoiding complications in order to enable implementation, these are typical characteristics of an entrepreneur and must-have attributes for making innovation happen.

When helping an organization prepare for transformation into an innovation-driven organization, one of the first steps in the journey is to create a "characteristic blueprint". This is what guides the creative ideation and the practical doing in order to make innovation real. Whenever I get teams engaged in producing this blueprint, I cannot tell if the words and phrases they come up with are describing an entrepreneur, creativity or a healthy, progressive empathetic culture and tribe. The overlap and similarities are fascinating.

Exploring this blueprint in the context of creativity, we can look at the need for creativity within the innovation eco-system. This isn't because you need creativity for having great ideas or for making innovatively designed products. I am interested in creativity because it perfectly explains the relationship between innovation and the innovation space! It makes it apparent why we need or believe to need a specific space to drive innovation.

23.2.2 Creativity

There is an endless supply of magnificent books, podcasts and other sources of information out there on creativity, so I am not planning to attempt another definition.

I recently ran a 12-month research project involving around 100 participants, from a range of different cultures and countries. We thoroughly discussed the question of "What is Creativity?" and believe me: there was never the one right answer.

What I am interested in, when we talk about creativity, is the list of the most typical characteristics we use to describe a creative person, or creative behavior. Creative people are visionary people; they want to be perfect, they try and experiment and never get tired. Creativity is put in place to help solve problems, find answers, provide new options and it helps to diversify. It is immensely based on empathy and it aims to arouse a set of emotions to satisfy, engage and integrate you. Creativity deals with the fear of failure and embracing resilience. Once you clearly distinguish between creativity and art, you realize creativity always strives to harvest the collective intelligence. It aims to interact with consumers and integrates them in the development process. It goes beyond any pre-set reality and very much explores the impossible.

I can go on and on about creativity. And I can argue that each and every characteristic of a creative individual, or act of creativity, aligns with the image we have of an entrepreneur. From there we can see how many of these attributes also correlate with the concept of innovation. This would however take time and would be a chapter in itself. So, for the sake of moving to the more exciting part, let's assume I've already convinced you of the fact that there is a massive overlap in attributes and characteristics between Entrepreneurship and Creativity and that many if not all these attributes are used to form the culture of innovation.

The key aspect here, relevant to our topic, is the nature of creativity. There is a period in our lives where creativity is a natural part of our development: our childhood. Remember the sandbox? Isn't it funny that the phrase "innovation sandbox" is regularly used to define the framework of an innovation space? Looking at it analytically, you'd be surprised to discover that a large segment of childhood and child-like behavior is embedded within the innovation process. The point I am making should be obvious. Think of the usage of Lego bricks to build stuff during a brainstorming process. Is it the brick itself that is so important? Or the fact that we are invited to be the child again? To let go of our fears, not overthink, let our imaginations fly, believe that anything is possible—that you can build a machine out of some pieces of cardboard and fly to the moon with it.

If you have ever been involved in an innovation sprint, I am certain you were set up in a space and armed with different colored pens, sticky notes, scissors, glue, etc. Basically, you could open the door to the room and minus some details and some sophisticated words here and there, you wouldn't be able to tell the difference between an innovation hub and a kindergarten.

The line of thought I'd like to hold on to is these child-specific characteristics. From the perspective of creativity, these are what provide us with the confidence to reach for the stars and to look around and to build something with whatever materials we have on hand. The fear of failure has not manifested itself yet and is not a barrier. The easiness, the playfulness, the fun we have in doing what we do and not getting tired of it. In this state, burnout has no meaning. Have you ever seen a child getting tired of playing? I have seen children literally fall asleep on their toys while playing and then wake up to immediately continue with the game! So, there is this natural relation to doing things, a curiosity, an excitement to explore the unknown and fully disregard any potential danger or consequences.

You see what I mean. We are looking at a rich basket of attributes and characteristics that we would wish every member of our team would bring along. Paired with the experiences gathered through the years, the knowledge and awareness of our environment, and the fact that at the corporate level we have specific goals to pursue, make these child-like attributes being an amazing added value. So if you are an individual who has managed to keep the inner child alive in yourself, or if you have no difficulties comprehending the concept of going back to your child-like state of being, you will observe how your lust and hunger for innovation grows. Most importantly, you suddenly realize it doesn't matter where and with what. If you have the goal and desire to innovate, it is not a task, it is a way of looking at your business, day in and day out. It is an attitude and you know how to approach it, naturally and by default. And this makes you independent to a specific space, tool or process.

23.3 Applicability

Let us translate this philosophy and theory into practical measures. So, what are the ingredients for innovation? On one hand, we have a set of characteristics that define entrepreneurship and creativity. On the other hand, we have the beauty of limitless opportunities and possibilities of doing based on our child-like set of behaviors. These are the essential components of innovation. If you have managed to make your people understand and embrace these ingredients, you are already in tune with establishing your culture of innovation.

If you need a recipe to cook this meal, the first step is to introduce these components and characteristics to your people. What about pre-designed tools? Yes, there is design thinking and similar devices, but once you understand innovation, can you not design your own tools and process? Is that not already innovation? Customized to your unique challenge, company, audience and more? I am sure you can anticipate, the more customization you add early on in the process the more unique your output will be.

The same would go with the space. You might believe that in order to have your people be more innovative, it helps to take them away from their working environment, from their daily routines or their phones and laptops. But frankly, these are just rules of engagement. If you are hard-wired with the right culture you can innovate anytime, anywhere.

Imagine you allow your people to write ideas on the walls anywhere inside your workspace. Imagine you permit your people to spend a portion of their workday sitting and just thinking, having a coffee, taking their socks off and putting their feet into warm water. I can provide you with a long list of easy and yet absolutely disruptive activities. But depending on your organization and circumstances, you would likely reject those, welcome them, find them funny, certainly often much cheaper than an agency designing an innovation space for you. And I have understanding for possible doubts. In order to make it more directed, I recommend the following three things to consider here.

23.3.1 Subject Vs. Object

One important factor, when talking about innovation, is to turn the focus from the subject to the object. What do I mean by this? Consider yourself as the subject and the challenge or the problem you face as the object. When I say 'yourself', I am including your entire organization. When it comes down to innovation and innovation space, we tend to look at ourselves first and with that, we limit ourselves to what we have, who we are and what we are capable of. This point of view already generates a barrier in terms of achieving innovation. We are only looking at solutions what we can make real. So, accordingly, if you have created and designed a specific space for innovation to happen, that space is a barrier to realizing innovative thinking. That you come up with depends on your tools, your environment, your "trained" resources and so on. But if you manage to change perspective and give priority to the object, and by object I mean the problem you want to solve, the challenge you are going to tackle or the goal you hope to achieve, you establish a different starting point. Your subconscious is not driven by the "What can I do?" question, but rather with "How can this be solved?" question. And these are two entirely different starting points. The latter provides you with the luxury of collaboration, freedom of space and freedom within the elements you are working with.

A true innovative process driven by objects, as the core point of focus, allows you to transport and realize your ideas beyond your closed eco-system and towards hitting much bigger targets. True Innovation adds something to your organization that you did not have before—new resources, new processes, new structures, you name it.

23.3.2 Categories of Innovation

We have a wide range of organizational structures and sizes. Your industry segment, the size of your business, the maturity of the organization, alongside a few other elements defining who you are and what culture you are driven by. There is also the market, consumers, competition and other external situations and influences. All these elements affect how your organization approaches innovation.

As a young company, you might already have the agility to act innovatively and your entire office might be designed as an innovation hub. Likely entrepreneurship focused; you are already sub-consciously unleashing the child in you. Larger and older organizations, with generations of employees and established success with products or services, are very likely in a comfort zone and don't possess the right culture.

If you aim to progress through innovation, it's important to understand that designing a specific space, training your people with certain tools or supporting them with lean, agile and fun processes, is nothing more than an attempt to wake the child in them. These efforts release the power of creativity or make your people believe in being a part of your brand's story and committing to it. Realizing this, you can clearly see that the space, the tools and everything else are simply used to implement and manifest culture. The starting point. So it's essential to make sure you know what the real priority is.

23.3.3 Trigger

This is the other key component. Every action has a trigger and the trigger needs to be rooted, it needs to be valid for the majority of those involved and it needs to relate to your intentions. Why do you want to innovate? Believe me, if you narrow your trigger down to a statement such as "my competition has a better product and I need to top that", you will fail. No process and no space will help you there.

Imagine a car manufacturer saying, "the reason I am after clean energy transportation, is that Tesla has electric cars in the market". Alternatively, imagine that the same car company claimed "I realized the world needs better concepts for transportation, with less harm to the environment and a new experience for the customers". Which statement triggers you more?

Having the right trigger and fully exploring and understanding where it comes from is an elementary step towards innovation. With the right trigger, you inspire and compel the right people to work on a challenge. And getting to know those right people, helps you provide them with the environment they need to explore potential solutions for the problem and increases their level of innovative output. You design your innovation space around your problem and those who work on it. You don't build a specific space to generally drive innovation. Space is always specific to a certain goal and challenge.

23.4   Conclusion

In summary, my recommendation is to start your innovation journey in a human-centric manner. This helps you better connect with your internal resources, better educate and prepare them and it also helps you to get a much better feel for the needs and desires of your customers. This also helps you to better identify the area of innovation you aim to focus on. You will have the right rationale for what you do and why you're doing it, which creates the right focus on your challenge. You can argue all efforts and costs involved, have the team with the right attitude and culture to do the job, and only then will you have the essential information to think of your "innovation space". When you design, taking into consideration all of the above factors, you maximize your chances for success.

Your space is more than some comfortable sofa, or a PlayStation, or boards on the walls and pens on the tables. This is the place where you can ask unlimited questions and aren't afraid of not knowing the answers. This is the place where your people can feel empowered and can grow with challenges they tackle. This is the place where they feel they are contributing to change something dramatically and leaving footsteps behind.

The innovation space is the place where you hack your own company. What's different in this space is not how it is designed but how you think and act when you are in it. So, if you can think differently anywhere in your company, anywhere is your innovation space. Make sure the design of your space puts humans first and make sure you aim to implement a culture, not a process. With that, you will see how the obvious design of your space becomes apparent to you.

Augmenting Machine-Human Intelligence with Human-in-the-Loop

Karina Grosheva

24.1 Innovation as a Design of Human-Machine Cross-Augmentation

Innovation, as a field of study or business practice, has historically been based on leveraging human ingenuity and creativity to deliver on business value. Product innovation design, in particular, evolves further into analysis of user experiences and business processes with the aim of introducing new products and services to the market.

Customer- and user-centeredness have typically been recognized as foundational principles of product innovation. Leading design agencies and management consulting firms focusing on product innovation, researched these principles over the years of practice.

However, classic innovation design theory has evolved in recent years, largely due to newly available massive volumes of data. In addition to data feeds extracted from conventional data-rich business processes such as supply chain or financial management, there has been an exponential growth of new data coming from embedded sensors in the production lines and operations (Saracco 2019). These sensors, located in factories, selling floors or warehouses, form a network of machines and devices that collects digital copies of the physical world. These emerging data sources pose a new design problem for businesses.

K. Grosheva (✉)
TaQadam, New York, NY, USA
e-mail: karina@taqadam.io

© The Editor(s) (if applicable) and The Author(s), under exclusive license
to Springer Nature Switzerland AG 2021
V. Nestle et al. (eds.), *Creating Innovation Spaces*, Management for Professionals,
https://doi.org/10.1007/978-3-030-57642-4_24

24.1.1 How Can These New Data Sources Can Be Used to Revolutionize the Business Process and Augment Human Performance?

Advancements in AI, including the emergence of deep learning, have allowed forming machine or algorithmic intelligence to exist side by side with human intelligence in business processes. The new innovation design paradigm is shifting from the design of a single product solution to the design of human-machine interaction, and further to the design of the human-machine ecosystem. Such emerging complex business ecosystems bring about multiple data communication patterns: human-to-machine and machine-to-machine.

In this emerging human-machine ecosystem, data requires a human interpretation to generate business value and an informed innovation process. The scenarios of such relationships are based on user-centered design, as well as practical application and maturity of AI systems, or *user-centered AI solutions*.

The design of a human-machine ecosystem may include the following steps of human-machine interaction:

- Developing unbiased and robust AI models using balanced and high-quality training datasets
- Setting human-in-the-loop or active learning systems to improve deployed AI solutions
- Creating a Digital Twin environment of cross fertilization between AI and human intelligence, where humans take on roles of performance analytics

24.2 Human-Machine Interaction in Development of AI Systems

This section explores two different models used to design AI using human-labeled data. The first model, *passive learning*, requires a large human-labeled training dataset to be fed into a machine learning model at the outset. The second model, *active learning,* or *human-in-the-loop* is used in less known business environments or for more complex use cases where outcomes are impossible to predict. In these circumstances, humans become a part of the feedback loop for the AI models.

24.2.1 Human Labeling of Training Datasets for Robust AI Models

Before a machine learning model is developed, a *training set* of manually labeled data is designed. The goal of AI is to augment human performance. Therefore, AI is built on work done by humans. The development of AI systems starts with asking questions which are innately human in reference to a specific business process. While there has been scientific progress in using semi-supervised and unsupervised machine learning models (Alloghani et al. 2020), the majority of market applications require humans to label training dataset.

24.2.1.1 What Are the Key Principles of Creating High-Quality Training Datasets with Human Labeling?

Custom Models and Unique Use Cases

All companies operate in individual and unique business environments. Companies with specific factory setup, gear, or industry risk operate in especially unique business environments. Companies in the sectors of agriculture, mining or industrial production require custom AI models for deployment of robots to understand and navigate specific environments, to evaluate safety risks, and to detect defects on assembly lines.

No AI Model Is the Same

In AI development practice, these tailored models are referred to as *custom models*. These custom models use custom training datasets. Custom training datasets cover classes and decision-making scenarios of a particular business process inherit to a company, industry or object. For example, a custom model for an automobile production company may require a custom training dataset that addresses a relatively uncommon scenario, such as distinct spare parts used. If these labor-intensive processes require timely human input, then the development of a training dataset for automation of such a process would likewise require significant effort. In developing a training dataset, this effort would be put toward class definition, labeling and interpretation.

Examples of Training Datasets for Computer Vision Models

Computer Vision is one of the fastest growing sub-fields of Artificial Intelligence. Different image processing techniques have been used prior to the proliferation of *Computer Vision,* but none reached the necessary scale for mass implementation (Bezdek et al. 1999). Now, Computer Vision, as a sub-field of AI, finds practical application in *robot vision* (e.g. navigating the ambient), *machine vision* (e.g. inspections and support of manufacturing processes), and *geo-spatial analysis.*

Image detectors, cameras and edge devices installed across business facilities have become extremely effective and cost-effective. Machine Learning algorithms interpret data from high-resolution and low-cost sensors at scale. Automated image recognition helps to address business problems or needs such as drone-based monitoring and surveying of wind turbines in need of maintenance, the development of intelligent traffic systems with detection of vehicle category or parking violations, or final production inspections on assembly lines.

Different Computer Vision models are in use, including *classification, object localization and detection,* and *semantic segmentation* models. Of these models, semantic segmentation models are the most advanced and the most difficult to develop.

Fig. 24.1 Semantic segmentation of the scene. (Source: Author)

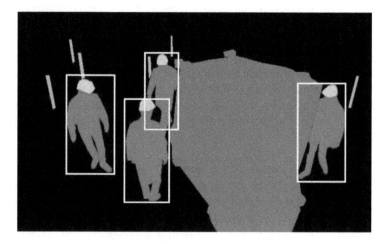

Fig. 24.2 Instance segmentation of the workers in the facility. (Source: Author)

As defined in (Thoma 2016) *Semantic image segmentation, also called pixel-level classification, is the task of clustering parts of image together which belong to the same object class.*

Semantic segmentation training set is performed by manually segmenting—with pixel precision—objects on the image with the intent of training a machine learning model to recognize pixel to class attribution. An example is depicted in Fig. 24.1.

Another type of Computer Vision practice, Instance segmentation as referred by (Chen et al. 2018) *allows solving the complexity of object detection or localization and segmentation jointly, specifying each individual pixel attribution as well as clustering it around specific instances of objects.* An example is depicted in Fig. 24.2.

Class Imbalance

Size and sampling best practices behind creating a training set vary and depend on the use case. Ideal training sets are required to maintain the class balance, which means feeding into the machine learning model a necessary number of instances for each class trained. In the real-world generated images upholding a strict class balance is nearly impossible. For example, street view cameras may collect a significantly larger number of *pedestrians* or *SUVs* as a class, than *bikes* or *fire hydrants*.

Human workers' engagement in labeling training sets cleans and tunes the dataset to the right class balance which optimizes the machine learning model's robustness. Engagement of human labelers helps to prevent commonplace disadvantages of AI, such as *overfitting*. As defined by Roelofs (2019), *overfitting is used to describe any unwanted performance drop of a machine learning model, which is a typical performance for low quality training dataset and class imbalance.*

High Cost of Error are the "Principles"

Human-labeled training datasets are beneficial to use when there is no margin for an algorithm's poor performance. For example, human-labeled training datasets should be favored over *synthetically generated data* when image processing is used for ensuring safety or assessing industry risks or fairness of job application screening or criminal justice applications.

These sensitive circumstances raise two major concerns: unbalanced data and algorithmic bias. To solve the problem of algorithmic bias, a manually trained dataset, diversification of labelers and maintenance of impartiality are all required in the original decision-making process.

Information on Ethics of AI: Biased Datasets

Ethics in AI has been broadly discussed in the past several years, with opacity and potential bias of AI systems being a main debate focus (Floridi, Taddeo, 2016). This debate peaked after the studies and media coverage of facial recognition algorithms, when a software used to predict future criminals showed bias against individuals of African American and of Asian descent. In 2016, ProPublica published a report which tested and demonstrated racial discrimination in criminal risk attribution to individuals (Angwin et al. 2016). This was but one of many cases that brought attention to the potential for bias in algorithmic training. This results from inherited imbalanced training sets as well as systems trained by humans, who, as a result of their own biases, may introduce bias.

24.2.2 Human-in-the-Loop or Active Learning Model

Another model of human-machine interaction is implemented as *Human-in-the-loop or Active Learning.* Generally defined, *Human-in-the-loop (HiTL) is a model of augmented intelligence that requires human interaction in the continuous feedback loop to machine learning models* (Zanzotto 2019). While an original human-labeled training dataset may result in a high accuracy- and confidence-level AI model, there is a high probability that data engineers are not able to define and consider all the possible scenarios and outcomes.

Introducing human intelligence into the continuous feedback loop of AI systems can help to realize a faster and verified analysis-response mechanism. Decision-making tasks, traditionally carried out by humans, are now handled through learning loops augmented by AI. These active learning loops make the development of AI solutions agile and iterative and in alignment with lean *startup principles*. Subsequently, active learning business process setup is less limited in terms of volume or speed than passive learning. Active learning allows the AI model to continue improving over time, selectively feeding low confidence predictions, or edge cases, to the human verification loops prior to automating the high-confidence predictions.

Notably, in active learning human-machine interaction, the original human-labeled training datasets become smaller, and data engineers' preliminary work on sampling is reduced. First iterations of the trained model, in practice referred to as a pre-trained *model*, allow us to gain insight into specific class performance.

The business value in an active learning approach lies in rapid prototyping and deployment of an AI model. Even in critical business applications, as discussed in Sect. 2.1.3, human engagement resolves the impasse of AI deployment, by augmentation instead of automating the process in its entirety. Interestingly, companies or institutions deploying such AI models retain critical personnel for human-in-the-loop processing (e.g. CT medical scan practitioners or safety professionals). This hybrid model is a great example of an *augmented intelligence* ecosystem with cross-fertilization of decision-making between AI and human experts.

24.3   Augmented Intelligence in Digital Twin Environments

Digital Twin business models are being used in increasing frequency as boundaries of machine and human in the business process become fuzzier.

As defined by IBM (2016) *"The digital twin is the virtual representation of a physical object or system across its life-cycle. It uses real-time data and other sources to enable learning, reasoning, and dynamically recalibrating for improved decision making."*

Generating digital twin models have only become possible in the era of connected devices and embedded sensors, where the data generated in the physical world is being copied into a virtual world. While generally referred to as *IOT, or Internet of Things*, and have its most popular references in a design of *a smart home*, the idea of a virtual copy of manufacturing process is drastically reshaping the industrial world.

The data streams at the virtual or digital copy of the physical process are generated at scale with computer vision, as well as applied AI models interpreting temperature, vibration or pressure data. These data points are critical for decision making processes in manufacturing processes. The digital copy - or full and continuous synchronization of the business, operational and industrial process -

allows not only to early detect defects or machine incidents, but also build analytics through predictive maintenance models developed using historical data.

Digital twins change human engagement to machines. Simulation and virtualization of the processes allow early testing and lower risks. The challenges referred to at Sect. 2 remain in advancing the digital twin model, and for its full implementation, there is a need for a thoughtful design of the human-machine ecosystem.

24.4 Conclusion

In the first part of this chapter, we explored evolving design disciplines and reviewed the growth of AI applications to business. We then delved into specific roles humans may hold within the field of AI, including their role in developing training sets for continuous human-in-the-loop models. We showed concrete examples of training sets for computer vision and discussed the key principles of human-machine interactions to build robust AI models. As an outcome, we examined digital twin setups, both as a forward-looking ecosystem and in relation to humans' increasingly analytical roles within industrial operations. Through these explorations, discussions and examinations, we broke down the idea of augmented intelligence as a human-machine ecosystem and gained an understanding of how human intelligence and artificial intelligence can complement each other and generate value for business.

References

Alloghani M, Al-Jumeily D, Mustafina J, Hussain A, Aljaaf A (2020) A systematic review on supervised and unsupervised machine learning algorithms for data science

Angwin J, Larson J, Mattu S, Kirchner, LP (2016) Machine bias. https://www.propublica.org/article/machine-bias-risk-assessments-in-criminal-sentencing. Accessed January 15, 2019

Bezdek JC, Keller J, Krisnapuram R, Pal NR (1999) Image processing and computer vision. Fuzzy models and algorithms for pattern recognition and image processing, The Handbooks of Fuzzy Sets Series, vol 4. Springer, Boston, MA

Chen L, Hermans A, Papandreou G, Schroff F, Wang P, Hartwig A (2018) MaskLab: instance segmentation by refining object detection with semantic and direction features

Floridi L, Taddeo M (2016) What is data ethics?

IBM (2016) Cheat sheet: what is digital twin? https://www.ibm.com/blogs/internet-of-things/iot-cheat-sheet-digital-twin/. Accessed December 28, 2019

Martin Thoma (2016) A survey of semantic segmentation

Roelofs R (2019) Measuring generalization and overfitting in machine learning

Saracco R (2019) Augmented machines and augmented humans converging on transhumanism

Zanzotto F (2019) Viewpoint: human-in-the-loop artificial intelligence. J Artif Intell Res

Innovation Spaces in the Global Environment

Karl H. Ohlberg

25.1 Introduction

Many entrepreneurs and leaders are so focused on their product or project that they do not find the time to deal with the big picture of their environment.

The global development of a business activity covering all major continents is one of the most fascinating tasks for an entrepreneur, but also one of the most challenging. Countless entrepreneurs who are successful in their home markets have already failed in this task. Those who have made it are admired.

In this chapter, we would like to show that the time has come to rethink internationalization. The currently developing innovation spaces in the global environment offer epochal new opportunities.

At the beginning of the chapter, we will briefly show how globalization is changing through new technologies. We will then present the drivers of global change and the role of the COVID-19 pandemic in this context. Next, we will describe how the local and global business environments differ and how innovation spaces can be configured. Then we look at changes in Silicon Valley. Finally, we discuss developments in the global startup economy.

25.2 How Globalization has Changed

The globalization of the world economy has so far progressed in phases. During a stable phase, the primary task of managers is to realize profits in existing structures (doing things right). During a phase change, it is the primary task of leaders to

K. H. Ohlberg (✉)
EmpraGlob GmbH, Duesseldorf, Germany
e-mail: karl@empraglob.com

V. Nestle et al. (eds.), *Creating Innovation Spaces*, Management for Professionals,
https://doi.org/10.1007/978-3-030-57642-4_25

develop business under the changing conditions of the new era (doing the right things) (Drucker 1967).

In the past decades we have had a stable phase in many parts of the world. The holistic use of the advantages of globalization has so far been largely reserved for large corporations in this period of stability. In simple terms, small and medium-sized enterprises (SMEs) could only use international sales markets (export/import) or they could become involved in supply chains.

For entrepreneurs, it is more difficult to build a globally active company in such a stable period. This is also one of the reasons why a country like Germany has not built up a pervasively globally active company in the last 48 years. The youngest fully globalized German company is SAP, founded in 1972.

A different path is being followed by the well-known up-and-coming companies from Silicon Valley and, especially recently, by tech companies from Asia, which have managed to build up world market-leading companies through the courageous use of future technologies combined with entrepreneurship, first with the market launch of the personal computer (PC), then through the development of the Internet, and since the turn of the millennium through new digital methods of social media (see Sect. 25.5). However, it must be taken into account that, with a few exceptions, these rising tech stars have so far only been active in a few service sectors.

Initially, the success of the tech upstarts only had the dimension of a good business, where some entrepreneurs and investors were rewarded with high profits. However, this success then developed into another dimension, which is that precisely these technologies have introduced nothing less than a new phase of globalization.

To better understand the current situation of upheaval, it is useful to take a brief look at the previous upheavals of globalization (see Fig. 25.1).

The first phase of globalization came about before the First World War through new forms of transport using mechanical power (e.g. steamship, railways). This new technology led to a rapid increase in international activities and then to two world wars. After the Second World War, globalization took place with national guidelines and rule-based international governance (especially UNO, IMF, World Bank, WTO) (Baldwin 2018).

Starting in the 1970s, global supply chain networks were established, which for the first time combined high-tech with low wages. With these supply chain networks, the first real 'world-wide-web' developed (Khanna 2016).

From around 2015, the digital *world-wide-web* began to gain such momentum that a new phase of globalization was initiated, Globalization 4.0 (Baldwin 2018).

It is to be expected that the upheavals that will take place in this phase will go far beyond the usual understanding of the upheavals brought about by digitization. So far, occupations in the service sector have only been marginally affected by the consequences of globalization. In future, it will be possible for more and more activities to be carried out remotely, e.g. by service personnel, skilled workers, office staff, but also doctors and lawyers.

The Internet of Things (IoT), Artificial Intelligence (AI), Virtual Reality (VR), Augmented Reality (AR) and human connectivity through improved telecommuni-

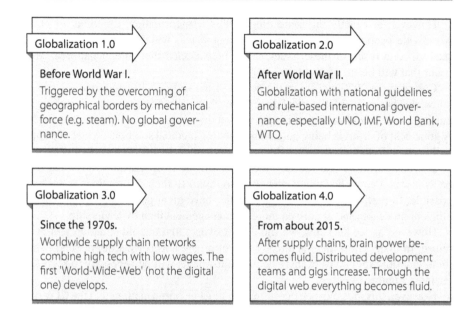

Fig. 25.1 The four phases of globalization. Categorization by R. Baldwin (2018). (Source: authors)

cation systems will enable teams to work together more easily without having to be in the same place. Distributed development teams and so-called gigs, i.e. work by freelancers, will also increase. In summary, a so-called virtual migration may be on the horizon, where skills and labor cross national borders but workers themselves do not (Baldwin 2019).

This transition will be a gradual process, although it has already started on a small scale. Many elements of the previous phase will remain for the time being. Observations have shown that the effects of new technologies are overestimated at the beginning and underestimated afterwards (Baldwin 2019).

However, the aspect of digitization described here is only one of several drivers of the global upheaval. Worldwide developments show that at this very moment, a number of other developments are simultaneously taking place that will make the upheaval even greater, and which represent no less than an epochal break. We will briefly explain the details in Sect. 25.3.

25.3 The New Epoch

The fourth phase of globalization (Globalization 4.0) outlined in the previous section describes how a new technology of massive worldwide digitization and networking is currently in the process of transforming the nature of globalization into a new form.

However, at exactly the same time as this transformation, a number of other worldwide problems and changes are taking place, which are presented in this section. As a result of these issues, it can be expected that an epochal break will occur that will be strong and fast.

Currently, in 2020, we are in the period of the COVID-19 pandemic. As we all know, this is a crisis of historical dimensions that is already changing everything in our lives, and it is affecting all people around the world practically simultaneously. A great deal of effort is being put into developing medical solutions, which we hope will soon be found.

It is easy to think that one day the crisis will be over and that everything will be as it was. People and companies want to return to their old routines as soon as possible. In particular, established companies have great persistence in their usual efficient processes and are driven more by management than by leadership.

However, as we all know, we should not expect that the old situation will ever return. In many areas there is already talk of a new normality. Entrepreneurs may think that only initiatives of incremental adjustments will be necessary to keep the business running as before.

However, this idea must be questioned. It must be borne in mind that the COVID-19 pandemic is an unexpected additional problem that overlaps with all other current geopolitical changes and problems. The COVID-19 pandemic can be seen as a catalyst or an accelerant, depending on which aspect is considered (Fig. 25.2).

Below is a brief summary of the geopolitical issues that are currently taking place practically simultaneously.

We will not go into details here. Changes in the world and international relations are certainly only of interest to some entrepreneurs and leaders. It has also been shown that those who do not often deal with this topic are finding it difficult to understand. This is not least because these issues are extremely complex. Above all, we do not want to cause fear, although some of these aspects may well have that effect. The sole purpose of this section is to make the reader aware of this historically unique situation in which we all find ourselves together in the world (!) and to open the reader's eyes to new perspectives. In this sense, we also want to show that the connection between globalization and innovation will always be there. Viewed in this way, the opportunities for entrepreneurs can be greater than ever before, simply because the number of very serious problems to be solved is higher than ever before.

In Sect. 25.7 we will mention some aspects of how entrepreneurs and leaders can take advantage of this situation.

In the following, we briefly describe the individual topics (bubbles) shown in Fig. 25.2. As already mentioned, these topics are complex and, in addition, they influence each other, sometimes to a great extent. Details can be found in the respective references.

In the list, the topics are roughly sorted in the order in which they gained momentum. Objective sorting is not possible because the topics have developed in a slow process and there are different interpretations of when relevance occurred. The graph should be interpreted in such a way that topics further to the left have

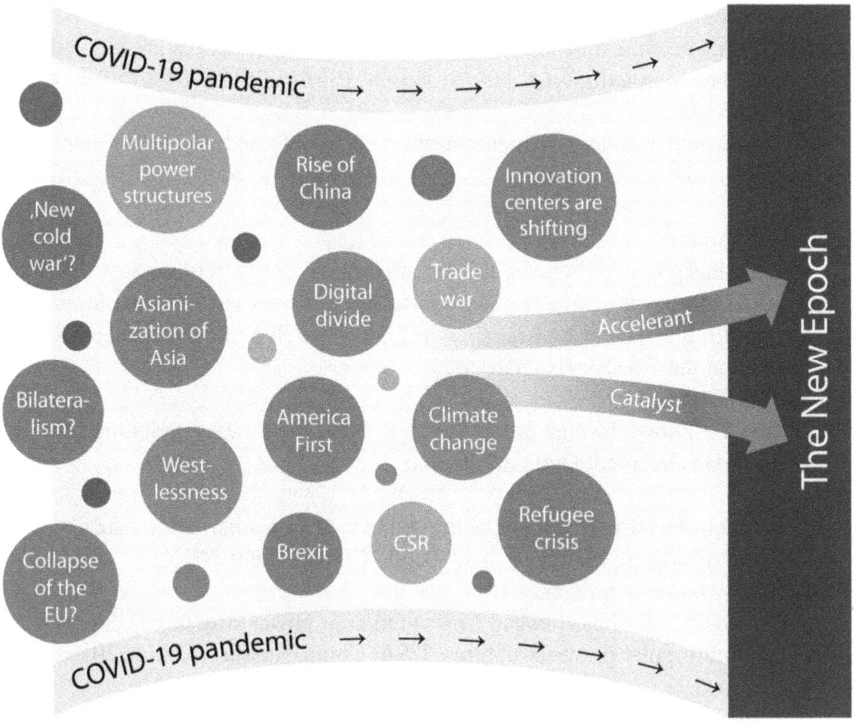

Fig. 25.2 Initializing a new epoch: the influencing factors. (Source: authors)

gained momentum or will gain it later. The first 12 topics have already become a reality; the last three (in the graph with question marks) are speculative.

- *Innovation centers are shifting*

  European innovation centers are shifting to Central Asia, Latin America and Africa ("Bundesministerium für Bildung und Forschung" (BMBF) n.d.). US Innovation Centers in Silicon Valley are moving within the US and are also migrating to all areas of the world, primarily to Asia (see Sect. 25.6).
- *Refugee crisis*

  80 million people are currently on the move worldwide. This figure has doubled in the last seven years (United Nations High Commissioner for Refugees n.d.). It can be assumed that the number will increase even more in the future, e.g. due to climate change.
- *Climate change*

  Many economies, even very large ones such as the USA, will suffer ever greater damage as the temperature rises (Nunn et al. 2020).
- *Trade war*

  This point refers to the trade war between China and the USA. An essential aspect of this conflict is the economic and technological competition between these two great powers (Lau 2019).

- *Corporate social responsibility (CSR)*

    CSR has become a business issue, in the way that investors are beginning to demand that companies contribute to society. (Sorkin 2018).

- *Digital divide*

    Large companies use digitization more effectively and efficiently than small and medium-sized enterprises (SMEs), which leads to division (Frietsch et al. 2016).

- *Rise of China*

    China has grown to become the second largest economy in the world, behind the USA. Moreover, China is now considered to be very strong in the innovation sector, with the second highest spending on research and development (R&D), also behind the US (Harris 2018).

- *America First*

    The well-known foreign policy stance in the United States under the administration of US President Donald J. Trump.

- *Brexit*

    The impact of Brexit will not be limited to the EU. Rather, effects are expected to be felt throughout the UK, EU, USA and China (Mitter 2020).

- *Multipolar power structures*

    The world order has changed from a unipolar power structure (US power) to complex multipolar power structures (USA, China, Russia) (Collins 2019).

- *Westlessness*

    Westlessness describes an internally divided West that is increasingly losing its claim to shape global governance (Munich Security Report 2020 n.d.).

- *Asianization of Asia*

    Almost five billion of the nearly eight billion people in the world live in Asia (1.5 billion of them in China). In the past, Asia was dependent on technologies from Western countries. This is no longer the case, especially due to China's technological progress. As a result, Asia is in a position to shape its own economic world (Khanna 2019).

- *New Cold War?*

    A *New Cold War* would be a future conflict situation, similar to the historical *Cold War*, between major powers, e.g. USA and China. This scenario is currently a matter for speculation.

- *Bilateralism?*

    Bilateralism would mean that the regulators of the global economy (e.g. UNO, IMF, World Bank, WTO, WHO) would lose more and more influence, and bilateral agreements between states would become an increasing priority. This is not the case at present.

- *Collapse of the EU?*

    Despite the UK's withdrawal from the EU and increasing conflicts, the collapse of the EU is only speculation.

25.4 About Local and Global Innovation Spaces

25.4.1 Innovation Space: Definitions

The term *innovation space* is used in the literature and in business language in very different contexts. In a common definition, it refers to places, e.g. buildings or metropolitan regions, which form an environment for innovation activities, such as co-working spaces, startup spaces, incubators, accelerators, maker spaces, and research institutes. Thus, it is increasingly the case that these innovation spaces are becoming blurred in their distinction (Wagner and Watch 2018). What these types of innovation spaces have in common is that they provide an infrastructure in a community locally at one location. Due to the COVID-19 pandemic, however, many of these innovation spaces are currently experiencing problems because people are no longer able or willing to use the facilities, as the example of the current major additional problems of WeWork shows (Inagaki 2020). Since the pandemic will not disappear quickly, these spaces may also undergo a fundamental change. Participants (tenants) now often use video communication in virtual spaces. Some of them experience that this technology can also work, although in a different way. The users learn that the disadvantage of the lack of physical proximity is offset by the advantage of independence of location. It is hardly to be expected that physical spaces will disappear, but perhaps virtual spaces will establish themselves as an extension, especially as new technologies such as VR and AR are now becoming suitable for mass use. This could promote spatial expansion, especially international expansion, and may open up new possibilities. It will be exciting to observe how this environment develops.

Another definition of the term *innovation space* is much broader. In this notion, there is no geographical limitation, but rather the connections and exchange are in the foreground, regardless of the medium and location. All stakeholders in the innovation process are possible participants, not only entrepreneurs and startups, but also, for example, multinational companies and policymakers. Providing access to knowledge and resources is one of the goals (McKelvey and Bagchi-Sen 2015).

In yet other publications, the term *innovation space* is used as a generic term and as a replacement for the term *innovation network* (Pyka and Scharnhorst 2009).

25.4.2 A Definition for This Chapter

In summary, the idea of an innovation space depends on what it is supposed to achieve. A co-working space has a different definition than an innovation ecosystem of a metropolitan region, and a startup has a different vision than a business unit of a large company.

Since entrepreneurship in the global environment is the priority in this chapter, we use the following definition:

Innovation spaces are location-independent structures where individuals and/or organizations come together to promote innovation. The main purpose of these spaces is to provide access to or share knowledge and resources, to exert influence, and to maintain and develop networks.

25.4.3 How to Configure Innovation Spaces

When addressing the topic of innovation spaces it very quickly becomes clear that it is a complex issue. In addition, international aspects increase the complexity even further.

Practice shows that suitably configured innovation spaces are of crucial importance for the success of innovation activities of any kind. The important question in an innovation project is how the innovation space is configured to achieve the planned goal. It is therefore necessary to decide which stakeholders and influencers should be involved and how the space should be organized. Figure 25.3 shows possible influencers and stakeholders.

Regarding the organization of the space, it is important to note that compromises must always be found between the use of open and closed structures and between the use of flat and hierarchical governance. More open is not always better than closed, and flatter is not always better than hierarchical (Pisano and Verganti 2015).

Innovation spaces give large companies the advantage of having the infrastructure, experience, and human and financial resources they need. For example, the takeover of the car manufacturer Volvo by the Chinese automotive company Geely

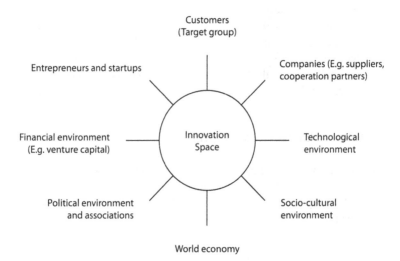

Fig. 25.3 Possible influencers and stakeholders of innovation spaces. (Source: authors)

in 2010 was considered a project in this context. At the time of the takeover, Volvo used a platform of the original owner, Ford. However, Ford did not want to create a major new competitor in the Chinese market. The resulting challenges were solved in an international innovation space (McKelvey and Bagchi-Sen 2015). It can be assumed that all the possible influencers and stakeholders in Fig. 25.1 played a role in this innovation space.

The situation is different for SMEs and startups. It is often the case that these companies configure their spaces in a very reduced way. This is often due to the fact that a maximum focus should be achieved with limited resources. However, it is advisable to define an appropriate innovation space on the basis of defined goals and to coordinate this with any existing investors.

In the startup environment, an innovation space that is too small (unsuitable) leads to the creation of startups that either

(a) develop only individual aspects of a larger whole (e.g. a new method for diagnosing X-ray images); or
(b) as a local solution provider (e.g. the German business network Xing) are unable to take the step toward internationalization.

The former are usually sold after a success and ideally give the investors a good exit, while the latter ideally offer the founders and investors good sources of income.

It is okay to proceed in this way if the result is the desired goal. However, really large organizations with a global impact, such as the US tech companies Amazon and Google, or the Chinese tech company Xiaomi, are not created in this way. Incidentally, such a limitation is a problem for an entire continent, namely Europe. This region is therefore in the process of missing its technological boat.

It is precisely at this time that startups have the best opportunities to build up their own innovation space in a borderless economy, provided they have the right mindset.

25.5 Silicon Valley: History and Future

If there is one truly world-class example of modern innovation, innovation spaces and global business expansion, it is Silicon Valley. This unique region in California, USA and the world-famous companies that have been established here over the last 70 years, such as Xerox PARC, Apple, and Hewlett-Packard, are widely known. Countless managers, researchers, entrepreneurs and capital investors visit the region each year not only for business but also to be inspired by the spirit of tech innovation.

This section, however, focuses on a slightly different aspect, namely the past and the future of this innovation region. The reason for this is that an epochal break in the worldwide uniqueness and significance of the Valley is currently becoming apparent.

25.5.1 The Waves of Silicon Valley

Throughout its history, the region has always been able to reinvent itself when competitors from outside became too strong. In the 1980s, for example, the Valley lost its global technological supremacy in semiconductors to Japan, leading to a recession and the loss of 25,000 jobs in just two years (Benner 2002). The region solved the problem by pushing through a new phase of innovation in the global market, namely by Intel's major development of its microprocessors. These components were crucial in initiating the strong growth area of the emerging PC industry, coupled with a large ecosystem of participating companies, many of them in the Valley. The next technological innovation followed in 1993 with the launch of the Internet and companies such as Netscape, Cisco, 3Com, and Google.

A striking feature of this development are the short innovation cycles of 10 to 15 years, known as waves, which are shown in Fig. 25.4 (Silicon Valley Competitiveness and Innovation Project n.d.).

This was followed in the early 2000s by the wave of the social media age, the so-called fifth wave, which is still going on today. In summary, this development resulted in the following waves (Fig. 25.4):

- 1st & 2nd waves (1950s–1980s): Defense & Integrated Circuits
- 3rd wave (1980s–1990s): Personal Computer
- 4th wave (1990s–2000s): Internet
- 5th wave (2000s–Present): Social Media

The website of the Silicon Valley Competitiveness and Innovation Project assesses the transition to the fifth wave as follows: "The rise of Social Media represented a shift in the region from engineering innovative technology products and services toward creatively applying that technology for consumer markets. Comparatively low barriers to entry (e.g. low costs) have helped to spur rapid

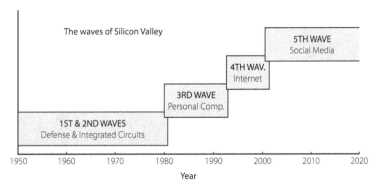

Fig. 25.4 The five waves of Silicon Valley. Adapted from the Silicon Valley Competitiveness and Innovation Project (n.d.). (Source: authors)

growth of startups, particularly in San Francisco" (Silicon Valley Competitiveness and Innovation Project n.d.).

Smartphones (Apple as of 2007, Google Android as of 2008) with their ecosystems of apps are part of the social media wave in this view, although the two system providers were and still are only responsible for technology, and hardware production takes place in Asia without exception. This constellation was a novelty, because in the past hardware was produced both in the Valley and in Asia.

This development of the division of labor with Asia, which was not so sharply defined before, seems to be very interesting economically in the short and medium terms, but it does have long-term risks. Experience in other industries over the past decades has clearly shown that outsourcing production to areas with lower labor costs leads to the gradual diffusion of all know-how to the regions of production (Pisano and Shih 2012). It is therefore questionable how long the duopoly of the smartphone operating systems of Apple and Google with exclusive production of the hardware in Asia can continue in this form. Asian software manufacturers such as Huawei are already working on an operating system alternative (Kotabe and Helsen 2020). The hurdle is certainly very high because of the closed ecosystems of the apps. However, the market pressure is also very high, because almost 5 billion of the world's population live in Asia (Khanna 2019).

25.5.2 Backlashes in the Valley

It is also not the case that Silicon Valley has been able to successfully implement all the planned business initiatives. In 2006, for example, the cleantech sector was to be the *next big thing*. Until the financial crisis of 2008, investors provided around USD 1 billion in venture capital to startups in this sector. However, the investment flopped. In particular, the long development times, but also the enormous capital requirements were not properly assessed, and companies were not able to develop suitable business models. Venture capital firms had planned too many quick exits, as was normal in the software industry. Instagram, for example, returned 29 times the amount of investment to its supporters within two years. This principle proved impossible to implement in the cleantech sector (Sivaram and Gaddy 2016).

25.5.3 Manufacturing Innovation Example: Tesla

In another area, entrepreneurs in Palo Alto in Silicon Valley took a completely new approach to developing mobility on the basis of electrical energy by founding Tesla, Inc. back in 2003. One year later, in 2004, Elon Musk joined the company as an investor, co-founder and chairman of the board of directors (Vance 2017). Tesla's approach was to completely rethink the software side of electric vehicles, which in the future should also be able to drive autonomously. Traditional car manufacturers such as Volkswagen or Toyota are up to six years behind Tesla in the development of these technologies, as a teardown of a Tesla Model 3 in

Japan at the beginning of 2020 showed. From a technological point of view, the central processing unit developed by Tesla proved to be particularly outstanding. At competitor Volkswagen, these tasks are distributed among around 70 control units running eight different operating systems. This example shows what technological achievements Silicon Valley is still capable of, and how willing they are to make major investments with a long-term perspective. It also shows how seriously modern manufacturing is taken there. Manufacturing startups require enormous investments and take a long time to become profitable. Tesla's manufacturing takes place mainly in plants at various locations in the USA. Only one plant is located in Shanghai, China, and a plant in Germany is planned. There is no sign of manufacturing taking place long term in low-wage countries as happens with smartphones. However, Tesla has not yet generated profits. But that exemplifies the heart of the mindset: growth over profitability. What is important is technological leadership and the early development of international markets.

With its highly hardware-intensive, high-tech manufacturing approach, Tesla has a completely different business compared to players in social media, the companies of the fifth wave. You could almost say that Tesla goes back to the roots of the early Silicon Valley. However, it is already the case that Tesla, in contrast to the early days, is building up its own ecosystems, e.g. for charging infrastructure, and has strongly internationalized at a very early stage. How this new automobile scene will develop in the future on a possible path to becoming an industry of mobility service providers cannot be predicted today. It is possible that in this regard Tesla has laid the foundation for a sixth wave of the Valley.

25.5.4 Thoughts on the Future of the Valley

If there will be a sixth wave in the Valley, it is likely to be related to AI in some way. This AI reference is particularly relevant to Tesla in the development of self-driving cars, and there are also strong orientations toward AI among social media companies.

However, the region will then no longer have the exclusivity to which it has been accustomed, as China is already in the process of overtaking the US as a pioneer in AI systems (Lee 2019).

Further details on the future of the Valley in the global environment will follow in Sect. 25.6.

25.6 The Global Startup Economy

In this section we will describe how Silicon Valley is developing in comparison to other innovation centers worldwide and what the global scene of innovation ecosystems is like. The current fifth wave of Silicon Valley (social media, see Fig. 25.4) has been going on for 20 years now, longer than any other previous wave, and

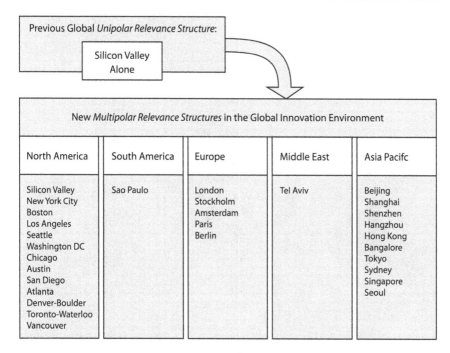

Fig. 25.5 New multipolar relevance structures in the global innovation environment. Data source regarding locations and ranking: The Global Startup Ecosystem Report GSER 2020 (n.d.). (Source: authors)

there is no end in sight. This could be an indication of an end to the typical short, centralized innovation cycles of the Valley.

In the first to fourth waves, Silicon Valley was characterized by worldwide exclusivity of the respective technologies, combined with the highest relevance as a center of innovation, and it is no exaggeration to say the Valley has changed the world from a central location. In reference to geopolitical power structures (see Sect. 25.3), we therefore speak of unipolar relevance structures in this period. Silicon Valley alone determined innovation in the tech sector at that time (see Fig. 25.5).

The question is whether and how this predominance of relevance as a center of innovation changed in the fifth wave. Here are some facts about this: Silicon Valley has slowed down its overall growth. For the last three years in a row, more people have moved away from the Valley than have moved in. The immigration of people from abroad is declining. Real estate prices fell by 7% in the last year under review. The costs of doing business in the Valley are among the highest in the US (Brennan 2020).

The 2020 Global Startup Ecosystem Report by Startup Genome LLC (The Global Startup Ecosystem Report 2020 n.d.) comments on the situation as follows: "There Will Be No "Next Silicon Valley. There Will Be 30.""

Table 25.1 Top 30 global startup ecosystems. (Data source: 2020 Global Startup Ecosystem Report (n.d.)

City	Ranking 2020	Change from 2019
Silicon Valley	1	0
New York City	2 (tie)	0
London	2 (tie)	0
Beijing	4	0
Boston	5	0
Tel Aviv	6 (tie)	0
Los Angeles	6 (tie)	0
Shanghai	8	0
Seattle	9	3
Stockholm	10	1
Washington, DC	11	8
Amsterdam	12	3
Paris	13	−4
Chicago	14	3
Tokyo	15	New
Berlin	16	−6
Singapore	17	−3
Toronto-Waterloo	18	−5
Austin	19	−3
Seoul	20	New
San Diego	21	−1
Shenzhen	22	New
Atlanta	23	5
Denver-Boulder	24	−3
Vancouver	25	−1
Bangalore	26	−8
Sydney	27	−4
Hangzhou	28	New
Hong Kong	29	−4
Sao Paulo	30	New

This quote clearly calls into question Silicon Valley's unique position. The authors of the report describe a situation in which the 30 most important startup ecosystems (see Table 25.1) address relevant technology areas at different locations worldwide. Performance (value creation and exits), funding, connectedness, market reach, knowledge, and talent were evaluated. The analysis is conducted annually. The change from the previous year is indicated. In addition, the report lists 15 other locations that have the potential to be among the top 30 in the following year.

As the facts and data show, there are many indications that Silicon Valley's unique position has changed fundamentally as the importance of other regions has increased. The resulting relevance structures can be described as multipolar (see Fig. 25.5). The resulting term *multipolar relevance structures* is also used in reference to multipolar power structures in geopolitics.

The groupings by world zones (see Fig. 25.5) show a fairly even distribution of locations in terms of geography, with the exception that Europe is severely underrepresented compared to economic performance. This is exactly in line with the analysis of *The Billion Dollar Startup Club*. Here too, the USA and Asia are in the lead, while Europe is lagging behind (The Billion Dollar Startup Club n.d.).

Geopolitical power structures became multipolar some time ago (see Sect. 25.3). At a very similar time, the relevance structures of the global innovation environment also became multipolar. Whether the approximate contemporaneousness of the changes is a coincidence or whether there is a causal connection cannot be answered here.

It is a fact that our entire world is becoming more and more multipolar, which is due to the ever-increasing networking of the global infrastructure (Khanna 2016). For entrepreneurs and leaders, this means that opportunities increase if they use international arbitrage with creativity and persistence (see Sect. 25.7).

25.7 Conclusions

In the previous sections, we have described the enormous changes that have taken place and continue to take place in many areas of globalization, geopolitics and entrepreneurship, and how these are interrelated. All these issues have a global dimension and invite entrepreneurs and leaders to take action like never before.

However, for many entrepreneurs the global environment is still something abstract, something difficult to understand, difficult to assess. It is something where entrepreneurs quickly lose their focus and for reasons of efficiency prefer to concentrate on their local environment in order to be successful there first. But that's where internationalization usually ends up. The reasons for this are many and varied.

We would therefore like to encourage entrepreneurs and leaders to rethink internationalization. Concretely, this means not just limiting business initiatives to sales and procurement markets alone, but also taking a holistic view of internationalization in connection with innovation. This begins with the targeted international expansion of the personal network in all relevant areas of the entrepreneurial innovation space (see Sect. 25.4.3). This process of expanding the personal network has never been easier, due to the international momentum of social media (e.g. Linkedin, Twitter, webinars). Interestingly enough, the COVID-19 pandemic has simplified this process even more, because due to travel restrictions all participants have become more accustomed to the possibilities of Internet communication. This is especially true for video conferences with screen sharing and collaboration tools. Of course, good will must be presumed on the part of all those involved. We are all learning that right now, at this particular time. The same applies to virtual teams, i.e. teams that work together via Internet communication regardless of location. This concept, which had already been developed at the end of the last millennium but did not catch on, can flourish with today's possibilities and in the current situation. Entrepreneurs can take advantage of the associated arbitrage in the global environment (see also Sect. 25.2).

In summary, waiting for better times during the COVID-19 pandemic and beyond is not an option. Only those who take active steps now will remain relevant to the market as well as society.

Entrepreneurs are now facing challenges as never before, but at the same time there are opportunities as never before. Google and Facebook, for example, have emerged from the dot-com crisis and have thus initiated the age of social media.

It is to be hoped that it will be entrepreneurs who will solve the really big problems of humankind such as climate change. It is even possible that it will have to be entrepreneurs, because world politics seems to be failing in some areas. There is a reason why investors are beginning to demand CSR from companies (see Sect. 25.3).

References

Baldwin R (2018, December 22) If this is globalization 4.0, what were the other three? https://www.weforum.org/agenda/2018/12/if-this-is-globalization-4-0-what-were-the-other-three/. Accessed 30 June 2020

Baldwin R (2019) The globotics upheaval: globalisation, robotics and the future of work. Weidenfeld & Nicolson, London

Benner C (2002) Work in the new economy: flexible labor markets in Silicon Valley. Blackwell, Malden, MA

Brennan B (2020, February 1) Silicon Valley competitiveness and innovation project—2020 update. https://www.svcip.com/files/SVCIP2020-FINAL3.9.2020.pdf. Accessed 30 June 2020

Bundesministerium für Bildung und Forschung (BMBF, Federal Ministry of Education and Research, a cabinet-level ministry of Germany) (n.d.) Vernetzung weltweit. https://www.bmbf.de/de/vernetzung-weltweit-268.html. Accessed 30 June 2020

Collins A (2019, January 15) The global risks report 2019. https://www.weforum.org/reports/the-global-risks-report-2019. Accessed 30 December 2019

Drucker PF (1967) The effective executive. Harper & Row

Frietsch R, Beckert B, Daimer S, Lerch C, Meyer N, Neuhäusler, P et al. (2016, November 15) Die Elektroindustrie als Leitbranche der Digitalisierung—Innovationsstudie. https://www.zvei.org/presse-medien/publikationen/die-elektroindustrie-als-leitbranche-der-digitalisierung-innovationsstudie/. Accessed 30 June 2020

Harris B (2018, February 7) China is an innovation superpower. This is why. https://www.weforum.org/agenda/2018/02/these-charts-show-how-china-is-becoming-an-innovation-superpower/. Accessed 30 June 2020

Inagaki, K (2020, May 29) SoftBank investment chief given 113% pay rise despite Vision Fund woes. https://www.ft.com/content/08248d28-b7b7-4809-8d78-d2df86944d40. Accessed 30 June 2020

Khanna P (2016) Connectography: mapping the future of global civilization. Random House, New York

Khanna P (2019) The future is Asian: commerce, conflict, and culture in the 21st century. Simon & Schuster, New York

Kotabe M, Helsen K (2020) Global marketing management. Wiley, Hoboken

Lau LJ (2019) The China-U.S. trade war and future economic relations. Chinese University Press, Hong Kong

Lee K (2019) AI SUPERPOWERS: China, Silicon Valley, and the new world order. MARINER Books

McKelvey M, Bagchi-Sen S (eds) (2015) Innovation spaces in Asia. Edward Elgar Publishing, Cheltenham, UK. https://doi.org/10.4337/9781783475681

Mitter R (2020, January 19) With Brexit imminent, what are the chances of a UK trade deal with China? https://www.theguardian.com/commentisfree/2020/jan/19/brexit-uk-trade-deal-china-us-compromise. Accessed 30 June 2020

Munich Security Report 2020 (n.d.). https://securityconference.org/en/publications/munich-security-report-2020/. Accessed 30 June 2020

Nunn R, O'Donnell J, Shambaugh J, Goulder LH, Kolstad CD, Long X (2020, April 6) Ten facts about the economics of climate change and climate policy. https://www.brookings.edu/wp-content/uploads/2019/10/Environmental-Facts_WEB.pdf

Pisano GP, Shih WC (2012) Producing prosperity: why America needs a manufacturing renaissance. Harvard Business Press, Boston, MA

Pisano GP, Verganti R (2015, July 15) Which kind of collaboration is right for you? https://hbr.org/2008/12/which-kind-of-collaboration-is-right-for-you. Accessed 30 June 2020

Pyka A, Scharnhorst A (2009) Innovation networks: new approaches in modelling and analyzing. Springer, Dordrecht. https://doi.org/10.1007/978-3-540-92267-4_5

Silicon Valley Competitiveness and Innovation Project (n.d.) By the Silicon Valley leadership group. http://www.svcip.com/. Accessed 30 June 2020

Sivaram V, Gaddy B (2016, July 26) Clean energy technology investors need fresh support after VC losses. https://www.ft.com/content/917de65a-4500-11e6-9b66-0712b3873ae1. Accessed 30 June 2020

Sorkin AR (2018, January 15) BlackRock's message: contribute to society, or risk losing our support. https://www.nytimes.com/2018/01/15/business/dealbook/blackrock-laurence-fink-letter.html. Accessed 30 June 2020

The Billion Dollar Startup Club (n.d.). https://www.wsj.com/graphics/billion-dollar-club/. Accessed 30 June 2020

The Global Startup Ecosystem Report 2020 (n.d.) Startup Genome. https://startupgenome.com/reports/gser2020. Accessed 30 June 2020

The Hamilton Project and the Stanford Institute for Economic Policy Research, Ten Facts about the Economics of Climate Change and Climate Policy. https://www.brookings.edu/wp-content/uploads/2019/10/Environmental-Facts_WEB.pdf

United Nations High Commissioner for Refugees (n.d.) Figures at a glance. https://www.unhcr.org/en-us/figures-at-a-glance.html. Accessed 30 June 2020

Vance A (2017) Elon Musk: Tesla, SpaceX, and the quest for a fantastic future. Ecco, an imprint of HarperCollins, New York

Wagner J, Watch D (2018, October 24) Innovation spaces: the new design of work. https://www.brookings.edu/research/innovation-spaces-the-new-design-of-work/. Accessed 30 June 2020

CPSIA information can be obtained .
at www.ICGtesting.com
Printed in the USA
LVHW022156170221
679360LV00007B/324

9 783030 576417